THE NEW BASIC READERS

CURRICULUM FOUNDATION SERIES

REG U.S PAT. OFF

GUIDEBOOK

to accompany

More Times and Places

The 1962 Edition

William S. Gray, Marion Monroe,

A. Sterl Artley, May Hill Arbuthnot

Scott, Foresman and Company

Chicago, Atlanta, Dallas, Palo Alto, Fair Lawn, N.J.

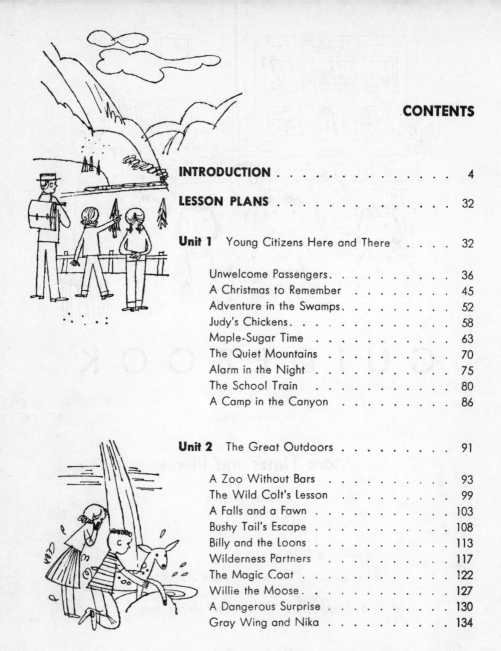

CONTENTS

READING IS A BASIC TOOL OF LEARNING

Since their first year in school, children have been engaging in learning experiences in the language arts, social studies, health, science, and other areas of the curriculum. In most of these areas, they have been interpreting printed symbols (pictures, text, or both). They have been using **reading as a medium of learning.**

Wherever reading has been the medium of learning, the goals have been the same: **Growth in** the use of reading as a learning tool and, simultaneously, personal **growth through** reading.

But throughout the primary grades, children have grown in and through reading at different rates. In the middle grades they will continue to grow at different rates. We may find any or all of these children in our classrooms:

David and Ellen read anything and everything. They are enjoying their first experience with the classics. From reading, from travel and other cultural advantages, they have a fund of information, which they contribute to the learning activities of their class at school.

Joe likes sports and games. He keeps up well with his class but does little reading on his own. He is a typical "average" pupil—energetic, responsive, likable . . . a real boy.

Susan has always been slow. She can read a third-grade book fairly well, but she finds middle-grade reading hard and frustrating. She can't keep up with David and Ellen and Joe. But her mother expects—even demands— that she keep up.

Michael flounders in any book beyond the Book Two level, and he flounders a bit even there. He definitely needs special help in reading—and something to read in place of all that "baby stuff" in second-grade readers.

By the time they are in the fourth year in school, Joe and Susan and their classmates are individuals, with distinct personalities of their own. Real abilities are becoming apparent; real interests are beginning to develop. Individual differences are distinct and clear.

I've always found that middle-grade youngsters are stimulating to work with—they're starting to think for themselves . . . to have their own ideas and points of view. They're keen about fairness . . . about right and wrong. I can talk things over with them and get some really good discussion.

Yes, I have found that they respond best to the adult who treats them as individuals and approaches them in a grown-up way. Don't you think it pays to include them in planning—above all, to take plenty of time to help them understand why we do what we do?

There's something I want to talk about. The standardized reading test showed that many of my pupils are below average grade expectancy. What can I do to bring them up to standard?

Let's remember that a standard score means the score made by the middle child in large numbers of children belonging to a grade. Most of us have pupils who are below grade level and others who are above.

Careful attention to readiness and to
individual differences pays off in the
primary grades. Isn't it just as
important in the middle grades?

Indeed it is! We're faced not only with
wide developmental variations among our
youngsters but with amazing differences
in background and experience.

I think we have to remember, too, that
the beginning of the middle grades is a
critical time for many boys and girls.
Those who are unhappy, unsuccessful,
insecure may develop severe reading
problems or serious personality problems
—or both.

I think one of our most important jobs
is to know our pupils as individuals.

And to provide the kind of classroom
atmosphere in which each child is
comfortable, so that he can respond to
guidance and grow in his own way.

Take time to know boys and girls as individuals

It takes time and patience to know youngsters as individuals. But, in trying to discover and provide for each pupil's needs, we can (1) examine carefully the child's physical well-being, (2) search conscientiously for emotional problems, and (3) ask ourselves, "Are the child's experiential background and his language ability adequate for the concepts to be developed at the middle-grade levels?"

Physical handicaps

Caroline has a visual defect. To her, the words on the page are blurred, and sometimes the letters look doubled. Often, while reading, she brushes her eyes to try to brush away the blur. After a short time her head begins to ache.

Bill had a severe case of measles in early childhood. Since then he has had frequent earaches. When he has a cold, he doesn't seem to hear well. Phonetic analysis has always been difficult for him. He has trouble in identifying vowel sounds, and he has never understood how vowels function in our language.

Physical factors may affect progress, and often we have to inquire back into a child's health history to evaluate the effects of physical well-being and past absences on his school work. If a child has missed out on basic skills developed at preceding levels or simply has not understood, we must help him catch up before we can expect him to succeed at a new level.

Emotional problems

Edward resents a dominating parent who is ambitious for him and who "makes" him read at home each night. At school he resists reading and does all he can to avoid it.

Evelyn dresses differently from most of her classmates; her hair is never tidy. The girls whom she would like to have as friends leave her out of playtime activities. She is ill at ease and never seems wholly "there" during class periods.

The thoughts and feelings of pre-teen-aged boys and girls may be embroiled in any number of emotional situations, which set up psychological blocks to learning in the classroom. The causes of such blocks may be hard to discover, especially if they go back into the child's preschool life.

Language and experiential deficiencies

Mary comes from a family where there's little time for children. She has never heard a bedtime story or seen anyone read a book in the home. In the first grade she lacked "readiness" in language and in the experiences that make reading meaningful. Although she has gained much from her few years in school, her difficulty in interpreting what she reads still reflects that early deprivation.

Without an adequate background of language and of experiences that make language meaningful, pupils have difficulty in developing interpretative skills in reading. We need to know the child's history in terms of his home environment and language background.

Establish a friendly, permissive atmosphere

To establish a friendly relationship, we make each child aware that we are interested in him—his likes and dislikes, his hopes and fears, his plans. We invite confidences, but we understand that confidences from a boy or girl are the rewards of friendship—that they must first be deserved.

What is meant by permissive?
Not doing as you please . . .   but being free to exercise self-direction . . .

A teacher creates a permissive atmosphere through understanding, not through inadequacy. That is, she permits freedom of action and initiative because she recognizes pupils' needs for growing in self-direction. She is fully capable, however, of directing the class and of commanding attention and obedience in any emergency in which prompt leadership is necessary.

A permissive teacher helps her pupils establish the limits of permission. They exercise freedom and initiative within the limits of regard for the rights of others.

In a friendly, permissive atmosphere boys and girls are comfortable and free to be their best selves. Only in such an atmosphere can learning activities be carried on in a spirit of enjoyment.

VARIED EXPERIENCES IN INTERPRETING LANGUAGE CONTRIBUTE TO GROWTH IN AND THROUGH READING

In various areas of the primary-grade curriculum, three basic types of experiences with oral and printed language contribute to the child's growth in and through reading. These same types of experiences are indispensable in the middle grades: (1) listening experiences, (2) guided reading experiences, (3) independent reading.

What kinds of listening experiences must we provide—and why?

Throughout the school day, in various areas of the curriculum, the child will listen to different types of materials. These will include:

The finest in children's literature—poems, stories, books

Passages from reference books—nature handbooks, encyclopedias, pamphlets, and the like

Stories and articles from newspapers and magazines

Records, films

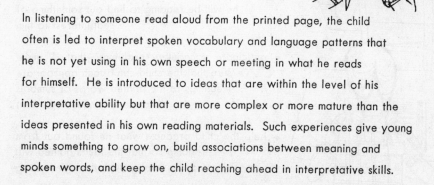

In listening to someone read aloud from the printed page, the child often is led to interpret spoken vocabulary and language patterns that he is not yet using in his own speech or meeting in what he reads for himself. He is introduced to ideas that are within the level of his interpretative ability but that are more complex or more mature than the ideas presented in his own reading materials. Such experiences give young minds something to grow on, build associations between meaning and spoken words, and keep the child reaching ahead in interpretative skills.

What kind of guided reading in each area of the curriculum—and why?

For guided reading experiences, we choose materials that the child is able to read successfully under guidance. Usually these are the textbooks provided in each area of the curriculum.

To do a good job of guided reading in each area, we must day by day . . .

- establish background for each interpretative experience—that is, (1) help the child call up and organize from his own background those ideas and experiences that will enable him to interpret what he reads and (2) ensure that he will be reading to find out something of real interest to him

- anticipate vocabulary problems—that is, make sure that the child can attach appropriate meanings to the printed words or symbols that he will meet in the text

- help the child organize what he found out from reading so that the ideas gained will contribute to his total growth through reading

Jimmy can't read his social-studies book (or his arithmetic or his science book). Why hasn't he learned to read something besides stories?

We, as middle-grade teachers, are aware of this kind of complaint. We know that it loses sight of certain fundamental ideas:

"Reading" in any area of the curriculum is much more than recognizing visual word forms and pronouncing them correctly. Jimmy may be able to recognize the word *fifth* and may understand perfectly what it means in the story context "Don was *the fifth skater* for the Blue Streaks." But the fact that he understands this sentence in the contextual orientation of a story in his reader is no guarantee that he will understand *fifth* in arithmetic—as a fractional part of a whole, for example. The arithmetic program, not the reading program, assumes responsibility for building readiness for, introducing, and developing the concepts that Jimmy needs to solve problems involving fractions.

Each area of the curriculum has a unique responsibility for the total picture of child growth in and through reading. The arithmetic program carries a major responsibility for developing the ability to perceive quantitative relationships and to engage in quantitative thinking. The social-studies program assumes major responsibility for helping the child grow in his understanding of man-land relationships. Here maps become an indispensable tool of learning. Developing the ability and the special background of concepts needed to interpret maps and map symbolism is the responsibility of the social-studies program, not of the basic reading program.

The basic reading program assumes major responsibility for developing the basic interpretative skills and the basic understandings of language that are common to the reading done in all areas of the curriculum. In response to passages in his reader, for example, Jimmy forms and reacts to vivid sensory images of scenes and events. Thus he is prepared, as a first step in interpreting symbols on a map, to associate imagery of his home community with the dot that stands for it on a map, but he is not likely to do so automatically. In the social-studies class, he must first be led to understand what the dot stands for—a real place with real people living in it.

If the child is to **grow in** and **through reading in the other areas of the curriculum**—if he is to read his social-studies or science or arithmetic book successfully—we, as teachers, must guide his interpretation of that textbook as carefully and intelligently as we guide his interpretation of his basic reader.

In the first place, we must be sure that he is **ready** to read his social-studies or his arithmetic book—in every sense of the word **ready** as it is understood in basic reading.

We must be sure that his reading is an active process of finding out something that is significant to him—a process that challenges his whole mind, not a passive process of sitting back and somehow "absorbing" or "being told."

And we must help him organize what he finds out from reading so that it will contribute to his growth through reading.

What kind of independent reading experiences—and why?

For independent reading experiences, we steer the
child to materials that he is ready to read on
his own. For all but the superior reader, the level
of difficulty of these materials is often below
that of the materials chosen for listening experiences
or for guided reading.

A major goal of the basic reading program is wide independent reading for
every child—to develop children who can read and who do read because they
like to. The materials that the child selects may be related to any one or all
of the areas of the curriculum, and they may go far beyond, including
special interests from astronomy to zoography.

THE BASIC READING PROGRAM
HAS UNIQUE FUNCTIONS IN THE CURRICULUM . . .

to develop the fundamental language understandings and the basic interpretative skills common to the reading done in all areas of the curriculum

to acquaint the child with his literary heritage, to mold tastes and promote love of fine literature

to provide leads to wide personal reading on his own for every child

to ensure continuous, sequential growth for every child in basic understandings and skills

. . . AND A CONTENT SUITED TO ITS FUNCTIONS

For guided reading experiences, the basic reader provides story materials **carefully selected** and **organized around broad unit themes** that comprehend all the major interests of pre-teen-aged boys and girls.

Careful selection of content ensures that each story . . .

- is at the reading level of the middle-grade child—he can read it and in the process he **grows in reading**

- is intrinsically interesting to the child—he wants to read it to find out something of interest and importance to him

- contributes something to each child as an individual—something that meets his personal and social needs—otherwise, there is no **growth through reading**

Skillful organization of content around broad unit themes ensures . . .

- leads to wide personal reading for every child

- the wide variety of materials needed to build, in natural and orderly sequence, the basic understandings and skills common to reading in all areas of the curriculum

- correlation with the content of other areas of the curriculum

Fine story materials—with lively plots, interesting and significant themes, memorable characters, and distinguished style—enable the basic reading program to fulfill its unique functions in the total curriculum of the middle grades.

THE BASIC READING PROGRAM IN ACTION

Developing fundamental language understandings

Throughout the primary grades, the basic reading program has been helping children develop serviceable understandings of the relationship between meaning and spoken language and between spoken and printed language and meaning.

Children have developed such fundamental understandings as . . .

- spoken words communicate meaning; printed forms represent the sound of spoken words and, in turn, meaning

- word meaning must always be determined in light of the context in which the word is used

- root words retain their meanings in inflected and derived forms; prefixes, suffixes, and inflectional endings are also meaning units in words

- consonants, vowels, and accent are the phonemic elements in our language

- accent significantly affects vowel sounds in words

- the separate consonant and vowel elements are blended into syllables, and the syllables are blended with appropriate accent into meaningful word wholes

- in printed words there are certain visual clues that aid in determining syllabic divisions, accent, and vowel sounds

Major understandings and principles developed at primary levels are of course reviewed at the beginning of Book Four[1] level. (See the exercises on phonetic analysis and structural analysis in the lesson plans for the first two units, as well as the Index of Skills, in the *Guidebook* for the new *Times and Places*.)

We, as middle-grade teachers, continue to help children extend, strengthen, and apply fundamental understandings of relationships between meaning, spoken words, and printed language symbols. Such understandings are emphasized both in a definite skills program in basic reading and as we guide our pupils' reading, thinking, and writing in each area of the middle-grade curriculum.

We emphasize at Book Four level . . .

- root words, prefixes, and suffixes as meaning units in inflected and derived forms

- visual clues to vowel sounds, syllables, and accent

- understandings that function in spelling as well as in reading; for example, by comparing such words as

> admitted—profited
> beginning—buttoning
> occurring—remembering
> propelling—labeling
> preferred—peppered

the child observes that a doubled final consonant is a clue to accent as well as a clue to vowel sound. (For a detailed outline of the understandings developed at this level, see the Index of Skills in this *Guidebook*.)

With emphasis ever on meaning, we introduced at Book Four[1] level a glossary and the dictionary as meaning tools. At Book Four[2] level we introduce them as pronunciation tools.

Skills and abilities developed at preceding levels ensure readiness for these big new steps toward independence in the use of reading as a medium of learning.

To enable boys and girls to locate entry words quickly and easily, we review and reinforce understandings of general alphabetical position and alphabetical order, and we develop understandings of entry words and guide words.

Even more important, we lead pupils to observe that the entry words in a glossary or dictionary are usually root words, not the inflected forms that they frequently encounter in reading.

Here we call into play and reinforce continuously the ability to identify root words as meaning units in inflected or derived forms—an ability that children have been developing since their first year in school.

As we teach the middle-grade child how to locate words, we bear in mind that his real motive for turning to a glossary or dictionary is to understand the meaning of the sentence or the passage in which he has encountered an unknown word, not to learn the meanings or pronunciations of lists of words (few children—or adults—have an overpowering desire just to know what words mean or how to pronounce them).

As pupils meet unknown words in their reading in any area of the curriculum, we guide them step by step in comprehending definitions of meaning.

We give pupils continuous guidance in selecting the definition that seems appropriate to a given context and testing its appropriateness by "tuning" it back into context and rethinking the idea in a meaningful way (here we call into play the ability to use context clues—an ability that children have been developing throughout the primary levels).

At Book Four[2] level we place special emphasis on helping children learn to use a glossary or dictionary as a pronunciation tool. We recognize that the ability to translate printed pronunciations into accurate spoken pronunciations rests on many phonetic skills and understandings that have been sequentially developed from the first day of school. Throughout Book Four level we continue in a planned sequential program to promote each child's ability to

  associate a given consonant sound with its most common symbol
  recognize vowel sounds and associate them with given pronunciation
    symbols
  use a pronunciation key to identify consonant and vowel sounds
  blend consonant and vowel sounds into syllables
  recognize the function of visual syllabic divisions
  recognize the function of the accent mark
  blend syllables into word wholes

We guide children in each area of the curriculum in their use of textbook glossaries and the dictionary as pronunciation tools. Quite as important as skill in deriving pronunciation is the child's attitude toward the dictionary as a highly personal and functional tool to be used when needed in any area of the curriculum.

Obviously, pupils do not learn in a day or a week or a year to use the dictionary as a tool of meaning, pronunciation, spelling. Rather they need a planned, sequential program of learning extending throughout the middle and upper grades—a program that develops powerful language and thinking skills as a result of, and in conjunction with, the use of the dictionary.

Developing basic interpretative skills and abilities

In the middle grades, as in the primary grades, the basic reader enables us to give pupils continuous, sequential guidance in the interpretation of printed language.

What does the name George Washington make you think of?

We, as teachers, set the stage so that the reading of each story will be an eagerly anticipated event in the school day. We know our pupils, and we know the story—its theme, its content, its values in the life of the pre-teen-aged child. We know that enthusiasm for reading is contagious, if not always self-generating.

Enthusiastically, with our eyes on each child as an individual who expects to understand and enjoy, we . . .

- lead pupils to call up, share, and organize those ideas and past experiences that will make the story meaningful

- anticipate vocabulary needs, presenting new sight words and using certain of the new attack words in informal discussion to make sure that pupils are familiar with the sound and the meaning of these words before they meet the printed forms in their reading

• ensure that each child will be reading with a definite and compelling purpose—to find out something that he wants to know, not letting his eyes wander idly over the page in the hope of stumbling upon something that we may ask him

While pupils are engaged in silent reading of any designated part of a story, we pass unobtrusively among them . . .

• giving needed help and jotting notes to be used later in planning special help to meet individual needs

• sharing chuckles or shivers of excitement when a child who is "living" the story and reacting to his vivid sensory images glances up to catch our eyes

Immediately after silent reading of a given part, we encourage pupils to . . .

• share reactions to what they have found out

• ask questions freely about anything that was puzzling or obscure

• find specific clues or "read between the lines" for clues helpful in anticipating next events or outcomes

I don't blame Ben and Jason for running off and leaving Robert.

I don't think Robert's really unfriendly— he's just lonesome for New York.

Since we know our pupils, we are able to guide the discussion of any part (or of the total story if it is read as a unit) in such a way that . . .

- each child contributes according to the present level of his interpretative ability but is challenged to reach a higher level of interpretation

After pupils have completed silent reading of the story and have talked over the events of greatest interest to them (in light of their own specific purposes for reading), we help them think through the total story to . . .

- heighten sensory images and their reactions to the dominant idea or theme

- appreciate subtle humor, figurative and picturesque language or other elements of style

- distinguish between main ideas and subordinate ideas and organize these ideas for the purpose of remembering; there are many ways to organize ideas easily and effectively, and we lead pupils to use the one appropriate to the material and to their purpose (see, for example, the exercise on pages 95-96 of this *Guidebook*)

- organize ideas or facts from the story with ideas or facts gleaned from other sources to enlarge their store of information (often pupils' ideas, especially of times and places remote from their own experiences, need to be clarified, corrected, and reorganized)

- compare the plot with situations in their own experience

- evaluate the theme of the story, the motives and the behavior of the characters, or the outcomes in terms of their own everyday needs

Through discussions of the author's purpose in different parts of the story, of the characters' motives and emotional reactions, of pervading moods or emotional tones, we point the way to meaningful oral reading—true **oral interpretation** that is fun both for the reader and for his audience.

For three long days the boys walked steadily. They camped out each night and built fires to heat their food. At dusk on the **third day** they arrived at the camp.

Finally, we recognize the need for continuous reinforcement and further development of basic skills and abilities through (1) exercises such as those suggested in this *Guidebook* and (2) use of specific pages in the *Think-and-Do Book*. (For a comprehensive listing of the skills and abilities common to reading in all areas of the curriculum that are developed, strengthened, and extended at Book Four² level, see the Index of Skills in this *Guidebook*.)

Acquainting the child with his literary heritage, molding tastes and promoting love of fine literature

From earliest pre-reading days, the basic reading program has assumed responsibility for bringing to children the best in poetry, stories, and books. Through continuous experiences in hearing fine literature and in reading stories and books for himself, the child has found satisfaction in vicarious experiences that meet his basic needs at each level of growth—his need to achieve, to love and be loved, and to belong; his need for security, for refreshing change, and for aesthetic satisfaction (for a discussion of these needs and the experiences with literature that help to meet them, see Chapter 1 of *Children and Books*, Revised Edition, by May Hill Arbuthnot [Scott, Foresman and Company, 1957]).

We, as adults capable of distinguishing between fine literature and intellectual chaff, know that only fine literature feeds the mind and the spirit of the child. And the child who has had continuous experiences with the best in stories and poetry knows it, too, though he is incapable of abstract discussion of the differences between the worth-while and the shoddy.

To satisfy the needs of the middle-grade child and keep him reaching ahead, with a growing delight in literature, we take time for poetry . . .

The poetry of early childhood, with its emphatic melody and rhythm, has the power of evoking vivid sensory images and strong emotional response. As the child progresses to poetry with more content, the melodies are more subtle, but in good poetry there is always a compatibility between what Walter de la Mare calls "the tune and runningness" and the action, mood, or meaning of the poem. Melody and movement, sensory imagery, and the associative values of words all work together with magical results to make experiences memorable and to give them a significance that was lacking when they were merely experiences.

TIME
FOR
POETRY

REVISED EDITION

A TEACHER'S ANTHOLOGY
May Hill Arbuthnot

A Teacher's Anthology to accompany The New Basic Readers

We read poetry to our pupils, talk it over with them, and provide many opportunities for them to . . .

- express motor responses to the beat of strongly rhythmic verses

- participate in saying favorite poems, for children who have the experience of hearing poetry and a chance to join informally in saying it soon know quantities of verse that linger in memory like a song

- participate in quiet listening times, which can soothe or stir them, carry them to the land of make-believe or give their everyday experiences a new kind of glory

. . . and we take time to bring children and books together

We do not leave it to chance that middle-grade children will become acquainted with stories and books that can minister most effectively to their maturing minds, growing responsibilities, and changing needs. Instead we . . .

- read to them stories and books of fine literary quality

- put before them an alluring array of fine books, related to the unit themes in the basic reader, that they can read for themselves (the listing "Books to Read" on pages 294-301 of *More Times and Places* suggests a variety of books—for slow, average, and superior readers—that should be available in the classroom)

- explore individual interests and provide for each child, or show him how to obtain, fine books and stories that not only satisfy and expand his immediate personal interests but also cultivate potential interests and develop new interests

- see to it that our pupils have many opportunities to talk over what they are reading

The "Enjoying literature" sections in this *Guidebook* are full of suggestions for ensuring that boys and girls have a wealth of experience with literature—both listening and reading for themselves. The primary objective of the literature program is the creation of an environment so rich in poetry and books, so mellow with the enjoyment of literature, that boys and girls develop a keen delight in stories and in poetry and a genuine desire to read—on their own.

Providing leads to wide personal reading on his own for every child

One of the most significant contributions of The New Basic Reading Program is that it provides for maturation of children's perennial reading interests and introduces new areas of interest appropriate at each level of growth.

In the basic readers at Book Four level, we find eight centers of interest—each intrinsically interesting to pre-teen-aged boys and girls, each skillfully linked with units that precede and follow, and each (with the exception of the purely literary units) correlated naturally with the content of other areas of the middle-grade curriculum.

The materials in the following four units provide for maturation of reading interests that have existed since early primary levels:

- "Young Citizens of Today"—the activities and experiences of typical present-day boys and girls
- "Storyland of Here and Now"—modern fanciful tales
- "The Great Outdoors"—animals and the world of nature
- "Old Tales from Everywhere"—the classics of children's literature

These units provide for maturation of interests introduced in transition units at Book Three[2] level:

- "Young Citizens of Early Days"—the activities and experiences of children in the historical past
- "Young Citizens Here and There"—the activities and experiences of children in diverse geographical settings

These units, introduced at Book Four level, initiate new areas of interest:

- "Wonders of Our Times"—the mechanical world of today
- "Famous Americans of Other Times"—authentic biography

These unit themes are sufficiently broad and general not only to ensure leads to wide reading of the finest in children's literature but also to motivate reading of many different types of material.

For most youngsters, we do not of course expect that significant interest in wide reading of many different types of material will be self-generating. Instead, through guided reading and discussion, we build the concepts and generalizations common to the stories in any given unit. In the process we explore each child's present and potential interests, drawing out the reticent child and giving the enthusiastic child an opportunity to spark the interest of his friends.

We recognize, for example, that stories based on the lives of American heroes and heroines have undeniable appeal for preadolescents, who are usually born hero-worshipers. Yet when the unit "Famous Americans of Other Times" is introduced, we may discover that children tend to think of historical personages in isolation—each as a kind of glorified exception to the run of humanity.

Through guided reading and discussion of the stories, we must arouse children's curiosity about a famous person's relationship to other people and to the times in which he lived. Incidentally, when pupils begin to see these relationships, they have acquired readiness for the intelligent reading of history and current events. Most important perhaps, is the fact that in stimulating interest in reading about the lives of others, we are offering preadolescents a means of understanding themselves and their problems.

Once curiosities are aroused, we must be quick to show pupils how to use source materials that are within the range of their abilities—encyclopedias; newspapers and magazines; historical and biographical materials.

As concepts and generalizations common to the stories in any given unit become apparent to boys and girls, added meaning, purpose, and motivation are given to their reading. They develop an inner drive to seek materials that satisfy their growing interest in some aspect of the general unit theme.

A strong motive for personal reading will have been established—personal reading for which a background of basic concepts, generalizations, and interests has been systematically developed.

Ensuring continuous, sequential growth for every child

As teachers, we know that in the middle grades the range of children's interests is expanding rapidly. If growth in and through reading is to keep pace with interests and needs, the more able readers must have careful guidance as they seek to satisfy their widening interests through reading. Those children with reading problems need equally careful guidance of a different sort to ensure their growth in reading power as well as in interests.

As we have used the new *Times and Places*, we have established a flexible classroom organization designed to meet the needs of different ability groups.

Those children who are not ready for *More Times and Places* will, of course, continue at whatever level they are reading successfully.

Although most of the children in the class are now ready for *More Times and Places*, we are aware that within this group there is a wide range of achievement and interests to which we will need to adjust our guidance.

The lesson plans in this *Guidebook*, as in preceding ones, take into account the need for different kinds of guidance with different individuals within the group of children working at the same general achievement level.

For use with accelerated readers, there are challenging interpretative questions. There are suggestions for guidance in special research projects and in wide personal reading.

For use with less able readers, who need special help with particular skills, there are suggestions for reteaching and for review. There are also suggestions for stimulating independent personal reading.

Differentiation in the use of the exercises designed to extend skills and abilities is suggested. For example, all children reading at Book Four[2] level need to gain independence in the use of the dictionary as a pronunciation tool. The exercises in the first part of this *Guidebook* introduce the use of complete pronunciation keys. Some children will need more teaching, more special guidance, and more reteaching of the skills involved in using a pronunciation key than will others, but all need the initial instruction suggested.

The lesson plans clearly indicate whether a given exercise is designed to introduce or to maintain a skill or understanding. Those exercises that obviously introduce a skill should be used with all children who are reading at this level. Those exercises that are obviously designed to reteach, review, or strengthen skills may be used in a special-help situation with only those children who need special guidance. (For example, see the exercise, "Interpreting Implied Ideas," page 116 of this *Guidebook*.)

Enrichment and thoroughness with provisions for individual needs are more important than the speed at which an ability group or a child advances at any level. Although individual rate of growth, present achievement, and potentialities vary, all children need to take the same basic learning steps and to engage in stimulating enrichment activities.

Unit 1
Young Citizens
Here and There

This first unit of *More Times and Places* contains lively, absorbing stories about contemporary boys and girls whose problems, reactions, and inner drives are typical of pre-teen-agers everywhere. The settings, each a different region in the United States or Canada, range from the seacoast to the desert and from lush swamplands to northern forests and mountains. During their imaginary travels children experience a variety of scenery, climate, and local color, and share the problems, interests, and activities of many different families. Youngsters will find the story situations doubly interesting, since each arises from a unique aspect of the regional setting.

While it would be unrealistic and unsound to expect one unit of a basic reader to assume the responsibilities of a developmental program in social studies, reading and discussion of these stories will build readiness for many geographic understandings. The skills and understandings emphasized in the lesson plans are basic to interpretation in any area of the curriculum but are especially vital to interpretation in the social-studies area. For example, to interpret these stories the child must be able to (1) form vivid mental images from pictures and text of places he has never seen, (2) compare his surroundings, experiences, and activities with those of a story character and (3) understand simple cause-effect relationships that influence a character's life and make it like or different from his own.

All the story situations will stimulate discussion about traits that exemplify good citizenship and fine personal relationships everywhere—fairness, consideration, reliability, resourcefulness. Such discussion can foster self-evaluation and understanding of others, promote personal and social growth, and lead children to draw guiding principles that have application to their lives.

As children leaf through their books, they will notice two new features that contribute to that cherished feeling of growing up: the annotations in the "Books to Read" section and the glossary that gives not only the meanings of entry words but their pronunciations as well.

Of course, mere reading of the stories and casual use of the bibliography and the glossary will not insure growth in and through reading. The key to full interpretation of stories, to wide reading, and to growth in language power is the wealth of learning experiences that you initiate and adapt to your pupils' needs with the help of the lesson plans in this *Guidebook*. That is why each plan has been worked out in careful detail. If, over a period of time, you dispense with any portion of these lesson plans, it will be difficult to attain the values and goals of The New Basic Reading Program. At the beginning of each lesson in bold-face type there is a brief overview, which points up the theme of the story and its values in the life of the pre-teen-aged child. In many lesson plans you will note brief italic inserts that highlight the philosophy of The New Basic Reading Program.

Each section of a lesson plan has a definite purpose. Under "Preparing for Reading" you will find practical suggestions for insuring readiness for reading a story. Vocabulary needs are anticipated, a background of pertinent concepts is established, and motivation for reading is provided.

The section "Interpreting the Story" contains helpful suggestions for guiding silent reading, for initiating discussion of what has been read, and for helping children draw from their reading and discussion values and guiding principles applicable to their everyday lives.

The third section, called "Extending Skills and Abilities," is designed to develop and strengthen language understandings and interpretative skills vital to all meaningful reading. The initial group guidance suggested here is important to the function of the *Think-and-Do Book*, which has a dual purpose: With new and fresh materials, it gives the child an opportunity to apply the skills and understandings taught in a group situation; it helps you analyze children's responses to decide which pupils need special help with certain skills and understandings.

The section "Extending Interests" is of prime importance to the ultimate goal of the reading program, which is voluntary wide reading for every child. You will want to scan the list of books and stories suggested for this unit under the headings "Selections from Other Readers" and "Library Books for Children" in the bibliography at the back of this *Guidebook*, obtain as many as possible, and display them as lures to independent reading.

As you develop the lesson plans, you will want to take every opportunity to individualize your instruction within the group using *More Times and Places*. You may need to adapt the suggestions under "Preparing for Reading" to make sure that all pupils bring to the story the concepts needed for full interpretation. Under "Interpreting the Story" you will take into consideration the wide range of interpretative abilities usually found within any group of youngsters. Direct the simple factual questions to those children who still interpret largely at the who-did-what level. Stimulated by the feeling that they have made a contribution, such youngsters may think harder next time to answer a question requiring a higher level of interpretation. Pupils who interpret at higher levels should be challenged by questions that require ability to see fairly complex or subtle relationships. In developing new skills or understandings suggested under "Extending Skills and Abilities," you will work with all children who are using *More Times and Places*. However, lessons that review, reteach, and strengthen understandings might be presented only to those pupils who need them while the rest of the group engage in wide reading or research activities. The "Extending Interests" suggestions are important for all children. Many of the activities provide opportunities for challenging the superior reader; others will enable the slow reader to make a real contribution. Furthermore, you may discover that some youngsters who test high in reading and who discuss a story fluently are not reading widely on their own. To help them get started, you will find valuable suggestions for cultivating and developing varied interests that serve as leads into the rewarding world of juvenile literature.

INTRODUCING THE BOOK AND UNIT 1

After copies of *More Times and Places* have been distributed, allow time for pupils to leaf through their books and to comment about whatever is especially appealing. Then invite discussion of the cover picture and its implications. If necessary, explain that the boy is young Daniel Boone, that he lived in Washington's time and became a famous pioneer woodsman who explored the wilderness where many people later settled. Ask, "What is Daniel looking at? Would he really have been able to watch a farmer use modern machinery? Why not? What was the artist trying to show?" Help children generalize that this cover picture, like the one on the new *Times and Places*, is symbolic. It shows what has been done with some of the wilderness that Boone and other early woodsmen once roamed. It raises the interesting question: What would young Daniel have thought if he could have seen into the future and watched modern farmers working with machinery on cleared land that was once a vast wilderness?

Ask, "From this picture and the title of the book what would you expect some of the stories to be about?" Then suggest that pupils turn to the title page and tell what contrast between the old and the new is shown. You will also want to discuss the purpose of the table of contents and to consider what each unit title and picture tells about the stories in that unit.

Next, have pupils turn to the section "Books to Read" at the back of their books and talk over the advantages of having a description of each book. If you have assembled some of the library books suggested for the first unit, comment, "Like the stories in the first unit, these books tell about interesting adventures of children who live in many different places." Lead pupils to note that the glossary has pictures to illustrate some of the entries and gives the pronunciation as well as the meanings for each word. Call attention to the full pronunciation key and explain that you will show children how to use it to help them pronounce words.

To introduce the unit, have pupils turn to the unit-title page and read the title. Say, "Here are some young citizens helping adults with some interesting work. Can you tell in what part of the country these people probably live and what they are doing?" If necessary, explain that the picture shows the tapping of maple sugar trees in Vermont. "There is an interesting story in this unit that tells about a boy who had just moved to Vermont and did not understand at first how important maple-sugar time was. Other stories take us to the desert, to the seashore, and to Canada. By the time you have finished these stories you will feel as if you had made a long and interesting trip. You will have shared the work, the play, and the problems of many different boys and girls. You will have seen all kinds of scenery, some very different from what we see every day. Do you suppose that boys and girls who live in other parts of this country or in Canada enjoy the same things that you do? Do you suppose they have the same sort of work to do? Do you think their problems are the same as yours?" Welcome the contributions of children who have lived or visited in different places. Then suggest that by the time pupils have finished the unit, they all will have a basis for deciding whether or not people are more alike than they are different and just how much the place where a person lives affects his activities.

Unwelcome Passengers PAGES 6-13

Sight Word[1]: sweater

Attack Words[2]: *brilliant* crabs* shallow* securely* frequently** (glossary)

motionless* (root + suffix; mo'tion—position of single vowel letter)

lap* va'cant* cap'ture* (position of single vowel letter)

guided* (root with *e* dropped + ending; guide—final *e*)

argued* (root with *e* dropped + ending; ar'gue—vowel followed by *r*)

moaning* (root + ending; moan—two vowel letters together)

mean'while'* (two vowel letters together; final *e*)

Catching crabs on their last day of vacation at the seaside was fun for Peter and Penny. But their plan for taking the crabs on a passenger train in spite of their mother's misgivings backfired with hilarious results.

The exciting action and hubbub of this story will provoke many chuckles, and will likely start a train of spontaneous reminiscences and maybe some self-evaluation; for few pre-teen-aged readers will fail to identify themselves with

---

[1] Sight words are words that pupils might have difficulty attacking independently on the basis of specific meaning clues or on the basis of structural and phonetic understandings. (For example, the new word *sweater* is presented as a sight word in this story since it is used in an unusual contextual setting.) In general, all sight words should be presented as suggested in the footnote on page 39.

[2] At the beginning of each lesson plan you will find a list of the new words that pupils at this level of reading can be expected to attack independently as they read. The attack words that appear in the glossary are listed first (in italic type). Every glossary word is starred as an attack word, since its pronunciation as well as its meaning appears in the glossary. The first few lesson plans review previously taught understandings about the function of a pronunciation key and teach the use of a complete pronunciation key. If an attack word is not listed in the glossary, the child can identify its meaning through use of context clues and can identify its pronunciation by combining context clues with specific methods of analysis. He may need to divide the word into syllables and use visual clues to vowel sounds, determining the accented syllable through use of visual clues to accent or of context clues. For your convenience, each attack word that is not listed in the glossary is divided into syllables, and the accent is shown. The notation in parentheses suggests the method of phonetic analysis that the child may apply to determine the vowel sound in the accented syllable.

the story characters and their plight. Some youngsters will be consoled by the idea that everyone at some time or other has had a "great" idea that back-fired; many boys and girls will be challenged by the way Peter and Penny handled the situation.

PREPARING FOR READING

Establishing background and anticipating vocabulary needs: You might begin by commenting, "Our first story whisks us to the seaside where two brothers, Peter and Penny, and their mother and father had been spending their vacation. Can you imagine why a boy might have the nickname Penny?" Allow time for pupils' surmises.

Explain, "The cottage where Peter and Penny spent their vacation was along the Atlantic Ocean—probably on the coast of the state of Massachusetts." Indicate the coastal area of Massachusetts on a large map, or if pupils have had experience in map reading, have them locate the area on a map in their social-studies book. If any pupils have visited or lived in that area or in any coastal region, encourage them to describe it.

Then ask, "What do you suppose Peter and Penny did to have fun during their vacation at the seaside? What would you be most interested in doing if you vacationed there?" After a brief discussion, comment, "Yes, the boys in the story liked to go out on the water in a boat, and they loved to fish. They also liked to catch _____. [Write the word *crabs* on the board and have pupils read it.] What are crabs and why are people interested in catching them? Let's turn to the glossary in our books and see whether it gives us a specific answer to that question." Suggest that pupils use the guide words to locate the page where the entry word *crab* may be found. After they have read the definition, invite discussion of the questions "What do crabs look like? Where do they live? Why do you suppose Peter and Penny liked to catch them?"

Continue, "Right after the entry word *crab* we see in parentheses the printed pronunciation of the word. What two letters in the pronunciation stand for the beginning consonant blend we hear in the word? [*kr*] How do we know that the vowel sound in the word is the short *a* sound?" If necessary, explain that the letter *a* without any mark above it is the symbol for the short *a* sound. Then ask, "What is the last consonant sound in the word? [the *b* sound] Were we pronouncing the word *crab* correctly before we checked its pronunciation in the glossary? Why did you expect that the letter *a* would stand for the short *a* sound in this word?"

Next, write the words *brilliant, shallow, securely, frequently* on the board and explain, "These words from today's story are in the glossary, too. Let's take a few minutes to look at the pronunciation of each one now." Use procedures similar to those on page 37 for the word *crab* to help pupils derive the pronunciation of each word. Before pupils find the word *securely* in the glossary, however, you might explain that they must "take off" the suffix *-ly* and find the root word. Note children's ability to interpret not only the letter symbols and the schwa symbol (ə), which represents the soft, unaccented vowel sound, but also the accent mark in the pronunciations. Conclude, "As you come to these words in the story, you may wish to refer to the glossary again to make sure of their meanings or pronunciations."

Pupils who have had the developmental training suggested in the "Extending Skills and Abilities" sections of the Guidebook *for the new* Times and Places *have had experience in locating entry words in a dictionary or a glossary, in deriving their meanings, and in interpreting simple pronunciation symbols. Such pupils should have no difficulty with the glossary words in this story. To derive the pronunciations for these words, pupils need only interpret consonant and vowel pronunciation symbols taught at the previous level. The dictionary exercises in the first unit of this* Guidebook *introduce the use of the complete pronunciation key on page 302 of* More Times and Places.

"Today's story takes place on the last day of Peter and Penny's vacation. What started as a rather dull day ended with much excitement and some embarrassment for the boys—all because they thought they'd dreamed up a wonderful idea, only to have it backfire. The title of our first story is 'Unwelcome Passengers.' Can you guess who the unwelcome passengers might be? Do you suppose Peter and Penny were embarrassed because they were unwelcome passengers? Let's read the story to find out."

INTERPRETING THE STORY

Pages 6-9: After pupils have turned to page 6, allow time for their comments on the picture at the top of pages 6 and 7. Call attention, if necessary, to such details as the wide, endless expanse of water, the sandy beaches, the scattered cottages and docks, the sea gulls, and the sailboats—all of which give a background for imagery of the setting and action of the story. Do boys and girls think they would enjoy a vacation in a spot like this? Why (or why not)?

Introduce the two main characters, Penny and Peter, and ask pupils whether they think the brothers look very happy. After a brief discussion of why the boys might be bored and discontented in spite of their delightful surroundings, comment, "Peter and Penny didn't sit on the dock looking bored for long. They decided to do something to surprise their mother. In fact, they got so interested in what they were doing that lunch time rolled around before they knew it. Their mother had to hang the time-to-eat signal on the porch to remind them that lunch was ready. The signal was an *old red sweater.* [Present[1] the italicized phrase.] Read the first four pages to find out what the boys decided to do. By the time you have finished page 9, you will probably guess who the unwelcome passengers are."

When pupils have read the first four pages, ask, "What did Peter and Penny finally decide to do to amuse themselves? Who will describe just how they went about catching the crabs? [Encourage any pupils who may have gone crabbing to compare their experiences with that of Peter and Penny.] Can you guess from the picture and from the definition of *crab* in your glossary why the boys scooped up the crabs with a net and not with their hands? Will someone read the sentence on page 6 that tells us how Penny got his name?"

To check further on comprehension of the plot of the story thus far and on the ability to anticipate outcomes, ask such questions as "Why couldn't the crabs be eaten for lunch? What did Peter and Penny suggest doing with them? What did their mother think of the idea at first? Under what conditions would she allow the boys to take the crabs with them on the train? Can you guess now who the unwelcome passengers will be? Do you suppose the boys can take charge of the crabs successfully on the train? Why [or why not]?" Then suggest that pupils finish the story to see whether they are right.

Pages 10-13: When pupils have finished, enter into the fun with some such comment as "Well, that *was* some train trip both for the boys and their mother and for the other passengers, wasn't it? Did the trip turn out just about the way you expected it would?" Since pupils will probably be eager to talk about this unusual and hilarious train ride, encourage them to talk freely. You might subtly guide their retelling of the story and make the action come alive by occasionally (don't overdo it!) injecting such questions

---

[1] As used in this *Guidebook*, the word *present* means that the teacher should write the italicized words, phrases, or sentences on the board as she uses them in meaningful oral context. Thus the child associates sound, form, and a specific meaning with each sight word. All words listed as sight words should be presented in this way.

as "How did _____ [Mother, Peter, Penny, or the passengers] feel when *that* happened? What could you see the others doing while *that* was going on? What could you hear then? Is that what *you* would have done?"

Often a child—or adult for that matter—does not realize what a good story-teller he can be. He may never think about how satisfying his emotional reactions to a story have been and what vivid sensory images he has formed until he is challenged to think about his reactions and images by a clever listener who asks just the right question at the right time. That kind of listener seems not to be interrupting the narration but rather to be participating in it and relishing it as much as the storyteller.

To point up the motives of the story characters, ask, "Why did the boys' mother, after first saying no, decide to let Peter and Penny take the crabs on the train? Why do you suppose people screamed when they saw crabs in the aisle? Why did Peter insist that he and Penny should catch them?" Encourage several pupils to respond to each question; you may thereby gain new insights into the character, background, and problems of various children. Opinions will likely vary, and pupils' opinions will be modified or changed as they listen to or participate in the discussion. Naturally you will respect all opinions unless they are completely inappropriate, in which case you will want to try to discover the reason behind them.

In conclusion ask someone to read aloud what Peter said after the crabs had been safely put back in their basket. To help pupils integrate as a part of their experience ideas gained from reading, ask, "Why *is* there a rule against taking animals into passenger cars? Do you think it's a good one? Why [or why not]?" If pupils are using the *Think-and-Do Book*, you might comment that on page 2 they will read an interesting story about what happened when someone tried to take some baby animals on a streetcar.

Extending interpretation: To point up without undue moralizing the lesson in responsibility and fair play implicit in this story, ask, "Do you think that the boys' idea of taking the crabs on the train was a wise one? When they got into trouble, did they take the responsibility for getting out of it? How? What lesson do you suppose they learned? No doubt some of you have been in a 'tight spot' because a good idea of yours went wrong. Would you like to tell us about *your* experience?"

Fairness plays a large part in the thinking of nine-year-olds, and they will often argue loud and long over fairness in games, for example. Too, they are usually reasonable and responsible. At nine years of age most children are beginning to understand right and wrong and are trying to develop standards. Therefore this is a good time to help youngsters develop standards that build character not by "sermonizing" but by encouraging informal discussion and evaluation of the behavior of story characters.

Oral interpretation: This story is a good one to read aloud for many reasons. It contains marked changes in mood, in setting, and in pace. There are many cues in the narrative text that indicate just how the characters felt and how they must have sounded as they talked. There are many opportunities for the reader to convey to his audience the tone of certain passages and to arouse vivid sensory images through his facial expressions, rate of reading, and tone of voice. Before oral reading, help pupils plan how to read certain passages. How should page 6 be read, for example? Lead pupils to note that there is no action here—the page sets the stage for the subsequent action. The last sentence on the page cues the reader to the way Peter and Penny felt and therefore to how they probably sounded. Page 7 provides a contrast to the mood of the previous page, and page 7 itself is full of contrasts. There is straight narrative text that describes this business of crabbing. Then we note that Penny's mood veers from one of enthusiasm to grumbling impatience, and the reader will want to convey those moods by the way he reads Penny's remarks.

Continue this type of informal analysis with succeeding pages. Then encourage pupils to "let themselves go" as they read aloud. If necessary, read some of the passages aloud yourself, to set the pace and to illustrate how much fun oral reading can be.

Following the oral interpretation of the story, you might suggest, "There are three whole books about Penny and Peter. You enjoyed this story so very much I'm sure you will want to read at least one of the books." Help children locate *Here's a Penny*,[1] by Carolyn Haywood, in the bibliography at the back of *More Times and Places*. Allow time for them to read the annotation describing this and two other Haywood books. If you have these books in the classroom, you might display them. If not, encourage children to obtain them from the library.

By suggesting appropriate books while children's interest in a story is still at its height, you are providing a strong incentive to further reading. An enjoyable story is one of the best recommendations for the book from which it was adapted or for other books by the same author.

[1] All books referred to in the lesson plans are listed with their publishers in the bibliography at the back of this *Guidebook*.

Using a pronunciation key: This exercise is designed to strengthen the following important understandings basic to the interpretation of the pronunciations in the glossary of *More Times and Places:* (1) Each symbol in a printed pronunciation stands for a sound (there are no silent letters in the printed pronunciations); (2) A consonant letter stands for its most common sound; (3) A vowel letter with no mark over it stands for its most common sound—the short sound; (4) The schwa symbol (ə) stands for the unstressed vowel sound heard in most unaccented syllables.

Have pupils turn to the full pronunciation key on page 302 of *More Times and Places.* Call attention first to the single consonant symbols printed at the left of each of the three columns and remind pupils that each symbol stands for one sound only, that when they see the symbol *b*, for example, in the printed pronunciation that follows an entry word, they will say the sound that the letter *b* stands for in the words *bad* or *rob.* Ask children to pronounce other words that begin with the *b* sound and then others that end with the *b* sound. Review the idea that in pronunciations the letter *b* is always used to stand for this sound. Continue with some or all of the other consonant symbols given in the key.

To point up the reason why the consonant letters *c*, *q*, and *x* are not used as consonant symbols in the key, write the following words on the board:

camp	city	quit	fix
come	cent	queen	coax

Have each pair of words pronounced. Then use the first two pairs to review the fact that *c* may stand for a *k* or an *s* sound; the third and fourth pairs to review the fact that the letters *qu* usually stand for the sounds *kw*, and *x* often stands for the sounds *ks*. Then lead pupils to generalize that when we pronounce words spelled with the letters *c*, *q*, or *x*, we say other consonant sounds for them.

Next, call pupils' attention to the group of symbols that represent *a* sounds in the key and ask, "We may speak of the *b* sound, or of the *k* sound, but why couldn't we speak of the *a* sound?" Recall with children that *a* is a vowel letter, and, unlike the consonant letters used in the key, it stands for no *one* common sound. The letter *a* may stand for a short sound as it does in *hat*, for example, for a long sound as it does in *age*, or for neither a short nor a long sound when it is followed by *r* as in *care* and *far.* The same things are true, of course, of the other vowel letters.

Next, write the following words, omitting the printed pronunciations:

crab (krab)	face (fās)	silent (sī'lənt)
stamp (stamp)	age (āj)	confess (kən fes')
lap (lap)	main (mān)	amuse (ə mūz')

Have the words in the first list pronounced. Then ask, "What sound does the letter *a* stand for in these words? [short *a*]" Explain that since the letter *a* stands for the short sound more often than for other sounds, this pronunciation key uses the letter *a* without any mark above it to represent the short sound. Lead pupils to notice that the same thing is true of the other vowel letters. Then write the printed pronunciations in parentheses after the words, cover the spellings, and have pupils pronounce the words again. Use similar procedures with the second list to bring out that a straight line over a vowel letter represents the long vowel sound.

As each word in the third list is pronounced, ask, "How many vowel sounds do you hear? [two] What vowel sound do you hear in the unaccented syllable? [the soft, unstressed vowel sound]" Remind pupils, if necessary, that we call this vowel sound the schwa sound and have them find the symbol in the key that stands for this sound (ə). Then write the pronunciations after the words and review the purpose of the accent mark and the space between syllabic divisions. Use the pronunciations in all three lists to reinforce the understandings that (1) every symbol stands for a sound, (2) printed pronunciations often look very different from the spellings of words, (3) the schwa symbol may stand for the sound represented by any vowel letter in an unaccented syllable.

Think-and-Do Book: Use pages 1 and 2. Page 1 represents an alluring travel advertisement for the Massachusetts seacoast. Interest is focused on interesting vacation activities. The page will stimulate additional contributions from children on things they like to do during a vacation at the seaside, as well as give practice in summarizing and organizing ideas. The discussion on the inside front cover and the detailed Teacher's Notes in the back of the *Think-and-Do Book* give helpful suggestions for the most efficient use of the *Think-and-Do Book*. Specific suggestions for the use of each page are given on the page itself.

EXTENDING INTERESTS

Enjoying literature: As pupils start reading the Haywood books mentioned earlier, they will want to describe some of Penny and Peter's other humorous experiences. In addition, "Unwelcome Passengers" suggests another story with quite the opposite problem—"Michael Who Missed His Train," by Dorothy and Marguerite Bryan. It can be found in *Time for True Tales*[1] and is a story children will enjoy hearing you read aloud.

Take some time now to go over the bibliography at the back of *More Times and Places* in more detail so that children can decide which books they would like to read. (There may be a few words, such as proper names, with which youngsters may need help.) There are many points of comparison and contrast between these library books and the stories in the unit, which should lead to some interesting discussions.

Setting up a "travel bureau": It might be fun for children to set up part of their classroom as a travel bureau, advertising each area they visit vicariously in the stories of this unit. Vivid visual imagery evoked by the stories may inspire some pupils to paint a travel poster or a mural for background, while others contribute pictures or material from travel magazines to make the display as alluring as possible. As a special feature, a child who has spent a vacation in one of the areas and has slides or snapshots at his disposal might enjoy showing them to his classmates.

Independent supplementary reading: Provide time for pupils to read and discuss the selections from other readers suggested in the bibliography at the back of this *Guidebook*. These selections include stories closely related in content to the stories in the text and thus serve to broaden children's appreciation of the unit theme. To help you adapt the independent supplementary reading program to the needs of individual pupils, three levels of difficulty are indicated:

Unstarred selections: Easy-to-read materials, which any pupil prepared to read *More Times and Places* can read without guidance. Many of the new words can be attacked independently even by slow readers.

Single-starred selections: Stories of average difficulty, which most fourth-graders should be able to read independently.

Double-starred selections: More difficult stories for superior readers who have developed a high level of efficiency in independent reading.

These classifications should serve merely as guides in recommending stories for children of different abilities. No attempt should be made to discourage slow readers from trying to read materials on a high level or to limit the reading of superior readers to the more difficult stories.

---

[1] *Time for True Tales, and Almost True*, Revised Edition, compiled by May Hill Arbuthnot (Chicago: Scott, Foresman and Company, 1961).

A Christmas to Remember PAGES 14-21

Sight Words: ruined forehead youngsters quarter

Attack Words: *cactus* mesquite* linger* apparently** (glossary)

    duties* (root with *y* changed to *i* before ending; du′ty—
      position of single vowel letter)

    pro vide′* (final *e*)

    or′na ments* (vowel followed by *r*)

    bitterly* (root + suffix; bit′ter—position of single vowel
      letter)

This heartwarming story tells how Jane Wallace, a newcomer to ranch life in the desert region of Arizona, solved a seemingly hopeless problem of providing a Christmas tree for her younger brother and sister. Young readers will be delighted and touched by the way Jane overcame her initial discouragement and ingeniously provided not only a Christmas tree but ornaments and gifts as well.

Without being overly sentimental this story exemplifies affection, consideration, and tenderness within the family circle. Young readers will feel a kind of glow as they finish the last page. And tucked within the plot is a subtle lesson on the real meaning of that overworked phrase "the Christmas spirit." Few children will leave this story untouched by the idea that after all it *is* more blessed to give than to receive.

PREPARING FOR READING

Establishing background: Since the pictures and text supply most of the background information about desert life needed for the interpretation of this story, you might keep the preliminary discussion brief. After pupils have studied the picture on page 14 and have read the page and the first half of page 15, they will likely have established for themselves the setting and background for the story and will have discovered the problem of the main character. During the discussion following the reading of these pages you may present the sight words and clarify concepts about the desert, as suggested in the next section of this lesson plan.

Middle-grade youngsters are eager for independence. Occasional use of the procedure suggested in this lesson plan helps put children on their own in an important aspect of interpretation—that of using pictures and text to discover for oneself the setting, background, and problem of a story. This story is so illustrated and constructed that it lends itself to fostering this type of independence. Page 3 of the Think-and-Do Book *gives interesting introductions to two other stories. The child is to decide what the story problem will probably be in each. You, the teacher, are of course the best judge of the maturity of a particular group of children and consequently of the amount of guidance that may be necessary in connection with this skill.*

You might begin by recalling with pupils that the previous story took them to the seaside. Then ask how they would like to travel on the magic carpet of printed words to quite a different part of the United States. Indicate on a large map the state of Arizona and comment, "If any of you have ever lived or visited in Arizona, especially this part of it [the general southwest area of the state], you know that this is interesting desert country. As you read today's story and look at the pictures, you may notice that this part of our country is different from the part where we live—that the weather is different, that the plants look different. You may decide that even Christmas would seem different on a ranch in the desert.

"But after you have finished the story, I wonder if you won't agree that Christmas is Christmas no matter where a person lives, and that it can never be *ruined* [present the word] if one remembers what Christmas means."

INTERPRETING THE STORY

After pupils have located the story, suggest that they study the picture on page 14 and read that page and through the sentence "Jane leaned on her broom, thinking hard" on page 15 to find out more about the place where this story occurs and what the problem of the main character is. "If you come to a word you can't 'figure out,' I'll be glad to help you."

If a pupil asks for help with a word during silent reading, it is usually a good idea to tell him the word so that his train of thought will not be interrupted. You may wish to jot down any words he asks for in a notebook beside his name. Is the word one you have just presented? Is it a word the pupil could have found in the glossary? Is it one that elementary knowledge of phonetic or structural analysis or use of context and word-form clues should have enabled the pupil to unlock? A quick analysis of the type of words a pupil asks about will enable you to individualize your instructions during lessons designed to foster independence in word attack.

Pages 14-15: When pupils have finished, heighten awareness of how much a picture can do to help us understand the background of a story by asking: "First of all, what does the picture on page 14 tell you about winter weather in the desert? [The way Jane is dressed and her tanned skin would indicate that the weather is warm and sunny.] How is this winter weather different from [or like] ours? Who can tell us something about weather, plants, and living conditions in the desert? How would you describe the view of the desert from the Wallaces' front porch? Who knows what those odd-shaped, tall plants in the distance are?" Write the word *cactus* and have pupils check its pronunciation and meaning in the glossary. Explain that there are many species of cactuses (or cacti)—the kind pictured in the glossary is similar to that growing by the porch post at the left in the picture. The tall cactuses in the distance are the largest of the cactus family— the saguaro cacti. The white blossoms they bear in May and June are the state flowers of Arizona.

Continue, "What are those scraggly, bush-like trees in the picture?" If no one knows they are mesquite, write the word *mesquite* on the board and have pupils check its pronunciation in the glossary. Then ask, "Can you tell from the definition of *mesquite* and the sentence printed in italic type, which helps explain the meaning of *mesquite*, why Jane's father would be glad that it grew on his ranch?" Write *linger, apparently* beneath *cactus* and *mesquite* and explain that these words are also in the glossary.

"What does the first paragraph of the story tell us about the way Jane felt? Did you notice that everything you read through the middle of the next page told you why Jane's thoughts were not cheerful? What were the reasons? What was Jane's main worry or problem?" After the discussion, ask, "What does the fact that Jane worried about the *youngsters* in the family and not herself tell you about her?"

Continue, "Do you suppose she leaned on her broom a *quarter* of an hour or so, thinking so hard that she wrinkled her *forehead?* What do you think Jane will do to solve her problem?" Suggest that children read to the bottom of page 18 to see if they have guessed right.

During silent reading, you will also want to notice which pupils indicate by their facial expressions that they are "living" the story—that they are truly reacting to the story plot as it unfolds.

Pages 15-18: After silent reading, comment, "When a person is able to work out his own problems and think of many things to do on his own, we sometimes say that person is resourceful. Was Jane resourceful? Why do you think so?" If necessary, help pupils organize their thinking by asking such questions as "What did Jane decide to do about the problem of providing a Christmas tree? What nearly upset her plan for trimming the tree with pretty ornaments? Who helped her solve that problem? How do you suppose Mrs. Wallace happened to remember that her granny made ornaments from eggshells? What other kind of Christmas tree trimmings did Jane think of to make? What kind of presents did she make for the twins and what gave her the idea for them?"

Call attention to the picture at the bottom of page 19 and ask, "What do you suppose Jane was thinking as she looked out over the desert on the night before Christmas? Do you suppose her plans for making a Christmas to remember worked out to her satisfaction? Let's finish the story to find out."

Pages 19-21: As children finish the story, watch for contented smiles and satisfied expressions that indicate reaction to the gratifying outcome of the story. Ask, "What do you like about the way this story ended? Why was this Christmas an especially happy one for the Wallaces?" If necessary, check interpretation of story events by asking, "How did Jane make the mesquite tree look like a Christmas tree? How did the twins feel about the Christmas Jane had prepared for them? What surprise did Jane get on Christmas day? What surprise did Mr. Wallace get?"

Call attention again to the picture on page 14 and ask, "How did Jane feel in this picture?" Then have pupils turn to the picture on page 19 and ask, "How did Jane feel on the night before Christmas? What had happened to change Jane's attitude?" During the discussion, bring out that Jane's attitude toward her new home and Christmas in the desert was not changed by any external circumstances. The change occurred within Jane once she realized that with a little ingenuity she could make a happy Christmas for her family with what was at hand.

Extending interpretation: Have the last two paragraphs of the story read aloud and ask, "Who do you suppose will remember longest this first Christmas in the desert? Who do you think enjoyed it the most? Why?" Most children will probably agree that it was Jane. If, however, there is a difference of opinion, encourage pupils to justify their opinions. During the discussion, help youngsters generalize in their own words that (1) we remember longest those events or occasions to which we personally contribute our efforts and good will, (2) our greatest happiness and enjoyment in life is likely to come from doing things for others.

Oral interpretation: Children will enjoy reading aloud this unique Christmas story. Help them plan how best to bring out the dominant moods of the story. For example, the first page and a half should be read to reflect Jane's despair. Then momentarily her spirits lift, but on page 16 her hopes are dashed, and we read "Jane sighed bitterly." From page 17 on, the mood of the story is happy, and the ending is positively triumphant. Briefly call attention, too, to the many cues to the way characters sounded as they spoke and to the italicized words that are cues to emphasis.

EXTENDING SKILLS AND ABILITIES

Identifying and evaluating character traits: The events and outcome of this story might have been different indeed if Jane had not been the kind of girl she was. To help children identify and evaluate Jane's character traits and note their effect on story events, have them turn back to page 15 and read the first paragraph. Then comment, "Suppose Jane had then said, 'It doesn't seem right for me not to have any Christmas this year.' How might this story have been changed?" Have the second paragraph read and ask pupils to think of words that describe or characterize Jane from what she did say (unselfish, considerate, thoughtful of others). "Would you like to have your friends use these words in describing you?"

Have pupils read the next to last paragraph on page 15 and ask, "Suppose at this point Jane had said, 'There *aren't* any real Christmas trees around here; so we just won't have a tree this year.' How would this story have been changed?" After the discussion, have pupils read the last paragraph on page 15 and think of words that characterize Jane from what she said (resourceful, imaginative, optimistic, determined). . "Would you like to have your friends use these words in describing you?"

Encourage pupils to think of other words that describe Jane and to justify their opinions by references from the story.

Using a pronunciation key: This lesson provides for a quick review of the understandings developed in the previous lesson plan and presents four vowel pronunciation symbols: oi (heard in *oil* and *boy*), ou (heard in *out* and *cow*), u̇ (heard in *put* and *took*), ü (heard in *rule* and *soon*).

1. Suggest that today the group might play a game called "Which Is It?" Remind pupils to refer to the full pronunciation key in the glossary, if necessary, and then write the following pronunciations on the board: (kwāk), (kwak). Ask, "Which of these pronunciations is the word for the sound a duck makes?" When pupils agree that the second is the pronunciation of

the word *quack* and therefore the correct answer, write the word *quack* before its pronunciation. Then ask what word the other pronunciation stands for. As pupils pronounce the word *quake*, write it before (*kwāk*).

Continue with the following pairs of pronunciations and questions:

(stem)	Which is part of	(lej)	Which is part of
(stēm)	a plant?	(leg̣)	your body?
(nēs)	Which is part of	(sal′ əd)	Which is something
(nōz)	your face?	(sāl′ ər)	to eat?
(kwit)	Which means stop?	(ok′ sən)	Which means more
(kwīt)		(ak′ səl)	than one ox?

2. To introduce the first of the new pronunciation symbols, pronounce the following words and tell pupils to listen carefully to the vowel sound in each: *put, hook, should.* Ask, "What do you notice about the vowel sounds in these words? [They are the same.] What symbol in the pronunciation key is used to represent this vowel sound? [*u̇*]" Next, write under the symbol *u̇* the pronunciations shown in the first column below, omitting the spellings of the words. As pupils say the word each pronunciation represents, write the word before its pronunciation.

u̇	*ü*	*ou*	*oi*
bush (bu̇sh)	glue (glü)	bound (bound)	voice (vois)
brook (bru̇k)	scoop (skü̇p)	drown (droun)	toy (toi)
hood (hu̇d)	suit (sü̇t)	scout (skout)	coin (koin)
could (ku̇d)	move (mü̇v)	doubt (dout)	noise (noiz)
full (fu̇l)	group (grü̇p)	town (toun)	joy (joi)

Continue similarly with the remaining three lists of words, pronouncing beforehand the words *blue, stoop, fruit* to introduce the symbol *ü; out, cow, gown* for *ou;* and *moist, join, boy* for *oi.*

3. If pupils are using the *Thorndike-Barnhart Beginning Dictionary,*[1] guide the use of page 57 with them at this time. If the dictionary is not available, write the following short vowel key on the board and explain to pupils that it will help them with printed pronunciations:

> oil   out   pu̇t   rüle

Then write the pronunciations given on page 51 and explain, "As I point to each pronunciation, you are to pronounce the word it represents." Then as children pronounce each of the words, write its spelling before the pro-

---

[1] *Thorndike-Barnhart Beginning Dictionary,* by E. L. Thorndike and Clarence L. Barnhart (Chicago: Scott, Foresman and Company, 1959 or 1962).

nunciation. When the exercise is completed it will look as follows:

bullet (bŭl′it)	clown (kloun)
cruel (krü′əl)	enjoyment (en joi′mənt)
fool (fül)	foot (fŭt)
crowd (kroud)	soup (süp)
destroy (di stroi′)	accuse (ə kūz′)

Think-and-Do Book: Use pages 3 and 4. Page 4 gives the child experience in using a simple key to derive the sound of printed pronunciations with no cue from word forms, since the word to be identified is pictured.

EXTENDING INTERESTS

Enjoying literature: Probably some of the children in the class have at some time moved to a completely strange place as Jane Wallace's family had in "A Christmas to Remember." Perhaps these youngsters can explain what made the new place seem like home to them: for example, having their own things around them or celebrating a special occasion, such as a birthday, in a traditional way. In *Time for Poetry*[1] there is a poem by Polly Boyden called "New Mexico," which brings out this idea. The child in the poem was evidently from another part of the country and frightened a bit by the desert at night. Let the pupils explain why "indoors is Home" to the child in the poem.

Then suggest, "Since you enjoyed the story of the Wallaces' Christmas, you'd probably like to read a whole book about someone who worked hard to make Christmas an especially happy time. See if you can find such a book in the section "Books to Read." [*Maggie Rose, Her Birthday Christmas* is a wonderful example of a happy Christmas following a tragic disappointment.] Do you see any other books that remind you of 'A Christmas to Remember' in some way? [Some children may see a relationship between the Larkin family in *Blue Willow* and the newly settled Wallaces.] Now let's look for a book that might have another story about the Southwest in it." When someone mentions *Told Under Spacious Skies*, suggest that the boys might like to look through that book and see if it does contain a story about the Southwest. ("Kip and the Red Tractor" takes place in Texas.)

Art activities: Youngsters who have shared Jane·Wallace's satisfaction in providing her family with a Christmas of her own making will be eager to try their hand at making similar decorations for an approaching holiday, or for a class party they may be planning.

---

[1] *Time for Poetry*, Revised Edition, compiled by May Hill Arbuthnot (Chicago: Scott, Foresman and Company, 1959).

Adventure in the Swamps PAGES 22-29

Attack Words: *swamps* alligator* coiled* cypress* tupelo* coon* panic* lunged** (glossary)

San'tee* 'ga'tor* moss*[1] blos'soms* hol'low* de fends'* (position of single vowel letter)

encouraged*[2] (root with *e* dropped + ending; encour-age—form of root word + meaning clues)

rattlesnake* (roots in compound; snake—final *e*)

grasped* (root + ending; grasp—position of single vowel letter)

In contrast to the arid desert of the last story, the setting of this one is the lush Santee River swampland in South Carolina. It is mysterious country, full of sights, sounds, and smells unfamiliar to the average reader. The problem in the story, however, is a familiar one. Young Johnny wanted to prove to himself that he was as able and self-reliant as his older brother, Henry. In spite of his mother's repeated warnings, Johnny set off alone into the dangerous swamps to catch an alligator. Through a narrow escape he learned why it pays to heed the advice of experienced adults.

Pre-teen-aged youngsters will be fascinated by the rich and colorful imagery this story evokes. Their craving for adventure will be satisfied, and they will applaud the unexpected twist at the end of the story.

PREPARING FOR READING

Establishing background and anticipating vocabulary needs: Recall with pupils the two widely separated areas of the United States in which the two previous stories have taken place (the coast of Massachusetts and

---

[1] The pronunciation of *o* in this word varies in different regions. In some sections short *o* is heard, but the broad vowel sound (*ô* as in *ôr*) is probably the more common. Children will, of course, use the sound common to their own speech patterns.

[2] Although the prefix *en-* has not been taught, the form, sound, and meaning of the root word *courage* is known. Therefore the new derived form *encourage* should be easily recognized when it is encountered in a context that forces its meaning.

southwestern Arizona) and locate them again on the map. Then comment, "Arizona, where Jane lived, is in the southern part of the United States, isn't it? It is also in the western part. So we say Arizona is in the Southwest. Today's story takes place in the southeastern part of the United States—way across the southern part of our country in the state of South Carolina [sweep your hand across the map from Arizona to South Carolina]." Indicate Massachusetts again and say, "As you can see, South Carolina, like Massachusetts, borders the Atlantic Ocean, but it is much farther south—as far south as Arizona."

Recall with pupils that Jane Wallace lived in the warm, dry desert in Arizona. Then explain, "Johnny, the boy we are going to read about today, lived in a moist region—on a farm near the Santee River in South Carolina. [Indicate the Santee River on the map.]" If any pupils have lived or visited in South Carolina or if the group has studied about this region in social studies, encourage them to tell what they know about it.

Continue, "Johnny had an exciting, dangerous adventure one day in the _____ [write the word *swamps* and have it read]." If necessary, refer children to the glossary for the pronunciation and meaning of *swamp*. Then ask, "Do you know what animals live in southern swamps? What trees and plants grow in swamps?" For answers to these questions, encourage children to draw upon their direct experiential background or upon what they may have learned about swamps from their science books or other sources. If no one mentions that alligators live in southern swamps, write the word *alligator* and have pupils check its pronunciation in the glossary. Then ask, "After looking at the picture of an alligator in the glossary, would you care to have one for a pet? Why [or why not]?"

INTERPRETING THE STORY

Page 22: Have pupils find "Adventure in the Swamps," in the table of contents and turn to the first page of the story, which establishes the problem and provides the motive for reading. Encourage discussion of picture details and speculations about why Johnny is practicing roping. Then comment, "I wonder if Johnny felt the way you do about alligators. Read the first page to find out." Write the word *coil* and remind pupils to check its meaning in the glossary, if necessary.

After pupils have finished, ask, "Why did Johnny want an alligator? Do you think he can get one all by himself? What do you think might happen to Johnny in the swamps?" After pupils have conjectured, suggest that they finish the story to see if they are right. Write on the board the words *cypress, tupelo, coon, panic, lunged* and suggest that as children encounter these words in the story, they use the glossary if they are uncertain how to pronounce them or do not know their meanings.

Pupils should not be given the impression that it is necessary or desirable to look up lists of isolated words in a glossary or a dictionary. Rather it is important that children are taught to regard a glossary or a dictionary as a highly personal and functional tool for checking pronunciations and meanings of unfamiliar words that they encounter in context.

If the group reading *More Times and Places* is composed of superior and average readers, they should be able to finish the story without much guidance. To encourage some critical reading, you might write the following question: *Was it a good thing that Johnny went off into the swamp alone?* Suggest that as they read, pupils think of reasons to support their answers to this question. Later, of course, you will want to use some of the questions suggested below to stimulate full interpretation of the story.

For slow readers, who need the stimulus of frequent discussion to follow the thread of the story, you may want to divide the story into reading units and discuss each part after silent reading as follows:

Pages 23-25: "Why did Johnny feel guilty as he headed for the swamp? Do you think he was a little afraid? What makes you think so?" Encourage comments about the picture on pages 24 and 25. Then ask, "If you had been walking along beside Johnny, what things would you have seen, smelled, and heard? Do you think he will be able to catch his 'gator? Let's read the next two pages to find out."

Pages 26-27: "What troubles did Johnny have trying to catch his 'gator? What did the alligator do after Johnny roped him? Why did Johnny stay out of reach of the animal's tail? Do you think Johnny will take that alligator home for a pet? Let's finish the story to see."

Pages 28-29: "Were you surprised at the way this story ended? Why [or why not]? What grave danger did Johnny encounter? What lucky happening saved Johnny? How did he repay the alligator?"

With children of all levels of ability, during the discussion following the reading of the story, ask, "Was it a good thing that Johnny went to the swamps alone?" Give all youngsters who desire it a chance to respond to this question. Conflicting opinions may emerge! Consideration of the following question may also spark a lively discussion: "If you had been in Johnny's place, would you have let the alligator go? Why [or why not]?"

EXTENDING SKILLS AND ABILITIES

Interpreting implied ideas: Recall with pupils Kitty's attitude toward her older brothers in the story "Too Many Brothers" in the new *Times and Places*. Then ask, "Do you suppose Johnny felt the same way about his big brother Henry?" Have pupils justify their opinions by reading passages from the story, for example, the sentence "He would show Henry!" on page 27. Although this story never states explicitly that Johnny was sometimes envious or jealous of his older brother or that Henry ever plagued him about being "too young," the implications are there.

The ability to catch implications and to read between the lines adds immeasurably to the enjoyment of reading. It is one of the abilities that distinguishes the imaginative, participating reader from the "plodder." Best of all, most youngsters can cultivate this interpretative skill, given suitable materials and the challenge of questions and discussions that carry them beyond the who-did-what level of interpretation.

Have the last two paragraphs on page 23 read aloud. Then ask, "What do these two paragraphs tell you about the way Johnny felt as he walked toward the swamp? Why did he argue with himself? Why did he whistle?

"When Johnny saw the rattlesnake [the last paragraph on page 26], does the story say that Johnny was afraid? How do you know that he was? Where in the story are you first told directly that Johnny was frightened? ["Panic seized Johnny. . . .", page 28] What does the word *panic* tell you about the kind of fear that he felt?" If necessary, refer pupils again to the glossary for the meaning of *panic*. You might point out the figurative use of the word *seized* in the sentence on page 28 by contrasting it with a sentence such as "The owl seized the mouse," in which it has its literal sense meaning. If possible, introduce page 5 of the *Think-and-Do Book* now. With new, exciting story situations, children are given experience in interpreting implied ideas and recognizing emotional reactions of story characters, skills in which most youngsters need abundant practice.

Using a pronunciation key: This exercise introduces the pronunciation symbols $\tilde{a}$, $\ddot{a}$, $\dot{e}r$, $\hat{o}$ and reviews the vowel sounds they represent. It also introduces the vowel pronunciation key printed at the bottom of every right-hand glossary page but the first.

1. To review previously presented pronunciation symbols and the sounds they represent, write the printed pronunciations listed on the next page.

Suggest that children refer to the full pronunciation key given on page 302, and pronounce each word. As they do so, write the word before its pronunciation. The completed exercise will look as follows:

brilliant (bril′ yənt)   arrange (ə rānj′)
announce (ə nouns′)   canoe (kə nü′)
bellow (bel′ ō)   stomach (stum′ ək)
below (bil ō′)   excuse (eks kūz′)
loyal (loi′ əl)   wooden (wůd′ ən)

2. Next, write in a column the following words and ask pupils to listen carefully to the vowel sound in each as you pronounce them: *hair, bear, dare, where.* Then ask, "What do you notice about the vowel sounds in these words? [They are the same.] What symbol in the pronunciation key stands for this vowel sound? [$\tilde{a}$]" Then write the symbol above the list of words, and write in parentheses after each word its pronunciation (*hãr, bãr, dãr, hwãr*). Cover the spellings and have pupils pronounce the words. Since it is doubtful whether children will recognize that in the word *where* the *h* sound actually precedes the *w* sound, you might present *hw* as the symbol used to represent the sound the letters *wh* stand for in such words as *when* (*hwen*), *whip* (*hwip*), and *wheel* (*hwēl*).

To present the symbols ä, ėr, ô, use procedures similar to those above with the following words:

ä	ėr	ô
calm (käm)	jerk (jėrk)	gone (gôn)
farm (färm)	earn (ėrn)	haul (hôl)
heart (härt)	squirm (skwėrm)	ought (ôt)
cart (kärt)	turn (tėrn)	for (fôr)

3. Call attention to the vowel key at the bottom of a right-hand page in the glossary and lead pupils to note that it contains all nineteen symbols that the glossary uses for vowel sounds. Conclude, "If we remember that in every printed pronunciation of a word a consonant symbol stands for its most common sound, we often need to use only this handy vowel key to figure out the printed pronunciation of a glossary word."

4. Pupils who are using the *Thorndike-Barnhart Beginning Dictionary* should be guided in the use of pages 56 and 58-59 at this time. If this dictionary is not available, write just the printed pronunciations listed at the top of the next page and use procedures recommended on pages 50-51 of this *Guidebook.* This time, however, have pupils use the vowel key on any right-hand glossary page as a guide to pronunciations.

carton (kär′tən)	furnace (fėr′nis)
wear (wãr)	zoom (züm)
could (kúd)	quarter (kwôr′tər)
couple (kup′əl)	journey (jėr′ni)
autumn (ô′təm)	gown (goun)

The goal in teaching a child to interpret a pronunciation key is, of course, to foster independent use of a dictionary for deriving pronunciations of words that he does not know how to pronounce. Exercises in which pupils must derive the pronunciation of a word from its pronunciation without first seeing the spelling are valuable for at least two reasons. They check whether or not children can interpret pronunciation symbols correctly. For example, the pupil who says "cartoon" when he sees the pronunciation (kär′tən) obviously needs help in interpreting vowel pronunciation symbols and the accent mark before he can succeed in independently deriving dictionary pronunciations. These exercises also point up vividly that a printed pronunciation is merely an exact representation of the sound of a word—that it often bears little resemblance to the spelling. Youngsters who are just beginning to consult a dictionary for pronunciations need much practice in seeing and interpreting printed pronunciations under teacher guidance.

Think-and-Do Book: Use pages 5 and 6. As children use page 6, they will acquire additional interesting information about the Santee Swamp from reading a series of informational sentences such as they might find in encyclopedias or informational text material. Each sentence contains an unknown word the meaning of which they can check by context clues, the pronunciation of which they derive from the use of a pronunciation key. After children have marked the correct pronunciation, it would be fun to have them summarize the information presented on the page.

EXTENDING INTERESTS

Enjoying literature: To people who do not live near swamps, they are terrifying places. But to the people who live in regions like the Santee River swamplands or the Florida Everglades, they are beautiful. A child who has read *When the Moon is New*, by Laura Bannon, will want to show the wonderful pictures of the Everglades and tell the story. You might want to read aloud the excerpt from Joseph Lippincott's *The Wahoo Bobcat*, in *Time for True Tales*. You can shorten it by explaining that this enormous bobcat has been named the Tiger by the hunters. Then begin your reading with the first complete paragraph on page 74. The book is difficult reading, but a few superior readers may be capable of reading it.

The same interpretative skills are involved in interpreting both written and oral materials. Since pupils' speaking-meaning vocabularies are larger than their reading vocabularies, they can often interpret oral material that is on a higher reading level than that which they can read for themselves. It is wise to keep children "reaching ahead" in their interpretative skills by reading to them stories like the excerpt from The Wahoo Bobcat.

For a little hilarity, try "The pickety fence," the third of the "Five Chants" in David McCord's *Far and Few*. (The five poems are also found in the revised edition of *Time for Poetry*.) After hearing it a few times, the children will be chanting it with you and working up speed. Nonsense it is, but excellent speech work, too. *Far and Few* is a delightful book of poems that you may wish to explore with the children over a period of time. It contains some unusually good nature poetry for seasons or science interests and some captivating nonsense verse.

Judy's Chickens PAGES 30-37

Sight Words: St.   Louis

Attack Words: *peered* convinced* region* tornado* syrup* ceased* hesitate* slashing** (glossary)

dimness* (root + suffix; dim—position of single vowel letter)

sped* (position of single vowel letter)

curved* (root with *e* dropped + ending; curve—vowel followed by *r*)

western* (root word + meaning clues)

Neither the title of this story nor the first two illustrations give the reader any inkling of the dramatic action about to unfold. The setting is placid enough—springtime on a small farm. No momentous problem confronted Judy Woods, the main character, until the elements conspired against her. With awful suddenness a tornado threatened. Alone on the road young Judy was faced with a difficult decision. Should she rush home to save her own precious chickens or stop to save those of her good friend, Mrs. Pepper?

The decision Judy made and her reasons for it will of course be commended and admired by pre-teen-aged readers. But, more important, they will likely raise the question in each youngster's mind "Would I have done as Judy did?" In other words, youngsters' reactions to the story character's behavior will probably culminate in self-evaluation. Self-evaluation which arises spontaneously from a story situation is much more likely to spark improved behavior patterns than "sermonizing" and exhortations from adults.

PREPARING FOR READING

Establishing background and anticipating vocabulary needs: Comment, "As you started to read a story, have you ever thought you knew what the story was going to be about and then had to change your mind? Or have you ever decided after reading two or three pages of a story that it was not very interesting or exciting, only to discover as you read on that it was most exciting?" After the discussion of such reading experiences, comment, "We can't always tell what a story is going to be like from its title, from the first picture or two, or from reading just the first two pages, can we? Some stories—some books—have many surprises in store. This is the kind of story we are going to read today.

"In this story some children are planning an Easter trip to *St. Louis* [present the name]." If necessary, help pupils locate St. Louis on the map. Continue, "Today's story is called 'Judy's Chickens.' Let's read it slowly, a page at a time, until we've all decided what the main problem is." Write the words *peered, convinced, region, tornado, syrup, ceased, hesitate, slashing* on the board and remind pupils to use the glossary to check their pronunciations or meanings if necessary.

INTERPRETING THE STORY

Page 30: After pupils have found the story, suggest that they think about the title a moment and study the picture on page 30 to see whether or not either gives them an inkling as to what the problem in the story is to be. Pupils probably will respond in their own words with the obvious—the story is about a girl named Judy who has some chickens. In the picture she seems to be either admonishing them or counting them. No particular problem is apparent. Comment, "It's hard to imagine what exciting action might take place or what the problem in the story is just from the title and the first picture, isn't it? Read the first page to see if it gives you an idea of what Judy's problem is."

When pupils have finished, ask, "What did you find out on this page that the picture didn't tell you? What is Judy's only problem so far? Do you think the story will be about the missing chicken?" Discussion of the last question may give you some insights into the maturity of pupils' reading interests. A few may be satisfied with a plot concerning a lost chicken, but most pupils will reject it as too "babyish."

Page 31: Continue, "Read the next page and study the picture to see whether this page gives you a better idea of what Judy's problem might be." After silent reading, ask, "Now does anyone still think the story is going to center around the missing chicken? Why not? What did you find out on this page? Have you any idea yet what Judy's problem is going to be? Do you think the story is going to be about the class trip to the zoo? Do you suppose Mrs. Pepper is going to have an important part in this story?" After pupils' conjectures, suggest that they read the next page to see if it gives a hint of any exciting action or important problem.

Page 32: When pupils have finished you might ask, "*Now* do you think you know what Judy's problem might be? What makes you think so?" Many children may reason that since a tornado is mentioned on this page and since the title of the story is "Judy's Chickens," the plot will center around Judy's chickens' being destroyed by a tornado. "Did you need to check the meaning of *tornado* in the glossary?" Through brief discussion of what a tornado can do, bring out that it is a more serious thing than Bob Banks' joking remarks would indicate. (The strange things that tornadoes sometimes do sound like fantastic tall tales. On page 7 of the *Think-and-Do Book* youngsters will find the six brief accounts of the effects of tornadoes exciting reading and will, incidentally, get excellent practice in interpreting the main idea.) Some pupils may advance the idea that since there was a tornado nearby the night before, there won't likely be another one so soon. Welcome all conjectures, and then suggest that pupils read the next page to see if it tells what Judy's problem will be.

Page 33: After silent reading, ask, "Now what is Judy's problem? Do you think she will get home in time to let her chickens into the chicken house? What kind of storm do you think will come from the huge purple cloud in the west? Read the next page and the first half of page 35. I think you'll change your mind again as to what Judy's real problem is."

Pages 34-35: When pupils have read to the middle of page 35, comment, "At last we know what the real problem in this story is! Would you call it a serious problem? Why? What do you think Judy will do?" After the discussion, have pupils read to the bottom of page 35 to find out. Ask, "What made Judy decide to turn back and save Mrs. Pepper's chickens? What prevented Judy then from hurrying on home? How do you suppose she felt as she stood alone with the chickens in the chicken house? Would this be a good place for the story to end? Why not? How do you think the story will end? Let's finish it to find out."

Pages 36-37: When children have finished, ask, "Were you surprised at the way the story ended? Why [or why not]? What lucky happening saved Judy's chickens? Would you say that Judy deserved her good fortune? Why? Would you have done as Judy did? Why [or why not]?"

EXTENDING SKILLS AND ABILITIES

Recognizing story problem or plot structure: Comment, "Although we wouldn't want to read all stories a page at a time and then stop for discussion, maybe reading this one that way has taught us something." To help children think about what they may have learned from this particular guided reading experience, ask such questions as the following: "Can we always tell what a story or a book is going to be about just from its title? Why not? What other title can you think of for the story we have just read?

"Do pictures that accompany a story tell us all we need to know about the action of the story or the problem of the main character? What are pictures for? Does reading the first page or sometimes even the first few pages always plunge us into the main action of the story or reveal the problem? What do the opening pages often contain?"

During the discussion, help children arrive at the following generalizations in their own words: (1) Sometimes the title of a story may tell us in a general way what the story is about. Sometimes a title may be purposely strange or mystifying. But we cannot usually do more than guess what a story is going to be about just from its title. (2) Pictures help us form visual images of story characters, settings, and bits of the action. Except in picture books for very young children or in comic books, one cannot usually tell what the main action or problem in a story is just from looking at the pictures. (3) The first page or pages of a story often set the background for a story—tell us things we need to know to understand the problem and subsequent actions and reactions of story characters. (4) If a person rejects a story or a book just on the basis of looking at the pictures, reading the title or the first few pages, he may be depriving himself of an enjoyable reading experience.

Reacting to specific word meaning: This exercise and page 8 of the *Think-and-Do Book* are designed to help children sense and react to the difference between a general word (*look*, for example) and a word that is more exact and colorful because it sparks a more specific image (*peer*, for example).

The ability to interpret the printed page fully and richly is dependent in no small part on the reader's ability to form the mental images that the author intended to stimulate. One way an author sparks vivid sensory imagery is by using words that call up sharp images. Unless, however, the reader can associate with such words not only their general meaning but the exact extra shade of meaning they suggest, he will not fully interpret—he will miss much of the flavor and the enjoyment the author had in store.

Begin by writing on the board the sentence *The boy looked at the house number*. Ask pupils to read it silently and then describe the mental picture the sentence stimulated. Then ask, "Can you tell from this sentence *how* the boy looked at the house number?" Change the word *looked* to *peered* and ask, "Now how does the picture in your mind change? How is the boy looking at the house number now?" If any pupils seem puzzled by the meaning of *peer*, have them refer to the glossary to check its meaning. You might let pupils take turns thinking of other words to substitute for *looked* that would carry the idea of *looked* but force a more specific image of the boy's action (*peeked, stared, glanced, gazed*, for example).

Use similar procedures to contrast the mental imagery evoked when the first of the italicized words in each sentence below is changed to the second.

He (*cut, slashed*) the bark off the tree.
The horse (*moved, lunged*).
He was filled with (*fear, panic*).
She (*stopped, hesitated*) at the door.

Think-and-Do Book: Use pages 7 and 8.

EXTENDING INTERESTS

Relating reading and life experiences: Ask, "Do you think Judy will be likely to forget her adventure the day of the tornado? Why not?" After pupils have discussed this question and given reasons for their opinions, ask them what they think is *their* most memorable adventure and why. Later, some children might like to write their story. Those who are artistically inclined will have fun telling theirs in pictures; however, the majority will probably be happiest telling it to an eagerly listening audience.

Enjoying literature: "Judy's Chickens" is perhaps a milder story than the preceding one, but it, too, shows courage and "stick-to-itiveness." Pupils can probably think of many examples of resourcefulness and courage from the library books they are reading. Just a few suggestions for discussion are given below. No matter which library book a child is reading, he will be able to contribute to the discussion by telling how some hero or heroine solved a difficult problem on his own or did something that took courage or resourcefulness.

Prairie School, by Lois Lenski. How did the teacher and the children manage when they were forced to stay inside the little one-room school during the blizzard? What character traits did some of the children and the teacher show?

Blue Willow, by Doris Gates. Time and again, Janey Larkin showed the same qualities that Judy displayed in "Judy's Chickens." Tell us about a few of those times.

Cowboy Boots, by Shannon Garst. Did Bob ever get discouraged about learning to be a cowboy? Why? How did Montana help him? Tell us how Bob finally earned the right to be called cowboy.

Maggie Rose, Her Birthday Christmas, by Ruth Sawyer. How did Maggie Rose show that she was resourceful?

Maple-Sugar Time PAGES 38-46

Sight Word: recognized

Attack Words: *sap* boring* spout* violently* arrival** (glossary)

Ver mont'* Ja'son* buck'ets* tank* gal'lons* bub'bles*
    pitch'er* (position of single vowel letter)

lonesome* (root word + meaning clues)

pipe* (final *e*)

containing* (root + ending; con tain'—two vowel letters
    together)

Few places are more appealing, more typically American, than the state of Vermont in maple-sugar time. In this story young readers participate in the fun, work, and excitement that pervades a rural Vermont district when the sap runs in early spring. The brisk air fairly vibrates with anticipation, old and young invade the maple groves to help scatter and empty the sap buckets, and tantalizing smells issue from the sugar house.

That Robert Huff, a young newcomer to Vermont, should at first resist participating in such delightful activities seems almost inconceivable. What was the matter with him? The answer to that question is implicit in the first part of the story. Robert's attitude is not likely to be a mystery to those youngsters who have moved from one locality to another. They will appreciate the difficulty of adapting oneself to an unfamiliar community, to new schoolmates and interests. How and why Robert's attitude toward his new surroundings changed from indifference to enthusiasm makes satisfying reading. The story may also provide for some youngsters at least one answer to that perplexing problem "How can I make new friends?"

PREPARING FOR READING

Establishing background and anticipating vocabulary needs: Recall with pupils that reading the first four stories of this unit took them to four widely separated parts of the United States. To help children see each of the story settings of the unit as a part of large geographic areas of this country, indicate each of these large areas on the map as you comment, "The first story 'Unwelcome Passengers' took us to the northeastern part of the United States. 'A Christmas to Remember' took us to the Southwest. 'Adventure in the Swamps' took us to the southeastern part, and the last story we read took us to the Middle West. Today's story takes us back again to the northeastern part of the country—to the section that is sometimes called New England. The name of the story is 'Maple-Sugar Time' and the main character is a boy who has just moved with his family to a New England state that is famous for maple syrup and maple sugar. Can you guess in what state today's story takes place?" If necessary, tell pupils that the state is Vermont and help them locate it on the map. Encourage children who have visited or read about Vermont to tell about it and to describe, if they can, how maple syrup is made.

> *It is not the purpose of this unit to teach geography with its many highly specialized skills such as map reading. A developmental program in social studies rightfully assumes that responsibility. However, pointing out on a map the settings of the stories may clarify the meaning of such terms as the* Southwest, New England, *and* Middle West, *which youngsters are likely to hear or read frequently.*

Continue, "As this story opens, you will discover that Robert Huff had lived in Vermont only two weeks—just long enough to make a few acquaintances and to be able to *recognize* some of the people he might meet on the street. I won't tell you how Robert felt at first about his new home town and what made him change his attitude. That's the whole point of the story!" Write on the board the words *sap, boring, spout, violently, arrival* and explain to pupils that the glossary will help with the meaning and pronunciation of these words.

INTERPRETING THE STORY

Pages 38-41: After pupils have turned to the story, call attention to the picture and identify the boy in the red cap as Robert Huff. After a discussion of what the picture tells about the season, the size of the Vermont town, and what the three boys are about to do, ask, "From the expression on his face, do you think Robert is unhappy about something? Let's read the first four pages to find out."

After silent reading, encourage discussion of Robert's attitude toward his new home and acquaintances and the reason for his attitude with such questions as "How did Robert feel about skating? about the fact that maple-sugar time was at hand? Did he seem to want new friends? What do you think were the reasons for his attitude and behavior? Do you suppose he was just naturally an unfriendly boy? Why [or why not]?" Have pupils justify their opinions by reading aloud parts of the story that tell what Robert said, thought, or did and then discussing his motives. For example, Robert's rude remark at the top of page 39 is an interesting one for discussion. Also, what do pupils think of Ben's and Jason's reaction to it? Why did Robert pretend he was too busy to help scatter sap buckets? How do you suppose the boys and girls on the sled felt toward him? How did he feel afterwards? What did he do afterwards that proved he was not so uninterested in the sap-run as he pretended to be? What was the real reason he didn't offer to help Ben and Jason with the work in Peters' Woods? Who was Robert hurting by his stubborn attitude? The answer to the last question is an emphatic *himself!* Robert has assumed what appears to be an unreasonable attitude toward his new surroundings and is "stuck" with it. The discussion suggested is valuable because it promotes understanding of the reasons for Robert's attitude and the effect of it on himself and others.

As interesting as the discussion of Robert's behavior is, you will not want to neglect discussing what youngsters have learned from the story and the pictures about the fascinating business of maple-sugaring. Refer pupils to the last sentence, page 38, and ask, "Did you understand Ben's remark when you first read it? If not, what helped you understand as you read on what

Ben meant when he said 'The sap will be running soon'? What is sap? Did you know before you read the story or did you look up the word in the glossary? Which entry word, sap^1 or sap^2, is the word used in this story? What kind of weather is good sap-running weather? How do people get the sap out of maple trees? In the picture on page 40, what does Mr. Peters have in his hand? [The boys will probably know that it is a brace and bit, a tool used for boring. A man can be seen using one in the right background of the picture.] Is maple sap the same thing as maple sugar? How do you know it isn't? What is a sugar house? In the picture, page 41, what is the tank on the sled used for?"

Pages 42-46: "Do you think Robert will change his attitude and offer to help Mr. Swift? Why [or why not]?" Suggest that pupils finish the story to see if their surmises are correct. After they have finished, ask, "How did Robert's attitude toward his new home town and maple-sugar time change? What happened to change his attitude?" After pupils have discussed the events that led to the happy change in Robert's attitude, suggest that they summarize what they learned about making maple syrup and maple sugar from reading the last part of the story and from studying the pictures.

Conclude the discussion by asking, "What do you suppose Robert will do next time he is asked to take part in some activity? What do you think Robert learned during maple-sugar time? What did you learn from reading this story that would help you make friends if you should move to a new town?"

Oral interpretation: The amount of time devoted to giving specific help in oral interpretation will depend, of course, upon the needs of your group of children. Many youngsters will profit from guidance that directs their attention to specific goals of projecting mood or tone in their oral reading. The oral interpretation of this story will be especially effective if the reader keeps in mind Robert's varying moods and reactions. Nearly every event in the story, interesting as it may be in itself, assumes a special significance because of Robert's attitude toward it. Help pupils prepare for effective oral reading by going through the story and noting Robert's moods, his reactions to characters and events. For example, how does Robert feel, how does he act, as the three boys head for the skating pond? How does Robert spoil the fun? What words can pupils think of to describe his various moods? (*discontented, rude, angry*) How do Ben and Jason react? How should this part be read to convey to the listener the unpleasantness of the situation? Briefly review with pupils the rest of the story, helping them pick out words that describe Robert and set the tone for oral interpretation.

Picking up interest leads from the story: Although this story describes in some detail how maple syrup and maple sugar are made, some youngsters may have questions that the story does not answer. "Do all maple trees produce maple syrup? What does maple sap look like? How long does a sap-run last?" If questions like these arise, write them on the board and use them as a lead into the exercise, "Locating source material."

EXTENDING SKILLS AND ABILITIES

Locating source material: To develop skill in locating and interpreting information in an encyclopedia, ask, "Does all maple sugar come from Vermont?" Write the question on the board along with other questions that pupils have raised concerning the production of maple sugar. Then ask, "Where could we find the answers to these questions?" When the encyclopedia is mentioned, display, if possible, a set of one of the children's encyclopedias. If a set is not available in the classroom, you will want to take pupils to the school library for a demonstration of how to use it.

Next, ask, "Where would we look in the encyclopedia to find the answers to our questions?" Lead children to note that since all the questions involve maple trees, maple sap, or maple sugar, they would probably look up the key word or topic "Maple." (Here the child is applying his skill in identifying main ideas or topics in connection with specific problems.)

Then call attention to the letters on the backbone of each volume of the encyclopedia. Explain that topics in an encyclopedia are arranged in alphabetical order, just as words are in a dictionary. Then ask pupils to indicate the volume in which the topic "Maple" can be found. Turn to the entry "Maple" and display the pictures. If *The World Book Encyclopedia* is being used, call attention also to the separate entry "Maple Sugar." If *Compton's Pictured Encyclopedia* is used, call attention to the sub-head "Making Syrup and Sugar from Maple Trees" under "Maple."

Next, ask pupils to listen for answers to their questions listed on the board as you read what the encyclopedia tells about sugar maples and the making of maple syrup and maple sugar. In conclusion, encourage discussion of those questions in light of information given in the encyclopedia.

Structural analysis: This exercise reviews the understandings that (1) a root word retains its meaning in a derived form, (2) a prefix or suffix may be a meaning unit. It also gives pupils practice in inferring the meaning of new derived forms of known root words used in context.

Awareness of root words as stable meaning units in derived forms is invaluable to youngsters, who are daily meeting new derived forms of root words. It prompts a kind of flexibility that fosters independence and self-confidence in reading. For example, the child who knows the word courage *(its meaning, its printed form, its sound) is not likely to be intimidated when he meets the words* encourage *or* encouragement *in context.*

Begin by writing the following words on the board:

disagree	bucketful	dimness	purposely
motionless	impatient	container	reappear
swampy	unbuckle	babyish	shorten

Have the first word pronounced. Then ask, "What is the root word in *disagree?*" To bring out the meaning of the root word and of the derived form, ask someone to use *agree*, then *disagree*, in oral sentences. Continue similarly with the remaining words.

Next, write the following paragraph and have it read (the root word *pack* and its derived forms are italicized for your convenience only):

Ben began to *pack* some glasses in a box. Then he *unpacked* them. Later he tried to *repack* them. Finally he said to his mother, "Either I'm just a poor *packer* or these glasses aren't *packable.*"

Then say, "There are four words in this paragraph that are formed from a root word in the first sentence. What is the root word? What are the four words that are formed from it?" As pupils mention each derived form, underline it and discuss its meaning. Note pupils' ability to infer from context the meaning of *packable*, which is the only new derived form.

Next, write the following pairs of sentences on the board and have them read. Have pupils tell what word in the second sentence of each pair is formed from a root word in the first sentence and discuss the meaning of the new derived form.

The train did not arrive on time.
I waited two hours for its arrival.

Mrs. Page was very patient with her child.
Mothers seem to have much patience.

The cat waited for the bird to move.
The cat watched every movement the bird made.

If pupils have the *Thorndike-Barnhart Beginning Dictionary*, use page 70, which deals with the concept of what is meant by a root word.

Think-and-Do Book: Use pages 9 and 10. As children use page 9, they are led to read definitions carefully and to derive generalized meanings for words as they evaluate the behavior of characters in "Maple-Sugar Time." Page 10 gives practice in identifying meanings of derived forms. This page gives you an opportunity to determine objectively which children in your group you will direct specific attention to in future exercises on root words.

EXTENDING INTERESTS

Extending concepts: As pupils read "Maple-Sugar Time," they may have felt somewhat as Robert Huff did—unfamiliar at first with the fun of making maple sugar and then fascinated by the process. Children will find much additional information in either of the two color films, "The Story of Maple Syrup"[1] or "Maple Sugar Time." You may want to show both films, if possible, to let children see the contrast between the modern equipment shown in the first and the older equipment in the second. Following the showing of the films, help pupils combine and organize the information they have gained from the story "Maple-Sugar Time," reference books, and the motion pictures.

If the April 1954 issue of *The National Geographic Magazine* is available, you will also want to refer pupils to the article "Sugar Weather in the Green Mountains." Some sections of the article are too technical for fourth-graders to read or understand, but superior readers might like to read parts of the text. Certainly all children will enjoy the excellent pictures in color.

Independent supplementary reading: Ask children whether they have noted any similarities in setting, plot, or characters between the stories read independently and those in *More Times and Places*. During the discussion, invite pupils to tell how the characters' problems differ from or resemble their own. In conclusion you might let your youngsters decide which of the stories discussed they would most like to hear read aloud. Then suggest that those pupils who have read that particular story meet as a group and prepare to read it to the class at a later time. Remind the children in this group of the discussion that preceded the oral interpretation of "Maple-Sugar Time," and encourage them to skim their story together, noting clues that will aid them in their oral reading.

---

[1] All films referred to in the lesson plans are listed with their producers in the bibliography at the back of this *Guidebook*.

Enjoying literature: In Elizabeth Yates' *A Place for Peter*, the boy's mother has been called away because of illness, and Peter takes complete charge of the sugaring off and boiling down of the maple syrup. His dog follows him and complicates matters by having puppies. The chapter, "Shep Has a Mind of Her Own," which describes how Peter manages, is well worth reading to the children. In *Told under Spacious Skies*, there is a story called "High Water—High Wind," by Cornelia Meigs, which tells of another sugaring under emergency conditions.

Perhaps the stories read so far in this unit have prepared children for a curious little poem by David McCord called "Tiggady Rue." (It is in the revised edition of *Time for Poetry* and in *Far and Few*.) Who or what is Tiggady Rue? Is she our conscience? Is she our inner self wondering how we'll meet difficult situations? Tiggady Rue would have been pleased with the children in this unit—even Robert, who seemed so disagreeable at first. Read the poem several times. If pupils ask for it on succeeding days, repeat it, but don't be concerned if it misses fire.

The Quiet Mountains PAGES 47-55

Sight Word: Stephen
Attack Words: *valley* slope* fossil* familiar* grizzly** (glossary)
railroad* (roots in compound; rail—two vowel letters together)
sea'son* (two vowel letters together)
lev'el* rum'ble* (position of single vowel letter)
peaceful* (root + suffix; peace—two vowel letters together)
buried* (root with *y* changed to *i* + ending; bur'y—meaning clues to determine vowel sound)
receiver* (root with *e* dropped + suffix; re ceive'—two vowel letters together)

The majestic Canadian Rockies often look deceptively peaceful to the tourist. Young Sarah, who lived in a small railroad town nestled in a valley between towering mountain ranges, knew differently. One day she and a friend accompanied an artist up the valley. While he tried to capture the silence and peace of the mountains on canvas, Sarah wandered off by herself and had two exciting adventures, which were in startling contrast to the apparent quiet of the mountains.

Many things about this story make it especially appealing—rugged mountain scenery, railroad lore, wild bears, a treacherous landslide, and Sarah's courage and resourcefulness in the face of danger.

PREPARING FOR READING

Establishing background: Since the first three pages of the story establish necessary background for understanding the story events, you might wait until after silent reading of these pages to clarify concepts about the setting according to the needs of your group. Write the story title on the board and encourage speculation about it. Ask, "Is this the kind of title that tells us what the story is going to be about? You may be surprised by the time you've finished the story to discover what excitement so-called quiet mountains can provide."

INTERPRETING THE STORY

When pupils have found the story, call attention to the picture, page 47, and identify the girl as Sarah, the main character. Explain that she is looking at one of her favorite mountains, *Mount Stephen*. Then ask, "How is the view from Sarah's bedroom window different from [or like] the view from yours? Can you guess from the picture where Sarah lives?" After pupils' conjectures, suggest that they read the first three pages and be ready to tell what they found out about the place where Sarah lives. Write the words *valley, slope, fossil, familiar, grizzly* and remind pupils to use the glossary to check the pronunciation and meaning of each if necessary.[1]

Pages 47-49: After silent reading of these pages, ask, "What is the name of the town where Sarah lived? In what country is it?" With a sweep of your hand, indicate the whole of Canada on the large map you are using. "What more did you learn about the location of Field?" As pupils mention the Rockies, the valley, and the river, indicate the general southwest area of Canada and comment, "Here is about where Field is located." (If your pupils are familiar with this part of the country, you may want to point out the exact location of Field in the center of Yoho National Park

---

[1] In succeeding lesson plans, unless otherwise noted, write the glossary words for each story on the board and call attention to them before silent reading of the story.

in southeast British Columbia.) What do the expressions "railroad town," "railroad yards," "roundhouse" tell pupils about Field? What is a roundhouse? What are railroad yards? Do pupils understand that Sarah and her father are referring to trains when they speak of Number Nine and Numbers Fifteen and Sixteen? Encourage comments about the details of the picture on page 49 that portray vividly part of the long valley in which Field is located. Can pupils point out in the picture the route over which Mr. Brooks and the girls have traveled so far? Where are they planning to go? Why? Then ask, "What would you be most interested in if you were going along with them? Let's finish the story to see what Sarah decided to do and what adventures she had."

Pages 50-55: When pupils have finished, invite them to recount Sarah's exciting adventures. Then to check the ability to see cause-effect relationships that are expressed in the story, ask, "How did it happen that Mr. Brooks and the girls were able to go up to a much higher point in the valley than they had planned? How did Sarah happen to walk up the curving mountain road by herself? Why did Mr. Brooks think his painting wasn't very good? Why did Sarah smile at his reason for not liking it?"

To challenge pupils who are interpreting at a higher level, ask such questions as the following (the answers require the ability to perceive cause-effect relationships that are implied): "Did the story tell you why Sarah was especially afraid of grizzlies? What did the glossary tell you about them that might explain her fright? What are fossils? Why do you suppose they are called 'stories in stone'?" In the first paragraph, page 54, call attention to the dots that signify that Sarah paused in her telephone conversation to listen to the remarks of the person at the station in Field. Can pupils infer from Sarah's conversation what the person probably said to her? Continue, "Why is it especially necessary to have track workers on mountain railroads? Why is it important to have a signal wire near the railroad track in the mountains? Was there really any danger of a wreck?" Conclude, "Do you think the story title is a good one? Why [or why not]?"

EXTENDING SKILLS AND ABILITIES

Citing passages to determine the validity of inferences: This exercise provides a check on the ability to make inferences from story material and to locate the passages that either justify or invalidate the inferences.

After you have written the statements listed at the top of the next page, ask pupils to decide which ones are true, which untrue. Suggest that pupils skim the story and be ready to justify each answer by reading aloud a passage or passages from the story.

1. Field was a very quiet town.
2. Sarah's and Molly's fathers worked for the railroad.
3. Sarah was thoughtful of other people.
4. The landslide worried Mr. Brooks and Molly.
5. The roads around Field were straight and level.

Using a pronunciation key: This exercise completes the introduction of all pronunciation symbols used in the glossary of *More Times and Places*. The dictionary symbols *ch*, *sh*, *zh*, *th*, ᴛʜ, and *ng* are introduced here, and the sounds they represent are reviewed.

Write the words *chain* (*chān*) and *coach* (*kōch*) on the board, omitting the pronunciations, which will be used later. Ask pupils to pronounce the words and to listen carefully to the beginning sound in the first word and to the final sound in the second. Then have them turn to the full pronunciation key and find the symbol used to represent this consonant sound. Put *ch* above the words and write the pronunciations after each word. Then cover the spellings and have children pronounce the words again.

Use similar procedures to introduce the symbols *sh*, *zh*, *th*, ᴛʜ, using the following words and pronunciations:

sh	*zh*	*th*	ᴛʜ
sharp (shärp)	pleasure (plezh'ər)	thick (thik)	there (ᴛʜãr)
push (push)	measure (mezh'ər)	month (munth)	smooth (smüᴛʜ)

With *zh* have pupils listen to the consonant sound in the middle of the two words. Be sure that pupils listen carefully to the difference between the voiced sound (ᴛʜ) and the unvoiced sound (*th*) that the letters *th* represent.

To introduce the symbol *ng*, write the pairs of words given below (omit the pronunciations) and have them pronounced. Ask pupils to listen carefully to the difference between the final consonant sounds. Then ask, "What symbol in the pronunciation key stands for the sound heard at the end of the first word in each pair? [*n*] What symbol represents the sound heard at the end of the second word? [*ng*]" Next, write the pronunciations after each word, cover the spellings, and have pupils pronounce the words again.

thin (thin)	lawn (lôn)	ran (ran)
thing (thing)	long (lông)	rang (rang)

It might be interesting to note with pupils that the *ng* sound is never heard at the beginning of English words.

If pupils are using the *Thorndike-Barnhart Beginning Dictionary*, you will want to use page 62, which will give further practice in associating sounds with the two-letter consonant symbols presented in this *Guidebook* exercise. As time permits, you may also introduce pages 60 and 63, which review the functions of the long and short pronunciation keys and give practice in using them.

Think-and-Do Book: Use pages 11 and 12. On page 11 four accounts of the slide on Mt. Stephen are given by various people who might have witnessed it. When youngsters have finished the page, suggest that they pretend they actually saw the landslide and write an account of it. On page 12 pupils will read several series of vivid descriptive phrases each of which is designed to stimulate vivid sensory images. This type of page strengthens children's appreciation of an author's use of effective language.

EXTENDING INTERESTS

Enjoying literature: Many of us have a favorite place outdoors with a lovely view where we like to sit and think. Sarah led the painter to such a spot. Perhaps children would like to describe their favorite views. Then you will want to read "This Is My Rock," by David McCord (found in *Time for Poetry*, Revised Edition, and in *Far and Few*). This poem has all the peace that Mr. Brooks thought his painting lacked.

Personal reading: At this level, children should engage in considerable personal reading in areas of their own interests. For example, the reading and discussion of this story may reveal that some pupils are greatly interested in railroads. Be alert to these areas of interest and help children locate books, pamphlets, and magazine articles that will serve to broaden their interests. Then, too, your personal recommendation of articles you have come across that are related to pupils' interests and not too difficult for them to read will do much to motivate reading. Also, give children frequent opportunity to discuss what they have read. Through talks of this kind new interest can be developed: A child may want to learn additional facts about something that interests him; another may reach for a story in which a character had to solve a problem similar to his own.

Some children may enjoy writing comments on their personal reading for a class booklet entitled "Good Books to Read." If Tom reads Peter's enthusiastic comment on a story, he might just try to read it himself—though reading isn't quite as easy for him as it is for Peter.

Alarm in the Night   PAGES 56-62

Sight Words: Southern   California   comforting

Attack Words: *temperature* orchard* belt* wick* relief* double** (glossary)

freezing* (root with *e* dropped +ending; freeze—two vowel letters together)

oil* (identify sound of *oi*)

lit* (position of single vowel letter)

torch* (vowel followed by *r*)

choking* (root with *e* dropped + ending; choke—final *e*)

throat* (two vowel letters together)

boomed* (root + ending; boom—meaning clues to determine sound of *oo*)

From the cool slopes of the Canadian Rockies, this story takes the reader south to the orange-growing region of Southern California. The night in this sunny, warm land had suddenly turned cold, and the Page family was quick to act when the ringing of the frost-alarm bell announced that their orange trees were in danger of freezing. With Mr. Page away from the ranch, the big job of lighting the orchard heaters had to be handled by Mrs. Page, thirteen-year-old Susan, and her younger brother, Joey.

This exciting story presents a vivid picture of one of the problems in raising oranges. Susan and Joey's ability not only to take responsibility in an emergency but to stick to a job until it's finished will be admired by all preadolescents.

PREPARING FOR READING

Establishing background and presenting vocabulary: Since the story setting and initial mood are brought out in the first picture, have children turn to page 56, and ask, "Where do you think this story takes place?" When pupils point out the palm trees as a clue to a warm part of the country, suggest that they compare this picture with the pictures on pages 14 and 24-25. Lead pupils to recall the setting of these two pictures as warm parts of the United States, and point out Arizona and South Carolina on the map. Continue, "Today's story takes place in a warm southern part of the country, too. We also say that this place is in the Far West—it's *Southern California*." As you speak, indicate on the map the southern part of California from Los Angeles to the Mexican border.

Have the story title read and comment, "An alarm in the night! That's not a very *comforting* thought, is it? Does the picture give you any hint that something is wrong?" Some children may suggest that the picture looks "spooky," but in general the scene is one of tranquillity as contrasted with the story title. Lead children to contribute their own motives for reading by asking, "What do you want to find out as you read this story?"

INTERPRETING THE STORY

Pages 56-57: Suggest, "Let's read the first two pages to find out if they give us any hint of what the alarm in the night was." After silent reading, ask, "Why was Susan frightened when she heard the radio announcement? How did she happen to hear the announcement? [Do youngsters recall from stories at earlier levels what a pinto is?] What do orange growers do when the temperature drops to freezing? Why didn't Susan tell anyone in the family about what she heard on the radio? What does the phrase 'orange belt' mean? What do you think the alarm in the night will be? What kind of heaters could keep an orchard from freezing? You'll find out as you read the rest of the story. There's a lot of activity on these pages that we'll want to talk about. Try to picture in your mind all that went on."

Pages 58-62: If children form vivid sensory images and share the emotional reactions of the characters, this portion of the story becomes so real that youngsters will enjoy recounting what happened from the standpoint of one of the characters. After silent reading, suggest, "Imagine that you are Susan or Joey telling what happened. Tell us everything you did— everything you saw and heard and smelled, and how you felt." Encourage pupils to look back at the text and at the pictures, if necessary, for help in recalling story events.

Then, encourage children's comments on Joey and Susan's surprise, which gives the story such a thoroughly satisfying ending. Ask, "What sentences did you read earlier in the story that tell you why Susan was so pleased to get a pony?" After discussion of story events, let children tell what they learned, from the text and from the pictures, about the phase of orange-growing described in this story.

Extending interpretation: Ask children what it means to "take responsibility." Help them generalize, if necessary, that it means doing what one is told to do or knowing what needs to be done and doing it. Ask, "How did Susan and Joey show that they could take responsibility?" Bring out that the need to get the heaters lit quickly was an emergency—that the children's help was needed immediately—and that being able to take responsibility in an emergency is an especially commendable trait. Continue, "Their father called Susan and Joey good ranch hands. Is it important for good ranch hands to be able to take responsibility? Why?" During the discussion of this question, lead children to point out that when Mr. Page was away from the ranch, Mrs. Page might often need the children's help. You might conclude by asking children to tell about times when they or someone they know has taken responsibility in an emergency.

Oral interpretation: This story gives pupils an opportunity to use many contrasting tones of voice to project the different feelings of the characters and the differing moods of the story. Skim the story with children, helping them note descriptive words and phrases that give clues to how certain passages should be read to bring out the meaning. For example, the words "sharp with sudden cold" and "turning the leaves . . . to bright silver" (page 56) should be read in such a way that the listener forms an image of a crisp, calm evening. This mood is suddenly broken by the last sentence on page 56, which suggests a mood of fear and excitement. At the top of page 58, the mood returns, for a moment, to peacefulness. The second paragraph on this page should be read with an air of urgency and excitement that sets the mood for the fast action of this and the next two pages.

These pages are particularly good for bringing out emotional reactions and the sensory imagery of the cold air, the gassy smoke, and the weariness in arms and legs. On the last two pages, Mr. Page's good nature and warm personality should be brought out in his speeches. Let children experiment with Susan's last speech to bring out just the right note of surprise and eagerness.

EXTENDING SKILLS AND ABILITIES

Structural analysis: This exercise and page 14 of the *Think-and-Do Book* strengthen the ability to identify the root word in an inflected form—an invaluable skill in determining the spelling of a root word and in locating it in a dictionary or glossary. The exercise also gives practice in adapting defined meanings to context.

Begin by writing the following lists of known words:

guided	starred	duties
capturing	whipped	buried
convincing	preferred	denies
recognizing	admitting	dizzier

Point to *guided* and have it pronounced. Then ask, "What is the root word in *guided?* [Write the root word before the inflected form.] What ending was added to the root word? [*ed*] What change was made in the root word before the ending was added? Did adding an ending change the pronunciation of the root word? Which of the two forms would you usually find in a dictionary?" Continue similarly with the remaining words.

Next, use the first list to review the generalization that final *e* is dropped before the endings *ed* and *ing;* the second to review the idea that a single final consonant after a single vowel letter is doubled before an ending in one-syllable words and in two-syllable words if the accent falls on the last syllable; the third to review the generalization that final *y* preceded by a consonant is changed to *i* before an ending beginning with *e.*

Then write the following sentences, underlining the italicized words:

1. Nothing exciting *occurred* while you were gone.
2. Joe sometimes *accompanied* his father on business trips.
3. The soldiers were *advancing* toward the city.
4. No one was *permitted* to leave.
5. Sarah was *relating* her adventures to her father.

Explain that the root words of all the underlined words are in the glossary. Ask pupils to choose the definition of each word that fits the meaning of the sentence in which it occurs and then to rewrite each sentence, using that definition instead of the underlined word.

Pupils who have had the developmental training suggested in the "Extending Skills and Abilities" sections of the previous Guidebook *have had much experience in adapting defined meanings to context. The preceding exercise requires the ability to do inflectional paraphrasing of glossary definitions. If some children in your group seem to have difficulty in doing so, you will want to give them special help, using the type of procedures suggested in the series of lessons noted below the heading "Adapting definitions in light of context," page 272 of the Index of Skills in the* Guidebook *for the new* Times and Places.

If pupils are using the *Thorndike-Barnhart Beginning Dictionary,* plan to use pages 71 and 72 as soon as time permits. These pages give further practice in identifying the root word in an inflected form and deriving the meaning of the inflected form from the definition of the root word.

Using a pronunciation key: In any reading group there are likely to be some children who have difficulty in mastering the use of a pronunciation key. It would be profitable to organize these children into a special-help group for additional guidance and practice. While you work with this group of children on such exercises as the one suggested below, the children who do not need this extra help might engage in the research activities suggested under "Extending concepts" in the next step of this lesson plan.

Suggest that pupils play the game "Which Is It?" described on pages 49-50 of this *Guidebook*. Write on the board or reproduce the following questions and printed pronunciations, and suggest that pupils refer to the full pronunciation key, page 302 of *More Times and Places*, as they play the game.

(kär tün′) (kär′tən)	Which is a funny drawing?	(fig′yər) (fing′gər)	Which is part of your hand?
(wôrm) (werm)	Which is a small creeping animal?	(klōTH) (klôth)	Which is used in making clothes?
(kə lizh′ən) (kə lek′shən)	Which is dangerous for automobiles?	(pik′chər) (pich′ər)	From which could you pour milk?

Think-and-Do Book: Use pages 13 and 14. On page 13 there are excerpts from informational material such as children frequently encounter in source books or books in the content fields. The page gives valuable training in forming vivid images and in perceiving cause-effect relationships from reading expository material.

EXTENDING INTERESTS

Enjoying literature: In *Time for True Tales*, there is a fine story, by Marguerite de Angeli, called "Yonie Wondernose," that tells of another child meeting an emergency bravely and competently. It is about a Pennsylvania Dutch boy, who was trying to grow responsible enough to do a man's work. This story might be read aloud over a two-day period.

Read "Every time I climb a tree," by David McCord. The child in this amusing poem is evidently another "Wondernose." You may also wish to read Mr. McCord's "The Newt," "Mr. Toad," or "Crows," if the children are interested. The last three poems are about other creatures that a "Wondernose" might stop to watch and think about. (All four poems are to be found in the revised edition of *Time for Poetry*.)

Extending concepts: In the stories "Judy's Chickens," "Maple-Sugar Time," and "Alarm in the Night" children became aware of regional occupations. Discuss with pupils some of the typical occupations or industries in the area in which *they* are living. You might interest them in finding out more about this aspect of their home district by talking with adults and by consulting encyclopedias. If you and the children happen to live in a fairly large town, a visit to one of its key industries will deepen youngsters' appreciation of what is going on around them and perhaps stimulate further reading about their own section of the country.

The School Train PAGES 63-71

Sight Word: Antoine
Attack Words: *dusk* wilderness** (glossary)
                northern* whom* (root word + meaning clues)
                No vem′ber* sup ply′* lum′ber* mes′sage* Chal′mers*
                  (position of single vowel letter)
                Papa* (meaning clues)
                Ace* pine* (final *e*)
                praised* (root with *e* dropped + ending; praise—two
                  vowel letters together)

Deep in the Canadian forests in a one-room cabin lived Tony and John with their father, a trapper. In this lonely wilderness about the only signs of human habitation were the widely scattered lumber camps. Although there was no regular school for the boys to attend, they were determined to learn to read and write. The story tells how they braved many obstacles to attend a "train school." There they not only realized their ambition to become literate but acquired the friendship of other children.

The unusual setting, the high adventure, and the warm human relationships depicted in this story make it especially appealing to preadolescents. Perhaps, too, Tony and John's almost reverent attitude toward learning to read and write will foster increased appreciation of the educational opportunities that most boys and girls take for granted.

PREPARING FOR READING

Establishing background and presenting vocabulary: Recall with pupils the setting for the story "The Quiet Mountains" and indicate south-western Canada on the map. Then comment, "Today's story takes place in Canada, too, but in a different part. [Indicate on the map the western part of the province of Ontario.] In this heavily forested area the winters come early and last late in the spring, and many fur-bearing animals live in the deep forests. Do you suppose many people live in this region? Why not? What do you suppose the few people who live there do for a living? Our story today is about two brothers who lived in these deep forests with their father *Antoine*. I think you'll be surprised when you discover what these boys wanted to learn how to do. It's something you do every day."

INTERPRETING THE STORY

The first two pages of this story not only present the problem but give much interesting background information that is likely to be foreign to most pupils' experience. Therefore you will want to guide carefully the interpretation and discussion of these pages so that all children will "get into" the story with understanding. Then they should be allowed to finish the story without further interruption.

Pages 63-64: After pupils have turned to the story and have read the title, encourage speculation as to what a school train might be. Then call attention to the picture and comment, "Here we see Antoine and his two sons and the interior of their home. Does their home remind you of any that you have read about or seen?" Some youngsters may be reminded of cabins in summer vacation spots, others of pioneer homes. To forestall a possible inference that this story takes place in "olden times," comment, "It may be hard for some of us who are used to electric lights and other modern conveniences to realize that even today many people live and get along very well without them."

After pupils have discussed what the picture tells them about this home and the region in which it is located, suggest that they read the first page to discover what the text tells them that the picture does not. If, during the discussion following silent reading, the following information is not volunteered, ask, "How big was this home? What did the boys' father do for a living? What is a trapper? [Did pupils who did not know the meaning of the word figure it out from context in the second paragraph or from consulting the dictionary?] What is a trap line? [a series of traps] Where did Antoine plan to sell his furs? What does the term 'trading post' tell you about this region? Why do you suppose Antoine banked the fire in the stove? [To answer this question, one needs to know the meaning of the word *bank* in this context. Did pupils use their dictionaries to find this meaning?]

"From the little you have read so far, would you say that Tony and John are responsible boys? What makes you think so? Has reading this page given us any hint of what the school train is? Let's read the next page to see if it does." After silent reading, ask, "How is a school train different from our school? Why was it necessary in the region where Tony and John lived to have a school train?" Do pupils understand what lumber camps are? What does the necessity for a supply train tell about the remoteness of the camps? Continue, "Who was Ace Stone and what did he suggest that the boys do during their father's absence? What did Tony think of the suggestion? Do you think that the boys will want to wait long before going to the school train? Why not? Let's finish the story to see how the boys got to the school train and what it was like when they got there."

Pages 65-71: After silent reading, pupils will be eager to tell what happened from the time the boys decided to go to the school train by themselves until the happy day when they read for their father. You will want to note how well children can retell the main events of the story with a minimum of prompting. (The next section of the lesson plan helps pupils to organize the story events according to time sequence.)

For those children who have already read the book, *The School Train*, by Helen Acker, the narrative paragraph on page 66 of *More Times and Places* that tells of the boys' three-day trip through the forest will call up vivid imagery. As youngsters read the passage, Tony and John's exciting experiences will come crowding into their minds and they will be eager to tell some of them. By all means, allow time for at least a few of these details to be told now. The story will be enriched for all children, and those who have not read the entire book will be clamoring to do so. These examples of additional interesting and exciting episodes to be found in the book provide an excellent incentive for independent reading.

To point up character traits and the fine human relations implicit in this story, invite discussion of such questions as the following: "What kind of boys were Tony and John? Would you enjoy having them for friends? Why?" As pupils mention words to describe the boys (responsible, self-reliant, friendly, considerate, bright), have them find examples of times in the story when the boys displayed these traits. Continue, "What kind of person was Mr. Chalmers? Would you say that he was a good teacher? Why? [Individual responses to this question may be illuminating. What teacher hasn't wondered at times just what qualities in a teacher youngsters most admire and desire?] How did Antoine feel when he heard his sons read for the first time?" Conclude the discussion by asking, "Besides learning many things, what else do you think Tony and John gained from attending the school train?"

Extending interpretation: The average child today probably takes it for granted that most children aged nine or ten and certainly all adults can read and write. Undoubtedly Antoine and Ace Stone's inability to read and the fact that Tony and John had never had an opportunity to learn came as a startling, if not shocking, revelation to some pupils. The reading of this story provides a natural springboard into a discussion of the value of knowing how to read. You might initiate the discussion by recalling how badly Tony and John wanted to learn to read and write and what a happy occasion it was when they realized their ambition. Then comment, "Maybe you've never stopped to think about it, but consider how fortunate you are that you can read and write. If you couldn't, what are some of the things you would not be able to do or would miss?" Give children a few minutes to consider the question and suggest that they jot down some of their ideas. Then encourage all pupils to participate in the discussion.

In conclusion, help youngsters generalize in their own words that if one were not able to read and write, (1) he would be deprived of much of the world's finest entertainment, (2) he would find it next to impossible to get what is known as an education, (3) it would be extremely difficult to earn a living, (4) his life might often be endangered if he were unable to read signs, labels, and printed directions.

EXTENDING SKILLS AND ABILITIES

Organizing ideas for the purpose of remembering: Comment that the events of this story cover a longer period of time than those of previous stories in the unit, and lead children to recall that the story action takes place over a period of about five weeks. To help pupils note clues to time sequence, suggest that they skim the story to find those time phrases that give an indication of approximately how many days the story covers: *One snowy November night*, page 63; *The next morning*, page 64; *Early the next morning*, page 65; *For three long days*, page 66; *Early the next morning*, page 68;

The next two weeks, page 69; *Two weeks later*, page 70; *Monday morning*, page 70.

After the phrases have been selected and written on the board, have the story reread aloud, choosing a different pupil to read each sequence. Pause briefly after each sequence to let children tell what they saw and heard in their minds as they listened. There are many opportunities for picturing and expanding action that is mentioned briefly in the text—for example, what might have happened during the two weeks that the supply train was away from Pine Camp?

In conclusion, let pupils retell the story from memory, using the time phrases on the board as a guide. Page 15 of the *Think-and-Do Book* enables you to check each child's ability to remember this time sequence.

Phonetic analysis: This exercise reviews fundamental understandings developed at previous levels about the relationship between vowel sounds and the printed symbols used to represent them.

Although at this level pupils are learning to use a dictionary to find the pronunciations as well as the meanings of unknown words, they are still encountering for the first time in print many words already in their speaking-meaning vocabularies. To recognize the majority of such words the child needs only to apply language understandings taught at previous levels. Therefore occasional review and refinement of fundamental language understandings and skills is advisable, particularly with slow learners. The ability, for example, to identify the root word in an inflected or derived form, to divide words into syllables, and to determine the vowel sound in a word or accented syllable is indispensable if children are to be independent readers.

Principles that aid in determining vowel sounds in words or accented syllables, which have been developed at previous levels, are:

Position: A single vowel letter usually stands for a short vowel sound unless the letter comes at the end of a word or an accented syllable. (*dusk, mu′ sic*)

Silent vowels: If there are two vowel letters together in a word or an accented syllable, usually the first stands for a long vowel sound and the second is silent. (*throat, con tain′*)

If there are two vowel letters in a word or an accented syllable, one of which is final·*e*, usually the first vowel letter stands for a long vowel sound and the final *e* is silent. (*pale, pro vide′*)

r as a vowel controller: If the only vowel letter in a word or syllable is followed by *r*, the vowel sound is usually controlled by the *r* sound. (*whirl, tur′ key*)

To begin, write the following known words on the board:

vacant	season	provide	purpose
capture	contain	complete	harvest

As each word is pronounced, ask, "How many syllables does this word have? Where does the first syllable end? Which syllable is accented? What vowel sound do you hear in the accented syllable? Why would you expect to hear that sound?"

To give children practice in applying vowel principles to words that have not been used in The New Basic Readers, comment, "In each sentence I say, I will leave out a word. I'll write that word for you to read."

Say	*Write*
The sick boy had a high _____.	fever
She started to _____ what she had written.	erase
No one was _____ from school.	absent
There were no _____ at the window.	curtains
The movie did not _____ to me.	appeal

If any pupils have difficulty with these new words or with those on page 16 of the *Think-and-Do Book,* help them analyze each one as suggested in the first part of this exercise. You may feel that some youngsters need more review and practice in applying the understandings reviewed in this lesson plan. If so, the procedures suggested on pages 160-161 and 174-175 in the *Guidebook* for *Just Imagine* and on pages 62-63 and 72-73 in the *Guidebook* for the new *Times and Places* would be helpful to use with these pupils. Chapter Five of *On Their Own in Reading,* Revised Edition,[1] also contains many helpful suggestions.

Think-and-Do Book: Use pages 15 and 16.

EXTENDING INTERESTS

Enjoying literature: At this time you will probably wish to discuss the book, *The School Train,* in more detail. Following this discussion, suggest, "Let's turn to the bibliography at the back of our books and see whether there is another book about Canadian children." When youngsters locate *Across Canada,* by Clare Bice, and read the annotation, ask if anyone has read the book. If some pupils are familiar with it, each might tell or read aloud the story he liked best. If not, you might read one of the stories aloud to arouse interest in the book.

---

[1] *On Their Own in Reading,* Revised Edition, by William S. Gray (Chicago: Scott, Foresman and Company, 1960).

A Camp in the Canyon PAGES 72-80

Sight Word: Howard

Attack Words: *canyon* trout* permit* permission* crickets* proved**
ranger* patrol* desperately* scorched* (glossary)
rod* tim'ber* (position of single vowel letter)
dain'ty* (two vowel letters together)
fought* (phonetic and meaning clues)

The fun of a camping trip in the mountains, together with the excitement of a forest fire, is captured in this story. The Howards, camped near a stream in a steep canyon, were thoroughly enjoying outdoor life when a treacherous forest fire broke out. With the help of campers, rangers, and ranchers, it was finally put out. And Louis Cook and his father, who hadn't permitted campers on their land, changed their minds about the Howards—the Howards had proved that they were good campers!

Children will appreciate the way in which the Cooks and the Howards forgot their disagreements and fought together against the common danger of fire. Thrilling and absorbing as this story is, young readers cannot miss its subtle but ever-timely lesson on the conservation of forests.

PREPARING FOR READING

Establishing background and anticipating vocabulary needs: Ask, "Have you ever been on a camping trip?" and continue with such questions as "What did you take with you? Where did you go? What did you do?" Encourage even those children who haven't been camping to contribute to the discussion by telling about campers they have read or heard about and by telling what they would like to do if they were to go camping.

Explain that the *Howard* family in today's story went camping in the mountains in Colorado. On the map, indicate the Rocky Mountains in northern Colorado and let children who have been in this area describe its appearance—the rugged terrain, the forests, the animals, birds, and so on. You might encourage brief comments on what camping in the mountains would be like and comment that the Howards found unexpected excitement and danger while camping in the mountains. Continue, "The title of the story will tell you where the Howards made their camp." Write *A Camp in the Canyon* for pupils to read and suggest, "Let's look up *canyon* in the glossary to see what we can find out about the place where the Howards camped." After children have read the glossary definition, ask them to describe briefly the images they have formed of a mountain canyon.

Then suggest that they turn to the picture on page 72 to see how the canyon pictured here compares with their images. Before introducing the characters shown in the picture, comment, "The Howards had a little trouble on their camping expedition and there is one word in this story that may cause you a little trouble because it may be pronounced either one of two ways. Let's look it up ahead of time. Will you find the word *permit* in your glossary?" Direct attention to the two pronunciations given in the glossary and explain the meaning of the phrases "for 1" and "for 2" following the pronunciations. Mention that this word always means "let" or "allow" in this story, and ask pupils which pronunciation will be used in the story. Then suggest that pupils read the first three pages to find out what trouble the Howards ran into.

INTERPRETING THE STORY

Pages 72-74: After silent reading, ask, "Why couldn't the Howards stay at their first camping place?" As children discuss the conversation with Louis Cook, ask, "Do you think Louis was more unpleasant than he needed to be? Why do you suppose his father felt the way he did about campers?" Continue, "What was the first thing the Howards did when they found another camping spot? Why is it a good idea to ask permission before setting up camp?" Have the last paragraph on page 74 reread and ask, "What picture does this make you see? How does it make you feel?

"In the last part of this story the family does some exploring and Tom discovers a *deserted* shack full of odd things. [Present the word *deserted*, for up to this time pupils may have encountered only the word *desert* meaning "dry, treeless region."] Later, Jill and Tom have an unexpected chance to prove that they are good campers."

Pages 75-80: After silent reading, ask, "How did Tom and Jill prove that they were good campers? What did Jill, Tom, and Louis do to fight the fire? How was it finally brought under control?" Continue, "How did Louis act when he first saw the fire? Why did he and his father change their minds about the Howards by the end of the story?"

Then ask, "What did the Howards see when they explored the canyon? [Do youngsters know what pack rats are?] What did Tom and Jill see from the top of the fire tower at the ranger station? What did the children learn from talking to Ranger Dick Sharp?" (As pupils use page 17 of the *Think-and-Do Book,* they will find out more about the duties of park rangers.)

Extending interpretation: You might use Dick Sharp's statement, "Electric storms and careless campers cause us the most worry" as a basis for discussing how forest fires are started and the seriousness of fires to both plant and animal life. Encourage children to suggest ways in which campers can help prevent forest fires.

EXTENDING SKILLS AND ABILITIES

Interpreting main ideas: Recall with children the purpose of subtitles in a story (to let us know what each part of the story is about), and suggest that they look through "A Camp in the Canyon" to decide where it could be divided into parts. Lead them to see that the first three pages tell about selecting a camp site and pitching camp; on pages 75-76 and in the first paragraphs of page 77, the Howards enjoy the canyon; the rest of the story concerns the fire. Help pupils think of appropriate subtitles, for example, "Finding a Camping Place," "Enjoying the Canyon," and "Fighting a Fire" for the three parts. As each subtitle is agreed upon, write it on the board, leaving space beneath. Then suggest that pupils reread each part to select the things of importance that occurred in each. After each part is read, lead children to tell, in a few short sentences, what happened, and write these sentences under the main points, or subtitles. The following is suggested for a completed outline (do not include the Roman numerals and the letters, as they are added later):

A Camp in the Canyon
I. Finding a camping place
    A. The Howards set up camp in a perfect place.
    B. Louis Cook told the Howards they had to move camp.
    C. The Howards found another camping place.
II. Enjoying the canyon
    A. The Howards explored the canyon.
    B. Jill and Tom visited the ranger station.
III. Fighting a fire
    A. Jill and Tom found a fire.
    B. Jill, Tom, and Louis tried to put out the fire.
    C. The fire was put out.
    D. Mr. Cook told the Howards they could camp on his land.

Explain that what you have put on the board is called an outline. Point to the first three subpoints and say, "These all tell what happened when the Howards were setting up camp, so we put them under the heading 'Finding a Camping Place.'" Continue similarly with the other two parts, leading pupils to see that the subpoints in an outline always give additional information about the main points, and that the main points and subpoints together give a brief, clear picture of the information in the story.

Then insert the Roman numerals and the letters, pointing out that we use Roman numerals to show which are the main points, and letters of the alphabet to show which are the subpoints of an outline. Explain, using the outline as an example, "The Roman numerals, as well as the letters, come under each other in a straight line, and there is a period after each. One of the easiest ways to remember a story, or something you have read, or a talk you want to give is to make an outline of it, because you can tell by glancing at an outline what the most important ideas are."

In conclusion, have "A Camp in the Canyon" retold from the outline you have put on the board. (As time permits during the next few days, you might call attention to other types of material that can be outlined and let children select main ideas that could go into an outline.)

Think-and-Do Book: Use pages 17, 18, and 19. Youngsters who are beginning to be interested in maps will have fun with page 18. Here the settings of the unit stories are noted on a map, and pupils can figure out the relative locations of the homes of the story characters. Page 19 follows up this interest by giving interesting accounts of activities that might occur in some of the areas children have been reading about.

CONCLUDING ACTIVITIES

Summarizing the unit: The reading of this unit has dramatized the concepts that, no matter where they live, people are more alike than different, that the region where a person lives influences his activities. Help children recall and summarize the stories they have read to arrive at these generalizations. Give pupils time to look over the story titles, think about the main events, and name the main characters. Then write the names on the board and ask, "In what ways do you think many of these children were alike?" Help pupils bring out that most story children acted quickly and were responsible and courageous when the situation demanded it. Continue, "Which of the characters would you call resourceful? Which showed kindness? Did any of them learn to adapt themselves to a new situation? In library books and in stories from other readers, what other story characters have you read about who were resourceful or who adapted themselves easily to a new situation?" From their answers, help pupils generalize that boys and girls, regardless of where they live, are much alike.

Next, invite discussion of such questions as "What kind of pet delighted Susan and Joey Page? What kind of pet did Johnny want? Do you suppose Susan and Joey would ever have thought of an alligator for a pet? Why not? Robert Huff could probably read, but would he have known how to provide for himself on a three-day trip through the forest as Tony and John did? Why not?" Then encourage children to imagine what might have happened to them and what they might have done if they had been confronted with the problems of specific story characters. After the discussion, help children generalize in their own words that (1) the region in which we live often influences our activities and experiences, and (2) unless we live in regions similar to those where the story characters lived and meet similar problems, we cannot always be expected to know how to handle such problems. In turn, pupils will be able to name things they can do that children from other parts of the country could not do.

Conclude by asking several youngsters to tell which of the story characters they would most like to have as a friend and why. Let others tell which part of the United States or Canada they would like most to visit.

Enjoying literature: A lively discussion can be stimulated with the simple remark, "Sue, you have read several of the books listed at the back of *More Times and Places*. Which one did you like best?" Surely someone who has also read a number of the books, including Sue's choice, will claim a different favorite. Let children discuss the books they like best and relate incidents from the most popular books.

The reading of the library books suggested for this first unit certainly need not end abruptly with the completion of the unit. It is quite possible that every child who wanted to read a very popular book did not have the opportunity. Occasionally, too, a child who has shown no desire to read independently may suddenly become interested only toward the end of the unit, after he has noticed the pleasure his friends derive from reading. In either case, encourage the continued reading of these library books and give the youngsters an opportunity to discuss the stories.

To conclude, you will want to read aloud some of the children's favorites from among the poems you have introduced during the unit.

Unit 2

The Great Outdoors

The stories in this unit, like those in Unit 1, take the reader to many different places—to northern forests, to broad western plains, to rugged, mountainous country. This time the purpose of the imaginary travels is to provide an opportunity for youngsters to observe wild animals in their natural habitats. In five of the stories pupils will encounter children who have interesting adventures while watching or protecting animals. The other five stories are entirely about animal life. Some of the stories depict picturesque aspects of the behavior of wild animals—the nocturnal frolics of rabbits, the early morning dance of the loons. In most of the stories the action centers around some aspect of the basic problem of wild animal life—struggle for survival.

Through the reading of these stories children should develop an increased appreciation of some of the natural laws that govern wild animal life in its unceasing fight for survival. Some of these laws or concepts emphasized in this unit are that many animals in their search for food prey upon other animals; that all animals have enemies and must constantly be on the alert to survive; that most mother animals care for their young and teach them how to protect themselves; that nature has provided animals with various means of self-protection; that the kinds of homes animals make or choose are often related to their need for protection. The pictures are beautiful as well as scientifically accurate and contribute greatly to the understandings developed in the stories.

Implicit in this unit is a great theme, animal conservation—"let them live." The goal to be attained through reading and discussion of good animal stories is not merely understanding of natural laws and the facts of animal life. The ultimate and most important goal is to engender sympathy and respect for all living things. Perhaps it is not too much to expect that many pre-teen-agers will begin to develop unconsciously what Doctor Albert Schweitzer calls "reverence for life."

Since animal stories are bound to arouse interest and stimulate curiosity, they are natural leads to wide reading. Before introducing this unit, therefore, you will want to assemble the suggested library books and selections from other readers that extend and enrich the unit theme, and, if possible, procure the suggested films.

Reading and discussing stories and books about animals is so provocative that you may expect a constant barrage of questions. You will want to be ready to guide pupils to encyclopedias and other reference works, to illustrated pamphlets and magazines that will satisfy this ever-growing curiosity. You will want also to enlist the help and coöperation of the school or community librarian in obtaining materials to satisfy the wide range of individual interests sure to be aroused. Among the many beautifully illustrated reference books you might assemble for the classroom library table are *Hammond's Nature Atlas of America*, by Emil L. Jordan, and *The Golden Treasury of Natural History*, by Bertha Morris Parker. In the lesson plans you will find helpful suggestions for promoting skill in choosing and using reference materials.

INTRODUCING THE UNIT

To observe wild creatures of the woods, plains, or fields in their natural habitats, rearing their young, searching for food, and fending for themselves against enemies is the privilege of very few. As children will discover in this unit, many wild animals come out to feed or roam only at night, and then they are extremely wary.

An excellent film that will give pupils the vicarious experience of being silent, unseen observers of wild animals is "Common Animals of the Woods." If possible, show the film as an introduction to the unit. After pupils have seen it, encourage discussion by asking, "What things did most of the animals seem to be doing? How did parent animals care for and protect their young? Which of these animals have you seen or read about? Tell us about them. Is it easy to get close to animals like these and watch them? Why not?" (If the film is not available, you might use pictures of animals from various sources to initiate the type of discussion suggested here.) During this discussion and those that arise during the development of the unit, you will want to be alert for opportunities to capitalize on the science knowledge that boys and girls have. Encourage youngsters to draw upon the science generalizations that they have made about animals to interpret animal characteristics and behavior depicted in the unit "The Great Outdoors."

Then call attention to the unit title in the table of contents and comment, "The stories in this unit will take us outdoors in different parts of the country and give us a chance to watch different wild animals doing the things all animals have to do to live and protect themselves. You may be surprised to see some of the things animals do. Sometimes it seems as if they are just having fun or amusing themselves. In some of the stories we'll meet boys and girls who have interesting experiences while watching or helping wild animals." Encourage children to skim the story titles and speculate about what animals they will read about in each story. Call attention, too, to the library books recommended for the unit on pages 296-297 and to the brief notation describing each book. The list may remind some youngsters of books in their own libraries that they would like to share with the class.

A Zoo Without Bars PAGES 82-89

Attack Words: *advancing* occasionally* paused* slight* gradually* fleeing* swooped* keen* bolted** (glossary)
skunk* in'sects* slim* (position of single vowel letter)
de serves'* (vowel followed by *r*)
movement* (root word + meaning clues)
twitched* (root + ending; twitch—position of single vowel letter)

A more satisfying and appropriate story with which to open this unit would be hard to find. It tells of the adventures of three children who start out one moonlit October night to watch the wild animals in a meadow near their home. The first picture and the almost lyric descriptions set the mood and tone of the story —stillness coupled with suppressed excitement. The children's patience is rewarded, as quietly and unseen, they watch a skunk, some rabbits at play, and even a fox. Then the spell is abruptly and humorously broken as the younger brother tumbles off a log and frightens the fox away.

As they identify themselves with the story characters, young readers will be quick to sense and appreciate an inquiring and sympathetic attitude toward wild life. The lesson in the story is very clear though never directly stated— the best way to learn about animals is to watch them.

PREPARING FOR READING

Establishing background: Ask, "Have you ever gone out into the fields or woods to watch wild animals?" Encourage those youngsters who have observed wild animals in their natural habitats to tell about their experiences. If children have seen the film "Common Animals of the Woods," encourage them to discuss what animals were shown and how seeing the movie made them feel that they were right there in the woods watching the animals. During the discussion, lead children to bring out the importance of being quiet and patient while watching wild creatures. Comment, "Whether you have watched wild animals or not, as you read this story I think you'll feel as though you're with Jim, June, and David, crouching on an old log and waiting patiently to see what wild things will appear. One animal comes so close that you will see its whiskers twitching!"

INTERPRETING THE STORY

Suggest that pupils use the table of contents to find the first story in the unit. After they have turned to page 82, have the title read and encourage comments on its probable meaning. Then call attention to the double-page picture and ask, "Does this look like a good place to watch animals? What animals might you see here? What time of the year do you suppose it is?" The first paragraph sets the mood so delightfully that you will want to read it aloud, or have it read by one of your skillful oral readers. Suggest, "Look at the picture as the first paragraph is read—you can almost see this scene come alive. I know you'll feel as though you're right there on the edge of the meadow." Then comment, "On the first three pages of the story, you'll find out why Jim was particularly eager to see as many animals as possible and which animal the children saw first in the 'zoo without bars.' "

Pages 82-84: After silent reading of these pages, ask pupils to discuss what the children saw first from their hiding place. Ask, "Why did Jane stiffen when she saw the skunk? Why do you suppose Jim chuckled and said, 'He [the skunk] isn't at all afraid of us'? What do skunks eat?" Continue, "Why had Jim picked this particular night to watch wild animals? Why do you suppose he decided to watch near the rabbit run?" As a check on the images that children have formed in the first part of the story, ask various pupils to describe the rabbit run, the children's hiding place, and what could be seen from the fallen log. What do pupils think of the hiding place?

Comment, "In the rest of the story, several other animals come to the 'zoo' and the children see a very unusual animal party."

Pages 85-89: After the story has been completed, use the picture on page 86 as a basis for discussing the rabbits' strange dance and why it ended suddenly. Then call attention to the picture on page 87 and ask, "What is the fox doing here?" Discuss the implications of the last sentence on page 87, bringing out that a fox's keen sense of smell enables him to protect himself and to find food. Continue, "What can you see the fox doing after he sniffed the air? How did Jim fool the fox? How do you suppose the children felt as the fox came closer?" Lead children to tell what happened to put an end to the animal-watching for that night. Encourage them to capture in their descriptions as much as possible of the tense excitement, the humorous letdown, and the feelings of the characters.

Extending interpretation: To bring out the constant alertness of wild animals and the importance of their keen senses to help locate food and natural enemies, ask children to recall the rabbits' danger signal and when it was given. Ask, "When the fox and the rabbits thought that danger was near, what did they do? Why are their noses and ears especially important to animals?" Then ask, "Why do many animals hunt for food at night?"

To stimulate discussion of animal conservation, ask, "What are some of the things that you should remember if you go into the woods or fields to watch wild animals?" As children discuss such things as remaining quiet and not frightening the animals, ask, "Why do many animals fear man? Did the animals in this story need to fear Jim, June, and David? Why not?"

EXTENDING SKILLS AND ABILITIES

Organizing ideas: Recall with children that Jim planned to give a talk in school about the wild animals near his home. Ask, "What things might Jim want to bring out in his talk?" After several suggestions have been made, continue, "What might Jim do beforehand to help him remember what he wanted to say?" When youngsters mention that he might make an outline, suggest, "What do you think the main points of Jim's outline might be? [The main points might consist of a list of the animals that Jim saw.]" When the main points have been agreed upon, suggest that pupils list these on paper, leaving space beneath each main point for subpoints. Then have children skim the story to note the passages that tell about each animal and decide on subpoints from each passage to complete the outline. The following is suggested for a completed outline:

I. The skunk
   A. It hunted for food.
   B. It caught a mouse.
II. The rabbits
   A. A rabbit sent a danger signal.
   B. The rabbits danced.
   C. An owl frightened the rabbits away.
III. The fox
   A. The fox sniffed the air.
   B. Jim imitated a mouse's squeak.
   C. The fox came toward the sound.
   D. It was frightened away.

Then comment, "If Jim used an outline like the one that we have just finished, he would be telling everything just as it happened. In what way might he organize his talk if he wanted to tell his listeners how to watch animals, what animals might be seen, and what could be learned from watching them?" Help children decide on such main points as those suggested below and guide them in selecting subpoints to complete the outline:

I. How to observe wild animals
   A. Choose a clear, moonlit night
   B. Find a place where animals might come
   C. Stay hidden and quiet
II. Animals you can see near here
   A. Skunk
   B. Rabbits
   C. Owl
   D. Fox
III. What you can learn from watching wild animals
   A. What they eat
   B. How they hunt for food
   C. How they protect themselves
   D. How they play

In conclusion, suggest that children use the outlines as guides and give the kind of talk they think Jim would give from each.

Structural analysis: This exercise, together with page 21 of the *Think-and-Do Book*, introduces the prefix *fore-* and the suffix *-ward* and reviews some known prefixes and suffixes. To begin the review, write the following:

	re-	-less	-er	im-	dis-
defend_____				someone who defends	
_____perfect				not perfect	
_____please				fail to please	
motion_____				without a motion	
_____capture				capture again	

Call attention to the familiar prefixes and suffixes at the top of the exercise. Recall with pupils that each may be added to a root word to make a new word. Then ask which suffix could be added to the word *defend* to make a word meaning "someone who defends." Write the suffix *-er* in the blank after the root word *defend* and have pupils use both the root word and the derived form *defender* in sentences. Use similar procedures with the remaining words.

Then write the word *forehead* and ask, "In what part of your head is your forehead, the front or the back? What prefix is added to the word *head* to make a new word meaning 'the front part of the head'?" Underline the prefix *fore-* in *forehead* and write the word *forenoon*. Ask, "When we speak of the forenoon, do we mean the part of the day coming before or after noon? What prefix is added to the word *noon* to make a word meaning 'before noon'?" Underline the prefix *fore-* in *forenoon* and help pupils generalize that *fore-* means "in front" or "before."

Then write the word *backward* and ask, "If you fall backward, do you fall toward the front or toward the back? What was added to the root word *back* to make the new word *backward*?" Underline the suffix *-ward* and lead children to understand that it means "toward" or "in the direction of."

In conclusion, write the derived forms *forefeet, upward, eastward, forepaw* and have children discuss their meanings and use them in sentences.

Think-and-Do Book: Use pages 20 and 21. On page 20 youngsters will find an interesting article that extends their understanding of why Jim made his observation trip after dark.

EXTENDING INTERESTS

Enjoying literature: There are several poems that you will find appropriate for the story "A Zoo Without Bars." "The Skunk,"[1] by Robert P. Tristram Coffin, is difficult, but it reads so melodiously that children like it even if they do not understand every word of it. It will require explanations of a few difficult words, such as *malign, undulates, fawn,* and *symphony.*

---

[1] Unless other sources are specifically mentioned, all poems referred to in this *Guidebook* may be found in *Time for Poetry*, Revised Edition.

Read the poem first, explain the words, and then reread. If it seems desirable, you might omit the third and fourth verses.

"The Little Fox," by Marion Edey, is a winter poem, but gives a fine picture of both the fox and the owl. Children may remember it from an earlier grade. This poem might be done in verse-choir form. The high voices ask the question at the beginning of each verse. Medium voices answer the question in the first verse; low voices answer in the second.

The situation in the story is reversed in Elizabeth Coatsworth's poem "The Rabbits' Song Outside the Tavern." In this poem, animals are observing human beings in a "cave" (house) where they have "suns" (electric lights) and "Stars, each on a tall white stem" (candles). To the rabbits, who are constantly·hunted by the fox and the owl, these people seem to have no cause for fear and no need to hunt their food. This is a wonderful poem by a fine writer. It may be difficult for some pupils in your group, but it is well worth trying. You will want to read the poem, talk it over with the children, and then reread it.

At various times throughout the unit, you may wish to refer to Dorothy Lathrop's book *Let Them Live* and to read portions of it aloud. This book makes a powerful plea for animal conservation and approaches its subject animal by animal. Probably only your most superior readers, or those with a particular interest in animals, will read it for themselves. However, it contains much interesting information about many of the animals covered in this unit, and all children will enjoy the beautiful pictures.

Applying ideas gained in reading: After reading "A Zoo Without Bars," children will probably be eager for another showing of the film "Common Animals of the Woods." (You might draw special attention to the mink and the river otter and tell pupils that they will meet some "first cousins" of these animals [weasel and sea otter] in later stories of the unit.) Both the film and the story may well lead children to seek further information about wild animals first-hand, as did the children in the story. Rural children, of course, have an advantage, but almost every area offers some opportunities for this type of observation. Squirrels and birds are to be found in nearly every city park. They are not as exciting, perhaps, as foxes and skunks, but they are fascinating to watch, nevertheless. Other pupils may wish to find additional facts in such reference books as those suggested in the overview to this unit and in the encyclopedias listed in the bibliography at the back of this *Guidebook*. Children might then take turns telling the class of their observations or findings.

The Wild Colt's Lesson ^{PAGES 90-94}

Sight Word: War

Attack Words: *gully* whinny* pounce* terror* crafty* intent* prey**
            enraged* mare* (glossary)
            forefeet* (root + prefix)
            part′ner* (vowel followed by *r*)
            cliff* fu′ry* res′cue* (position of single vowel letter)
            injured* (root with *e* dropped + ending; in′jure—position of single vowel letter)
            gleamed* (root + ending; gleam—two vowel letters together)

All young animals are appealing, but none more so than a leggy, frisky colt. War Paint, the wild colt in this story, roamed the vast western plains with a herd of wild horses. One day his carefree existence was threatened in a terrifying encounter with a prairie wolf. The grim struggle ended when the mare came rushing to the rescue of her colt. The whole impact of this story is one of untrammeled animal life in the great outdoors. Here the eternal struggle for survival is vividly portrayed—the strong prey on the weak and unwary, constant vigilance against natural enemies is necessary, and the mother animal faces extreme danger to protect her young.

PREPARING FOR READING

Establishing background and anticipating vocabulary needs: You should have little trouble arousing interest in a story about horses! Tell children that today's story is about a colt, and encourage a discussion of colts or ponies that children have seen or read about—their appearance, their actions, and so on. Say, "Today's story is about a wild colt named *War Paint* that lived with a herd of wild horses on the western plains. Like all young horses, War Paint spent most of his time playing with other colts. But one day his playfulness led him into danger." After pupils have turned to page 90 and read the story title, encourage comments about the broad expanse of land shown in the picture and its suitability as a home and ranging ground for wild horses. Since the picture on page 91 is sure to arouse interest and curiosity, suggest that pupils start to read immediately to find out what War Paint's dangerous adventure was and what lesson he learned from it.

INTERPRETING THE STORY

Children should be able to read this five-page story without much guidance. During silent reading, notice which children seem to have difficulty with words, which children are consulting the glossary, and which children seem to be reacting to the exciting events.

Pages 90-94: After silent reading, children will be eager to discuss the battle and the mare's rescue of the colt. To guide the retelling of the main events and keep the narration lively, you might inject such questions as "How did that part of the story make you feel? What could you see and hear as you read this part? Why did the wolf keep lunging for the colt's hind legs?" Explain, if necessary, that the wolf was trying to cripple or break a leg so that it would be impossible for War Paint to escape. After the discussion of the mare's part in the battle, encourage children to recall from observation or from their reading, other instances of animal mothers' protecting their young, and lead pupils to conclude that mother animals often will face great danger to protect their young. Then ask, "How do wild horses protect themselves? What lesson do you think War Paint learned from his experience with the wolf?" Thoughtful readers may decide that War Paint learned not only to obey his mother's warning whinnies but also to be on guard against enemies, even when at play.

Oral interpretation: Ask, "Did you feel as though you were right there as you read this story—seeing and hearing everything that happened? What made you feel that way?" Point out that the author has used many vivid words to describe the animals and the action, and that these words make the story come alive. Ask pupils to describe the mental pictures they formed of the wild colts in the first part of the story and suggest that they turn to pages 90-91 to find the words and phrases that prompted their images (for example, *as free as the wind, frisky colts, lively animals, pranced boldly*). Encourage children to look through the rest of the story to find words that describe the wolf, the battle, and the mare, and to discuss what pictures these words bring to mind. Then suggest that pupils who read aloud try to project the exciting action and the vivid imagery to those who listen.

Stimulated by the excitement of "The Wild Colt's Lesson," pupils will likely be looking for more books about wild horses. Several such books are suggested in the bibliography at the back of *More Times and Places*. This would be a good time for children to look over the annotations again to decide which of these books they wish to read.

EXTENDING SKILLS AND ABILITIES

Using context clues: To focus attention on the use of context clues to determine which of two possible pronunciations of a word is appropriate, write the word *permit* and ask pupils to check its pronunciation in the glossary. When pupils have located it, ask, "How many pronunciations are given for this word? When it means 'let' or 'allow,' how is it pronounced? When it means 'written order giving permission,' how is it pronounced?"

In our language there are many words (object, *for example*) *whose pronunciations depend upon their meaning in a given context. If the word* object *means "thing" (noun use), it is pronounced* ob'jikt. *When it means "be opposed" (verb use), the accent shifts to the second syllable, and it is pronounced* əb jekt'. *When one looks up a word of this type in a dictionary or glossary, the clue to which pronunciation of the word is appropriate is its meaning in a given context. Although it is perhaps too difficult a concept to develop at this level, it is interesting to note how often it is true in our language that words whose pronunciations depend on their meanings usually are accented on the last syllable when used as verbs.*

Continue by writing the following sentences, underlining the italicized words:

He would not *permit* me to go alone.
He needed a *permit* to enter the building.

Ask pupils what the underlined word means in each sentence and how it should be pronounced. Then have the sentences read. Use similar procedures with the following pairs of sentences:

People who like to read *frequent* libraries.
Mary made *frequent* visits to the doctor.
Before the men build the highway, they have to *survey* the land.
The men found it hard to make *surveys* in the mountains.
At first, I did not *suspect* that the cave was a dangerous place.
The police named two men as *suspects* in the bank robbery.

Since this lesson is the first presentation of the use of context clues to determine appropriate dictionary pronunciations, you will want to note carefully which children have grasped the idea quickly and have no difficulty with page 22 of the *Think-and-Do Book*.

Whenever a new skill or understanding is introduced in a group situation, you will note that the Think-and-Do Book *usually provides an immediate opportunity for children to apply independently that skill or understanding. Analysis of pupils' responses on that page enables you to check each child's mastery of the new skill and to determine which pupils need special help.*

If pupils are using the *Thorndike-Barnhart Beginning Dictionary,* have them do pages 61, 74, and 75, which give additional practice in using context to determine appropriate pronunciation and meaning.

Think-and-Do Book: Use pages 22 and 23. Page 23 gives valuable training in locating information in an encyclopedia. Below the picture of an eight-volume encyclopedia are questions that children might raise about animals. To locate the desired information, pupils are to decide what topic they would look under and in which volume they would find it.

EXTENDING INTERESTS

Enjoying literature: Among the books about wild horses listed in the bibliography, one of the most touching is Glen Rounds' *The Blind Colt.* The opening chapters are in *Time for True Tales.* You might read any or all of these aloud as a lead to the whole book. Be sure to call children's attention to the way in which the author describes the country from the standpoint of the colt—in terms of sound, smell, taste, and touch, but never sight. It is a remarkable feat of describing sensory imagery. If youngsters shut their eyes and try to describe their surroundings without mentioning anything visual, they will discover how skillfully Glen Rounds has led us into the sightless world of a blind wild colt on the range.

Youngsters who are reading or have read *Star of Wild Horse Canyon,* by Clyde Bulla, will arouse the interest of their classmates with a discussion of the roundup of wild horses, the training of Star, and his later disappearance. Don't let children disclose Star's whereabouts at this time. Keep the solution of the mystery fresh for those who have not yet read the book.

A good description of a mustang is contained in the poem "Noonday Sun," by Kathryn and Byron Jackson. This poem, together with the books suggested, are valuable because, like many of the stories in the unit, they arouse admiration and compassion for wild animals.

Independent supplementary reading: The selections from other readers, suggested in the bibliography at the back of this *Guidebook,* are a good source of material for oral reading. Because the stories are numerous, short, and varied in content and difficulty, they provide material for children of varying abilities to read aloud without much repetition in content. Using these stories for oral-reading activities will give you an opportunity to observe pupils' ability to apply the skills emphasized in the oral-interpretation sections of the lesson plans.

A Falls and a Fawn PAGES 95-101

Attack Words: *pity* risk* glimpse** (glossary)

splen'did* dis'tant* knelt* (position of single vowel letter)

downward* (root + suffix)

passageway* (roots in compound; pas'sage—position of single vowel letter)

directly* (root + suffix; di rect'—position of single vowel letter)

encircled (root with *e* dropped + ending; encircle—root word + meaning clues)

This story with its exciting plot has an idyllic setting. In rescuing a fawn caught in some rocks near a waterfall, Joyce and Phil get very close to nature, even to walking in the shadowy passageway behind the falls. There is a tenderness and compassion in the children's attitude toward the helpless fawn and its bewildered mother, whose instinct to protect and help her baby was of no avail. Besides admiring the story characters' resourcefulness in meeting an unusual emergency, young readers can hardly fail to recognize the satisfaction that results from protecting and aiding wild creatures.

PREPARING FOR READING

Establishing background: Comment that today's story is about an unusual adventure two children had while trying to help a fawn, and lead pupils to discuss what they know about fawns and deer from their reading or from seeing these animals. Doubtless pupils will agree that the timid deer is one of the most interesting and likable wild animals.

After youngsters have found the story, invite their comments on the picture. Ask, "What sounds can you hear as you look at this picture?" Encourage children who have seen waterfalls to compare them with the one in the picture and to tell what it is like to be near a waterfall. "How would the children on the cliff have to talk when they spoke to each other?" Introduce the children as Phil and Joyce and suggest, "Would you guess that this waterfall has something to do with a rescue? As you read the story you'll find out that although the waterfall proved dangerous to the fawn, it helped the children rescue the frightened animal. If you need help with these words [write *pity, risk, glimpse*], you'll find them in the glossary."

INTERPRETING THE STORY

Pages 95-101: After silent reading, you might organize the discussion of the story around this question: "What problems did Phil and Joyce have to overcome to rescue the fawn?" As pupils decide on the difficulties faced by the story children, write them on the board:

> getting to the bottom of the falls
> getting to the other side of the stream
> freeing the fawn
> rescuing the fawn from the whirlpool

Then encourage children to tell briefly how each problem was solved. As the solutions are given, write them on the board. When the main events have been reviewed in this way, help children think about the sensory images they formed as they read by asking, "If you had been with Joyce and Phil what unusual things would you have seen, heard, and felt?" You might use the picture on page 99 as a basis for visualizing and have various pupils give their impressions of what it would be like to walk through the tunnel behind the waterfall—watching the sparkling waterfall, hearing the roar of the water, feeling the dampness of the low, cool tunnel and the spray, and so on. "What do you think Joyce might answer if someone asked her why she thought a waterfall was the most beautiful thing in the world? What are some of the words she might use to describe the waterfall?" Remind children of her statement on page 99, "It sparkles like diamonds" and see what other descriptive words and phrases they can suggest. To check cause-effect relationships you might ask, "Why was it a good idea for Phil to let his father know that he and Joyce wanted to go down to the fawn? Why do you suppose the fawn jumped into the stream after Phil freed its leg from the rocks? Why is a whirlpool dangerous? Why did Phil use a slipknot in the rope? Why do you suppose the mother doe did not stay right beside her baby?"

To bring out the character traits of the story children, ask, "What kind of children did Phil and Joyce show themselves to be in this situation?" As descriptive words are mentioned (resourceful, careful, responsible, sympathetic, for example), have pupils justify their opinions by specific references to incidents in the story. Then ask, "How do you suppose Phil and Joyce felt after they had rescued the fawn?" During the discussion, encourage pupils to tell about times when they may have rescued an animal.

EXTENDING SKILLS AND ABILITIES

Comparing and contrasting story situations: Ask, "In what way is this story like the previous one, 'The Wild Colt's Lesson'? [It is about a young animal that gets into a dangerous situation.] In what way does the doe in this story remind you of the mare in the previous story? In what way does the rescue of the fawn differ from the rescue of the colt? Why wasn't the doe able to help her fawn? What might have happened to the fawn if Phil and Joyce had not come along?"

At this point you might present the term *animal conservation*, discussing some of its simpler implications and Phil and Joyce's attitude toward conservation of wild life. What have pupils learned about animal conservation from their independent reading? Those who have read or are reading Dorothy Lathrop's *Let Them Live* or other library books about animals should have much to contribute to this discussion. In conclusion, lead pupils to generalize that (1) although most mother animals are quick to protect and help their young, there are situations in which a mother animal is helpless, (2) one of the important aspects of conservation of wild life is people's willingness to protect and aid wild animals and to restore them to their natural habitats rather than hunting or molesting them.

Using a pronunciation key: This exercise and page 25 of the *Think-and-Do Book*, in which two different pronunciation keys are used, strengthen three basic understandings, fundamental to the use of any pronunciation key: (1) Each symbol in a pronunciation key stands for one particular sound; (2) In printed pronunciations a consonant letter stands for its most common sound; (3) Since each vowel letter in our language may stand for more than one sound, a system of diacritical marks has been devised to show the variant sounds that vowel letters represent. Because vowel sounds in accented syllables are heard more distinctly than those in unaccented syllables, this first exercise in comparing pronunciation keys deals only with diacritical marks commonly used in accented syllables.

> *Thus far in this* Guidebook *understandings necessary to the use of a pronunciation key have been developed on the basis of the key in the glossary of* More Times and Places.[1] *However, children are sure to encounter pronunciation keys that employ different symbols in other textbook glossaries, in encyclopedias, and in different elementary dictionaries. Therefore, it is important that pupils develop facility in using any pronunciation key. Obviously, they should never be expected to memorize any one key.*

You might begin by writing first the two keys for *a* given below, omitting the words and pronunciations below them. Lead pupils to note that the one on the left is from the complete vowel pronunciation key at the bottom of every right-hand page in the glossary of *More Times and Places*. Explain that not all dictionaries or glossaries use the same diacritical marks, and call attention to the key for *a* at the right. Have the words in each key pronounced and lead pupils to note that although there are some differences in the pronunciation symbols, the vowel sounds they stand for in each key are the same. Next, as you write each word at the left, have pupils pronounce it. Then write its pronunciation under each key and lead pupils to compare the two printed pronunciations.

	hat, āge, cāre, fär	ădd, āle, câre, ärm[2]
square	(skwãr)	(skwâr)
crab	(krab)	(krăb)
prey	(prā)	(prā)
card	(kärd)	(kärd)
calm	(käm)	(käm)

Next, write the following on the board and use procedures similar to those suggested above:

	cup, pùt, rüle, ūse	ŭp, fŏŏt, fōōd, tübe[2]
dusk	(dusk)	(dŭsk)
huge	(hūj)	(hūj)
prove	(prüv)	(prōōv)
juice	(jüs)	(jōōs)
bush	(bùsh)	(bŏŏsh)

[1] The key for the glossary of *More Times and Places* is identical to that in the *Thorndike-Barnhart Beginning Dictionary*.

[2] By permission. From *Webster's Elementary Dictionary, A Dictionary for Boys and Girls*, copyright, 1935, 1941, 1945, 1949, 1953, by G. & C. Merriam Company.

In conclusion, lead children to note that (1) the consonant pronunciation symbols used in the two lists of pronunciations are the same and (2) a given vowel sound may be represented by different pronunciation symbols in different keys.

Think-and-Do Book: Use pages 24 and 25.

EXTENDING INTERESTS

Enjoying literature: After reading "A Falls and a Fawn," someone will want to show the exquisite pictures in *Dash and Dart*, by Mary and Conrad Buff. They catch the beauty of the wild forest and the small creatures that live there. *Spike, the Story of a Whitetail Deer*, by Robert McClung, is short and would be a fine story for someone who is familiar with it to read aloud. Pupils might then discuss the many things a young deer learns during his first year of life and the dangers he faces.

If some of your average and superior readers show particular interest in these stories about deer, you might recommend *Deer Mountain Hideaway*, by E. H. Lansing. After the idyllic forest picture of *Dash and Dart*, the forest of Fred, Hank, and the little nuisance, Janey, will seem at once more realistic and more dangerous. Mrs. Lansing's intelligently planned mystery is excellent reading. Moreover, as it is discussed by those who read it, the book will intrigue your most reluctant readers because of its high interest quality and suspense.

Using reference materials: The informational material presented on page 24 of the *Think-and-Do Book* may arouse some youngsters' interest in learning more about Niagara Falls. Help children follow up their curiosity by guiding them to encyclopedias and other source materials.

You might also stimulate some thinking about the value of certain magazines as source material. Ask pupils to think of magazines that they have seen at school, at home, or in the public library that contain information and pictures about animals and the great outdoors. As magazines are mentioned, list them on the board (you might make suggestions, too). A typical list could read: *Life, National Geographic, Junior Natural History, Natural History, Field and Stream, Science, My Weekly Reader, Holiday*. Encourage youngsters to bring from home magazines containing information and pictures dealing with animals and the great outdoors.

Since "A Falls and a Fawn" probably takes place in a state or national park, some children might be interested in knowing more about such places.

Most encyclopedias contain information under such entries as "National Park" or "National Park System." Pupils may also want to find out about national or state parks in their own section of the country. *The World Book Encyclopedia* carries a brief discussion of state parks. To find this information, pupils can locate the appropriate heading under the entry for their state. (This heading is "Interesting Places to Visit.") Locating and organizing this information would provide a worth-while research project for a group of superior readers to pursue independently. At a suitable time, help them plan how to present their information to the class.

Bushy Tail's Escape   PAGES 102-107

Attack Words: *midsummer* ventured* weasels* prowled* dread* fled* rustling** (glossary)

sneaking* (root + ending; sneak—two vowel letters together)

force* (vowel followed by *r*)

greedy* (root + suffix; greed—two vowel letters together)

roots* (meaning clues to determine sound of *oo*)

increased* (root with *e* dropped + ending; in crease′— two vowel letters together)

The forest on a midsummer night may seem a peaceful place to people, but actually it is full of activity and soft mysterious sounds as wild creatures bustle about in search of food. Full interpretation of this story brings the reader, a silent, unseen onlooker, into the midst of the forest—even into the snug den of a chipmunk family. On this imaginary excursion the reader witnesses the chipmunks' breath-taking escape from a weasel and the weasel's capture by a great horned owl. Children's sympathies are likely to lie with the chipmunk family. Yet few young readers will miss the implication that the law of the forest is struggle for survival. Owls, weasels, and other wild creatures, not so endearing perhaps as chipmunks, must eat; and smaller, weaker animals are their natural prey.

Establishing background and anticipating vocabulary needs: Suggest that children glance briefly at the pictures on pages 82-89 and recall the setting and the animals mentioned in this story. Remind youngsters, too, of page 20 in the *Think-and-Do Book* that explains how darkness helps animals. Then comment, "Today's story takes us into the forest on a summer night. Listen as I read the first paragraph; then be ready to tell what it makes you see, hear, and feel." After children have had an opportunity to describe their imagery and reactions—the hushed sounds, the animals to be seen, the pale, glimmering sky, and the air of mystery and expectancy— suggest that they look at the illustration on page 102 to see how the artist pictures a midsummer night in the forest. Can pupils infer what time of the year midsummer is? If not, suggest that they consult the glossary. Encourage youngsters to identify the animals. If necessary, explain that the brown animal at the right is a weasel, write the word, and have pupils look up *weasel* in the glossary to find out more about this animal. Then, to complete the description of the picture, read the last paragraph on page 102 aloud, emphasizing by your oral interpretation the atmosphere of lurking danger amid the beauty of the summer night. Discuss the effectiveness of the words *pounce, ventured, prowled,* and *preying* to describe how owls, mice, wood rats, weasels, and foxes act at night. (If pupils seem uncertain of the meanings of these words, suggest that they consult the glossary.) Then ask, "Which animals seem to be bold? Which, timid?"

INTERPRETING THE STORY

Call attention to the picture on page 103 and comment, "Here we see Bushy Tail with his family. They certainly look snug and safe, don't they?" After children have identified the animals as chipmunks, help them visualize this picture as a cross section of a chipmunk's burrow and make sure that they understand the general plan—the tunnels leading into it, the grass-lined den, and the storage bins for the animals' food supply. Ask, "Do you know why the burrow has two doorways? You'll find out for sure as you read." Then have the story title read and comment, "The chipmunks were not to spend the night safely. One of their worst enemies was roaming the forest that night. Let's read the rest of the story to find out about the chipmunks' narrow escape."

Pages 103-107: After silent reading, you might comment, "The forest is hardly a peaceful place at night, is it?" and lead children to discuss Bushy

Tail's escape. Then ask, "How did the weasel find the chipmunks' burrow? Why did the father chipmunk keep watching the door of the tunnel? What did he do when the weasel started into the tunnel?" Have pupils turn back to the picture on page 103 and show how the chipmunks got out of their burrow. "Why was Bushy Tail frightened when he came out of the burrow? How did he feel by the end of the story? Why? Were you glad that the owl caught the weasel? Why? What do you suppose the other small animals did when they heard the owl's hunting cry?"

Extending interpretation: Children at this level are not too young to realize that all wild animals must maintain a constant struggle for survival and that all animals have enemies and must be constantly on the alert. To point up these concepts, comment, "We were glad that the owl caught the weasel, and Bushy Tail was saved, but what was the weasel's reason for hunting chipmunks? the owl's reason for seizing the weasel? Can you think of other animals or birds that Bushy Tail and his family might fear? In what ways can chipmunks protect themselves from their enemies?" From the text and the pictures in this story, pupils can conclude that the chipmunks' means of protection included their underground den with its two entrances and narrow tunnels, and fleeing and hiding. Then ask, "What other means of protection do animals have against their enemies?" During the discussion, lead pupils to bring out the importance of the keen sense of smell and hearing that most animals have, and help children conclude that animals must be always alert if they are to survive. If you can do so with a light touch, help youngsters realize that actually there is no standard of right or wrong involved in the behavior of animals. The fact that animals prey on each other is an objective fact of nature. They do so by instinct in order to eat and survive.

EXTENDING SKILLS AND ABILITIES

Interpreting descriptive language: Remind youngsters that if we form vivid mental images as we read, a story becomes more real—we feel as though we are actually seeing and hearing the story action. Explain that the author of this story has used many words that help us see and hear the actions and that even make us feel a certain way. Ask, "How did you feel about the weasel in this story?" Doubtless children will agree that they disliked the weasel; suggest that they find descriptive words and phrases that the author used to create an impression of an unpleasant, cruel animal (*preying on weaker animals, sly, sneaking, greedy eyes shone cruelly*).

Then encourage children to find words and passages (examples are given in parentheses for your convenience) that show that:

the forest was a dangerous place for small animals (*crept cautiously out, unable to defend themselves, risking their lives*)

night in the forest was usually quiet (*soft, mysterious sounds, silence of the night*)

the chipmunks were very frightened when the weasel found their den (*woke in terror, frantically*)

Bushy Tail was afraid when he came out of the tunnel (*filled with fresh terror, increased his panic*)

the horned owl would be a fearful enemy of small animals (*fierce hunting cry, swooped*)

Since page 26 of the *Think-and-Do Book* will further strengthen appreciation of vivid words, you may want to use it before introducing the exercise suggested below.

Using a pronunciation key: This exercise and page 27 of the *Think-and-Do Book* will strengthen understanding of the function of a pronunciation key and point up the idea that pronunciation symbols may differ in different keys. Write the following on the board:

let, bē, tėrm; it, īce; hot, ōpen, ôrder

(hol′ō)	(in′sekt)
(skwėrm)	(dis gīz′)
(skôrch)	(sô′si)
(griz′li)	(in dēd′)

ēve, ĕll; bīte, pĭn; nō, ôr, tŏp; bûrn[1]

(hŏl′ō)	(ĭn′sĕkt)
(skwûrm)	(dĭs-gīz′)
(skôrch)	(sô′sĭ)
(grĭz′lĭ)	(ĭn-dēd′)

First, have the two keys compared and recall with pupils that different pronunciation keys may use different symbols for some vowel sounds. After the words in each key have been pronounced, lead children to note that although different key words and in some instances different symbols are used, the two keys represent the same eight vowel sounds. Using the first key, have pupils look at the first word in the list below it, tell what two key words indicate the two vowel sounds in the word, and what syllable is accented.

---

[1] *The Winston Dictionary for Schools*, The John C. Winston Company, Philadelphia, Pa., Copyright 1954.

Then have the word pronounced and write *hollow* in front of the pronunciation. Repeat the procedure, using the second key.

Continue in like manner with the printed pronunciations for *squirm, scorch, grizzly, insect, disguise, saucy, indeed,* having children use both keys for each word. Lead pupils to note that different keys not only use different symbols but also indicate the divisions between some syllables in different ways.

Think-and-Do Book: Use pages 26 and 27.

EXTENDING INTERESTS

Recalling stories: If possible, present the film "Chumming with Chipmunks," which shows a chipmunk being tamed by means of nuts tied to the branch of a tree. The charm and humor of the situations and the text will make seeing this film an enjoyable experience for you and the youngsters. It will also lead to a discussion of the fact that some animals of the woods may overcome their instinctive fear of human beings if treated with kindness and approached very slowly. See whether pupils can recall examples of stories in which animals lost that fear. They may suggest such stories as "Skinny Takes His Own Picture," in the new *More Streets and Roads*, "Salt for the Deer," in the new *Streets and Roads*, and "The Wahoo Bobcat," which you may have read aloud from *Time for True Tales* during the preceding unit. Library books and selections from the independent supplementary reading may also provide examples.

Enjoying literature: "Bushy Tail's Escape" was adapted from *Bushy Tail,* by Alice Gall and Fleming Crew. The book, unfortunately, is out of print and therefore not listed in the bibliography. However, if a copy is available in your school or public library, you will want to mention it to any superior readers who may be interested. The book reveals a great deal of information about the habits of many small animals of the woods. Children should understand by this time that animals do not talk, as they appear to do in this book, but you might remind them, beforehand, that this is simply the author's way of telling the story.

The section of *Time for Poetry* called "The Animal Fair" contains many poems that are appropriate to this unit. You might like to read "The Jolly Woodchuck," by Marion Edey, for its description of another underground den, snug and secure during the winter months. It would be a good idea, too, to reread the poems presented with the first story in the unit.

Billy and the Loons PAGES 108-115

Attack Words: *loons* companion* swirling* opposite** (glossary)
lan'tern* mist* (position of single vowel letter)
upward* (root + suffix)
dawn* (*a* followed by *w*)
lane* (final *e*)
foam* ea'gle* (two vowel letters together)

What could be dearer to the heart of a young boy than being considered a real woodsman? While camping with his parents in the north woods, Billy Grayson realized that desire. He was fortunate in having as a companion a remarkable Indian guide, whose attitude and expert instruction taught Billy what being a woodsman means.

As young readers identify themselves with Billy, they, too, will experience the thrill of living close to nature—of fishing for one's supper, eating and sleeping outdoors, and watching the loons dance at dawn. The story contains all the appeal of the great outdoors plus affectionate, kindly human relationships. The dignity, wisdom, and humanity of the guide make him an unforgettable story character.

PREPARING FOR READING

Establishing background and anticipating vocabulary needs: Recalling the Howard family's camp will provide an interesting lead into this story about another camping experience. Show the picture on page 72 and lead pupils to discuss where the Howards went camping and what their camp was like. Comment, "In today's story you'll read about another family that went camping—Billy Grayson and his mother and father were spending their vacation in the north woods." Encourage children to recall what they know from previous stories, from books and pictures, or from their own experience about the north woods—it is a sparsely populated forest and lake region. During the discussion, you might indicate the general area of northern Minnesota and Wisconsin and explain that it was in this region that the Graysons were spending their vacation.

Then suggest that youngsters turn to the picture on pages 108 and 109. Introduce the two people in the canoe as Billy Grayson and the Indian guide, Chief. If any pupils have fished in the lakes of northern Wisconsin, Minnesota, or Canada, or if they know anything about fishing in this region, they might like to venture guesses about the kind of fish Billy has caught and what he had to do to catch such a fish. Ask, "Why do you suppose the Graysons had an Indian guide?" After children have had an opportunity to comment on the camp and the dense forest in the background, have the story title read and comment, "If you camped near a lake in the north woods, you might very likely see or hear a loon. Do you know what loons are? The glossary will tell you." It is to be hoped that you or one of the children can imitate the wild, eerie laughter of a loon. Even a fair imitation will add to the effectiveness of the story.

Continue, "Billy wasn't satisfied just to fish—he wanted to be a real woodsman. What do you suppose one has to learn or do before he can be called a woodsman?" Welcome conjectures and then suggest, "Read the story to find out how Billy earned the right to be called a woodsman."

INTERPRETING THE STORY

Pages 108-115: After silent reading, ask, "How did Billy prove that he was a real woodsman? How did he probably feel when the Indian guide said 'I believe you're a grown-up woodsman now!'?" Then suggest that children imagine that they are Billy, telling a friend about everything that happened in this story. Let pupils refer to the text when necessary as an aid to recalling events and sequence, but encourage them to use their own words as much as possible to describe Billy's feelings, the sights and sounds of the forest and the lake, and the loons' dance. Suggest that several children give their impressions of what it would be like to lie beneath the great pine and to wake up in the gray, misty dawn. Then ask children whether the loons' dance reminded them of a wild-animal dance in another story in this unit, and lead them to compare the rabbits' dance in "A Zoo Without Bars" with the loons' dance. In conclusion, you might ask, "Do you think June and Jim might enjoy having Billy with them on their trips to the zoo without bars? Why?"

From his statements in this story we sense that the Indian guide had a deep interest in, almost a reverence for, nature. And though Billy is only a boy, we can imagine that he, too, shared that respect for the ordinary sights and sounds as well as for the wonders of nature. To make children aware of this attitude, suggest that they read the last two paragraphs on page 109. Then ask, "Do you suppose Chief had slept outdoors many times? What makes you think so? How do you think he felt about sleeping out? How do you think his voice sounded as he talked?" Help pupils see that his voice probably reflected the pleasant experience of sleeping near the lake and hearing its sound and the sound of the wind. You might call on several youngsters to read these paragraphs to bring out how they think the Indian talked—even looked—as he spoke. Then have them read the paragraph on page 115 beginning "Chief turned slowly, . . ." and discuss the question "How do you suppose Chief felt about seeing the loons dance?" Again suggest that pupils experiment with reading the Indian's words aloud. Continue, "We describe a person like Chief, who spends much time outdoors and who enjoys watching animals and birds, as someone who is 'close to nature.' In what ways do you suppose Billy felt close to nature during his night outdoors?" Conclude the discussion by asking, "How did Billy feel toward Chief? How do you know? Would you like to know Chief? Why?"

Oral interpretation: The rich descriptive language, the moods, and the contrast between Billy's excited eagerness and the Indian guide's calm and quiet manner can best be brought out through oral interpretation. Before oral reading, you will want to go through the story with children, helping them plan how to bring out these qualities. For example, how should the first paragraph on page 112 be read to bring out the mood of an evening in the north woods? Remind pupils that oral reading is more effective if the reader forms pictures of what he reads and projects these images to his audience through softness or loudness of voice, rate of reading, facial expressions, and pantomime. After the discussion suggested in the preceding paragraph, children probably will have decided how the Indian guide's speeches should be read, but you might lead them to point out clues to how he sounded—"soft voice," "eyes intent and serious." Throughout the story, Billy's excitement and enthusiasm are evident, and the exclamation points following his speeches on pages 113 and 115 tell us that this excitement was reflected in his voice and they serve as clues to how he sounded.

EXTENDING SKILLS AND ABILITIES

Locating source material: Loons are fascinating water birds, and this story may arouse curiosity about them. "How long can a loon stay under water? Are loons fast birds? Where do they build their nests? What do they eat?" If such questions arise, suggest that pupils look for answers in one of the children's encyclopedias and in available nature reference books. Recall with children how to use the guide letters on the backbone of an encyclopedia to find the correct volume.

Then to point up the value and the method of using an index, open a single-volume reference book and ask, "How can we tell quickly whether there is any information about loons in this book?" When someone suggests the index, turn to it and lead children to note that all entries are alphabetized and that each is followed by a number or numbers that indicate on what pages the desired information can be found. Explain, too, that many indexes have a way of indicating on what page one can find a picture of a particular entry. Before a page number following an entry word there may be the abbreviation *ill.* or the words *color plate.* Some indexes simply use an asterisk after a page number to indicate an illustration.

Part of an index from a reference book about animals is reproduced on page 29 of the *Think-and-Do Book.* As a child uses this page, he applies his skill of comprehending abbreviation and phrase meaning to the problem of locating source material in an index.

Interpreting implied ideas: This exercise might be used with the whole group or reserved for a special-help session with those pupils who have exhibited difficulty in answering questions involving implied ideas or relationships. As children discuss the answers to the questions below, note individual weaknesses in this skill. During the discussion of succeeding stories plan to give those pupils who need it many opportunities under guidance to read between the lines.

What did Chief mean when he said that Mr. Grayson was a wise man and would let Billy sleep outdoors by himself?

Why did Mrs. Grayson exclaim, "Oh, Billy!" when she heard he was going to sleep outdoors?

Why did Chief say, "Good boy!" when Billy said he did not want to keep the lantern?

Why was Billy glad that he had not awakened in the dark?

How do you know that Chief was up and about at dawn, too?

Think-and-Do Book: Use pages 28, 29, and 30. As youngsters use page 28 they will acquire and organize interesting information about the warning signals of various animals from reading expository material such as might be found in encyclopedias or in single-volume reference books.

Enjoying literature: The Indian guide and the subject matter of "Billy and the Loons" suggest Longfellow's "Hiawatha's Childhood." Children may remember having heard this poem at an earlier level. If you decide to use it at this time, read it aloud on several successive days. Youngsters will enjoy Nokomis' explanations and names for the sights and sounds of the forest.

Entertaining a guest speaker: Should there be someone in your community who is greatly interested and well informed in nature lore, perhaps he could be invited to speak to the class. He might tell a few of his experiences, for example, and explain some of the habits of the wild animals he has observed. If the speaker is a camera enthusiast as well, he may also wish to show some of the animal pictures he has taken. Children can plan questions they would like to ask during a question-and-answer period to follow the talk. The entire event might be planned as a class activity. The class could compose the letter of invitation, select a committee to greet and introduce the speaker, and appoint another committee, perhaps, to arrange for simple refreshments.

Wilderness Partners PAGES 116-120

Attack Words: *considered* roamed* solid* alert* Husky* heeding* sensed* ambled** (glossary)
forepaws* (root + prefix)
chose* (final *e*)
an'ger* na'ture* (position of single vowel letter)
swallowed* (root + ending; swal'low—meaning **and** phonetic clues)

Those who have been fortunate enough to observe animals in the wilderness know that they do not always seem frightening or cruel. In this charming, comical story a young Husky puppy discovers that a huge grizzly bear, who catches trout for his dinner, is very generous with the discarded fish tails. Besides being entertained by the humor of the situation, young readers will be impressed by wild animals' ingenuity in getting food and their apparent willingness to share if their immediate needs do not conflict.

PREPARING FOR READING

Establishing background: A film that you might use to introduce this story is "Giants of the North," which shows a group of men "hunting" bears with cameras in the wilds of the north. The wilderness setting and the scene showing a bear catching fish make this film especially valuable for building background for "Wilderness Partners."

Recall with pupils how Sarah in the story "The Quiet Mountains" felt about grizzly bears. Then ask, "What did the glossary tell you about grizzlies that helped you understand why she felt that way?" Continue, "In today's story you'll travel in your imagination to the northern wilderness and watch one of these huge bears as he goes about the important business of getting a meal. You may be surprised at how he gets his dinner and at what happens when another animal tries to interfere! And by the end of the story I think you'll agree that the grizzly doesn't always act fierce."

INTERPRETING THE STORY

After children have turned to the story and commented on the picture, have the title read. Ask, "Do you suppose this grizzly will be one of the partners mentioned in the title? You'll find out as you read the story who the wilderness partners were and how this partnership came about."

Pages 116-120: After silent reading, give youngsters who are still interpreting largely at the factual level a chance to contribute by asking them such questions as "How did the Husky puppy and the grizzly bear become partners? How did the bear get his meal? Why was the grizzly good-natured most of the time?" Then ask, "In what ways did the puppy remind you of other young dogs that you have seen?" After the discussion of these questions, encourage children to read aloud those parts of the story that they liked or thought particularly amusing. Since much of the humor stems from the mental pictures that children formed as they read, ask each child who selects a part to read aloud to tell what he could see happening in that part. Visual images that certainly should be shared by all youngsters are those evoked by the last paragraph on page 118, the first line on page 119, and the contrast between the small puppy and the huge bear as the grizzly sniffed at his "partner."

Pupils who have read or are reading *Snow Dog* from which this story is taken will probably be eager to tell of other adventures the Husky had, especially with grizzlies. Encourage them to do so, for nothing quite recommends a book like the spontaneous, enthusiastic comments of its readers.

EXTENDING SKILLS AND ABILITIES

Using a pronunciation key: This is the third in a series of lessons designed to strengthen understanding of the function of pronunciation keys and to promote awareness of likenesses and differences in the pronunciation symbols used in various dictionaries and glossaries. Attention is focused in this exercise on noting how the schwa sound heard in unaccented syllables is represented in different pronunciation keys.

Have pupils turn to the full pronunciation key on page 302 of *More Times and Places*. Call attention to the schwa symbol (ə) and have the five key words pronounced. Recall with pupils that the purpose of the key is to show that the schwa symbol stands for the unstressed vowel sound represented by any vowel letter in an unaccented syllable. Then call attention to the vowel key at the bottom of a right-hand glossary page and have pupils note which key word is used for the schwa sound (*takən*). Next, under the key word *takən*, write just the pronunciations shown below:

	takən	ăccount, sofȧ, silĕnt, makēr, charĭty, cŏnnect, circŭs[1]
canyon	(kan′yən)	(kăn′yŭn)
patrol	(pə trōl′)	(pȧ · trōl′)
moment	(mō′mənt)	(mō′mĕnt)
cactus	(kak′təs)	(kăk′tŭs)
convince	(kən vins′)	(kŏn · vĭns′)
terror	(ter′ər)	(tĕr′ēr)
arrival	(ə rīv′əl)	(ȧ · rīv′ăl)
engine	(en′jən)	(ĕn′jĭn)

Then, with the vowel key as their guide, ask pupils to say the word each printed pronunciation represents. As they do so, write the word to the left of the parentheses. Next, write the unaccented vowel pronunciation key to the right and explain that some dictionaries and glossaries use a different method of representing the soft, unstressed vowel sound heard in unaccented syllables. As the key words are pronounced, lead pupils to note that a different pronunciation symbol is used to represent the soft, unstressed

---

[1] By permission. From *Webster's Elementary Dictionary, A Dictionary for Boys and Girls*, copyright, 1935, 1941, 1945, 1949, 1953, by G. & C. Merriam Company.

sound that each of the various vowel letters may stand for, and that with the exception of the symbol used for the unstressed vowel sound before *r*, the symbols consist of the five vowel letters printed in italics plus diacritical marks. Then write the pronunciations below the key as indicated and lead pupils to compare the pronunciations for each of the eight words.

In conclusion have pupils pronounce the words listed below at the left and lead them to compare the printed pronunciations. Explain that for some words containing the schwa sound, certain dictionaries and glossaries use an apostrophe to represent the schwa sound.

weasel	(wē′ zəl)	(wē′ z'l)[1]
eaten	(ēt′ ən)	(ēt′ 'n)
person	(pėr′ sən)	(pûr′ s'n)
apple	(ap′ əl)	(ăp′ 'l)

Page 32 of the *Think-and-Do Book* is the third in a series that checks ability to use a pronunciation key different from that in the glossary in *More Times and Places*. It emphasizes the importance of referring to a key when one encounters unfamiliar pronunciation symbols. Pupils who have difficulty with the page should be placed in a special-help group and given step-by-step guidance in auditory perception of vowel sounds, in association of sounds with pronunciation symbols, and in deriving the pronunciations of words from their printed pronunciations. For helpful suggestions, see pages 215-228 of *On Their Own in Reading*, Revised Edition.

Think-and-Do Book: Use pages 31 and 32. The covers of various magazines are reproduced on page 31, and pupils are given practice in the elementary but important research skill of deciding which magazine they might consult first to get certain types of information.

EXTENDING INTERESTS

Extending concepts: Though you may have used the film "Giants of the North" to introduce "Wilderness Partners," you will want to show it again. In the excitement of seeing a bear charge toward the camera, children may have misinterpreted the use of the gun, which was fired only to frighten the bear. This is a good point to discuss with youngsters at the close of the film. Another film, "The Bear and Its Relatives," shows various kinds of bears in captivity, but the narration describes the habits of the animals in their natural habitats as well. This film, too, is worth showing twice. It

---

[1] By permission. From *Webster's Elementary Dictionary, A Dictionary for Boys and Girls*, copyright, 1935, 1941, 1945, 1949, 1953, by G. & C. Merriam Company.

will give children an excellent picture of the size of bears, and of the details of their appearance.

Either or both of these films will provide material for lively class discussion. However, if neither film is available, some superior readers might look up information about various kinds of bears, their habits, and the regions in which they are found and present the findings to the rest of the class. *Hammond's Nature Atlas of America* includes the black and the grizzly bear. Most encyclopedias contain interesting information about other kinds as well.

Personal reading: Pupils should be given opportunities to tell about the books, magazine articles, etc. that they have been reading in connection with their own personal interests. You might devote some time each week to discussions of this type. At all times you will want to be alert for opportunities to broaden children's current areas of interest and to develop new ones. Such opportunities arise not only from discussion of the type suggested above but also from class discussions of all kinds, your personal conversation with individual children, and your awareness of the youngsters' backgrounds of experience.

Enjoying literature: Like all Jim Kjelgaard's stories, *Snow Dog*, from which "Wilderness Partners" is taken, is a thrilling and beautifully written tale. So is Harold McCracken's *The Biggest Bear on Earth*. The children will not want to miss either of these fine books. Various episodes from both stories might be recounted by youngsters who have read them.

Both books mentioned above are difficult for fourth-grade children and will be read principally by your superior readers. However, you may find several of the average or even slow readers reaching for them after their interest has been aroused by the glowing enthusiasm of their classmates. Often avid interest in a subject or story character will carry a child through a book that would ordinarily be considered much above his reading level. Certainly he should be encouraged and helped in his efforts—not only to prevent his lack of fluency in reading from overcoming his desire to read the books, but also to give him the sense of accomplishment that will come with the realization that he has read a longer, more mature book. If he succeeds once he will try again. Then you may begin to notice a change in his attitude toward reading as well as in his ability to read.

Time for Poetry contains a poem about another wild creature that likes fish. It is "The sea gull curves his wings," by Elizabeth Coatsworth. This poem is another example of contrasting rhythm and melody to suggest contrasting moods and action. Notice that the first couplet of each verse has a smooth, sailing movement that is like the soaring, floating motion of the sea gull's flight. The second couplet of each verse is harsh in sound and staccato in movement like the cry of warning that it really is. There is also an element of surprise in those second couplets that children enjoy. If your youngsters like choral speaking, this poem lends itself to two choirs. The first couplet in each verse will be spoken by the high-medium group, and the second by the low-medium group. Be sure to speak the second couplets with humorous gusto rather than ominous seriousness.

The Magic Coat   PAGES 121-127

Sight Word: Leone's
Attack Words: *ledge* shove* crouched* coyote* despair* threatened**
                confused* (glossary)
                Taw'ny* (*a* followed by *w*)
                pitched* humped* hissed* uttering* (root + ending;
                    pitch, hump, hiss, ut'ter—position of single vowel
                    letter)
                purred* (root + ending; purr—vowel followed by *r*)
                but'ter fly'* (position of single vowel letter)

Safe in a rocky den on a steep ledge, Tawny and Leone, two mountain lion cubs, frisked and tumbled in the playful manner of all young kittens. Then one day Tawny fell from the ledge and was introduced to danger in the form of a coyote sneaking toward him. Instinctively, Tawny climbed a tree and was saved for the moment. But it was his mother's response to his desperate cries that rescued him from the hungry coyote. Back at the cave, the mountain lion played an important game with her cubs—a game that would teach the kittens that their reddish-brown coats could camouflage them from their enemies. It may come as a surprise to some young readers that even the large and powerful mountain lion must be wary of enemies—that the law of the forest, constant struggle for survival, affects all wild creatures.

Establishing background and presenting vocabulary: Ask, "What are some of the animals that you might see in the mountains in the western part of our country? Which of the animals that we have read about might live in the mountains?" After the discussion, continue, "Today's story takes us to a rocky cave on Mount Grizzly in Colorado where a mother mountain lion and her two babies had their den." You might indicate the central, mountainous part of Colorado on the map and encourage children who have lived or visited in this area to tell about wild animals they may have seen. Then have children turn to page 121, and encourage them to comment on the lions' appearance—the white undersides of the mother and the kitten, the babies' spots, and so on. During the discussion, explain that since mountain lions belong to the cat family, their young are often referred to as kittens and that these kittens' names are Tawny and *Leone*. Then have the title read and ask, "What does this title make you want to find out as you read the story?" After children have had an opportunity to state their reasons for reading, you might stimulate further interest by commenting that there is an exciting and dangerous adventure in this story.

INTERPRETING THE STORY

Pages 121-127: After silent reading, ask, "What was the magic coat in this story? Why was it called 'magic'? How did the mountain lion teach her babies about the magic coat?" Then lead children to discuss Tawny's adventure with the coyote—how the kitten happened to fall off the ledge, how he tried to protect himself from the coyote, and how he was rescued. Ask, "How did this part of the story remind you of 'The Wild Colt's Lesson'?" To heighten awareness of story structure, ask, "Where does the story action really begin? [the last paragraph on page 122] What does the first part of the story tell about?" Remind pupils that an author sometimes puts an introduction at the beginning of a story to tell us things that we need to know to understand the story or to present interesting action or ideas that make us want to read on to find out what the story problem is. To encourage discussion of the information given in the introduction of this story, ask, "How did Tawny and Leone remind you of ordinary kittens? How were they different? How were they like other baby animals that you have seen or read about?"

While children are still visualizing Tawny and Leone as playful kittens, ask, "Has anyone read a book in which there is a full-grown mountain lion?" Any youngster who is familiar with *Brighty of the Grand Canyon*, by Marguerite Henry, will enjoy describing Brighty's first encounter with one of these large animals. This episode will give children an idea of the kittens' potentialities as mature mountain lions. Continue, "Does hearing about Brighty's fight make you feel the same toward mountain lions as reading the story 'The Magic Coat'? How has your feeling changed?" The more immature youngsters may have difficulty expressing their reactions. With these children, specific questions will help: "How do you feel toward Tawny and Leone? toward the mountain lion that Brighty fought? Do you think that Tawny and Leone will grow up to be like that lion?" Such questions will help pupils realize that although most wild animals are appealing when very young, many grow up to be fierce and predatory.

It is quite possible that pupils who have read Brighty of the Grand Canyon *will have seen no relationship between the mountain lion in that book and the apparently harmless kittens in "The Magic Coat." The value of such discussions immediately following the interpretation of a story lies in the fact that they help children form the habit of integrating the information they have gained from various sources.*

Extending interpretation: This story provides an excellent lead for a discussion of protective coloring. Ask, "How does the mountain lion's coat protect it from its enemies? What other animals have 'magic coats'?" If children have seen the movie "The Bear and Its Relatives," recalling the polar bear's white coat will prompt other examples of animals whose coloring blends with their surroundings. Page 33 of the *Think-and-Do Book* presents additional information about animals whose coloring or general appearance provides protection. If pupils want to find out more about animal camouflage, suggest that they consult some of the available reference materials. (*The World Book Encyclopedia*, for example, contains interesting information under the entries "Animal" and "Protective Coloration.")

EXTENDING SKILLS AND ABILITIES

Organizing ideas: Since this story divides easily into three main parts, it is a good one for pupils to organize and retell from memory. Have them look through the story and decide where it can be divided into parts. Remind them that they have already discussed one part—the introduction. After they have decided on the division between the second and third parts (the bottom of page 125), suggest that children read each part aloud and discuss what mental pictures they formed and what sounds they heard as they read. Then have them decide on subtitles that point up the main action of each part, for example, "Growing up in the den," "Mother to the rescue," "An important game." In conclusion, have pupils retell the story from memory, using the subtitles as a guide.

Structural analysis: This exercise strengthens the understanding that root words are meaning units and retain their meaning in inflected and derived forms. The use of page 35 of the *Think-and-Do Book* before presenting this exercise will help you decide which pupils need this review. Those who have no difficulty with the page might engage in extension reading or research activities while you work with the special-help group.

Youngsters who have formed the misleading habit of looking for little words in big as a method of word analysis are those who have not yet grasped or have not been taught the significance of the word word—*a speech sound or a series of sounds that has meaning and is used as an independent unit of language. For example,* car *is not a "little word" or a root word in* carpet; *it is merely the first syllable or pronunciation unit.* Pup *is not a word in* pupil; *nor is it a syllable, the first syllable being* pu. *Children who may be using this unsound method of word analysis need reëducation in the skills and understandings that enable them to analyze the structure of an unknown word—to identify root words in inflected and derived forms and to recognize compound words before applying phonetic analysis to get the pronunciation of the root words.*

To point up the understanding that a root word retains its meaning in derived or inflected forms, write the words *appeared, disappear, reappear, appearing* and ask pupils to tell from what root word they are all formed and what prefix or ending has been added. Then have pupils use the words in oral sentences. Next, write the sentence *Tom was puzzled by his dog's disappearance* and have it read. Ask pupils to tell from what root word *disappearance* is formed and discuss its meaning.

Then to emphasize the understanding that it is *meaning*, not visual form, which determines whether or not words are formed from a common root word, write the following on the board, underlining the italicized words:

The *car* was new.
Father took a *carful* of boys to the game.
The new *carpet* covered the floor.
Three *cars* sped by us.

Have the sentences read and discuss with pupils the meanings of the four italicized words. Lead pupils to note that one of the words, *carpet*, is not related in meaning to the other three words—that it is not formed from the root word *car*. Use similar procedures with the lists of words given below:

sad	need	care	amuse
sadden	needles	careless	unamused
saddle	needy	scare	used
sadly	needless	careful	amusement

Think-and-Do Book: Use pages 33, 34, and 35. Page 34 calls pupils' attention to the power of descriptive writing to call up vivid sensory images that establish a dominant mood.

EXTENDING INTERESTS

Extending concepts: Since the mountain lion is just one of the many wild animals that have become scarce in this country, children might be interested in finding out why various animals have almost disappeared and what is being done to preserve them. *Saving Our Wildlife*, by Bertha Morris Parker, explains these points clearly and in addition tells what we can do to help. (One section is devoted specifically to a discussion of the mountain lion.) This book is easy enough for most children to read independently.

The encyclopedias also contain information on this subject in sections devoted to the conservation of wildlife under the more inclusive entry "Conservation." If youngsters are interested in knowing what animals are still fairly numerous in their own state, suggest that they read the section "Natural Resources" (one portion is devoted to animal life) under the entry for their state in *The World Book Encyclopedia*. Your superior readers might well engage in such research activities while you are reviewing and reteaching skills and understandings with special-help groups.

Enjoying literature: After the earlier discussion of Brighty's encounter with the mountain lion, readers of *Brighty of the Grand Canyon* will certainly want to have an opportunity to describe Uncle Jim's humorously tender but practical treatment of the little burro's wounds. The accompanying pictures are delightful and should be shown for the whole class to enjoy. Youngsters then will have had a taste of the excitement, humor, and pathos of this story, and the book will probably be in great demand.

Independent supplementary reading: A section of the board might be set aside for listing pupils' favorites from the selections from other readers. (See the bibliography at the back of this *Guidebook*.) When a child particularly likes a story that he has read, he can list it in this section of the board together with its page numbers, the book in which it is found, and the kind of animal it concerns. He might also add his own name. All pupils can refer to this list and select the stories they think they will enjoy. This type of independent reading list will not only stimulate interest but will also increase the likelihood of several children's reading the same stories and thereby serve as a springboard for good discussion.

Willie the Moose   PAGES 128-135

Attack Words: *determined* concern* flapjacks* overcome* strutted**
(glossary)
Wil'lie* flung* (position of single vowel letter)
Her'bert* Char'lie* (vowel followed by *r*)
attending* (root + ending; at tend'—position of single vowel letter)
freedom* appearance* (root word + meaning clues)
skillfully* (root word + suffixes; skill—position of single vowel letter)

This isn't a story about an ordinary moose. Willie was Herbert and Kitty Clayton's pet—that is until he accidentally kicked the children's father. "This is the last straw!" Mr. Clayton announced and marched Willie into the woods. How Willie saved the Clayton's logging camp from fire, thereby earning an important title, provides the climax to this comical story.

The delightful incongruity of keeping a huge moose for a pet and the antics of unquenchable Willie make this story unusual and appealing to preadolescents. Comical as Willie is, the story events are likely to raise the question of the advisability of trying to make pets of wild animals.

PREPARING FOR READING

Establishing background: Few specific concepts need be presented to ensure readiness for this amusing story. Pupils have already visualized the wilderness setting and isolation of a lumber camp in the story "The School

Train" in the preceding unit. You might comment briefly that today's story is about a moose that was the pet of Herbert and Kitty Clayton, two children who lived in a logging camp in northern Minnesota (point out this area on the map). Encourage children to recall from other books and from stories (for example, "A Visitor in Camp" in the new *More Streets and Roads*) what they know about moose—their size, appearance, and so on—and ask them whether they would like a moose for a pet. Say, "The moose in this story proved to be an amusing and unusual pet; I think you'll be chuckling all the way through this story at his funny actions."

INTERPRETING THE STORY

After the title has been read and children have commented on the picture, say, "As you read, you'll find out how Willie the moose became a hero!"

Pages 128-135: After silent reading, children will be eager to retell this delightful story from beginning to end. Suggest that before they do so, they look through the story to refresh their memories about the mental pictures they formed as they read. You might ask one of those youngsters who showed by his facial expression and amused chuckles that he was truly "living" and thoroughly enjoying the story to start telling it. During the narration, you might casually inject such questions as the following to bring out emotional reactions and to make the action come alive: "How did Herbert and Kitty feel when their father said he intended to get rid of Willie? How do you suppose Charlie sounded when he said 'I'll *moo* you!'? What did the men sitting around the fire probably think when they heard Willie moo and saw him start toward them? How had Mr. Clayton's attitude toward Willie changed by the end of the story?"

Some of the most amusing visual images can be formed by reading between the lines in this story and visualizing incidents and action that are only briefly mentioned. Encourage youngsters to discuss the mental pictures they formed as they read such passages as the second paragraph on page 128, the second paragraph on page 130, the first sentence in the second paragraph on page 132, and the last paragraph on page 135.

Extending interpretation: For all its hilarity, this story does pose a sober question: Is it a good idea generally to try to make pets of wild animals? To stimulate some thinking on the subject, ask, "How did it happen that the Clayton children had a moose for a pet? Why did Mr. Clayton want to get rid of Willie? Do you think his reasons were good ones? Why [or why not]?" Encourage children who have had wild-animal pets or have read about them to discuss whether or not wild animals are likely to be good pets. Then ask, "What is the difference between taming wild animals and keeping them for pets?" (The stories "Chip, the Baby Chipmunk" and "Salt for the Deer" in the new *Streets and Roads* provide material for discussion of this question.)

In conclusion, help pupils generalize in their own words that (1) although it is usually easy to make pets of young wild animals, once they are grown they are likely to become troublesome or dangerous; (2) unless one has the proper place to keep them and knowledge of how to care for them, it is cruel and senseless to remove wild animals from their natural habitats; (3) taming animals so that they will eat from one's hand is fun and quite a different thing from capturing them and restricting their freedom.

Think-and-Do Book: Use page 36. This page focuses pupils' attention on the importance of stressing appropriate words to make oral interpretation of a selection become meaningful and alive.

EXTENDING INTERESTS

Making judgments: It would be interesting now for children to look back over the stories in the first unit and decide which of the story characters might be likely to see some of the animals that have appeared so far in this unit. If you are using the *Think-and-Do Book*, have pupils refer to page 18 and recall where story characters lived. Then have children indicate where they live by the words "our home" on the map. Then ask, "Do you think Jane Wallace, in 'A Christmas to Remember,' would be likely to see a moose anywhere near her home? Which children in the first unit of stories do you suppose might see one? [Tony and John, in "The School Train"; Sarah, in "The Quiet Mountains"] Which animals that we have read about do you think Jane Wallace might see? Look at the pictures in 'A Christmas to Remember' and in 'A Wild Colt's Lesson.' Perhaps that will help you decide on one animal Jane might see [wild colt]." (Mountain lions and coyotes might also be seen in the southwest.) . Continue similarly with questions about other animals and the stories in the first unit, using the pictures when helpful. Then ask, "What animals that we've read about might we see?" To settle disputes and to verify opinions, youngsters can turn to the encyclopedias for information about the regions in which the various wild animals are found. *Hammond's Nature Atlas of America* shows the boundaries of these regions on maps of the United States and the southern portion of Canada. Some pupils will be more adept at interpreting these maps than others. These children might like to draw maps of their own, indicating the regions in which the stories of the first unit took place and the animals of this unit that inhabit those regions.

Preparing for audience reading: Suggest that children look over the selections that they have read independently and choose one that they think would be fun to read aloud. Discuss with pupils such things as descriptive words and phrases, italics, dashes, and exclamation points that help one know how a passage should be read. Also emphasize the idea that if we want others to enjoy a story as much as we do, we must read it in such a way that our listeners will know how the story makes us feel. In other words, we must read it as if we were telling something that we saw or that happened to us. To illustrate this point you might read one of the selections aloud. Then go back and read parts of it with little or no expression and poor phrasing. Ask children to criticize your second reading and tell why it sounded uninteresting to them.

Enjoying literature: There is something touching and comic about a huge animal like Willie making himself into a pet. Phil Stong's *Honk, the Moose*, with its remarkably funny text and pictures, is one of the best stories on this theme. During the discussion of the book, youngsters will probably compare Honk and Willie. Certainly few children will want to miss this amusing tale of a moose that was adopted by a town.

A Dangerous Surprise   PAGES 136-142

Attack Words: *glossy* cove* brief* recovered* snout* pierce* faltered* suckers* octopus** (glossary)
gliding* (root with *e* dropped + ending; glide—final *e*)
forbidden* (root with final consonant doubled + ending; for bid'—position of single vowel letter)

This exciting narrative emphasizes the idea that in the sea, as well as on land, the constant struggle for survival prevails for wild creatures.   In the story the plump baby sea otter, learning to swim under the watchful eye of his mother, immediately wins the reader's affection and sympathy. The day he slipped away from his mother and set off to explore a forbidden ledge the playful young otter discovered the reason for his mother's warning barks. A hungry octopus lived in the dark waters beneath. Young readers will be wide-eyed with excitement as they read about the otter's struggle with the octopus, and they will breathe a sigh of relief at the otter's narrow escape from the octopus' eight arms with their deadly suckers.

PREPARING FOR READING

Establishing background and anticipating vocabulary needs: Comment, "Today's story is about one of the most playful animals in the great outdoors—the otter." If possible, obtain a copy of the new *More Streets and Roads*, show the picture from "An Otter's Busy Day" on page 175, and lead pupils to recall that this otter amused himself by sliding down a steep icy bank. If youngsters have seen the film "Common Animals of the Woods," this picture will remind them of the film otter's glide down the waterfall. Then suggest that children look at the picture on page 136 of their book. Explain that the otter in the film and the one in "An Otter's Busy Day" were river otters, whereas the otters in this story are sea otters and live in a rock-walled cove by the sea. Write the word *cove* and suggest that pupils turn to the glossary and check the meaning of the word and study the accompanying diagram to visualize the place relationship between the cove pictured on page 136 and the sea. You might indicate the Pacific Coast from about San Francisco to Alaska on the map and explain that sea otters are found in this region. Then say, "Like most young animals, the baby sea otter in this story was curious as well as playful. He liked to explore the rocky ledges beneath the water. One day when he went exploring, he had a fearful adventure." Then ask youngsters to read the story title. Since this title is sure to arouse interest, suggest that children start reading immediately to find out what the dangerous surprise was.

INTERPRETING THE STORY

Pages 136-142: Since children are likely to be reacting to the tense excitement of the last two and a half pages of the story, ask immediately following silent reading, "What was the dangerous surprise? How did you feel as you read this part of the story?" Allow a few moments for youngsters to share their individual reactions before you check on comprehension of story events leading up to the exciting encounter.

As pupils talk over the first part of the story, guide the discussion to bring out what the baby otter enjoyed most and how things must have looked to him as he explored underwater. Ask, "Why did he want to go to the ledge? What prevented him from going? How was he finally able to go? As he came close to the ledge, how did he feel?" Then encourage children to tell about the struggle, bringing out all the things the exciting action made them hear and see as they read. In conclusion, lead pupils to compare the lesson the otter must have learned with that learned by War Paint.

EXTENDING SKILLS AND ABILITIES

Drawing conclusions: This story provides many opportunities for reading between the lines and drawing some conclusions about sea otters. As you repeat each of the following statements, suggest that children skim the story to find passages that provide a basis for making each statement:

Sea otters are playful animals.
Sea otters do not know how to swim when they are born.
Sea otters cannot breathe under water as fish do.
Sea otters can see under water.
Mother sea otters usually keep close watch over their babies.

The stories in this unit and many of the Think-and-Do Book *pages have provided numerous vicarious experiences with wild animals. These experiences have added to children's knowledge of animals and the great outdoors, and at the same time have aroused curiosity that has sent pupils to source materials to gain further experience. Much of the guidance suggested in the lesson plans and for the* Think-and-Do Book *pages has been to help youngsters organize their thinking—to see relationships, to draw conclusions, to form valid generalizations on the basis of these vicarious experiences. In other words, one of the important goals has been to strengthen certain thinking skills and to set a pattern for the type of thinking that pupils should employ as they seek information independently, whether in books or by direct observation.*

Comprehending special meanings of entry words: This exercise strengthens awareness of the idiomatic use of words and introduces special meanings that are listed as definitions of entry words. It also gives practice in adapting definitions to context.

Begin by writing the following on the board:

Tall grass grew *in* the meadow.
The fox began to *advance* toward me.
If I had known *in advance* that I might see a fox, I would have brought my camera.

Have the first two sentences read and comment that pupils undoubtedly know the meanings of the italicized words in the first two sentences. Then call attention to the italicized phrase in the third sentence and say, "When the words *in* and *advance* are used together this way, they have a special meaning. Look up the entry word *advance* in the glossary and find the definitions of the phrase *in advance*, which is printed in heavy, black type. Which definition fits the meaning of this sentence?" When pupils have agreed that "ahead of time" is the appropriate meaning, have them restate the third sentence using this definition in place of *in advance*.

Then write the following sentences, underlining the italicized phrases. As each sentence is read, suggest that pupils use the glossary to find the special meaning of the phrase and restate the sentence using that definition.

The mother sea otter was usually *on the alert*.
The weasel tried *in vain* to catch Bushy Tail.
Billy was very much *in earnest* about becoming a woodsman.
Mountain lions and house cats *are related*.
There are few people *in our midst* who would want a moose for a pet.

If pupils are using the *Thorndike-Barnhart Beginning Dictionary*, you will want to guide the use of pages 66, 67, and 68 as soon as time permits. Pages 66 and 67 will give further practice in comprehending special meanings of words and phrases and in adapting defined meanings to context. Page 68 introduces special meanings of words and phrases that are listed as entries below a main entry word.

Page 38 of the *Think-and-Do Book* provides experience in using context clues to select the appropriate special meaning of words.

Think-and-Do Book: Use pages 37 and 38. Page 37 presents interesting information about animals' defense mechanisms, and pupils are asked to select the sentence that best summarizes the main idea of the article.

EXTENDING INTERESTS

Extending ideas gained from reading: Children who have read the new *More Streets and Roads* may recall the river otter's encounter with a wolf in the story "An Otter's Busy Day." Ask someone to retell or reread the story aloud and show the pictures. The similarity in the appearance of this otter and the sea otter in "A Dangerous Surprise" may raise a question as to how sea and river (or land) otters differ. Other questions may arise concerning the rarity of both kinds of otters and the locality in which each might be found. Superior readers might look up the information in reference books and discuss their findings with the class. It may confuse young-sters to discover that all books do not agree upon the size of otters. Explain that authorities do not always agree on facts of this kind and that it is usually wise to look in several reference books before drawing conclusions. In this case, the class will probably conclude that river otters range in size from two and one-half to five feet.

Enjoying literature: It is to be hoped that some of your superior pupils have read *An Otter's Story*, by the naturalist Emil Liers. If so, have them tell something about the appealing river otters and bring out the point Liers makes about the danger of destroying them.

Some children may wish to find out whether *The Last of the Sea Otters*, by Harold McCracken, is available in the library so that they can read the entire story of the young sea otter that appears in "A Dangerous Surprise." Besides enjoying the touching story, pupils will find many points of com-parison between the sea otters in the McCracken book and the river otters that Emil Liers describes.

Gray Wing and Nika   PAGES 143-152

Sight Word: Nika

Attack Words: *wedge* gander* concealed* reeds* drake* vain**
faithful* harsh* blasts* (glossary)
southward* (root + suffix)
rays* (two vowel letters together)
rice* (final *e*)
fowls* (meaning clues to determine sound of *ow*)
Frank* Liz'zie* (position of single vowel letter)
Gor'don* (vowel followed by *r*)

This touching story is a particularly fitting one with which to conclude the unit, for it contributes much to the ultimate goal for reading realistic animal stories—to engender sympathy and respect for living things. In contrast to previous stories in the unit, it shows man as both hunter and protector of wild animal life. As a wedge of Canada geese were flying south, one of their number, Nika, was crippled by hunters and unable to go on. Gray Wing, her faithful mate, deserted the flock to remain with her. Later the geese were coaxed into a barnyard by a farm boy and spent the winter penned up but safe and well fed.

By spring Nika's wing had healed, and she and her mate tried vainly to escape. Young readers will rejoice at the unexpected accident that freed the wild creatures and sent them on their way to rejoin their flock. Few children will miss the point that capturing wild animals can be almost as cruel as shooting them, for they are usually happiest in their natural habitats.

PREPARING FOR READING

Establishing background and presenting vocabulary: Since the story action centers around the migration of wild birds, you might name some of the common birds in your area and ask children to tell at what time of the year they see these birds. Develop the idea that many birds spend each winter in the south and fly north again in the spring. Bring out the fact that some birds fly thousands of miles on these journeys. Ask, "Where do you suppose the birds rest and get food on the way? What dangers might they meet as they travel? What might happen to a bird that was hurt and couldn't fly south with the flock in the fall?" Allow time for conjectures and then comment, "You'll have a chance to find out in this story about two Canada geese—Gray Wing and *Nika* [pronounced nē′kə]." Next, call attention to the picture on page 143, and lead pupils to discuss briefly how the Canadas look in flight—their formation, the feeling of movement expressed in the upward and downward beat of the wings and in the way the feet are held back and the neck is stretched forward. Then suggest that children read the story to find out what happened to Gray Wing and Nika when they weren't able to continue the southward flight with the flock of geese.

INTERPRETING THE STORY

Pages 143-152: As children are reading, write on the board:

How was Gray Wing and Nika's flight interrupted?
How did the geese spend the winter?
How were Gray Wing and Nika finally able to rejoin the Canadas?

When pupils have finished silent reading, ask them to read each question and decide how they would answer it as briefly yet as clearly as possible—in such a way that a person who had not read the story would know just what happened. Encourage youngsters to look back through the story, if necessary, to help them organize their ideas and formulate answers. You will want to obtain several responses to each question, to lead children in friendly criticism of one another's responses, and to help them decide on the most concise, complete answer for each question. When all questions have been discussed, you might lead children to see that the answers form a brief summary of the story.

Then, to bring out reactions to specific passages, have pupils read aloud the last paragraph on page 146 and tell in their own words what picture they see, what sounds they hear, and how it makes them feel. Then ask them to read the last paragraph on page 152 and tell how the last sentence makes them feel and why they think it is a good ending for the story. You might also ask, "Did you admire Gray Wing? Why?"

With those children who need a more detailed discussion of story events and who need further practice in interpreting implied ideas and drawing conclusions, ask such questions as "Why do you suppose the Canadas had always felt as secure on the lake as in their northern home? How do you think the shooting might make a difference in the way the geese acted when they came to the lake again? How did Gray Wing and Nika feel in their winter home? How did the geese act when spring came? Why?"

In conclusion, lead pupils to compare the attitudes of the different people toward the wild geese—the hunters, Frank Gordon, Aunt Lizzie, and Uncle Peter. Then ask, "Do you think that Frank did the right thing in keeping the geese at the farm during the winter? Why [or why not]?" While most children will commend Frank's action, there may be some who point out that the birds had lost their freedom, and though the geese were well treated, they were still unhappy in captivity.

EVALUATING SKILLS AND ABILITIES

Throughout the lesson plans for the first and second units there has been much emphasis on developing skills and understandings necessary for interpreting dictionary pronunciations. Doubtless by now you have noted which children have grasped those understandings and are deriving pronunciations of unfamiliar words, using any given pronunciation key. Evaluation of each pupil's responses on pages 4, 6, 25, 27, 32 of the *Think-and-Do Book* plus your day-by-day observation of children may reveal those who are still unable to pronounce a word after referring to its printed pronunciation in a glossary or dictionary. Such pupils may well profit by more developmental teaching of the type suggested in the skill sections headed "Using a pronunciation key" in units one and two of this *Guidebook*. You might also use the lessons that are indexed under "Deriving pronunciations," page 272, in the *Guidebook* for the new *Times and Places*. Additional help is to be found in Chapter Seven of *On Their Own in Reading*, Revised Edition.

Think-and-Do Book: Use pages 39 and 40. Page 40 helps children summarize and organize in simple outline form what they have learned about ways in which animals protect themselves from their enemies.

EXTENDING INTERESTS

Extending concepts: The story "Gray Wing and Nika" provides an excellent interest lead into some research about bird migration. You will want to refer your superior readers to a section devoted to bird migration under the more inclusive entry "Migration" in various children's encyclopedias. Most youngsters will be able to read for themselves the section covering bird migration in *Animal Travels*, by Bertha Morris Parker and Thomas Park. On the inside back cover of this book, there is a map showing the principal flyways traveled by migrating birds. From this map and information to be found in *Hammond's Nature Atlas of America*, children might like to determine which birds are likely to pass over the region where they live. Suggest that pupils save their lists until the migrating seasons and see how many different kinds of birds they can observe at those times.

Enjoying literature: *The Wild Little Honker*, by Dorothy Childs Hogner, brings out the wild goose's need to travel with the flock. It might be reviewed by a pupil who has read the book.

There is an exceptionally beautiful poem in *Time for Poetry*—"Something Told the Wild Geese," by Rachel Field. The children may remember hearing it read at an earlier level. It conveys something of the mystery and poignancy of that yearly migration to the south of great flocks of wild geese. Ask children if they have ever seen a vast flying wedge of migrating geese and heard their wild honking. Their cries send a little shiver up one's backbone, and so does this poem when it is read with imagination.

"The Great Outdoors" has been a rich unit indeed. The stories in *More Times and Places* are authentic nature lore and absorbing tales. They have furnished leads into more related books and poetry than any one group of children could cover. And they should have aroused children's interests in and increased their sympathies for wild creatures of many kinds. Dorothy

Lathrop's fine plea for conservation in *Let Them Live* sums up what might well be the resultant attitude after interpretation of these stories, library books, and poems.

CONCLUDING ACTIVITIES

Summarizing the unit: This unit has been rich in examples of many aspects of animal life. Suggest that children glance through the stories to recall them, and write the following titles on the board: "A Zoo Without Bars" and "Billy and the Loons." Then initiate discussion by asking in what ways these two stories are alike. If necessary, to point up similarities, comment, "These two stories tell about different animals, but they both have people in them. What were the people doing in each story? [watching wild animals] Did the children in these two stories enjoy observing the animals? Then what could we say that these stories show us? [It is interesting and often exciting to observe wild animals.]" In a similar manner, discuss each of the next three groups of stories and lead children to make the generalizations indicated:

Group 1: "A Falls and a Fawn," "Willie the Moose," "Gray Wing and Nika." These stories are alike in that they are about people protecting or helping wild animals. They show, too, that wild animals sometimes need the help of human beings.

Group 2: "A Wild Colt's Lesson," "Bushy Tail's Escape," "The Magic Coat," "A Dangerous Surprise." The four stories in this group show that many animals prey upon other kinds of animals. ("Bushy Tail's Escape" also shows that some animals that prey upon other animals are themselves hunted.)

Group 3: "A Wild Colt's Lesson," "The Magic Coat." The common element in these stories is the mother animal's protection of her young.

The story "Wilderness Partners" stands alone in showing that all animals are not enemies. See whether children can explain why this story is different from all the others in the unit.

The discussion suggested in this summary of the unit may be difficult for some children. It requires a rather high level of reasoning for fourth-grade youngsters and may necessitate detailed guidance of the kind indicated at the beginning of this summary. If, however, you have a group for whom discussion is obviously too difficult, you might summarize the unit by supplying the generalizations given above and letting children think of the stories that illustrate them.

Unit 3
Famous Americans
of Other Times

This unit, which introduces the child to authentic biography, initiates a new area of interest in The New Basic Reading Program. Capitalizing on preadolescents' natural interest in heroes and famous people, the stories deal with revealing incidents in the lives of nine famous Americans, beginning with Washington as a lad of thirteen and ending with Edison, America's "electrical wizard."

Aside from the sheer enjoyment these stirring biographical stories provide, they have long-range values in the lives of pre-teen-aged children. Through reading and discussion of the stories in this unit, pupils begin to develop awareness that famous people of the past were once living, active human beings— not just "names" whose birthdays are celebrated, or pictures in a book, or statues in the park. Then, because in these stories famous people seem to live again and because living people do not exist apart in time and space, young readers begin to see the relationship between the man and the time in which he lived—the place where he lived, and his relationship to his contemporaries and those who came after him. The ability to perceive these relationships is one of the most important prerequisites to real understanding of history and current events. Furthermore, although it is not the goal of this unit to teach history, as pupils read these nine stories, which cover a period of almost one hundred fifty years, they will get at least incidental insights into many different facets of a growing democracy—the exploring and settling of the wilderness, educational and cultural advancements, science and invention, wars, the beginnings of organized philanthropy, and developments in the field of entertainment.

Of paramount importance is the contribution that biographical materials make to molding character and arousing new ambitions and hopes. Someone has said that character is caught, not taught. As a youngster identifies himself with the famous people who walk through the pages of this unit, whose childhood interests, hopes, and traits show promise of their later accomplishments, he, too, grows a bit and gains faith in himself.

No other unit at Book Four level provides more natural motivation for voluntary wide reading than these biographical stories. Reading one story woven around an incident in the life of a person arouses curiosity and speculation that can be satisfied only by learning more about him and the times in which he lived. Therefore, before you introduce the unit, you will want to assemble as many as possible of the suggested library books and supplementary readers. Then, too, as questions arise and interest is high, be ready to guide pupils to source materials—encyclopedias, magazines, and other reference materials that will satisfy these newly roused curiosities.

INTRODUCING THE UNIT

You might begin by commenting, "Stories about the lives of real people are often stranger and more exciting than any stories that writers make up. What *famous Americans* [present the words] who have lived before us do you know about or would you like to know more about?" As names are mentioned, encourage pupils to tell of these people's achievements and to relate interesting anecdotes about them that they have read or heard. (If, as suggested in Unit 3 of the *Guidebook* for the new *Times and Places*, you read aloud *The Wright Brothers*, by Quentin Reynolds, pupils should be able to recall incidents from that book.) Ask, "Did you ever wonder what famous people were like when they were young? Do you suppose they enjoyed many of the things you do—had hobbies, problems, and interests like yours? Do you think that things were always easy for them as they grew up? that they must have been unusually smart and lucky? Or do you suppose they sometimes made mistakes and got into difficulties, as you and I do?"

During the foregoing discussion, welcome conflicting opinions, but do not attempt to settle any now. Instead, ask, "How do we learn about the lives of famous people of other times?" Talk over all possible sources of information that pupils are familiar with—radio, television, movies, museums. When books, stories, and articles in magazines, newspapers, or reference works are mentioned, explain that this type of writing is called biography. Then have pupils turn to the table of contents and call attention to the unit title "Famous Americans of Other Times." Comment that each of the stories is biographical; that is, the main incidents in these stories really happened. As pupils read the story titles, encourage conjectures as to what famous American might be the subject of each story. Then let children satisfy their curiosity by leafing briefly through the unit.

Call attention, too, to the library books suggested on pages 298-299. Allow time for comments and recommendations from those who already may have read some of these books or other biographies not listed here. Conclude, "As you read the stories in this unit and some of these library books, you will live in your imagination over a period of one hundred thirty-five years and will visit many different places. There you will meet many famous Americans when they were young. You'll see how they dressed and lived, what their families and friends were like. You'll share their fun, hopes, problems, and disappointments. I wonder if you won't decide that they were like you in many ways."

George Grows Up   PAGES 154-162

Sight Words: Lawrence   England   Byrne   Virginia

Attack Words: *tedious* surveying* boundary* future* surveyor* lord**
   accompany* abroad* (glossary)
   Ver'non* (vowel followed by *r*)
   tramping* (root + ending; tramp—position of single
   vowel letter)
   de scribe'* (final *e*)
   Wil'liam* (position of single vowel letter)
   Fair'fax* (*ai* followed by *r*)

This story makes George Washington, the teen-ager, seem singularly alive and provides some interesting sidelights on life in colonial Virginia. It may surprise young readers to learn that at sixteen Washington was considered a grown-up, that he commanded the respect and deference of men twice his age and older. Implicit in this lively story are some of the reasons and circumstances that brought about this early maturity: young George's natural curiosity, determination, and persistence; the time and place in which he lived; his association with wise and understanding adults. Preadolescents will find it far easier to understand and identify themselves with the young Washington pictured here than with the paragon of the timeworn fable of the cherry tree.

PREPARING FOR READING

Establishing background and anticipating vocabulary needs: Ask pupils what the name George Washington makes them think of. (The contributions that pupils make to this discussion will give you valuable insights into their experiential backgrounds, and you will be able to adjust your guidance accordingly.) Recall that the Burds (Unit 2 of the new *Times and Places*) started moving West when Washington was President, and write the dates 1789-1797, explaining that those were the years of his Presidency. Then say, "Today's story, however, begins when Washington was only thirteen years old. He was born in 1732. Can you tell then in what year our story begins? That's right; it begins over two hundred years ago in 1745 in what was then the colony of *Virginia* [indicate on a large map the present states of Virginia and West Virginia]. Perhaps you know that before the War for Independence, sometimes called the Revolutionary War, this part of our country [with a sweep of your hand, indicate the territory between the Appalachian Mountains and the Atlantic Ocean from New Hampshire through Georgia] was divided into thirteen colonies that belonged to *England*."

Full interpretation and enjoyment of authentic biography requires the ability to form vivid sensory images and to perceive time and place relationships. Otherwise, the reader is not ready to understand cause-effect relationships, a must in the interpretation of biography and historical material. For example, in reading about a famous person of the past, one tries to discover why he thought and acted as he did—why he chose this and rejected that. But unless one is able to visualize the period and environment in which the person lived, it is difficult to appreciate his motives and reactions. Therefore, although it is not important that pupils remember exact dates or localities in which these famous people lived, it is important that children are helped by every means possible—pictures, trips to museums, simple source materials, and your frequent explanatory remarks—to form vivid images of the settings for each of the stories in this unit.

Continue, "The story title 'George Grows Up' is the kind that arouses curiosity. When you've finished the story, I think you'll be able to tell in what ways George Washington grew up in three years' time and what helped him to do so. As you read, you'll meet some interesting men who had a great influence on young George—his half-brother *Lawrence, Mr. Byrne,* William Fairfax, and Lord Fairfax. Let's open our books to the story and step back in time to the colony of Virginia in the year 1745."

INTERPRETING THE STORY

Pages 154-158: Call attention to the picture on page 154, and explain that the setting is Ferry Farm on the Rappahannock River in eastern Virginia. After identifying the characters as Mrs. Washington and her son, George, suggest that children read the first five pages to find out how something his mother asked him to do aroused new dreams and ambitions in young George.

After silent reading, ask how it happened that cleaning a storehouse turned out to be important in the life of young Washington. To check general comprehension of story events, ask such questions as "What was the strange thing that George found in the storehouse? What is a surveying chain used for?" You might pause to ask whether pupils used the glossary to check the pronunciation of *surveying* and whether they used picture and context clues or the glossary to derive the meaning of *surveying.* Continue, "Why did George want to give up school? What two things did Mrs. Washington forbid him to do? Why did Mr. Byrne try at first to discourage George from learning surveying? [Do pupils get the significance of the word *gentleman* as Mr. Byrne used it? If not, discuss the first definition of the word in any elementary dictionary and then ask pupils to infer from Mr. Byrne's remarks what kind of work he thought fitting for a gentleman.] How do you know that George was not easily discouraged?"

Pages 159-162: Call attention to the picture on page 159, which shows young Washington on a surveying trip. Then ask pupils to read page 159 and be ready to discuss whether or not they think surveying would be child's play. After the discussion, recall the title "George Grows Up" and suggest that children finish the story to find out in what ways George had grown up by the time he was sixteen and what helped him to do so.

After silent reading, encourage discussion of the events that led to George's going on the surveying trip, what he learned as a result, and why he was recognized as a grown-up after the trip. Discussion of such questions as the following should prove challenging to those in your group who are interpreting at high levels: "Why do you suppose that in Washington's time many young men who could afford it went to England to finish their education? Why was there need for many surveyors during this time?" Recall that Mr. Burd (Unit 2 of the new *Times and Places*) bought a hundred acres of land near Trader's Point on the Ohio River and ask, "Do you suppose the land Mr. Burd bought had been surveyed? What makes you think so? Why do you suppose the wilderness land in the West was cheap?"

The stories in this unit are so written that they provide innumerable opportunities for pupils to read between the lines, see relationships, and draw conclusions about the period in which each story takes place. You will want to capitalize on these aspects of interpretation throughout this unit. At the same time you will be individualizing your instruction and providing for individual differences within the group of pupils reading this unit.

In conclusion, have the last paragraph of the story read aloud. Interesting questions for discussion would be "In what ways did Lawrence's prediction that Washington would have a big part in Virginia's future come true? From what you know about Washington, would you say that he played a big part only in Virginia's future? Why [or why not]?"

EXTENDING SKILLS AND ABILITIES

Identifying and evaluating character traits: To initiate a discussion of Washington's character as it is revealed in this story, ask, "Would you like to have known Washington when he was in his teens? Why? What things did he do that you would have enjoyed doing, too?" Then encourage pupils to think of words or phrases that describe young Washington and to justify their opinions by references to specific passages in the story (for example, he was curious, resourceful, self-reliant, persistent, and observant). You might conclude the discussion by asking, "Do you think these character traits helped Washington in later life? How?"

Meeting individual needs: If some of your pupils are having difficulty interpreting pronunciation symbols that are different from those used in the glossary of *More Times and Places*, you might organize a special-help group, and plan several brief sessions in guided use of the key in question. Use procedures suggested for the game "Which Is It?" (pages 49-50 and 79 of this *Guidebook*), this time writing the paired pronunciations in the symbolism of the pronunciation key that the group finds difficult to interpret. Be sure that pupils refer to the key as they play the game.

Think-and-Do Book: Use pages 41 and 42-43. Page 41 gives interesting information about the sources that the author of "George Grows Up" used to make the story authentic. It will reinforce the concept that biography is based on fact and not made up by the author. Since youngsters may have been surprised to read in the story that Mount Vernon was once the home of Lawrence Washington, the pictures and explanatory text on pages 42-43 will help clarify the history of its ownership and structural changes.

EXTENDING INTERESTS

Enjoying literature: In *Time for True Tales*, there is an excerpt from *George Washington, Leader of the People* that leads up to the episode with which the unit story begins. Read this aloud, explaining that it is from the same book from which "George Grows Up" was taken. When you have finished, see whether pupils can tell some of the characteristics of the boy Washington that show signs of the great man he was to become. Recommend to pupils who have enjoyed Mrs. Judson's accounts of young Washington the entire book she wrote about him. Encourage them to look in the bibliography to find this book and others about Washington or about famous people of Washington's time that they might like to read (*Benjamin Franklin, The Story of John Paul Jones, The Story of Mad Anthony Wayne*).

Children will probably recall having heard the poem "Washington," by Nancy Byrd Turner. Whether or not the poem is familiar to your class, it is well worth reading at this time.

Courageous, heroic, and selfless as most of the heroes in this unit are, don't let them seem too good to be true. Be sure that from their independent reading and from your frequent comments, children realize how much Washington loved his farm at Mount Vernon, his stepchildren, and the adventure of soldiering. Boone loved hunting and the vast, lonely solitudes of the wilderness, yet he could dance at a party until dawn. Lincoln's humor is usually stressed, but he loved learning with lifelong devotion. No one brief story can show the versatility of these famous Americans.

Perceiving relationships: Throughout this unit pupils might be on the alert for newspaper and magazine articles concerning living Americans whose lives or activities in some way resemble those of the famous people described in this unit. The bases for comparison should be left to youngsters themselves. For example, as a pupil reads an article about a famous person who started his career as a surveyor, he may be reminded of George Washington. At various points in the unit, have some of the articles read aloud and let the listeners decide which famous American each article makes them think of and why. The articles might then be put on a portion of the bulletin board labeled "Americans of Today."

The Boy Hunter   PAGES 163-168

Sight Word: Daniel
Attack Words: *reckon* drawled* weapon* opportunity* plume**
    midst* (glossary)
    Boone* (meaning clues to determine sound of *oo*)
    ri'fle* slen'der* ab'sent* (position of single vowel
    letter)

Daniel Boone has become one of the folk heroes of American history.   Woodsman, hunter, explorer, and frontiersman, he typifies the hardy, unquenchable
pioneer spirit.   This spirit seems to have been born and bred in Boone, as this
story illustrates.   At twelve he proved he could take care of himself in the
forests with only his rifle and hunting dog for company.

Young readers will discover that although Boone and Washington were contemporaries, their early lives and surroundings differed in many respects, just as
did their later achievements.   In addition to providing absorbing reading about
young Boone's adventures in frontier country, this story gives children some
insight into the contrasts in early American life and culture.

PREPARING FOR READING

Establishing background and presenting vocabulary: Recall with
pupils that in the story "Billy and the Loons," Billy Grayson wanted above
all to be considered a woodsman, and ask what he did to earn that title.
Then tell pupils that today's story is about a real woodsman, who lived at the
same time Washington did and whose boyhood adventures were quite different from Billy's. Present his first name, *Daniel*, and ask pupils to supply
his last name and to tell what they know of Boone. Suggest, "Even as a boy,
Daniel Boone explored the woods whenever he had an _____ [write
opportunity]." Suggest that pupils locate this word in their glossary and
check its pronunciation and meaning. Call attention to the two accent marks
and remind pupils that some words have two accents, a heavy one and a
lighter one, as indicated by these marks. Ask a few pupils to pronounce the
word. Then comment, "This second biographical story opens in the year

1744 in a forest region in Pennsylvania, where Daniel Boone spent his early boyhood. The main incident in this story, 'The Boy Hunter,' is an exciting one; it shows that even at twelve Daniel had many of the characteristics that made him one of the greatest woodsmen of all time."

INTERPRETING THE STORY

When pupils have located the story, call attention to the first picture and identify the people standing by the fireplace as Mr. Boone and his son, Daniel. Suggest that pupils read the story to find out what it was that Daniel was asking for and what happened when he finally got his wish.

Pages 163-168: When children have finished, you might comment that Daniel Boone certainly started early in life to be a woodsman, and allow time for children's spontaneous reactions. Then, to help children think about cause-effect relationships that are dependent on time and place relationships, ask such questions as the following: "Why did Daniel's father think it would be all right for Daniel to have a gun when he was twelve? What kind of weapon did Daniel use for hunting until he got his rifle? Would most boys of today be able to kill game with a homemade weapon like Daniel's? Why not?" Suggest that pupils skim the story and read aloud the passages that explain how it happened that Daniel was an unusually skillful hunter and woodsman by the time he was ten.

Then ask, "What did Daniel do after he got his rifle that proved he could take care of himself? Would most parents today allow their twelve-year-old son to go on a hunting trip alone? Why not? Why didn't Daniel's family worry about him when he started out? Why do you suppose that they did begin to worry, however, when Daniel did not return the second day?" Then suggest that pupils experiment with reading aloud page 167 and the first half of 168 to bring out the marked contrast between the emotional reactions of the frantic searchers and the calm boy. Remind children that they can show this contrast by the way they read not only the conversations but also the narrative text.

Call attention to the last two paragraphs of the story and ask pupils why they think the author included them and what relationship they have to the rest of the story. Conclude the discussion by asking, "Even if you read nothing else about Boone, could you explain why he is called a famous American? What contribution to the building of America did he make?"

Extending interpretation: Remind children that Boone grew up at the same time that Washington did. Then suggest that pupils refer to the first two stories in this unit, pay particular attention to picture details, and be ready to discuss the following questions: In what ways were young Washington and young Boone alike? Was the life that Washington led as a boy much like Boone's boyhood? How was it different? Can you think of reasons why their lives were different in many ways? (Note whether pupils draw upon their independent reading for answers to the last question.) From the discussion, help children generalize in their own words that (1) people of a particular period in past times did not all live in the same manner, have the same customs, backgrounds, and opportunities; (2) the place where these people lived affected their mode of living, customs, and opportunities. (For example, Washington grew up in a relatively well-established and civilized area of colonial America; Boone was a product of the frontier.)

Simple as these generalizations appear, they are significant and represent a step up in perceiving relationships about past times. Beginning with Book Three[2] level of The New Basic Reading Program, pupils have had much experience in comparing and contrasting past times with the present and should continue to do so. Now they should also begin to become aware of contrasts within a given period of past time as they are revealed in these biographical stories and in related independent reading. Youngsters who develop the habit of noting these relationships will be able to interpret biography and other historical materials with increased understanding.

EXTENDING SKILLS AND ABILITIES

Perceiving time relationships and interpreting the main idea: To help pupils see how the lives of famous people were related in time and to promote awareness of their lives as part of a broad historical setting, reproduce the chart shown on page 149, showing only the names at the left and the dates across the top that indicate decades of time. (The completed chart is shown for your convenience only. The chart appears also on page 62 of the *Think-and-Do Book*.) Place the incomplete chart on the bulletin board or in another convenient place.

After the chart is displayed, lead pupils to note that the names listed at the left are those of the famous Americans in Unit 3. Then point to the dates at the top of the heavy black lines and explain that the space between dates represents ten years' time, or a decade, that the lighter line between the heavy lines represents the middle of a decade, 1735, 1745, and so on. Then say, "As we read about each famous American, we will fill in the chart to show the time during which he lived."

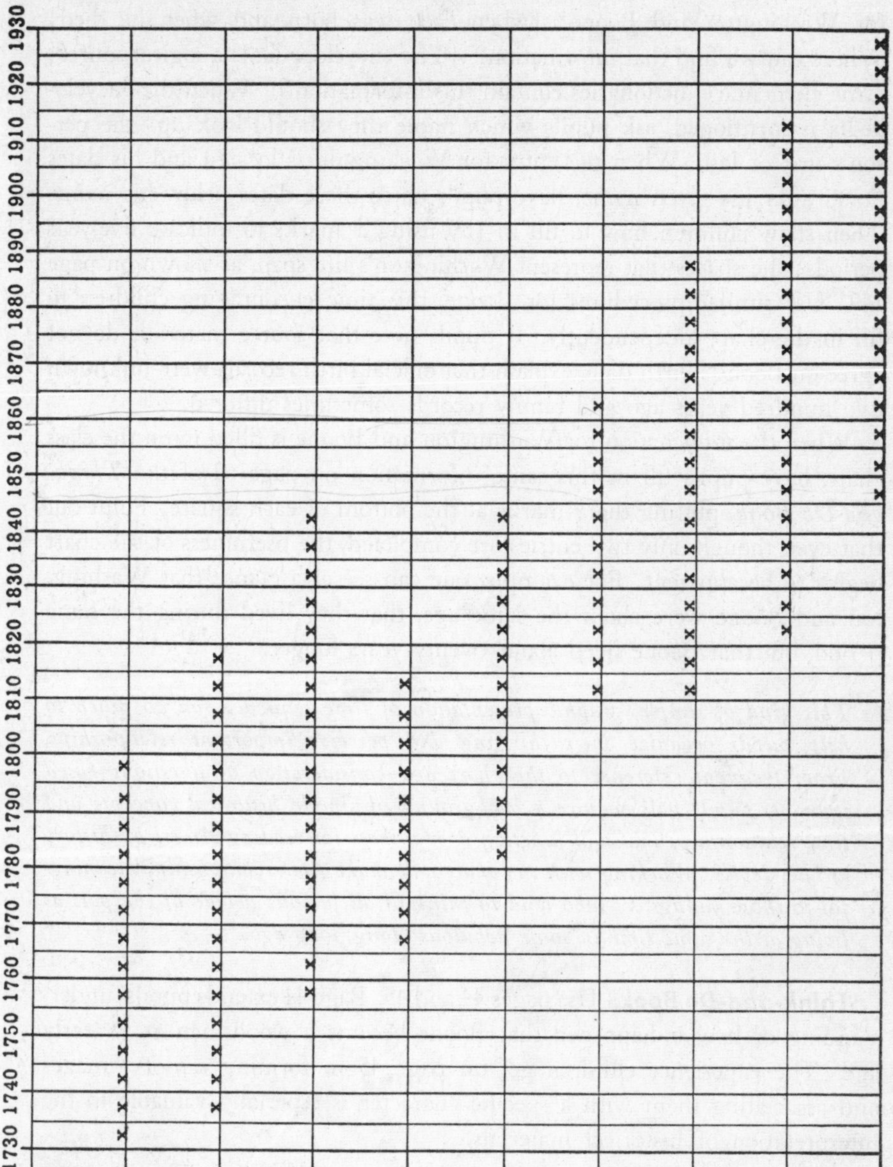

1730 1740 1750 1760 1770 1780 1790 1800 1810 1820 1830 1840 1850 1860 1870 1880 1890 1900 1910 1920 1930

Washington
1732-1799

Boone
1734 or 35-
1820

Webster
1758-1843

Fulton
1765-1815

Key
1779 or 80-
1843

Lincoln
1809-1865

Barnum
1810-1891

Barton
1821-1912

Edison
1847-1931

Next, ask, "What will you have to find out before you can fill in the chart for Washington and Boone? [when each was born and when he died] Where can we find that information? [The encyclopedia is a logical source; some elementary dictionaries contain this information.]" When the encyclopedia is mentioned, ask pupils which name they should look up—the person's first or last. When the entry for Washington is located and his dates noted after his given name, have pupils enter those dates below his name. Then show children how to fill in (by using *x* marks to indicate five-year periods) the spaces that represent Washington's life span, as shown on page 149. Use similar procedures for Boone, this time encouraging children to fill in the chart independently. If pupils note that source materials do not agree on Boone's birth date, explain that official birth records were unknown two hundred years ago and family records sometimes differed.

When the information for Washington and Boone is filled in on the class chart, have pupils fill in this same information on page 62 of the *Think-and-Do Book*, putting the *x* marks at the bottom of each square. Point out that even though only two entries are completed, the usefulness of the chart begins to be apparent. For example, one can see at a glance that Washington and Boone were about the same age, that they lived during the same period, but that Boone lived about twenty years longer.

This kind of simple, graphic presentation of time sequence can do much to help pupils organize their thinking and perceive important relationships. From frequent reference to the chart and consideration of questions based upon it, pupils will acquire a background of simple historical concepts and time relationships that will function as readiness for reading American history at later levels. Working with the chart will make time relationships meaningful to those youngsters who tend to think of all famous people of the past as living at the same time in some nebulous "long, long ago."

Think-and-Do Book: Use pages 44 and 45. Page 44 extends pupils' understanding of how it happened that Boone became a woodsman at an early age. The experience children get on page 45 in forming sensory images and associating them with a specific character is especially valuable to the interpretation of historical materials.

EXTENDING INTERESTS

Enjoying literature: In direct contrast to the daring exploits that children associate with Daniel Boone, is the reflective quality of his nature in later life. You might point up this quality by reading aloud "Long After-noon," from James Daugherty's *Daniel Boone*, found in *Time for True Tales*. This excerpt again illustrates versatility of a famous American.

Continue to encourage pupils to use the bibliography to find books they would like to read. You might suggest, "Those of you who want to read more about Daniel Boone can find the title of a book about him in your bibliography. Can you find another book about a man whose life might have been somewhat like Boone's?" Next, tell pupils that after the next story in *More Times and Places*, they will have an opportunity to discuss the books they are reading. Suggest that they be ready to describe some of the in-cidents in the lives of the famous people they have been reading about.

Personal reading: The wide variety of occupations and interests rep-resented by the famous Americans in this unit may well foster in young readers the development of new or latent individual interests and lead to wide personal reading. Youngsters may become interested not only in the lives of other famous people but also in stories or information about circuses, exploring, nursing, inventing, and so on. Therefore, it would be well to enlist the aid of the librarian in securing books, stories, pamphlets, magazine articles, and suitable research materials at various reading levels and to keep such materials accessible throughout this unit and beyond. Be alert to pupils' current reading preferences and give each child an opportunity to share the content of his personal reading with his classmates.

The Spelling Bee PAGES 169-175

Sight Word: Noah

Attack Words: *dreary* odor* audience* departed* wits** (glossary)
in'vi ta'tion* taf'fy* Web'ster* Re bec'ca* Je ru'sha* man'ner* a rith'me tic* Bi'ble* (position of single vowel letter)

Here is another story of an illustrious American whose boyhood interests and inner drives foreshadowed his later accomplishments. All his life Noah Webster was interested in words, a preoccupation that resulted in the first American dictionary and the immortal blue-backed speller, used by generations of American school children.

Set in colonial New England, the story provides a fascinating glimpse of children of the period at school and at play. Quaint as the customs and costumes appear today, preadolescents will recognize many points of similarity between themselves and the story characters. And, like Noah Webster's schoolmates, they are sure to be impressed by the precocious boy whose enthusiasm for words and whose desire to share that enthusiasm with others made him a delightful teacher at the age of twelve.

PREPARING FOR READING

Establishing background and presenting vocabulary: Recall briefly with pupils the achievements of the famous Americans, Washington and Boone. Then comment that the American in today's story became famous for his contribution to learning. Present the name, *Noah Webster*, and ask whether the name doesn't make children think of something they have been using quite a bit lately. When the dictionary is mentioned, explain that Webster made the first American one and that the Webster Dictionary used today is an outgrowth of the one Noah Webster made long ago. Then say, "Today's story, which tells about another contribution he made to education, opens in the year 1770 in a country schoolroom in New England. There you will meet young Noah, his sister, Jerusha [jə rü′ shə] and their classmates. You'll find that they were paying little attention to the teacher, for they were excited about something that Noah Webster was planning. Noah's friends all admired his ability and intelligence, and I think you will, too. The story tells what Noah was especially interested in and how his boyhood interest helped make him a famous man in later years."

INTERPRETING THE STORY

Page 169: Invite comments about details of the first picture and then suggest that pupils read the first page to find out what it tells that the picture alone cannot convey. Encourage children to tell how this classroom and the method of teaching spelling differs from what they are used to. Identify the boy in the blue stockings as Noah Webster and comment, "Noah did not think the schoolmaster's way of teaching spelling was a very good one. Let's finish the story to find out what Noah's ideas were. Be ready to tell how they helped not only his friends but many American boys and girls whom he could never possibly know."

Pages 170-175: After silent reading, ask, "Why was spelling at the Websters' a jolly party and not a tedious task? How did Noah's ideas about spelling and the way to teach it differ from the schoolmaster's? What did the guests talk about on the way home from the party? Were you surprised at the boys' and girls' reactions to Betsy Hand's remark? Why [or why not]? What did Noah do when he was older that enabled him to teach thousands of boys and girls he never met?" Tell children that page 46 of the *Think-and-Do Book* presents two pages from *Webster's Spelling Book*, which will give them some idea of the kind of textbooks that were used by boys and girls a hundred years ago.

Evaluating ideas: Recall with children the character traits and interests that Washington and Boone displayed as boys. Then ask, "Was young Webster like them in any way? How? How was he different? In what way was Webster's contribution to America different from theirs? Which traits of these famous Americans do you most admire? Which traits do you think are especially important for Americans to have today? Why?"

EXTENDING SKILLS AND ABILITIES

Locating and using source materials: Write the following questions and any others that pupils may have raised about Webster: How old was Noah Webster in 1770? In what part of New England did the story take place? What else did Webster do besides write a speller and a dictionary? Then ask where pupils could find this information. When the encyclopedia is mentioned, ask what key word they will look up and in what volume they will find it. After the entry on Webster is located, read it aloud and ask children to listen for information that will answer the questions on the board. To point up the difference between the biographical information in an encyclopedia and in a short biographical story, ask, "From which did you learn the most facts about Webster? Which made him seem more alive and real?" In conclusion, have pupils fill in Webster's dates and the appropriate spaces on the biographical chart displayed on the bulletin board as well as on the one on page 62 of the *Think-and-Do Book*.

The effective use of source materials is dependent not upon a specialized body of "research skills" but upon the application of specific interpretative skills that are common to reading most types of printed material. For example, deciding what source material to use for specific kinds of information requires the ability to identify and react to ideas in light of the author's purpose. Using an index requires the ability to interpret word and phrase meaning in a specialized context. Deciding upon a key word or topic to look up is dependent on the ability to identify main ideas. Once the source material has been located, one must be able to interpret main ideas, see relationships, and evaluate ideas in light of the author's purpose.

Combining structural and phonetic analysis: This exercise is the first in a series that review understandings of how visual clues to vowel sounds and syllabication may also function as clues to accent. To strengthen the understanding that a clue to a short vowel sound may also serve as a clue to accent, write these words in columns:

(1)	(2)	(3)	(4)
mask	strutted	happen	forbidden
bib	stopped	otter	propelling
fuss	bigger	mutter	permitted
fern	starring	horror	preferring
spur	furry	hurry	occurring

To introduce the exercise, you might comment, "In Webster's day, vowel sounds and accented syllables were often marked in the stories that boys and girls read in school. That would look very odd to us today, wouldn't it? We can usually tell by looking at words like these I've just written what the vowel sound will be and which syllable will be accented." Then, as the words in each column are pronounced, use them to review the following understandings:

Column 1: A single vowel letter usually stands for a short vowel sound unless it comes at the end of a word (or accented syllable). Exceptions are vowel sounds controlled by *r*.

Column 2: A single vowel letter followed by two like consonant letters before an ending or a suffix is a clue to a short vowel sound in the root word unless the vowel sound is controlled by *r*.

Column 3: Two like consonant letters following the first vowel letter are a clue to an accented first syllable and to a short vowel sound in that syllable unless the vowel sound is controlled by *r*.

Column 4: Two like consonant letters before the ending or suffix are a clue to an accented final syllable in the root word and to a short vowel sound in that syllable unless the vowel sound is controlled by *r*.

Meeting individual needs: The foregoing exercise and pupils' responses on page 47 of the *Think-and-Do Book* may reveal children who need further help with the understandings reviewed. The Index of Skills in the *Guidebook* to accompany the new *Times and Places* gives specific page references to developmental exercises that can be used in special-help situations. For example, if some pupils have difficulty hearing accent, use procedures like those suggested on pages 45-46 in the *Guidebook* for the new *Times and Places*. You will also find many valuable procedures in Chapters Four and Five of *On Their Own in Reading*, Revised Edition.

Think-and-Do Book: Use pages 46 and 47.

EXTENDING INTERESTS

Applying ideas gained from reading: After reading about Noah Webster's unique way of entertaining his friends, youngsters might like to present chalk talks. Give a short demonstration and then let children draw upon their imaginations, their independent supplementary reading, or their personal reading for stories to present to the class.

Enjoying literature: Briefly review the stories read so far in this unit. Ask children to tell what biographies they are reading (or have read) about these famous Americans, people who lived in their time, or people who were much like them. Encourage pupils to explain what kind of person each was and to relate an incident in the life of each one. A few suggestions for a general discussion of various books are also given below:

The Story of Mad Anthony Wayne. What did Wayne learn from his surveying and settling in Nova Scotia that helped him in fighting later on? Why was he called the cow-chasing general and why did his men like and respect him so much?

The Story of John Paul Jones. How did John Paul Jones get his name? What was he like as a boy? Tell us about the great sea victory that made him famous.

Kit Carson, Mountain Man. How did Kit Carson get his start as a mountain man? Why did he resent being told to wait when the mountain men were chosen? Why did he become one of the most famous of them all?

The Story of Daniel Boone. Tell us about the incident in which the women went out from the fort for water, knowing that the Indians were there and ready to attack.

Benjamin Franklin. Why is Benjamin Franklin sometimes said to be the most many-sided of all Americans? (interests, types of work, abilities in different fields, ways of enjoying life)

All children should be encouraged to contribute to the discussion. Pupils who have shown little inclination to read the library books may want to do so after they hear the biographies discussed with enthusiasm.

Fulton's Folly PAGES 176-183

Sight Word: Christopher

Attack Words: *folly* renewed* attacked* jeered* completion* throngs**
deck* triumph* echoing* (glossary)
Ful'ton's* (meaning and phonetic clues)
crank* in ven'tion* ship* France (position of single
vowel letter)
speechless* (root + suffix; speech—two vowel letters together)
invented* tested* (root + ending; in vent', test—position
of single vowel letter)

America owes a great debt to mechanical geniuses like Robert Fulton, whose claim to fame rests not only on his invention of the first commercially successful steamboat but also on his lifelong devotion to finding improved methods of doing many things. This exciting story deals first with his invention at fourteen of a boat with hand-cranked side paddles and his dreams of the day when boats would be powered by steam and then with his part in hastening that day. The story theme is one of courage and self-confidence in the face of doubt and incredulity.

Even nine-year-olds are not too young to sense the importance to America of men like Fulton and to draw inspiration from his life and character. The idea that fame and success usually come only after years of struggle, hard work, and discouragement is one of the lessons that biography gives young minds to ponder.

PREPARING FOR READING

Establishing background and anticipating vocabulary needs: Write the story title on the board and encourage pupils to tell what famous American they think will be the subject of this biographical story. Then have pupils turn to the story and allow a few moments for comments about the first picture. Identify the boy at the right as young Fulton and the other boy as his friend *Christopher*. You will also want to talk over the implication of the intriguing story title, and suggest that pupils consult the glossary for the meaning of *folly*, if necessary. Then comment, "Let's read the first four pages to find out if they give any hint as to why this story is called 'Fulton's Folly.'"

INTERPRETING THE STORY

Pages 176-179: After silent reading, ask whether the story events so far make Fulton seem foolish or talented. Do pupils detect any hint yet as to why the story is called "Fulton's Folly"? For youngsters who need more specific questions to stimulate discussion, ask, "What did Fulton invent as a boy? How did he happen to think of the idea? Was the invention a success? What other idea did he have for moving boats? What did Christopher's father think of it? How did Fulton earn his living when he first started to work?" Then ask whether pupils think Fulton forgot his idea for a steam-powered boat and suggest they finish the story to find out. Comment that the significance of the story title will become clear as pupils read on, and ask them to be ready to tell why the title is a good one.

Pages 180-183: When pupils have finished, point up the irony in the story title by inviting discussion of these questions: "Was Fulton a foolish person? Whose folly do you think this story really emphasizes?" Then encourage pupils to recount Fulton's experiments and experiences that culminated in proof that a steamboat would really go. Ask, "How did the people in France regard the idea of a steam-powered boat? Why did people in this country call the new steamboat 'Fulton's Folly'? How do you think you would have felt if you had been one of the passengers on the trial run? How did the people on the shore feel at first? How did their attitudes change when the boat moved upriver?" In conclusion, ask, "What traits and abilities did Fulton have that made him a famous American? Why are those same traits needed in America today?"

Oral interpretation: Children will enjoy rereading this story aloud to bring out its element of suspense, its interesting human relationships, and the vivid sensory imagery. Talk over these particular qualities and the ways in which they can best be conveyed to those who listen. Remind pupils that once they have formed clear images of the action and understand why story characters felt and acted as they did, they should be able to make the story come alive for their audience.

Extending interpretation: This story provides an excellent lead into discussion of the human tendency to view with suspicion and sometimes to ridicule inventions and innovations. Recall with pupils what the crowd said about Fulton's steamboat ("It will never work."). Then invite discussion of these questions: "Why do you suppose the crowd jeered at Fulton's boat? What other inventions do you know about that people made fun of at first? Can you think of anything that might be invented in the next one hundred years that we might find hard to believe possible?"

EXTENDING SKILLS AND ABILITIES

Perceiving relationships: Have pupils find the necessary information and fill in the biographical chart for Fulton. Then ask them to refer to the dates given in the story and tell how old Fulton was when he invented the hand-crank paddles, when his steamboat made its successful run upriver in America. In conclusion, have pupils use the chart as a basis for answering these questions: "Could Webster and Fulton have known Washington? Might Washington ever have ridden on a steamboat? Webster? Boone?"

After youngsters have used page 48 of the *Think-and-Do Book*, refer again to the chart and have pupils indicate which years of Fulton's life represent each of the four stages presented on this *Think-and-Do Book* page.

Meeting individual needs: The evolution of the steamboat is an interesting and romantic chapter in American history, and it is perennially appealing to most youngsters. To provide a stimulating and challenging research project for three or four of your superior readers, you might ask them to find out about the history of the steamship—who besides Fulton worked on its invention, when the first steamship crossed the ocean, and so on. In addition to consulting encyclopedias, these pupils might ask the librarian to show them how to use the card catalog and *Readers' Guide* to locate books and magazine articles dealing with the subject. Suggest that once the material is located, these youngsters select the information they think is most interesting, organize it, and present it to the class.

Combining structural and phonetic analysis: This exercise reviews basic understandings about visual clues to a long vowel sound that may also function as clues to accent. You might begin by briefly checking youngsters' ability to apply to unknown words the clues to short vowel sounds that were reviewed in the exercise on page 154. Say, "If you saw this word _____ [write *gull*], what vowel sound would you expect to hear? Why? Pronounce the word." Continue with *clerk*. "If you saw this word _____ [write *blotting*], what vowel sound would you expect to hear in the root word? Why? Pronounce the word." Continue with *jarring*. "If you saw this word _____ [write *comma*], which syllable would you try accenting first? Why? What vowel sound would you expect to hear in that syllable? Why? If you saw this word _____ [write *rebelling*], which syllable would you try accenting first? Why? What vowel sound would you expect to hear in that syllable?" Continue with the word *deferring*.

After this brief review, say, "There are some other clues that tell us that we might expect to hear a long vowel sound in a word or in a syllable, and that also tell us to try accenting that syllable." Write the following:

(1)	(2)	(3)	(4)
bite	taking	desire	uniting
lane	roping	amuse	surprising
hope	siding	complete	relating
cute	using	invite	escaping
mice		advice	producing
prince		necklace	practicing
cage		engage	engaging
ridge		cabbage	managing
five	living	behave	forgiving
have	diving	native	arriving

As the words in each column are pronounced, use them to review the following understandings:

Column 1: If there are only two vowel letters in a word, one of which is final *e*, usually the final *e* is silent and the first vowel letter stands for a long vowel sound unless final *e* is preceded by the letters *c*, *g*, or *v*.

Final *e* preceded by the letters *c* or *g* is a clue to the soft sound of *c* or *g* but not necessarily a clue to a long vowel sound. In English the final letter *v* is always followed by *e* but final *e* preceded by *v* is not necessarily a clue to the long vowel sound.

Column 2: A single vowel letter followed by one consonant letter before an ending is a clue to a dropped final *e* and to a long vowel sound in the root word unless final *e* is preceded by *v*.

Column 3: Final *e* in the last syllable of a two-syllable root word is usually a clue to an accented final syllable and a long vowel sound in that syllable unless final *e* is preceded by *c*, *g*, or *v*.

Column 4: A single consonant letter following a single vowel letter before an ending in a two-syllable root word may be a clue to a dropped final *e* and to a long vowel sound in an accented last syllable of the root word unless the single consonant letter is *c*, *g*, or *v*. (You might, at this point, explain that in a great many root words a single consonant letter following a single vowel letter before an ending may also be a clue to an unaccented syllable. Comment that this pattern will be reviewed in the next lesson.)

Then write the columns of words shown below:

(5)	(6)
toad	repeat
keen	complain
treat	approach
trail	succeed
boot	
crowd	
boy	
ground	

Explain that these words also contain visual clues to a long vowel sound and to accent, and use them to review the understandings listed:

Column 5: If there are two vowel letters together in a word, usually the first stands for a long sound and the second is silent unless the vowel letters form such special combinations as *oo, ou, oi, ow, au, aw,* and so on.

Column 6: Two vowel letters together in the last syllable of a two-syllable root word is usually a clue to an accented final syllable and a long vowel sound in that syllable.

If pupils have difficulty with this exercise or with page 49 of the *Think-and-Do Book,* see the Index of Skills in the *Guidebook* for the new *Times and Places* for page references to developmental exercises that could be used with a special-help group. Many suggestions may also be found in Chapters Four and Five of *On Their Own in Reading,* Revised Edition.

Think-and-Do Book: Use pages 48 and 49. Page 48, which contains interesting additional information about Fulton's experiments and triumphs, provides experience in applying interpretative skills to expository material.

EXTENDING INTERESTS

Recalling stories: See whether children can recall two stories from the new *Times and Places*—one that shows how people traveled on rivers before Fulton's successful invention of the steamboat ("The Long Journey") and another that tells of the excitement caused by the first steamboat on the Ohio River ("Steam Comes Upriver"). Briefly review "The Long Journey" through page 97 and have pages 98-100 read aloud. Also ask someone to read "Steam Comes Upriver" aloud. Then discuss the following questions: In what way would the Burds' journey have been different if there had been steamboats on the Ohio River at that time? Why is the last word in the title "Steam Comes Upriver" important? Do you think the story "Steam Comes Upriver" took place right after "Fulton's Folly" or quite some time later? Why?

Enjoying literature: While interest in Fulton is high, call attention to the book about him in the bibliography. Encourage pupils who have read *Boat Builder, the Story of Robert Fulton* to tell what Fulton was like as a boy and to recount one or two episodes that they particularly enjoyed. You might also resume the discussion of the other library books begun earlier.

How a Song Named a Flag PAGES 184-188

Sight Word: prisoners
Attack Words: *regarded* banner* spangled* Dr.* truce* fleet**
                    (glossary)
                    Bal′ti more (*a* followed by *l*)
                    Pick′ers gill* Fran′cis* Scott* bat′tle* bomb* (posi-
                    tion of single vowel letter)
                    tune* (final *e*)

These familiar words, "Oh, say, does that Star-Spangled Banner yet wave," take on new meaning when one knows how they came to be written. The action of this story, which is part of every American's rightful heritage, centers around the perilous but stirring events that prompted Francis Scott Key to write "The Star-Spangled Banner." Of all stories about our flag, this is surely one of the most thrilling. It tends to lift the spirits and quicken the pulse of those who interpret it fully. Every time they sing or hear our national anthem, youngsters will remember with pride and gratitude the man who anxiously watched the "broad stripes and bright stars through the perilous fight."

PREPARING FOR READING

Establishing background and presenting vocabulary: In order that pupils may discover for themselves the main character and the point of this memorable story, you will want to keep the preliminary discussion as brief as possible. To introduce the story, you might ask, "Can you imagine what it would be like to be on a ship with some *prisoners* of war, watching an enemy fleet attack an American fort? How do you think you would feel?" After the discussion, say, "You may be surprised to find out in today's biographical story that just such an experience prompted a famous American in 1814 to write a song that we all know and love."

INTERPRETING THE STORY

When pupils have turned to the story, discuss briefly the first picture, leading children to note the details that give the impression of an early American seacoast town and the fact that the flag is the focal point of interest. Mention that the city is Baltimore (have pupils locate it on a large map, or locate it for them, if necessary) and identify the people in the foreground as Mary Pickersgill and her daughter Caroline. Then have the title read aloud and suggest that pupils read the story to find out what the song is and how it happened to be written.

Pages 184-188: When pupils have finished, allow time for their spontaneous comments and reactions. Then have children tell how our national anthem came to be written. To check ability to perceive cause-effect relationships, ask, "Why was the year 1814 a time of anxiety for Americans? Why did the people of Baltimore think, 'As long as it [the flag] waves, we'll be safe'?" Call attention to the pictured flag, page 185, and ask, "How large was this flag? Why were Mary and Caroline Pickersgill especially proud of it? In what ways was the American flag in Key's time different from ours? Why do you suppose it was different? [The history of the changes in our flag may be found in any children's encyclopedia. Finding that information and reporting it later to the class would be an interesting project for superior readers.] Why was Key sailing under a flag of truce to meet the English fleet? [Did pupils use the glossary or context clues to derive the meaning of the words *truce* and *fleet?* How did those who used the glossary decide which glossary entry, *fleet*[1] or *fleet*[2], is the word used in this story?] Why do you suppose the English fleet did not let the truce ship return at once to Baltimore? Why was it so important to the Americans that they see the flag still flying over the fort?"

As a check on pupils' ability to form sensory images and to recognize emotional reactions of story characters, suggest that they listen carefully as one pupil reads the last two pages of the story aloud and imagine they are one of the Americans. Ask children to be ready to tell what they saw, heard, and smelled. How did they feel in body and in mind as they stood on deck all those hours? as they sang for the first time "The Star-Spangled Banner"? Comment that on page 50 of the *Think-and-Do Book*, pupils will find out more about the history of the song and how and when it was officially named our national anthem. In conclusion, ask, "Why is 'The Star-Spangled Banner' a particularly fitting name for our flag? What are some of the other names we sometimes use to refer to the flag?" (Stars and Stripes, Old Glory, The Grand Old Flag)

Extending interpretation: Have pupils fill in the biographical chart for Key and suggest that they use it as a source for answering these questions: "How old was Key when he wrote 'The Star-Spangled Banner'? Was Key living when Washington was President? Did Washington ever sing 'The Star-Spangled Banner'? Is it possible that Key ever rode on a steamboat?"

EXTENDING SKILLS AND ABILITIES

Identifying and reacting to ideas in light of author's purpose: This exercise is designed to help youngsters interpret the ideas expressed in our national anthem and note what those ideas reveal about the author. You might begin by asking, "Did you ever realize that to understand fully the first two stanzas of our national anthem, one needs to know the story of how Key happened to write it? Listen closely as I read, and see if you don't agree." As you read the first two stanzas, pause when necessary to discuss the meaning of such phrases as "the foe's haughty host" and "the towering steep." Then ask, "What did you hear and see in your mind as I read? How did the stanzas make you feel?" Lead pupils to note that the first two stanzas tell of Key's reactions to the attack on the American fort.

Before reading the last stanza, explain that it reveals Key's hopes for America's future. When you have finished, have children tell in their own words what those hopes were. In conclusion, ask, "What does this great song that he wrote tell you about the kind of man Key must have been? Does America still need people who feel about her as Key did? Why?"

Combining structural and phonetic analysis: This exercise reviews visual clues that aid in determining unaccented syllables. You might begin by briefly checking children's ability to apply to unknown words the visual clues to vowel sound and to accent that were reviewed in the exercises on pages 154 and 158-160. Use the following words for review:

channel	repelling	propose	competing
glitter	regretting	reveal	igniting

Continue, "There are also some visual clues that can tell us that a final syllable in a word is probably unaccented." Write the following columns of words:

(1)	(2)	(3)
turtle	wooden	opening
candle	fearful	pardoned
sparkle	farmer	pedaled
rumble	politely	blossoming
bugle	anxiously	peppering
thimble	darkness	labeled
needle	childish	glittering

Have the words in the first column pronounced. Ask, "What do you notice about the way each of these words ends? [They each end in the letters *le* preceded by a consonant.] Does this consonant go with *le* to form the last syllable in each word? Is this last syllable accented?" Lead children to recall the generalization that if a word ends in *le* preceded by a consonant, that consonant begins the last syllable and the final syllable is unaccented.

Have the words in the second column pronounced and ask, "Is the last syllable accented in any of these words? Can you tell me why not?" Lead children to note that the last syllable in each word is a suffix. Then ask, "Could we say that usually suffixes are unaccented final syllables?"

Then say, "You remember that a single consonant letter following a single vowel letter before an ending in a two-syllable root word may be a clue to a long vowel sound and a dropped final *e* as in *competing* and *igniting*." Have the words in the third column pronounced and then ask, "Do these root words have a dropped final *e* before the ending is added? Is the last syllable of the root word accented? Do you hear a long vowel sound in the last syllable of the root word? What sound do you hear? [the schwa sound]" Lead children to recall the generalization that a single consonant letter following a single vowel letter before the ending may also be a clue to the schwa sound in an unaccented final syllable of the root word. The immediate use of page 52 of the *Think-and-Do Book* will provide practice in applying the understandings reviewed in this exercise.

Think-and-Do Book: Use pages 50, 51, and 52.

EXTENDING INTERESTS

Enjoying literature: Children will sense a remarkably fitting climax for the Francis Scott Key story as they listen to the well-known poem by Henry

Holcomb Bennett called "The Flag Goes By."[1] This poem is a memorable one for children to hear, and will bear repeating.

The story of our first American flag is well told in the book *Betsy Ross and the Flag*. It is well worth discussing if some children have read it. You may also want to mention another great patriotic song, "The Battle Hymn of the Republic." Read aloud the story of how it happened to be written and how it became famous—the excerpt from Louise Tharp's *A Sounding Trumpet* in *Time for True Tales*—and encourage children to sing it.

Independent supplementary reading: From the selections they have read in other readers suggested for this unit, pupils might be asked to keep a brief written record of those stories in which some childhood event in the life of a famous person hints of the greatness that he showed later in life. As the unit proceeds, these notes might be used to help children choose selections for oral reading in a program with some such title as "Small Signs of Big Things to Come."

A Boy and His Book PAGES 189-194

Sight Words: pigeon   Indiana   youth   honest

Attack Words: *sturdy* community* fodder* toiled** (glossary)

A'bra ham* Lin'coln* (position of single vowel letter)

Abe* (final *e*)

illness* (root + suffix; ill—position of single vowel letter)

death* (meaning clues to determine vowel sound)

combing* (root + ending; comb—meaning and phonetic clues)

Set in a lonely pioneer community of Indiana, this story presents in dramatic fashion the hardships, the sorrow, and the few pleasures that helped mold the

[1] This poem is so well-known that it can be found in numerous poetry anthologies. It appears, for example, in the General Edition of *Time for Poetry*, which includes some poems that are not in the Teacher's Anthology that accompanies The New Basic Readers.

character of young Abraham Lincoln. Young readers will be touched by the determination of this lad whose hunger for book learning was never quite satisfied. The incident of the borrowed book will arouse admiration for young Lincoln's honesty and sense of responsibility. Most of all, perhaps, youngsters will be moved by the realization that neither poverty, hardships, nor any material lack prevented Lincoln from rising to the highest office his country had to offer. It is a story to strengthen one's faith in democracy.

PREPARING FOR READING

Establishing background and presenting vocabulary: The impact and effectiveness of this story will be increased if the preliminary discussion is kept as brief as possible. Comment, "Today's biographical story will take you back almost one hundred fifty years to a pioneer community called *Pigeon Creek* in *Indiana* [locate Indiana on a large map]. There you will meet an *honest*, hard working *youth*, who later became President of the United States. You'll find out how bare his life was of the comforts and advantages that we take for granted and that many people of his day took for granted, too—how he toiled long hours to earn a weather-beaten biographical book that had a great influence on his life."

INTERPRETING THE STORY

Pages 189-194: After silent reading, allow time for pupils to express their reactions to the story as they choose. Then invite discussion of the following questions, encouraging pupils to read aloud specific story passages to justify their answers: "What was probably Lincoln's greatest ambition as a boy? What made it impossible for him to completely satisfy that ambition? What opportunities and comforts do you have that Lincoln never knew? What hardships and sorrow did he know as a youth? When did he seem to be the happiest? What does the incident of the damaged book tell you about the kind of boy Lincoln was? What other character traits that helped him become a great American did Lincoln display in his youth? Do you suppose the people who knew him then ever dreamed that Abraham Lincoln would one day be President? Why [or why not]?"

In conclusion, it would be interesting to point up some comparisons and contrasts in the lives of Washington and Lincoln. Have pupils use both pictures and text of the stories "George Grows Up" and "A Boy and His Book" as sources for discussing such questions as "In what ways was Lincoln's boyhood different from Washington's? How did their boyhood ambitions differ? In spite of the differences in their backgrounds and opportunities, what character traits would you say they had in common? How do you suppose reading about Washington helped Lincoln become President?"

EXTENDING SKILLS AND ABILITIES

Perceiving time relationships: Suggest first that pupils find the necessary information and fill in the biographical chart for Lincoln. Then have them use the chart as a basis for answering these questions: "Was Lincoln living when Washington was President? Which famous Americans that we have read about lived during Washington's Presidency? Do you suppose Lincoln ever sang 'The Star-Spangled Banner'? Might Lincoln have learned to spell from Webster's speller? Could Lincoln have ridden on a steamboat?" Explain that Lincoln was President from 1861 until his death and ask, "Did any of the people we've read about know him as President? Are there people living today who knew Lincoln as a little boy? Was he President during your parents' lifetime? Do you think there might be people living today who knew Lincoln as President?"

Phonetic analysis: You might begin by explaining to youngsters the function of this exercise. Comment, "In the last few lessons we have been discussing how certain clues to vowel sound and accent can help us pronounce words. As we apply these clues to syllables in a word, we usually divide the word into syllables. Today let's review some of the clues that will help us divide a word into syllables, and see whether we also find clues to accent and vowel sounds."

Write these lists of words, one column at a time, without syllabic divisions or accent marks (these are shown for your convenience only):

(1)	(2)	(3)	(4)	(5)	(6)
cac' tus	va' cant	bub' ble	de scribe'	tax' i	buck' et
blos' som	sea' son	rum' ble	re ply'	anx' ious	reck' on
splen' did	fa' mous	cir' cle	kitch' en	ex act'	pack' age
con fuse'	a maze'	bat' tle	or' chard	e' ven	crack' le
con ceal'	se cure'	no' ble	wheth' er	serv' ant	chuck' le
per form'	re' gion	ea' gle	a shore'	fe' ver	pick' le

Use each column of words to review the understanding or syllabic principle that is indicated on the next page. With each column, as soon as each understanding is reviewed, go back to the first word in the column and ask pupils to pronounce it and tell which syllable they accented. Then ask them to point out any clue to the accented syllable they may see in the word, and indicate the accented syllable with an accent mark. Finally, have young-sters tell what vowel sound they hear in the accented syllable, and why they would expect to hear that vowel sound. Repeat this procedure with each word in the column.

Column 1: Ask, "How many consonant letters do you see after the first vowel letter in each of these words? Where does the first syllable end? Does the second consonant letter begin the second syllable?" Lead children to recall that if the first vowel element in a word is followed by two consonant letters, the first syllable usually ends with the first of the two consonant letters.

Column 2: Ask, "How many consonant letters do you see after the first vowel letter [or letters] in each of these words? Does the consonant letter begin the second syllable?" Lead pupils to recall that if the first vowel element in a word is followed by a single consonant letter, that consonant letter usually begins the second syllable.

Column 3: Recall that if a word ends in *le* preceded by a consonant, that consonant begins the last syllable.

Column 4: Lead children to recall that the syllables in a word often do not break between consonant blends or special two-letter consonant symbols (*ch, sh, th*). (You might point out that column 4 illustrates one exception to the principle illus-trated by the words in column 1.)

Column 5: Recall with pupils that (1) the letter *x* always goes with the preceding vowel to form a syllable, and (2) the letter *v* may go with the vowel that precedes it or the vowel that follows it. (This list of words illustrates two exceptions to the general principles illustrated in columns 1 and 2.)

Column 6: Recall that the letters *ck* go with the preceding vowel and end the syllable. You might also point out that the letters *ck* are a clue to an accented syllable. (Here the last three words illustrate an exception to the principle illustrated in column 3.)

To check youngsters' ability to note visual clues to syllabication and vowel sounds, ask, "Do you think the clues we have learned will help us in determining syllables in words of more than two syllables?" Write the fol-lowing words, showing syllabic breaks and accent marks. With each word have pupils tell why they would expect the syllables to end where they do and what vowel sound they would expect to hear in the accented syllable

or′ na ment	oc ca′ sion
tor na′ do	oc′ to pus
No vem′ ber	e lev′ en
wil′ der ness	max′ i mum
ca′ pa ble	a rith′ me tic

Think-and-Do Book: Use pages 53 and 54. Page 53, which contains six revealing incidents from Lincoln's boyhood, provides valuable experience in recognizing emotional reactions of a story character and projecting those reactions effectively in oral interpretation. Careful analysis of pupils' responses on page 54 will provide an objective check of their ability to apply independently the phonetic understandings that were reviewed in the preceding exercise.

EXTENDING INTERESTS

Enjoying literature: Of the many poems about Lincoln that you might read to complement this story, probably the most appropriate is Nancy Byrd Turner's "Lincoln"; one of the most touching is the Benéts' "Nancy Hanks." Before reading the latter, tell pupils that when the children in one classroom heard the poem read over the radio, they were so moved that they decided to write their own answers to Nancy Hanks' question, "You wouldn't know about my son?" Each child's reply was a sincere attempt to comfort the wistful ghost of Abe's mother. Two of these answers are found in the revised edition of *Time for Poetry*—"A Reply to Nancy Hanks," by Julius Silberger, and "I saw a Ghost," by Joan Boilleau. Don't expect youngsters in your class to emulate these responses—the poems were written by a group of slightly older children.

Any story about Lincoln leads into many stories and books. The bibliography in *More Times and Places* lists only a few of the many books about Lincoln that have been written for children. In addition to those listed, there is the very fine *Abraham Lincoln*, by Ingri and Edgar Parin d'Aulaire, which contains some of the most humorous stories and situations that have ever been recorded about Lincoln. This you might recommend to your average and superior readers who, later, can tell some of the amusing incidents and show the fine pictures.

Martin and Abraham Lincoln, by Catherine C. Coblentz, is a touching, true story that children like. One of the youngsters might show the pictures and read or tell the story. If the book itself is not available, the entire story can be found in *Time for True Tales.*

After several of the Lincoln biographies have been discussed, have children compare the kind of boy Lincoln was with the kind of man he later became. Lead pupils to realize that the traits he displayed as a boy remained with him throughout his life—such traits as gentleness, honesty, kindness, humor, compassion, and love of learning.

A Great Showman PAGES 195- 202

Sight Word: Phineas

Attack Words: *occurred* exhibiting* museum* swarmed* freaks**
midgets* required* (glossary)

en'ter tain'* (position of single vowel letter; two vowel
letters together)

Tay'lor* (two vowel letters together)

Bar'num* (vowel followed by *r*)

amusement* (root word + meaning clues)

col lec'tion* at tract'* thumb* Jum'bo* (position of
single vowel letter)

This story about the fabulous P. T. Barnum has all the gaiety and ebullience
that characterized that great American showman. It begins with Barnum at
fourteen, already interested in exhibiting things, and ends with him as co-owner
of the Greatest Show on Earth. In between is a colorful array of the exhibits
and trappings that belonged to the entertainment world of Barnum's making.
Aside from the sheer pleasure the story provides, youngsters will remember it
for the vivid and accurate picture it paints of the amusement world of another
day and of the man who contributed the most to it. Barnum's career teaches
no lofty moral lesson. But even nine-year-olds are canny enough to sense
that the secret of Barnum's success lay in his remarkable understanding of what
the public finds amusing and in his flair for advertising.

PREPARING FOR READING

Establishing background and presenting vocabulary: In keeping
with the spirit of this story, you will want to introduce it with a light, gay
touch and keep the discussion lively. To begin, you might comment, "Today's biographical story is so full of fabulous events and creatures that it
might seem to belong to the world of make-believe—but it all really happened! In a moment now, we are going to visit the entertainment world,
where we'll meet the greatest showman who ever lived. His name is still
familiar to all of us. In his later years people fondly called him 'Old P. T.'
Can you guess who he was?" When youngsters mention Barnum, explain

that the initials P. T. stand for his given name, *Phineas Taylor*. Then comment, "Perhaps you think of Barnum as a circus owner, and he was. But running a circus was not his only claim to fame, as you will see."

INTERPRETING THE STORY

Pages 195-199: Identify the boy in the first picture as young Taylor Barnum, and say, "Strange as it may seem, a joke that one of these men played on Taylor started him thinking about show business. Let's read the first five pages to find out how Barnum got his start as a showman."

After silent reading, enter into the fun by commenting, "That was a pretty silly joke John played on Taylor Barnum, wasn't it? What thought occurred to Taylor before he found out that the strange and wonderful dog was just a joke? Why wasn't he angry with John? When he was a store clerk, what talent or trait did Taylor display that helped him in show business later on?" Then have pupils tell how Barnum got his start in show business. Ask, "What would you have seen and heard if you had stood outside Barnum's American Museum? if you had gone inside?" Have the last paragraph, page 199, read aloud and talk over the meaning of the figurative phrases "the talk of New York" and "on everybody's tongue."

Pages 200-202: Comment, "Like the people of New York, we wonder what Barnum will do next. Let's finish the story to find out." When pupils have finished, ask, "What were some of the things that Barnum did next that brought him more fame than ever before? Which of the unusual things that Barnum exhibited would you most like to have seen? Why?" In conclusion, ask, "What kind of person was 'Old P. T.'? Would you have enjoyed knowing him? Why? What contribution did he make to America?"

Extending interpretation: Suggest that pupils find the necessary information and fill in the biographical chart for Barnum. Then ask, "How old was Barnum when the idea of exhibiting the strange dog occurred to him? Could Lincoln have seen Barnum's traveling circus? Could your parents have known Barnum? Could people in Barnum's day go to movies or have radio and television sets? In what way did the time in which Barnum lived account for part of his spectacular success?"

EXTENDING SKILLS AND ABILITIES

Recognizing inner drives and character traits: The activity suggested here will be fun for youngsters and will, at the same time, check their ability to identify and evaluate some of the inner drives and traits that contributed to the success of a famous person. Call attention to the picture on page 202 and then suggest, "Pretend that you are Barnum and that after the circus one of these children asked you, 'Mr. Barnum, what are the reasons for your success?' What would you reply?" Suggest that in preparation for the impersonation, youngsters (1) skim the story to recall the main things that Barnum did, (2) read between the lines to discover the reasons for the various things he did, and (3) think about the kind of person he was. Then encourage children to throw themselves into the performance with gusto, reminding them, if need be, that Barnum was not the least bit shy.

Adapting definitions to context: After a brief review of the simplest levels of adapting definitions to context, this exercise focuses attention on the more difficult level in which pupils must paraphrase both context and definition in order to grasp the meaning of a given word in its context.

It is important to keep in mind that a youngster's real motive for turning to a dictionary or glossary for the meaning of an unknown word is to discover the total meaning of a sentence or passage in which the unknown word appears. At Book Four level pupils have had much experience in applying such basic dictionary skills as selecting the definition of an unknown word that fits a given context and "tuning" that definition back into the original context. The simplest levels in adapting a definition to context are direct substitution of a definition for the unknown word, changing the inflectional form of words in the definitions, and transposing the order of a few words in the definition or in the context. Sometimes, however, to understand the meaning of a sentence in which an unknown word appears, one must first get a general idea of the word meaning from reading all the definitions. Then to fuse the meaning of that word with the context in which it appears, one must completely paraphrase both the words of the definitions and the original context. For middle-grade youngsters that means "telling in your own words" what a sentence or passage containing a given word means.

To begin the review, write these sentences on the board, underlining the italicized words:

1. Abraham Lincoln was a *sturdy* youth.
2. He *toiled* for two days to pay for a book.
3. Barnum thought he could make money *exhibiting* the strange dog.

As each sentence is read, have pupils find the underlined word in the glossary and restate the sentence, using the definition instead of the underlined word. Then talk over with children what is involved in "tuning" each definition back into the sentence. These sentences will provide a quick review of the use of (1) substitution, (2) inflectional adaptation, and (3) transposition in adapting definitions to context.

To introduce complete paraphrasing, you might comment, "Those definitions were easy to fit back into the sentences, weren't they? Sometimes, though, we have to do more rewording when we look up the meaning of a word and try to fit the definition back into a sentence." Then write the following sentences, underlining the italicized words:

Key showed his song to his *companions*.
To protect itself, Key's ship carried a flag of *truce*.
When people saw Fulton's steamboat move upriver, they shouted in *triumph*.
The whole *community* laughed at the joke about the two-tailed dog.
Barnum often sat in the *audience* at his circus.

Have the first sentence read and suggest that pupils read the complete definition of *companion* in the glossary. Ask if it is possible to fit either part or all of the definition back into the sentence. Lead pupils to note that to do so results in an extremely awkward and unintelligible sentence, even if grammatical forms are changed and words are transposed. Explain that in this case the general idea about the meaning of the word is what counts— not the exact wording of the definition. Then ask how pupils would explain to someone what the sentence means without using the word *companions*. Encourage several pupils to try; some attempts will be smoother than others. Let children decide which recasting of the sentence best clarifies the meaning of the original sentence. Perhaps pupils will agree that something like the following is satisfactory: *Key showed his song to the men who were with him.*

Continue similarly with the remaining sentences, emphasizing each time that pupils should read the complete definition of the word in question to get a general idea of its meaning. On page 55 of the *Think-and-Do Book*, children are asked to interpret definitions and then to rewrite in their own words sentences containing the defined words. This page will give you an objective check of each child's ability to use context clues to select appropriate meanings and of his ability to adapt defined meanings in light of sentence context.

As time permits, you will also want children to use pages 69 and 78 of the *Thorndike-Barnhart Beginning Dictionary*, which give further practice in paraphrasing to adapt defined meanings to context.

Think-and-Do Book: Use pages 55 and 56. The content of page 56 is based on the story "A Great Showman." The page provides an objective check of the child's ability to remember specific cause-effect relationships that were stated or implied in the story.

EXTENDING INTERESTS

Extending concepts: Most children know something about a circus performance whether or not they have ever attended one. Few youngsters, however, are familiar with the development of the circus or its intricate and highly efficient operation. This is a fascinating story in which P. T. Barnum played an extremely important role. Under the entry "Circus," the three encyclopedias listed in the bibliography at the back of this *Guidebook* contain a wealth of information that pupils will read and discuss with enthusiasm. (Additional facts about P. T. Barnum can also be found under his name.) After several superior readers have finished the articles in one or more encyclopedias, give them an opportunity to tell the class the behind-the-scenes story of the circus including the life of circus performers and the problems and method of moving a circus from city to city. You may wish to read parts of the articles aloud to the entire class so that all children may participate in the discussion.

Enjoying literature: One characteristic of American life has been its remarkable showmen from the time of Barnum to the present day. If any children have read the d'Aulaires' *Buffalo Bill*, they will be eager to tell the story of this great showman and display the pictures, which miss none of the hero's flamboyance. Later, lead pupils to contrast the Barnum circus with the wild West show of Buffalo Bill.

Independent supplementary reading: From the selections they have been reading in other readers, pupils might select for oral interpretation one story, or part of a story, which shows an outstanding character trait of some famous American. The listeners might then try to identify or describe the personal quality or strength that the famous American showed. A spirited and valuable sharing of ideas can grow from such questions as "Which of the people we've read about so far in this unit showed the same character trait? In what way is this quality needed by a young person today? Can you think of an incident in which someone you know showed that he was _____? [name the character trait that is under discussion] How might a person go about developing this character trait?"

Nothing for Herself PAGES 203-210

Sight Word: Clara
Attack Words: *frame* improve* earnestly* feebly* undertakes* assist**
           government* (glossary)
           Bar'ton* nurse* (vowel followed by *r*)
           bet* hos'pi tals* (position of single vowel letter)
           obtained* (root + ending; ob tain'—two vowel letters
           together)
           aid* (two vowel letters together)

"Coming events cast their shadows before." No other story in this unit better exemplifies the truth of that statement. Clara Barton's long career of service to others began when, as a child, she devoted almost two years to nursing a sick brother. As youngsters read this inspiring story of the founder of the American Red Cross, they will be impressed by the remarkable fact that the very qualities and traits that led Clara Barton to seek nothing for herself were the ones that brought her lasting fame and honor the world over.

PREPARING FOR READING

Establishing background and presenting vocabulary: Tell pupils that today's biographical story is about a famous American woman whose life was devoted to helping others. Present the name *Clara Barton* and note whether it calls up any associations in children's minds. Then comment, "Like most of the famous Americans we have been reading about, Clara Barton exhibited as a youngster many of the characteristics that later made her famous. The story title, 'Nothing for Herself,' gives you some hint of the kind of person Miss Barton was. Let's read the story to find out how a shy little farm girl from Massachusetts became a famous woman who was loved and admired in America and abroad."

INTERPRETING THE STORY

Pages 203-207: Encourage comments about the situation that the first picture depicts and identify the girl in the blue dress as eleven-year-old Clara

Barton. What do pupils think might be the outcome of this situation? Suggest that they read the first four pages to find out what happened and what effect the events had on young Clara's life. After silent reading, invite pupils to tell about David's accident and its effect on his sister's life. Ask youngsters to point out text and picture clues that help the reader know that this story took place many years ago. Then ask, "What kind of girl was Clara? What qualities did she have that made her a good nurse? Why did her mother worry about her?"

Pages 207-210: Comment, "About this time a family friend made a remarkable prediction about Clara. Read just the first two paragraphs on page 207 to find out what it was." Then discuss briefly with pupils Mrs. Barton's concern for her daughter's future and what the friend predicted would be true of Clara's life. (Did pupils consult the glossary to get the full significance of the new word *undertakes?*) Suggest that as they finish the story, youngsters keep in mind the things the friend predicted about Clara and note whether or not they came true.

When children have finished, you might use the family friend's predictions about Clara as a framework for helping pupils summarize and organize the story events. Have the second paragraph on page 207 read aloud and list the five statements or predictions on the board. Then have pupils use each of the predictions as a basis for discussing Clara Barton's accomplishments and character traits. A lively discussion and difference of opinion may ensue as children discuss the first prediction, "She may always be shy." However, most children will perhaps agree that a woman who went fearlessly onto battlefields and who talked with Presidents had probably overcome her shyness. In conclusion, have the last sentence in the story read aloud and ask, "Do you suppose most of the people who knew Clara when she was a girl, thought that one day she would become famous? Why [or why not]? Why is 'Nothing for Herself' a good title for this story? By wanting nothing for herself what did Clara Barton gain?"

Extending interpretation: Have pupils find the necessary information and then fill in the biographical chart for Clara Barton. Then ask, "How old did Miss Barton live to be? Are there people living today who might have known her? We know that she knew Lincoln. Which other famous people that we have read about might she have known? Was the American Red Cross founded during Lincoln's lifetime?" Next, recall with pupils that Clara Barton's fame rested on service to others. Then ask, "In what ways did some of the other famous Americans we have read about serve or help other people? What lasting contribution did Clara Barton make to America? How does the American Red Cross affect our lives today?"

It would be well to introduce pages 57 and 58 of the *Think-and-Do Book* now while the story of Clara Barton is fresh in pupils' minds. Page 57 contains additional incidents from Miss Barton's life and helps pupils note further how her childhood foreshadowed her future. On the basis of the informational article about the American Red Cross on page 58, pupils are asked to complete a simple outline, summarizing the peacetime and wartime services of that organization.

EXTENDING SKILLS AND ABILITIES

Structural analysis: This exercise introduces the suffix *-or* and reviews the understanding that suffixes, like root words, are meaning units. It also directs attention to the understanding that although a root word retains its meaning in a derived form (the root *dance* in *dancer*, *quick* in *quickly*, for example), the function of the derived form in context (its part of speech) is different from that of the root word.

This type of exercise, which directs attention to the ways words are used in sentences, promotes language facility and builds readiness for the study of grammar. Too often, as their first introduction to grammar, children are expected to memorize rules and definitions without first acquiring an adequate background of language experiences of the type suggested here. Since pre-reading levels in The New Basic Reading Program, youngsters have been developing awareness of correct language patterns and of the way in which words function in sentences. Without introducing grammatical terms or definitions, this exercise develops the understanding that, in addition to being meaning units, suffixes also have a grammatical function.

Begin by writing the following pairs of sentences, underlining the italicized words. As each pair of sentences is read, ask, "Which of the underlined words is the root word? In the second sentence, what suffix was added to the root word to make a new word? What does the new word mean?"

People often *freeze* food for future use.
Mother took the strawberries out of the *freezer*.

Miss White will *teach* the fourth grade next year.
She is a good *teacher*.

Use similar procedures with the pairs of sentences shown on the next page. Lead pupils to note that the suffix *-or* has the same meaning and pronunciation as the suffix *-er*, the only difference being the spelling.

Bob will *sail* his boat in the race.
He is a good *sailor*.

Fulton began to *invent* things when he was young.
He became a famous *inventor*.

Bring out that the root word *freeze* tells what people do—*freezer* tells what they use to do it with; *teach* tells what Miss White will do—*teacher* tells what we call a person who does that. Continue with the root words *sail* and *invent*. In conclusion, help pupils generalize that when we add the suffix -er or -or to a root word that expresses an action, we make a new word that tells what we call the person or thing that performs the action.

Next, write the following groups of sentences and use procedures similar to those suggested above. Use the underlined words in each column to help children generalize as follows: Column 1—When we add the suffix -y, -ly, or -less to a root word that names a person or a thing, we make a new word that describes someone or something. Column 2—When we add -ly to a root word that describes something or someone, we make a new word that tells "how" or "in what manner" something is done.

(1)	(2)
The *wind* blew.	Jane's answers were *correct*.
It was a *windy* day.	She answered the questions *correctly*.
Tom is my *friend*.	Her voice was *soft*.
He is a *friendly* person.	She spoke *softly*.
Tom will never be *friendless*.	

Think-and-Do Book: Use pages 57 and 58.

EXTENDING INTERESTS

Enjoying literature: Heroines like Clara Barton appeal greatly to girls of nine and ten who often are beginning to develop a sense of idealistic service. They will enjoy reading and discussing the longer account of Clara's life contained in the Stevenson book listed in the bibliography of *More Times and Places*. Arthur Guiterman's verse, "Of Giving," speaks for Clara as well as for many other famous Americans. Read the lines twice and let children say them with you. Then look back over the stories in this unit and the library books children have been reading and have pupils tell ways in which the heroes—Washington, Franklin, Wayne, Boone, Carson, John Paul Jones, Lincoln, and Clara Barton—gave of themselves and so helped make this country what it is today. Such discussion will provide an excellent review of almost the entire unit.

Night Is Turned into Day PAGES 211-218

Sight Words: Edison   Huron   electricity
Attack Words: *lamps* experimenting* extremely* material* trials**
 display* (glossary)
 Al′va* bulb* cot′ton* (position of single vowel letter)
 Eve* (final *e*)

No one can fully estimate the debt that the world owes Thomas Edison. His numerous inventions have made life simpler, more productive, and more enjoyable for millions. After giving readers a tantalizing glimpse of Edison as a youth, this story dramatizes his invention of the electric light bulb. It is a realistic story of hard work, disappointment and eventual triumph. It is an inspiring one of genius coupled with imagination, patience, and persistence. It will kindle sparks of ambition in some young readers and will give all young minds something to grow on.

PREPARING FOR READING

Establishing background and anticipating vocabulary needs: To introduce the story, ask, "How did people light their homes before they had *electricity?*" Recall what Lincoln read by at night, the kind of lighting Noah Webster's family used, and the kind of lights that shone outside Barnum's museum. Then comment that about one hundred years ago a boy living in *Port Huron*, Michigan decided there ought to be a better way to light houses than with oil lamps. Refer pupils to the picture of an oil lamp on page 308 of the glossary and ask them to tell why this type of lighting is inferior to electric lights. Continue, "The boy who complained about oil lamps became one of the world's greatest inventors. Today's biographical story tells about one of his most important and useful inventions. Perhaps you have already guessed that our story is about *Thomas Alva Edison.*"

INTERPRETING THE STORY

Pages 211-214: Have the title read aloud and ask which of Edison's inventions it suggests. Identify the people in the picture as Mrs. Edison and her son Tom, and talk over the ways in which this kitchen differs from a modern one. Suggest that pupils read the first four pages to find out why young Tom was dissatisfied with the methods people used to light their houses and what he tried to do twenty years later to give them a better way.

After silent reading, ask, "Why did Tom dislike oil lamps? What did he think of gaslights? What was his reason for wanting money? What does that tell you about the kind of boy Edison was?" You might mention that page 59 of the *Think-and-Do Book* tells about an unusual job that Tom took about this time to earn the money that he needed for his experiments. Continue, "After twenty years, how had Edison realized his youthful ambitions? Was he entirely satisfied? Why not? Why did he want to invent a good electric light? Why was he discouraged? What do you suppose was the biggest difficulty in the invention of the electric light bulb?" Suggest that pupils finish the story to find out what the difficulty was, how Edison overcame it, and how he seemed to turn night into day.

Pages 215-218: When children have finished, invite them to tell the dramatic story of the invention of the light bulb. Encourage those who have read Enid Meadowcroft's book about Edison to tell more details of how he prepared the cotton thread so that it would glow. Do pupils know what is used in bulbs today? If not, suggest that someone find out and tell the class. Continue, "If you had been in that throng of people who flocked to Edison's display on New Year's Eve, what would you have seen and heard? How do you think you would have felt about the wonderful new invention? Why do you suppose that the crowds called Edison a wizard? Was he really one?" In conclusion, ask, "What other things besides electric lights do we have in our homes today that would seem like magic to those people who called Edison a wizard?"

Extending interpretation: Suggest that pupils complete the biographical chart by filling it in for Edison. Then ask, "How old was Edison when he invented the electric light bulb? Which of these people listed on the chart lived to see or hear about electric lights?" Recall that Clara Barton talked with President Lincoln in 1865 and ask, "How old was Edison then? Might Edison have known Barnum? Clara Barton? Were your parents living during Edison's lifetime?"

This biographical chart, which represents simply and concretely the time relationships emphasized throughout this unit, has served to help children summarize and organize ideas for the purpose of remembering them.

Comment that it has been stated that no other inventor has had so great an effect on people's lives as Edison. Then ask, "How does the story we have just read help prove that statement? What else did Edison invent that justifies the statement?" Suggest that during the discussion of the last question, pupils use the illustrations on the end sheets of the book *The Story of Thomas Alva Edison*, by Enid Meadowcroft, or those in the article about Edison in any children's encyclopedia (*The World Book Encyclopedia* is excellent for this purpose) to dramatize Edison's inventive genius.

EXTENDING SKILLS AND ABILITIES

Evaluating inner drives and character traits: Recall with pupils that many people were so astounded at the idea of electric lights that they called Edison a wizard. Then comment, "We know, of course, that he did not possess magical powers. What traits did he possess that enabled him to become a successful inventor?" Then ask, "In what ways were Edison and Fulton alike when they were young? From what you know about Fulton, Edison, and other inventors, would you say that being an inventor is an easy life? Is it a satisfying one? Why?" In conclusion, it would be interesting to discuss with children two of Edison's most famous statements: "I owe my success to the fact that I never had a clock in my workroom" and "Genius is 2 per cent inspiration and 98 per cent perspiration." What do they reveal about the kind of man Edison was? What bearing do they have on the events of the story that pupils have just read?

Think-and-Do Book: Use pages 59, 60, 61, and 62. Page 60 gives pupils experience in deriving general meanings from definitions of words that characterize the famous Americans in this unit. The nine interesting incidents on page 61 further the understanding that some of these famous Americans were contemporaries or that their lives touched upon one another's in some way. As youngsters answer the questions below the biographical chart on page 62, they will become increasingly aware of time relationships implicit in this unit.

EXTENDING INTERESTS

Enjoying literature: Children who have read the Guthridge book about Edison will want to relate some of his lively boyhood escapades and to tell about his numerous inventions. Also discuss Edison's love for his work, and suggest that those pupils who have read *Tom Edison: Boy Inventor* describe episodes from the book that point up this characteristic.

This would be a good time for children to discuss more fully the library books they have read. Let youngsters relate some of the episodes that interested them most, and suggest that they tell which of the books they liked best and would recommend to their friends. The activities described in the section "Summarizing the unit" should also be based on the library books suggested for this unit.

CONCLUDING ACTIVITIES

Summarizing the unit: To conclude this first excursion into biography, children might review the stories in one of several different ways. First of all, you will want to give pupils an opportunity to express their personal preferences and reactions to stories they have read by asking such questions as the following: "Which story did you enjoy most? Why? Which famous American did you admire the most? Why? Which one would you most like to have known as a child? Why? In what ways were some of these famous Americans as children like boys and girls of today?" Then the class might be divided into groups, with each group dramatizing a scene from one of the stories in the unit or from a library book they have read. See whether the others in the class can name the hero. Another possibility would be to have each group form a silent, living picture of one episode to be guessed by their classmates. If you prefer, you might play the game "Who Am I?" In this game, a child is selected to be "It." He steps out of the room while the rest of the class decide which famous American he is to represent. "It" returns to the room and asks questions of his classmates to determine his identity. When he correctly identifies the person he represents, he may choose another pupil to take his place.

Unit 4
Old Tales
from Everywhere

This final unit provides an opportunity for youngsters to leave the present-day world behind and enter the world of "Once upon a time" where fun and fancy reign, where magic is commonplace, where evil comes to a bad end and virtue is invariably rewarded. Old tales will not be new to middle-grade youngsters, for most children begin to find satisfaction and release in the world of fairy tales around the age of seven or eight.

As youngsters have sampled the old folk and fairy tales, each child has, in all probability, found a type that appealed to him—perhaps a fable, a talking beast story, or a tale of magic. This unit contains a variety of stories designed to appeal to this diversity of tastes, which is more evident in imaginative fiction than in any other field of children's literature. Included are three fables, four folk tales, an Indian "why" story, and one of Hans Christian Andersen's best-loved allegories. The source of each tale is included in the table of contents, and children will be interested to learn even more about the sources of their favorite stories.

The old tales are usually the first samples of real literature that a child comes to know, and they form an important part of his literary heritage. The lesson plans for these nine stories are designed to help you promote preadolescents' awareness of the old tale as literature—as a form of language, not merely a series of incidents that go to make up a plot. You will find suggestions for helping youngsters recognize characteristic form, style, and content of various types of old tales and for developing appreciation of the colorful language in which they are written. Since the fun of old tales is heightened by hearing their picturesque language, many opportunities should be provided for lively oral interpretation.

In view of the popularity of old tales and the diversity of children's interests in this form of literature, you will want to scan the bibliography for this unit at the back of *More Times and Places,* obtain as many as possible of the individual tales and collections, and make them and other old tales available to youngsters. The "Extending Interests" sections also suggest records to be used in connection with the stories in this unit. For your own use as you approach the teaching of this unit, you will find many suggestions in the folklore sections of *Children and Books.*[1]

INTRODUCING THE UNIT

To lead children into the delightful world of make-believe, you might begin by asking, "When you hear or read the words 'Once upon a time,' what kind of story do you expect? Those are the kinds of stories we'll read in this last unit. One of the stories is about a lad who wins a rich reward and marries a king's daughter; another tells about a merry fellow who makes a promise that gets him into trouble; and still another tells about heaps of gold big enough to fill a room!"

Have pupils turn to the unit title page. After the title has been read, encourage comments on the picture, and arouse interest by explaining that it illustrates an amusing event in one of the stories. Suggest that children look at the unit story titles in the table of contents. Which fairy tale does the picture suggest? As you read through the titles with youngsters, let them tell which tale they have read or heard, and call attention to the source of each story. Comment, "You probably know many Grimms' fairy tales, Aesop's fables, and Hans Christian Andersen's stories. But at first most of these old tales didn't appear in books as stories today do. They were told aloud over and over and passed on from one family to another; no one knows who first told them. Finally people became interested in collecting and writing down some of the old tales."

To point up the "everywhere" in the unit title, comment, "Every part of the world has its old tales that were told over and over again before being written." Help children identify the parts of the world represented in this collection (Germany, France, England, North America, and so on), and

---

[1] *Children and Books,* Revised Edition, by May Hill Arbuthnot (Chicago: Scott, Foresman and Company, 1957).

comment that during the reading of the unit, youngsters will have a chance to learn more about the sources of these stories.

In conclusion, read through the titles and annotations for the library books suggested for the unit on pages 300-301 of *More Times and Places*. Lead children to see that these stories, too, are from many different countries. Encourage discussion of books that sound especially appealing, and display pictures from those you have collected for the library table.

The Four Musicians   PAGES 220-227

Sight Words: musicians   therefore   thieves

Attack Words: *dismal* spirits* fortune* possess* proceeded** (glossary)
accepted* (root + ending; ac cept'—position of single vowel letter)
mis' tress* Chan' ti cleer* (position of single vowel letter)
cock'-a-doo' dle-doo'* (position of single vowel letter; meaning clues to determine sound of *oo*)
perched* (root + ending; perch—vowel followed by *r*)
hor' ri ble* (vowel followed by *r*)

For over a hundred years youngsters everywhere have counted the Grimms' stories among their favorite fairy tales, for whether they are somber or rollicking, the Grimms' tales are highly entertaining and have a universal appeal for young readers.   In this story, a donkey, a dog, a cat, and a rooster set off for the city to earn their living as musicians, but they secure such fine quarters en route that the journey is never completed.   How this is accomplished forms a plot that is sure to delight any fun-loving preadolescent.

PREPARING FOR READING

Establishing background: To begin, you might mention some of Grimms' tales ("Snow White and the Seven Dwarfs," "Hansel and Gretel," "The Elves and the Shoemaker," for example) and let children indicate which they have heard or read and which are their favorites. Comment, "We have already talked about how people in all parts of the world told old tales like these over and over for many years. The name you see after the title of this first story [refer children to the table of contents] is the name of two brothers who traveled about in Germany listening to people tell stories and then writing them down. The Grimms were among the first people to collect old tales this way. Their tales were written in German, but they have been retold in English and in many other languages." You might tell children that when they read page 71 of the *Think-and-Do Book*, they will learn more about the lives of the Grimm brothers.

Presenting vocabulary: Comment, "Maybe you've heard today's story at some time; even if you have, you'll enjoy reading it for yourself. It's about four animals that believed that they had very good voices and, *therefore*, considered themselves fine *musicians*. What happened in the story reminded me of what happened in another old tale. ["A Home in the Wild Woods" in the new *More Friends and Neighbors* tells of the adventures of some animals that built a home in the woods.]" Suggest that pupils turn to page 220 for a glimpse of one of the musicians (doubtless they will also spy the picture on page 221 and conclude that here are two more of the musicians). Then suggest, "The animals in these pictures look quite woebegone, don't they? But from what you know about fairy tales, do you think they'll still be so downcast and miserable at the end of the story?" Lead children to recall this especially satisfying characteristic of folk and fairy tales: the misunderstood and wretched triumph, and good wins over evil. Continue, "During the story, the musicians meet a band of *thieves*, and what happens makes hilarious reading!"

INTERPRETING THE STORY

Pages 220-221: To acquaint children with the cumulative structure of the story, you might suggest that they read through page 221 to find out why the animals decided to become musicians. After silent reading, ask, "How were the dog's and the donkey's stories alike? What do you suppose the cat's story will be?" Encourage pupils to find and read the two phrases that prompt vivid mental images of how the cat looked and felt ("as dismal as three wet days," "out of spirits"). Continue, "In the rest of the story you'll find out who the other musician was and how the musicians triumphed over the thieves."

Pages 222-227: After silent reading, allow a few moments for children to give their spontaneous reactions to the story. To help the fun along, you might comment, "Were these the kind of musicians you like to listen to? What do most people think of these animals' voices?" Then say, "The last paragraph tells us that the animals were pleased with their quarters. Just what does that mean?" (If pupils seem uncertain of the meaning of the word *quarters* in this context, suggest that they look it up in their dictionary.) Continue with a discussion of how the four animals happened to find the house in the forest.

Suggest that pupils turn to the picture on page 225 and ask, "What kind of music can you hear as you look at this picture? How do you suppose it sounded to the thieves? What can you see them doing when they first heard it? Why do you suppose the thieves thought a troll was about to attack them?" (Do youngsters recall trolls from other folk tales, for example, "The Three Billy Goats Gruff"?) Then encourage pupils to tell what the returning thief thought had happened to him and what really happened.

In their personal reading, some children already may have encountered the name Chanticleer, which appears in this story. Certainly all youngsters will be interested in knowing the derivation of this name for a rooster. Explain that the name comes from two old French words, *cler* and *chante*, that mean "clear" and "singer," and ask pupils to decide why this is a good name for a rooster.

In conclusion, comment, "Some of you might like to read more of the Grimms' stories. Let's look in the 'Books to Read' section of our book to see where some of these stories can be found." After children have read the titles of the Grimm collections, encourage them to tell which books they have read and which stories they enjoyed the most. After this introduction to Grimm, the books probably will be in great demand.

Oral interpretation: This old tale is a favorite for dramatization. Children might act out the story, without costumes or stage properties, reading the conversations from their books. Go through it briefly with children, helping them plan how best to bring out the broad humor of the story situations for the enjoyment of the audience. For example, let pupils experiment with the animals' speeches in the first part of the story ("My body may have grown feeble, but my voice is as strong as ever," "Upon my word, you make a fine noise!" and so on) and with the noisy "Heee-eee-aw," "Bow-wow," "Meow," and "Cock-a-doodle-doo" on page 225. Tell youngsters that there is another version of this story that describes the rooster as crying "Cuck-cuck-cuck-cudooooo!" The robber then says that the creature cried "Cut the man in two-ooo!" Let children choose the version they prefer. Also suggest that children try pantomiming the action and assuming the facial expression of the characters to show how they felt. For example, how would a cat look that was "quite out of spirits," and "as dismal as three wet days"? Have youngsters find other passages that give an opportunity for pantomiming action and facial expression. Then encourage children to throw themselves into the dramatization with gusto.

EXTENDING SKILLS AND ABILITIES

Memory based on association: Children will enjoy this exercise, which checks recall of well known folk tales, and it will enable you to determine pupils' backgrounds in this area of literature. As you mention each of the items listed below, ask children to tell which story it makes them think of. Continue by having youngsters name an object and see whether the others can supply the story title or plot.

a magic tablecloth ("The Lad and the North Wind")
a wicked witch at a spinning wheel ("The Sleeping Beauty")
a golden fish ("The Fisherman and His Wife")
a talking mirror ("Snow-White and the Seven Dwarfs")
a glass slipper ("Cinderella")
a gingerbread house ("Hansel and Gretel")

Think-and-Do Book: Use page 63. Page 63 provides valuable language experience in choosing the appropriate conjunction to express the relationship between ideas in a sentence or sentences.

EXTENDING INTERESTS

Enjoying literature: The resourceful animals of the Grimm story bring to mind that smartest of all cats, "The Master Cat," found in *Time for Fairy Tales*.[1] Read this aloud or, if you have the excellent picture edition by Marcia Brown (more familiarly titled *Puss in Boots*), let one of your superior readers read the story to the class and show the pictures.

Children will find the annotations in the bibliography helpful in choosing books they wish to read. The picture books containing just a single tale will be especially good for your slow readers to enjoy. During class discussions, these stories can be told from the pictures. The story collections will yield a choice of delightful stories for the average and superior readers. Frequently during the unit, devote time to discussions of the library books. Some pupils will be capable of telling an entire story so well that it will hold class interest throughout. Less able youngsters might be encouraged to tell part of a story and let their classmates guess the ending. Others may show the pictures and tell why they enjoyed the story.

---

[1] *Time for Fairy Tales, Old and New*, Revised Edition, compiled by May Hill Arbuthnot (Chicago: Scott, Foresman and Company, 1961).

A Barber's Discovery PAGES 228-231

Sight Word: Garo
Attack Words: *observe* acorns* lo* behold* marvel* meekly**
               solemn* (glossary)
               bar′ber's* snore* sore* (vowel followed by *r*)
               e′qual* slum′ber* plop* (position of single vowel
               letter)

In their original verse form, the La Fontaine fables have delighted generations of French children, and in translation, they have long been enjoyed by English-speaking youngsters. This fable tells about a know-it-all, who decided that he could set Nature straight and improve on her processes. But when he saw how his plan might endanger his comfort and safety, he decided Nature knows best, after all. Children will enjoy the homely humor of this tale and all those who have been subject to unwanted advice are sure to relish the moral.

PREPARING FOR READING

Establishing background and anticipating vocabulary needs: Tell children that the name of today's story is "A Barber's Discovery" and suggest that they refer to the table of contents again to find the source of the story and to learn what kind of old tale it is. To refamiliarize youngsters with the fable style, ask them to recall other fables they have read (for example, "The Hare and the Tortoise"). Ask children how they would expect a fable to be different from a story like "The Four Musicians." Lead them to recall that a fable teaches a lesson, which is clearly pointed out in the moral at the end of the story. Continue, "La Fontaine, the writer of this fable, was a Frenchman who lived about 300 years ago. Just as the Grimms went about collecting old German folk tales, La Fontaine was interested in collecting fables and putting them into books. One of his best-known fables is the story 'The Grasshopper and the Ant.'" Let youngsters recall this fable, or if it is unfamiliar to them, read or tell it to them.

Continue, "The barber in this fable we are going to read today is named *Garo*. Garo liked to give people advice. Everyone thought he was very wise; and he really felt he had no equal. But one day something happened that made the barber decide that his advice wasn't always so wise after all. You'll be chuckling as you read, and remember there'll be a lesson in this fable that we'll want to talk about after we've finished."

INTERPRETING THE STORY

Suggest that children turn to page 228, and encourage them to comment on the old-fashioned costumes and the amusing characters in the picture. After the plump man at the left has been identified as Garo, suggest that youngsters read the story to find out what the barber's discovery was.

Pages 228-231: After silent reading, guide the discussion to bring out Garo's two discoveries. Ask, "What lesson did the barber learn?" and have youngsters find and read aloud the moral of this fable. Continue, "What did Garo think he had discovered as he lay under the tree? Why was he pleased that he had thought of a way to improve Nature? How did Garo happen to reach his decision that Nature knows best?" Continue, "Why was Garo's advice considered excellent? [Make sure that children understand that since Garo was a traveling barber, he had many opportunities to pick up all the news and gossip.] Why did people think that Garo was very wise?" Have youngsters read the first paragraph on page 229 and ask, "How is La Fontaine poking fun at the barber in this paragraph?" With more mature readers, you might extend the concept behind this question by asking how the author pokes fun at people in general in this paragraph. To bring out the amusing imagery in this story, encourage pupils to tell what they could see and hear as they read the description of Garo lying under the oak tree. Youngsters will be eager to share their images of the barber's fat, pumpkin-like stomach, his acorn-colored nose, the beard stroking that accompanied his discovery, and the loud snores.

Extending interpretation: Recall with pupils why Garo was thought to be so wise, and ask, "How do you feel toward people who are constantly trying to give you advice?" As children express their opinions, guide the discussion to bring out that it makes a difference who is giving the advice, how important it is, and whether or not one has asked for the advice. Children might enjoy telling about times when they, like Garo, gave someone the wrong advice, or when they received some wrong advice.

Oral interpretation: Youngsters will enjoy reading this story aloud to portray the pompous character of the barber. As they prepare to read, encourage them to bring out the self-satisfied way in which Garo made his observations, and his meekness as he went home.

EXTENDING SKILLS AND ABILITIES

Comprehending the main idea: Tell children that there are many old sayings about wisdom and that some of these can be applied to the barber. As you read each of the following, ask pupils to tell how it fits Garo:

It is easy to be wise after the event.
It is not wise to be wiser than is necessary.
No one is wise at all times.
It is easier to be wise for others than for yourself.
It is better not to know so much than to know many things that aren't so.

On page 64 of the *Think-and-Do Book* further experience in interpreting generalizations and applying them to new situations is provided as pupils decide which old sayings apply to four incidents from modern life.

Imagery of word form: Specific practice in calling up visual images of word forms is often helpful for the slow reader who tends to scrutinize each word as he reads. Suggest that children look at the picture on page 231, and point out that the artist didn't need to paint a picture of the acorn on the tree, and another of the acorn hitting the barber's nose to suggest to us all that happened. Comment, "The same is true with words. We do not always need to see every single part of a word to recognize it. Many times when we are reading rapidly, seeing only certain letters or a portion of the word helps us recognize the word. Let's try an experiment."

Suggest that pupils take a piece of paper or a card about the width of the page in the book. Direct them to slip the card down over the type at the top of page 229 until they see just the top of the first line. Let them experiment with how far down they need to slide the card before they can recognize the words in this line. Explain that often a glimpse of a word can make us see the whole word in our mind's eye, but only if we are familiar with how the word looks. Have children continue with the four lines in the first paragraph on page 229, possibly with the first four lines on page 230.

This experiment will aid you in determining those youngsters who are slow, word-by-word readers. Such pupils should be organized into a special-help group and given practice in using this technique with unfamiliar material.

Next, explain that when we read, we grasp the meaning of many words with just a glimpse. We are really reading by just noticing significant parts or shapes of words. Since the vowels, with the exception of *y*, are all little letters about the same size and shape (jot *a, e, i, o, u* on the board), we are more apt to notice the consonants than we are to notice the vowels when we read. Then say, "I'll write a sentence leaving out all vowel letters. See if you can read it." Write the following:

Th_ Gr_mm br_th_rs h_rd s_m_n_ t_ll th_ st_r_ _f "Th_ F__r M_s_c__ns" b_f_r_ th_ _ wr_t_ _t.

Comment, "You know who the four musicians in the story were. I'll write the words without any consonants, just with vowel letters. I think you can tell me which is which." Write:

_a_   _o_   _o_ _ey   _oo_ _e_

Next, write the following sentence and let youngsters try to read it:

"Th_ B_rb_r's D_sc_v_r_" _s _n _ld f_bL_.

Then, to point up the understanding that we are more often cued to word form by the consonant framework than by the vowel letters, rewrite the sentence, using only the vowel letters, and let pupils try to read it. Note whether children recognize that both sentences should read *"The Barber's Discovery" is an old fable.*

Conclude, "Many times when we read we can skim over words seeing only parts of them, but sometimes we have to look very carefully at the details of words. I am going to write a sentence that tells about something that happened in 'The Four Musicians.' There will be four mistakes in words in the sentence. Let's see how many of you can picture words clearly enough not only to fill in the missing parts but also to find mistakes in word forms." Write the following sentences one at a time:

The for thieves though one of the musicans was a which.
The barbor gave advice to his costumers.

As youngsters discover the errors in the first sentence, have them cross out the incorrect forms and write the correct forms. Repeat with the second sentence.

Think-and-Do Book: Use page 64.

EXTENDING INTERESTS

Enjoying literature: You will want a good collection of fables to complement "A Barber's Discovery" and the two other fables in this unit. The edition of *Aesop's Fables*, by Townsend and James, is fairly complete and easy to read. It contains amusing illustrations by Glen Rounds.

The idea of changing Nature around suggests those queer never-never beasts in *Time for Poetry*—"The Purple Cow," "The Bumblebeaver," "The Octopussycat," and "The Kangarooster." Though these may be familiar to your class, they are always a source of amusement. Youngsters will enjoy hearing them again. Perhaps pupils will want to try some scrambled beasts of their own, either in words or in drawings.

Independent supplementary reading: Fanciful stories are excellent material for oral reading. Children with imagination, a sense of humor, and a flair for the dramatic delight in interpreting the voices of the talking animals and the other fantastic characters of the old tales. Encourage youngsters to read many of the fanciful selections from other readers (see the bibliography at the back of this *Guidebook*) and to choose their favorites to read to their classmates. Your own oral reading of the old tales suggested under the heading "Enjoying literature" will set a pattern for children, and the procedures suggested under "Oral interpretation" will aid pupils in planning the reading of the selections they have chosen.

Tyll's Masterpiece   PAGES 232-239

Sight Word: punished
Attack Words: *nobleman* humbly* portrait* distress** (glossary)
        Tyll's* mem'bers* blank* com'mon* (position of single vowel letter)
        refused* (root with *e* dropped + ending; re fuse' (final *e*)
        punishment* truth* (root word + meaning clues)
        cur'tains* (vowel followed by *r*)

Tyll Eulenspiegel, a legendary mischief-maker, who was the hero of a series of German tales, is the main character in this story. Finding himself at the court of a nobleman, Tyll offered to paint portraits of the court members. After he heard how each person wanted his portrait painted, he found that being a painter was more than he had bargained for. How Tyll used his wits to save himself from dire punishment will delight preadolescent readers. Tyll's final remark "Laughter makes life easy and gay" is the sort of moral that youngsters will find appealing and useful.

PREPARING FOR READING

Establishing background and anticipating vocabulary needs: Tell children that today's story is about an amusing fellow named Tyll who lived by his wits. Ask pupils to tell what sort of person they would expect Tyll to be. Suggest that they use their glossary, if necessary, to decide what the expression "lived by his wits" means. To add to the interest of this old tale, explain that Tyll may really have lived, several hundred years ago in Europe, that he was a mischievous fellow who traveled about playing tricks on people. Many stories were told about his pranks, and these tales were collected and written in German. Continue, "Although Tyll lived by his wits, he sometimes made mistakes. In this story, it appeared for a while that Tyll's wits had failed him and that he would be *punished* for not doing exactly what he was told to do." Then ask children to turn to page 232, read the title, and discuss the meaning of "masterpiece," referring to a dictionary, if necessary. Encourage comments on the picture—Tyll's appearance and what he seems to be doing. Then suggest that pupils read the first two pages to find out more about what kind of fellow Tyll was.

INTERPRETING THE STORY

Pages 232-233: By the time they have finished these pages, most children will be chuckling at Tyll's roguish ways and will be eager to read on to learn the outcome of his portrait painting venture. To make sure that all youngsters enjoy the special flavor of this story, pause for a brief discussion that will bring out Tyll's chief interest, how he accomplished his aim, how he has already shown that he is sharp-witted, and what arrangements he made with the nobleman for painting the court portraits. Then ask, "Do you think Tyll really is a painter? Do you suppose that he will manage to paint the portraits? Finish the story to find out."

Pages 234-239: After children have commented on the outcome of the story, suggest that they reread the first paragraph on page 232 and then ask, "What trick did Tyll play to help the people in this story recognize their folly? Why were the people afraid to say that they saw nothing on the wall? Why did Tyll have to play the trick? Why couldn't he have pleased everyone?" Children will enjoy looking at the picture on page 235 and speculating about how these people would like to have had their portraits painted. To help youngsters understand the jester's role in the exposure of Tyll's trick, explain that the court fool was a person at the court of a king or nobleman who amused people with tricks and witty sayings. The court fool could often say things that other people didn't dare say.

In conclusion, lead pupils to recall the meaning of the word *masterpiece*, and comment, "Tyll didn't paint any portraits, did he? Why do you suppose this story is called 'Tyll's Masterpiece'?" During the discussion, help children see that Tyll's "painting" was a masterpiece of cleverness.

Extending interpretation: Pupils might consider whether Tyll's conclusion "Laughter makes life easy and gay" is really the moral of this story. Youngsters might decide that Tyll's burst of laughter did enable him to escape from what could have developed into an unpleasant situation. And it is the merry folk, like Tyll, who generally get along best in the world. Other children might suggest that the vanity of the members of the court or the trouble Tyll got himself into as a result of posing as a painter is worthy of a moral. You might let them phrase their own endings to this moral: "If you pretend to be something you aren't, . . ." Children will likely suggest such conclusions as ". . . you'll get into trouble," or ". . . you'll be found out."

Oral interpretation: To help pupils make oral interpretation of Tyll's speeches and actions more lively, you might use the exercise "Recognizing and inferring motives of story characters" (see the next section of this lesson plan) before oral reading. In addition, have children experiment with some of Tyll's speeches, using different tones of voice and pantomime to show how he must have sounded and looked as he talked.

EXTENDING SKILLS AND ABILITIES

Recognizing and inferring motives of story characters: The fun of this story is heightened when the reader sees through Tyll's actions and recognizes the real motives of this clever, impertinent fellow. Ask, "How does this story show that Tyll lived by his wits?" Doubtless children will respond with the obvious—the trick he played on the court members and the nobleman, the clever plan he devised to coax his donkey down the road. To point up Tyll's sharp-wittedness further, ask the following questions. Not all answers are directly stated in the story, and individual answers will be interesting and varied, depending on what the child inferred.

When Tyll first talked to the nobleman, do you think he was really humble?
    Why did he pretend to be humble?
Why did Tyll tell the nobleman he was a portrait painter?
Why did he consent to be the court painter?
Why did Tyll stay so long in the room where he was supposed to be painting?
Why did Tyll burst out laughing after the Court Fool said that he saw only
    a blank wall instead of a painting?

Structural analysis: This exercise stresses the grammatical function as well as the meaning of the suffixes *-ness* and *-ful*. Write the following pairs of sentences, underlining the italicized words, and use procedures similar to those suggested on pages 177-178 of this *Guidebook*.

(1)	(2)
The man was very *kind*.	The *force* of the waves knocked me down.
I thanked him for his *kindness*.	The waves are not often that *forceful*.
The child was *sick*.	She filled a *cup* with milk.
His *sickness* kept him indoors.	She poured a *cupful* of milk into a pan.

As pupils discuss the meanings of the italicized words in each pair of sentences, help them arrive at the following generalizations: Column 1— When we add the suffix *-ness* to a root word that describes someone or something, we make a new word that names something. Column 2—When we add the suffix *-ful* to a root word that names something, we make a new word that (a) describes someone or something and means "full of" or "having _____" (whatever the root word is); or (b) names something and means "as much as a _____ (whatever the root word is) will hold."

Think-and-Do Book: Use page 65. The use of this page will further strengthen the language understanding that, in addition to being meaning units, suffixes have a grammatical function.

EXTENDING INTERESTS

Listening to music: Richard Strauss' colorful tone poem, *Till Eulenspiegel's Merry Pranks*,[1] though advanced for many fourth-grade children, will nevertheless convey to them at least some of the spirit of mischief for which this impudent prankster has been known for generations. Before presenting the music, you might read aloud a few more stories about Tyll's antics which are found in the book, *Tyll Ulenspiegel's Merry Pranks*, by M. Jagendorf, from which "Tyll's Masterpiece" is taken.

[1] All records referred to in this *Guidebook* are listed with their recording companies and catalog numbers in the bibliography.

Strauss' music is based on tales of Till Eulenspiegel, but Strauss himself preferred to let the listener decide which pranks the music suggests. Present the tone poem without limiting pupils to a definite program of events. With a background of several of Tyll's escapades and the information that the music is about the same story character, children will enjoy the listening experience. Some may even invent their own tales about Tyll based on their interpretation of the music. Since the tone poem is rather long, you may wish to play only a portion of it.

Enjoying literature: "Tyll's Masterpiece" suggests another tale with the same idea—Hans Christian Andersen's *The Emperor's New Clothes*. If you have the edition with Virginia Burton's delightful illustrations, let some child show it to the class and read it aloud. If you do not have this edition, tell or read the story from *Time for Fairy Tales*.

Chanticleer and the Fox   PAGES 240-248

Attack Words: *beheld* lurking* scornful* relate* wallow* pursuers* hither* thither** (glossary)
fuss* a las'* a lack'* (position of single vowel letter)
cackling* (root with *e* dropped + ending; cack'le— position of single vowel letter)
friendship* (root word + meaning clues)
flattered* (root + ending; flat'ter—position of single vowel letter)
rate* (final *e*)

This fable about the vain, pompous fowl who succumbed to the flattery of the conniving fox provides a delightful introduction to that master storyteller, Chaucer.   Preadolescents will find this an unusually satisfactory version because the silly rooster catches on and turns the tables on the wily fox.   Even at the age of nine or ten, children are often exposed to flattery and are quick to detect its insincerity.   Consequently, they will relish the gratifying outcome of this fable and will enjoy discussing its moral.

PREPARING FOR READING

Establishing background: Recall with children the moral of the fable "A Barber's Discovery." Then comment that today's story is also a fable, but one in which the characters are animals that behave like people. Explain that it was written by a famous English storyteller, Chaucer. Then write his name on the board, and help youngsters find the Chaucer tale in the table of contents. Comment that Chaucer's fable reminds you of another old fable. Read either the La Fontaine or the Aesop version of "The Fox and the Crow" found in *Time for Fairy Tales,* and discuss the moral with pupils. After children have heard this fable about the vain crow that trusted a flatterer, encourage them to guess what is going to happen to Chanticleer in this story. Then suggest that youngsters read the story to see whether they were right.

INTERPRETING THE STORY

Pages 240-248: After they have finished reading, children will be eager to talk over the surprise ending in this story and the way in which the fable differs from "The Fox and the Crow." Ask, "In which fable did the flatterer have the tables turned on him?" Continue, "What kind of rooster was Chanticleer? Do you think that he deserved to be taught a lesson? Why?" Suggest that youngsters read passages from the story that support their answers and opinions.

This is the kind of story that most children enjoy retelling, for it affords many opportunities for comical gestures and lively, exaggerated dialogue. As a part of the narration, you might have pupils read aloud the fox's speeches on pages 245-246 to bring out his crafty insincerity and the exaggerated politeness used to flatter Chanticleer. The pursuit scene (the last two paragraphs on page 246 and the first three paragraphs on page 247) prompts such merry, noisy imagery that youngsters will enjoy reading it aloud. Encourage those who listen to describe their mental images of this frantic chase. After the story has been retold, have the last paragraph read aloud and ask, "What do you suppose the fox might have promised *himself* when he got home?"

Since the vivid illustrations add much to the enjoyment of this story, encourage discussion of how the artist has brought out the emotions of the principal characters in each picture. (For example, suggest that children compare how the fox looks on page 244 with his appearance on page 248—what details in each picture emphasize how the fox felt?)

Extending interpretation: Ask, "Why was it so easy for the fox to fool Chanticleer? What lesson did Chanticleer learn from his experience with the fox? What lesson did the fox learn?" Then ask, "In what ways did the fox's and Chanticleer's behavior remind you of the way people sometimes act? Can people sometimes be fooled as easily as these animals were? How? What lesson was the author of this fable trying to teach?" During the discussion, encourage children to phrase a moral for this fable. They might like to try making their own rhymed proverbs from the moral of this fable. To begin, you might suggest, "A flatterer usually wants a prize, / . . . if you are wise." The missing words might be "So you won't believe him" or "So be on your guard."

EXTENDING SKILLS AND ABILITIES

Identifying figurative language: Recall with children the phrase *as dismal as three wet days* used to describe the cat in "The Four Musicians," and explain that authors often describe something by saying it is like another thing in some way. Comment that such comparisons help a reader visualize what the author is describing and add to the interest of a story or book. Ask pupils to tell how the phrase *as dismal as three wet days* gives a better picture of how the cat looked than does such a phrase as *extremely dismal*. Then suggest that children look at page 240 and find two sentences in which things are described by saying they are like another thing (*as red as fire, as yellow as gold*). Discuss how these comparisons help the reader form a clear picture of the color of Chanticleer's comb and feathers. Continue by having children skim the next three pages in the story to find other comparisons, and encourage pupils to think of additional descriptive comparisons the author might have used in place of those in the story. (Page 66 of the *Think-and-Do Book* provides further experience in identifying and interpreting figurative and picturesque language.)

Phonetic analysis: This exercise is designed to make children aware of one common pattern of accent in multisyllabic words in the English language. You might begin, "We know that in two-syllable words, one syllable is stressed or accented more than the other syllable. We have also talked about certain clues that tell us which of the two syllables may be accented. Let's see if we can discover a pattern that can help us determine which syllable is usually accented in words of three or more syllables." Write the following words, showing syllable breaks (the accent marks are for your convenience and should not be used in the initial presentation):

ac′ ci dent	ac com′ pa ny
hos′ pi tal	ap′ pe tite
col lec′ tion	car′ pen ter
o pos′ sum	im me′ di ate
de ter′ mine	ri dic′ u lous
tem′ per a ture	des′ per ate

Have the words pronounced and ask children to tell which syllable is accented. As they respond, mark the accented syllable. Lead pupils to note that the first or second syllable in each word is accented. Say, "Usually in our language, we find that the first or second syllable of a long word is accented because the word is easier to say that way. Two or more unstressed syllables rarely come at the beginning of a word but are often found at the end of a word because they are easier to say at the end."

Children might enjoy pronouncing the words again and attempting to accent the third or fourth syllable. They will readily agree that the words "sound funny" and not at all like familiar English words.

If time permits, it would be well to introduce immediately page 67 of the *Think-and-Do Book*. This page gives pupils an opportunity to apply independently to unknown words the understanding about accent developed in this exercise.

Accent is an important element in our language, but all too frequently continuous sequential instruction in this aspect of word perception has been neglected. As children progress at middle-grade levels, they are encountering multisyllabic words more and more frequently—and they need to develop increasingly mature understandings if they are to cope with such words independently. The type of understanding presented in this lesson will be extended throughout succeeding levels of The New Basic Reading Program.

Think-and-Do Book: Use pages 66 and 67.

EXTENDING INTERESTS

Enjoying literature: Another version of Chaucer's fable that children will enjoy is *Chanticleer and the Fox*, adapted and illustrated by Barbara Cooney. The pictures are especially delightful and everyone will want to see them.

Personal reading: Pupils' personal reading should continue to be encouraged during this fanciful unit. Provide time for children to talk about their interests and to discuss the reading they have done in connection with their hobbies and other after-school activities.

The falling Star — I saw a star slide down the sky, Blinding the north as it went by, Too hurrying and too quick to heed, too lonely to be sought or seed, good only to make wishes on, and then forever to be gone. Sara Teasdale

The Seven Dancing Stars
PAGES 249-253

Attack Words: tribe* dwelt* squaws* wigwams* eldest* beware*
pleaded* (glossary)
hawk* (*a* followed by *w*)
joyous* (root word + meaning clues)

This Onondaga Indian legend is typical of the American Indian "why" stories, told to explain some natural wonder that the Indians found mystifying. Long ago an Indian storyteller invented this story about eight disobedient boys to explain how the constellation Pleiades appeared in the sky. The descriptive form and rather loosely knit plot of this tale form an interesting contrast to the condensation of description and incident in the fables that children have read. The implied lesson also forms an interesting comparison with fable morals.

PREPARING FOR READING

Establishing background and anticipating vocabulary needs: To introduce this "why" story, tell children that the Indians of long ago in our country spent much of their time outdoors. As they hunted in the forests or wandered across the plains, they saw many things that caused them to wonder. They wondered why there are four seasons, or why the woodpecker has a red head, or how the Great Spirit had created the small creatures of Nature. (If youngsters seem unfamiliar with the term *Great Spirit*, which appears in this story, refer them to the first definition for *spirit* in the glossary, and help them conclude that Great Spirit was the Indians' title for God.) Then, because they couldn't find out the real reason for these things, the Indians made up stories to explain the things they wondered about. Such stories are sometimes called "why" stories. Continue, "Like the folk tales and fables we've read, these stories are very old, and the Indians told them over and over through the years. Many people believed them, and so these old stories are now called legends. Our story today is an Indian 'why' story or legend." Have children find the story title in the table of contents, and suggest that they read the story to find out an Indian tribe's explanation for a certain group of seven stars that they could see in the sky.

INTERPRETING THE STORY

Pages 249-253: After children have finished reading the story, you might explain that we call this group of seven stars the Pleiades. Then encourage youngsters to tell briefly what happened to Little Eagle and his brothers the last time they danced in the forest. Since the story plot is rather loosely knit, you will want to discuss such questions as the following to check comprehension of story events and to bring out implied ideas, sensory imagery, and picturesque language: "Why did the Indians keep seeking new hunting grounds? To what sort of land did the Great Spirit lead the Indians?" During the discussion of the latter question, have the fourth paragraph on page 249 read aloud, and encourage pupils to explain it (especially such phrases as "toward the setting sun," "as eagerly as bees seek blossoms," "grow fat in the forest") and tell what mental pictures it makes them see. Continue, "How did it happen that Little Eagle and his brothers went deep into the forest?" Then discuss what the Indian boys found and what they did in the forest. "Who do you think the mysterious stranger in the forest was? Why do you think so? Why do you suppose the boys' mother didn't want to prepare food for them? Why are there seven dancing stars in the sky instead of eight?"

In conclusion, you might lead children to compare the form of this story with the fable form. Recall with pupils that a fable teaches a lesson and ask, "Do you think that as the Indian children of long ago heard this legend, they discovered a lesson in it? What lesson does this story seem to teach?" Perhaps youngsters will decide that the story might have been told to the children of the tribe not only to explain the seven stars in the sky but also to increase their respect for the Great Spirit.

Meeting individual needs: The Indian legends may open up a whole new area of reading interest particularly for superior readers. Encourage those who exhibit special interest in Indian legends to read and report to their classmates the Indian explanations for the four seasons, the woodpecker's red head, and so on.

EXTENDING SKILLS AND ABILITIES

Making inferences: In contrast to the clear-cut, definite form of the European folk tales, the plots of the Indian tales are loosely organized and incompletely developed. The reader must often read between the lines for ideas that are inferred but not directly stated. As children answer the following questions, have them read passages from the story that support their answers:

Did the Indians usually pay attention to the Great Spirit?
Did the squaws of the tribe have many tasks?
Were Little Eagle and his brothers frightened by the stranger's warning?
Was the squaw sorry that she had been cross to the boys? Why did she think they were rising into the sky?
How did Little Eagle's interest in food keep him from becoming a star?

Phonetic analysis: This exercise is designed to extend children's awareness of patterns of accent in our language. (See the italic insert on page 200 of this *Guidebook*.) You might begin by saying, "We have noticed that in a long word in our language, the accent usually falls on the first or second syllable because the word is easier to say that way. Some words in our language have two accents. One of these accents is not stressed as much as the other. We call this lighter accent a *secondary accent*. [Write the term.] The stronger accent we call a *primary accent*. [Write the term.] Dictionaries and glossaries use two kinds of marks to distinguish these accents. Let's turn to our glossary and find all the words that have these two accents. As you find these words, tell them to me and I'll write them on the board." As children respond, write:

al' li ga' tor	op' por tu' ni ty
earth' quake'	o' ver come'
flap' jack'	thun' der bolt'
mid' sum' mer	un' der take'

Continue, "Many words in our language in addition to having one heavy stress may have one or more lighter accents. You notice that these words have one primary and one secondary accent. Let's pronounce these words again and see if we can hear the two accents." Lead pupils to note also that in each of these words the first or second syllable has a primary or secondary accent—a further illustration of the generalization developed in the exercise on pages 199-200 of this *Guidebook*.

If pupils are using the *Thorndike-Barnhart Beginning Dictionary*, have them use pages 64 and 65, which deal with words containing primary and secondary accents.

Think-and-Do Book: Use pages 68 and 69. The implied and expressed comparisons used in the sentences on page 68 provide further experience in interpreting figurative language.

Listening to music: After reading an authentic American Indian legend ("The Seven Dancing Stars"), children will probably enjoy hearing examples of the music of various Indian tribes as well. If the record album *Music of American Indians* is available, play a few of the songs and dances for the class. The "Notes for Teachers" that accompany the album contain interesting information about Indian customs and the significance of each selection which you will want to refer to before introducing the music.

Enjoying literature: Sara Teasdale's poem "The Falling Star" is very appropriate to "The Seven Dancing Stars." It is an example of how most of us carry over some of the superstitions that existed in the days before people knew why things happen. The poem is so lovely that it is worth learning. By the time you have read it three or four times, youngsters will know it and will say it with you.

Rumpelstiltskin PAGES 254-267

Sight Word:	Rumpelstiltskin
Attack Words:	*lass* fetch* withered* wisp* dwarf* suspected* madam* steed* vow's** (glossary)
	rusty* (root+suffix; rust—position of single vowel letter)
	stool* (meaning clues to determine sound of *oo*)
	spun* sprung* mes′sen ger* (position of single vowel letter)
	heap* nay* (two vowel letters together)
	compared* (root with *e* dropped + ending; com pare′— *a* followed by *r* and final *e*)
	wealth* (meaning clues to determine vowel sound)

This story, like "Hansel and Gretel," is one of the perennial favorites from the Grimm brothers' collection of folk tales. It has the kind of characters that make a fairy story unforgettable—an ugly dwarf with magical power, who is comical, irascible, kind, and grasping by turns, a fair maiden in distress, a king who loves the maiden and gold with equal fervor. Its cumulative plot structure, typical of many folk tales, adds to the suspense. And for the sheer fun of rolling the queer names on the tongue, for savoring its quaint language patterns and the dwarf's incantations, youngsters will want to read it aloud over and over again.

PREPARING FOR READING

Establishing background and presenting vocabulary: Comment, "Today's story may be one of your favorites from the Grimm brothers' collection of folk tales. It's about an odd-looking dwarf with a most peculiar name, who made several bargains with a beautiful maiden in distress." Have pupils turn to the table of contents to find the picture of the dwarf and to learn his name, which is the story title. Then comment, "Yes, *Rumpelstiltskin* was his name, and he possessed strange, magical powers as you will see."

INTERPRETING THE STORY

Pages 254-260: When pupils have located the story, have the subtitle read, and suggest that they read the first part of the story to find out what magical powers the dwarf possessed and how he used them to bargain with a fair young lass. After silent reading, let children relate the main events. Then ask, "What kind of person was the miller? the king? What did the dwarf look like? How many bargains did he make with the maid? Why did she readily promise to give him her first-born child? How do you know she must have forgotten her promise when her first child was born?" (Discuss the meaning of the phrase "beyond compare.")

Pages 261-267: Have pupils read the subtitle on page 261 and discuss the implications of the picture. Then suggest that pupils finish the story to find out what the new bargain was and whether it enabled the queen to keep her child. When pupils have finished, allow time for their spontaneous comments on the satisfactory outcome of the story. Then encourage discussion of the new bargain and the queen's desperation as she tried to guess the dwarf's name. Youngsters will enjoy trying to pronounce the silly sounding names she guessed the first time. Have someone read aloud pages 264 and 265 to bring out the marked contrast between the eeriness of the scene in which the dwarf dances in the firelight and the wild speed of the messenger's two rides. Then ask, "What did the queen do to deceive the dwarf before and during their last meeting? Why do you suppose she did so? Did any of you feel sorry for the dwarf? Why [or why not]?"

Extending interpretation: Ask, "What character in this story will you remember the longest? Why? [Pupils will probably agree that the dwarf is the most memorable character because both his behavior and his appearance are not only more unusual but are also described in greater detail than are the other story characters'.]" You might point out that vividly portrayed "bad" characters are typical of folk tales, and encourage pupils to mention other "villains," male or female, that immediately come to mind when one thinks of fairy stories. Then ask, "Why do you suppose the dwarf wanted the queen's child? What other fairy tales have you read in which a wicked character wanted to take someone's child?" During the discussion of these questions, point out that this situation or theme is another characteristic of folk literature.

Oral interpretation: In preparation for the puppet dramatization of the story suggested in the last section of the lesson plan, help pupils decide into how many parts or acts the story can be divided. Then have children skim the story for clues that tell how the various characters felt and must have sounded as they talked. For example, how should the part of the maiden be read in the first part of the story to bring out her great despair? Encourage pupils to expand the dialogue by making up speeches that are merely indicated by narrative text. (On page 256, for example, what did the girl say and how did she sound when she told the dwarf the truth? when she promised to give him her necklace?)

EXTENDING SKILLS AND ABILITIES

Identifying elements of style: If the old tales are read aloud, as of course they are meant to be, children cannot help becoming aware of the distinctive style that is one reason for their ageless charm. Already youngsters have talked over the use of figurative language, characterizations, and certain plot situations common to the old tales. To promote further awareness of the picturesque language and the frequent poetic devices used in folk tales, have youngsters read aloud such sentences as "Well and fair . . . Only one more trial, my dear, and you shall toil no more" (page 259) and "Nay, nay! . . . A princess is a princess, and a promise is a promise" (page 262). Discuss the quaint and unusual phrasing, the repetition of the *pr* blend (alliteration), and encourage youngsters to find other examples of words, phrases, or conversations that are picturesque or poetic ("a lass in a thousand," page 254; "Alas and alack! But lo!" page 258; the verses, pages 264 and 266, for example).

Next, recall the repetition of the story incident at the beginning of "The Four Musicians," and ask which important incidents in "Rumpelstiltskin" were repeated three times (the spinning and the name-guessing incidents). Explain that this repetitive style of telling a story is another characteristic of many old tales, and encourage children to think of other examples of old tales they have read or heard that use this repetitive or cumulative type of plot structure ("The Gingerbread Boy," "Three Sillies," "Goodbrand-on-the-Hillside," and so on).

Phonetic analysis: This exercise and page 72 of the *Think-and-Do Book* check pupils' ability to interpret pronunciation symbols quickly and to blend into meaningful word wholes the vowel and consonant sounds that the symbols represent.

You might begin by saying, "Today, we are going to play a game. I'll write a pronunciation on the board. [Write (*hat*).]" Ask children to pronounce the word and use it meaningfully in a phrase or sentence, for example, "a hat on his head." Continue, "Now I'll change one pronunciation symbol and substitute a symbol that stands for a different sound [quickly erase the *a* in (*hat*) and substitute ē making (*hēt*) and have *heat* used meaningfully]. One sound can entirely change the meaning and pronunciation of a word, can't it?" Continue forming the following pronunciations by substitution and having pupils use each new word in a phrase or sentence. Suggest that pupils refer to the short pronunciation key at the bottom of a right-hand glossary page for any help that they may need with vowel symbols. (You will note that each of the following pronunciations is formed from the preceding one by merely changing one symbol; the spellings are given merely for your convenience.)

(hit)	hit	(hed)	head	(bēd)	bead	(kôl)	call
(hīt)	height	(led)	lead	(bud)	bud	(kōl)	coal
(hăt)	hate	(lēd)	lead	(bid)	bid	(kül)	cool
(hot)	hot	(lĭd)	lid	(bil)	bill	(fül)	fool
(hut)	hut	(līd)	lied	(bel)	bell	(foil)	foil
(hüt)	hoot	(lad)	lad	(bôl)	ball	(foul)	fowl
(hėrt)	hurt	(lād)	laid	(bōl)	bowl	(fôl)	fall
(hėrd)	herd	(lōd)	load	(bùl)	bull	(fāl)	fail
(hùd)	hood	(loud)	loud	(bāl)	bale	(fel)	fell
(had)	had	(boud)	bowed	(boil)	boil	(fēl)	feel
(hid)	hid	(berd)	bird	(koil)	coil	(fùl)	full
(hīd)	hide	(bad)	bad	(kėrl)	curl	(fil)	fill
(hēd)	heed	(bed)	bed	(kil)	kill	(fīl)	file

Use similar procedures with these words, which review certain *r*-controlled vowel sounds:

(fär)	far	(kãr)	care	(bôr)	bore
(fãr)	fare	(kär)	car	(dôr)	door
(fôr)	four	(bär)	bar	(dãr)	dare
(kôr)	core	(bãr)	bear	(pãr)	pear

Think-and-Do Book: Use pages 70, 71, and 72. After pupils have read the article about the Grimm brothers on page 71, they are asked to decide on the basis of that information whether or not certain ideas are implied—an ability vitally necessary to the intelligent use of source materials.

EXTENDING INTERESTS

Reproducing the story: "Rumpelstiltskin" is a favorite folk tale that lends itself to dramatization with puppets even more effectively than if the children themselves were to play the parts. Hand puppets are easier to make and handle than marionettes and are especially good for this story in which the puppets can wear flowing capes that will cover the arms of the children. (For books about making puppets, see page 428 in the revised edition of *Time for Fairy Tales*.) It is wise to have several casts for your puppet play so that every child has a chance to play a part.

Shy children, who find it extremely difficult to perform in a play, forget themselves in the unseen role of puppeteer and truly enjoy themselves. Little, timid voices often boom forth boldly, and the withdrawn child will sometimes put his puppet through amazing antics. A good puppet theater is great fun, and once you create such a stage, you can use it again and again for other plays. Not only is a puppet theater enjoyable for children but it also serves as an incentive for clear speech and for inventiveness in many fields—art, music, costuming, and the like.

Enjoying literature: Ask children who are reading *English Fairy Tales* if they have read a story that is very much like "Rumpelstiltskin." If one of your good oral readers knows "Tom Tit Tot," suggest that he read it to the class. If not, you might read it aloud from *Time for Fairy Tales*. It is as humorous as "Rumpelstiltskin" is somber. When youngsters have become familiar with both versions of the story, they might discuss the little magic-maker. What is he—an elf, a goblin, an imp, or what? Two amusing poems in *Time for Poetry*, "The Goblin" and "A Goblinade," may help answer the question.

The Ugly Duckling PAGES 268-278

Attack Words: *gloriously* properly* endure* swans* sought**
rapture* (glossary)
duckling* (root word + meaning clues)
cheep* (two vowel letters together)
hatched* (root + ending; hatch—position of single vowel letter)
tur′key′s* (vowel followed by *r*)
dazzling* (root with *e* dropped + ending; daz′zle—position of single vowel letter)

This version of the famous story that symbolizes Hans Christian Andersen's life has been adapted with every effort to bring out the pathos and the lyric descriptions of the original. Preadolescents will pity the persecuted, lonely duckling, and they will rejoice when he grows up to be a noble swan. Most young readers who have felt inadequate at some time will identify themselves with the duckling and will sense the larger meaning of this allegory.

PREPARING FOR READING

Establishing background: Comment that although we may think of today's story as an old tale, it really isn't a very old story. The man who wrote it was living at the same time as Abraham Lincoln. Continue, "You have probably heard the name of this author, and I'm sure most of you know many of his stories." Mention several of Andersen's fairy tales (especially "The Emperor's New Clothes" if youngsters heard or read it as suggested in the lesson plan for "Tyll's Masterpiece"), and then tell children, if necessary, that the author of today's story is Hans Christian Andersen. Next, have them find the title of the Andersen story in the table of contents, and suggest that they turn to page 268. Ask, "What kind of life do you suppose an ugly duckling would have? You'll find out as you read this story." Then have the first subtitle read aloud and encourage children to read the first part of the story to find out why Mother Duck's baby was considered queer looking. To cue youngsters to the picturesque language in the story say, "Notice the way the author uses words that make you see, hear, and feel things almost as if you were taking part in the story events."

INTERPRETING THE STORY

Pages 268-273: Since children will be eager to finish the story to see what happened to the duckling when he went out alone into the world, you will want to keep the discussion of these pages brief. Encourage children to tell about the hatching of the ugly duckling and his reasons for leaving the duck yard. Ask, "What reason did Mother Duck give for the duckling's looks? How did you feel as you read this last part? [page 272 and the first paragraph on page 273]" Then have the subtitle on page 273 read and suggest, "Let's finish the story to find out about the ugly duckling's search for a home and friends." While pupils are finishing the story, you might write the following phrases on the board:

soft air filled with the odor of clover blossoms
among some slender reeds near a deep, blue lake
hissing, biting, pecking ducks
November wind whistled fiercely outside a hut
dead leaves, icy blasts, dark clouds heavy with snow
dazzling white swans with long, gracefully curved necks
big warm kitchen, laughing, shouting children
dazzling sunshine, joyously singing birds, bright butterflies, flowering bushes, trees
   in full blossom, a glorious sweetness
dazzling white swans, floated lightly as butterflies
glossy feathers, handsomer than the others

Pages 273-278: Encourage pupils to give their reactions to the conclusion of the story by asking, "How did the end of this story make you feel? Why does it make you feel happy that the ugly duckling found out that he was a swan?"

Then, to help children organize the story events on the basis of the vivid sensory imagery that the descriptive language evokes, call attention to the phrases that you have written on the board. Comment, "One of the reasons for Hans Christian Andersen's success as a storyteller was his use of descriptive language that makes his stories come alive for the reader." Then point to the first two phrases on the board and ask, "What can you see, hear, and smell when you read these words? What story events do these words make you think of?" Continue with the remaining words and phrases, encouraging children to describe the sensory images each arouses and to tell how it makes them feel and what story event it recalls.

Then lead children to note that they have retold the story, just from several short phrases—that these words call up a series of vivid images that make it easy to remember the whole story. As the story events are reviewed, you may want to ask such questions as these to check comprehension and to emphasize cause-effect relationships: "Why was Mother Duck relieved that the ugly duckling could swim? What did you think of the way the cat and the hen talked to the duckling? Why do you suppose the duckling was so interested in the swans he saw flying South? Why do you think the duckling felt that he had to go to the swans? Why did the three swans glide out to greet him in such a friendly fashion?"

Extending interpretation: Comment that the story of the ugly duckling's life is much like the story of Hans Christian Andersen's own life. Ask, "Do you think that Andersen had a very happy boyhood? Why not? How did his life finally turn out?" Comment that a great many people who have or have had difficulties early in life find comfort in this story. Then encourage several superior readers to look up Andersen's life in one of the children's encyclopedias. After they have reported to the class, let pupils decide whether Andersen's life was really like that of the ugly duckling.

Oral interpretation: Recall with children that Andersen used many colorful words in this story that help the reader see and hear what was happening, and remind pupils that oral reading is much more effective if the reader visualizes what he is reading and conveys what he sees, hears, and feels to his audience. In preparation for oral interpretation, have youngsters experiment with some of the passages that spark vivid images (for example, the first paragraph on page 268, the fifth paragraph on page 274, and the second paragraph on page 277). Let them plan, also, how to read the conversations in the first part of the story to bring out the gossipy, chatty tone of many of the speeches. Since the story is full of picturesque language that offers many opportunities for effective oral interpretation, you will want to give as many children as possible a chance to read aloud.

EXTENDING SKILLS AND ABILITIES

Using context clues: This exercise, together with page 73 of the *Think-and-Do Book*, is designed to strengthen the ability to discriminate between words that have identical pronunciations but different spellings and meanings (homonyms)—an ability needed as much in spelling as in reading. Begin by writing the words *cheap* and *cheep*. Have the words pronounced and comment, "These two words are pronounced the same, aren't they? But how are they different? Which word am I using in this sentence, ' "Cheep!" said the baby duckling'?" Use similar procedures with the following sentences and words:

The lass _____ a rustling noise. (herd, heard)
The maiden and the prince were a happy _____. (pare, pear, pair)
The dwarf disappeared down the _____. (lain, lane)
The ugly duckling did not _____ what to do. (know, no)
The duckling began to _____ at the swans. (stair, stare)

Immediately following the completion of this exercise, you will want to introduce page 73 of the *Think-and-Do Book* to give pupils an opportunity to apply independently the understanding reviewed in this exercise.

Adapting definitions to context: This exercise strengthens the understanding that to adapt the meanings of words to context, it is sometimes necessary to (1) get a general meaning of the word from reading all its definitions and (2) paraphrase both the definitions and the context in order to fully grasp the meaning of the word in its context (see the italic insert on page 172 of this *Guidebook*). Write the following sentences, underlining the italicized words. As each sentence is read, use procedures similar to those suggested on page 173 of this *Guidebook*.

The cat and the hens showed no *pity* toward the ugly duckling.
Even the children would *sneer* at him.
A falling acorn showed Garo the *folly* of his ideas.
The angry dwarf began to *threaten* the queen.
The messenger was willing to *risk* his life for the queen.

Meeting individual needs: It would be well to plan a special period for talking over with pupils any problems or difficulties they have encountered in using the dictionary. For helpful procedures to use with children who have difficulty in locating entries, in deriving meanings or pronunciations, refer to the appropriate subheads under "Developing and applying dictionary skills and understandings" in the Index of Skills at the back of this *Guidebook*. The page references indexed in lightface type refer to numerous exercises that will provide effective patterns for teaching and reviewing skills and understandings fundamental to using a dictionary.

As you evaluate children's growth in and through reading and plan special-help groups to meet particular needs, you will find the Index of Skills especially helpful. The exercises indexed in lightface type provide valuable teaching techniques and patterns for developing and strengthening specific skills and understandings vital to the total process of interpretation. Moreover, if you wish to use content that pupils have not read for reviewing and strengthening certain skills, these same techniques can be used with many types of reading material (library books, supplementary readers, for example). The pages indexed in boldface numbers refer to pages on which the guidance is directed toward helping the child apply particular skills and abilities during the introducing, reading, and discussing of a story. This type of guidance is as important to growth in and through reading as are the developmental exercises and should be used in connection with reading in all areas of the curriculum.

Think-and-Do Book: Use page 73.

EXTENDING INTERESTS

Enjoying literature: Of all Hans Christian Andersen's stories, "The Ugly Duckling" is probably the best known and most loved. If you have the beautiful edition of this tale that is illustrated by the Danish artist Johannes Larsen, explain that this book was issued in commemoration of the one hundred fiftieth anniversary of the birth of Hans Christian Andersen. Then let someone show the pictures and encourage youngsters to retell the story from the illustrations.

Another Andersen story, which you may wish to read aloud, is "The Real Princess," found in *Time for Fairy Tales.* Although this story is an allegory that pokes fun at foolish beliefs about royalty, children interpret it literally and enjoy its humor. Comment that artists have always enjoyed illustrating this story and show the picture in *Time for Fairy Tales.* Then suggest that pupils make their own pictures for it.

Records: The record *Hans Christian Andersen* has the song version of "The Ugly Duckling" that was presented in the full-length motion picture of the same name. Youngsters will find this adaptation of the story highly entertaining. If there is time, you might play the record, with the brief comment that someone has rewritten Andersen's story of "The Ugly Duckling" as a song, and you think the class will enjoy hearing it.

Many of the old tales have been recorded in various forms. *The Emperor's New Clothes,* for example, has been written in the form of an opera for children; Shakespeare's *A Midsummer Night's Dream* has been adapted as a musical play appropriately set to Mendelssohn's incidental music; and of course, Prokofieff's musical setting of *Peter and the Wolf* is a favorite.

The Golden Eggs PAGES 279-282

Attack Words: *lacked* neglected* bewitched* glittered* rare**
(glossary)
stuttered* (root + ending; stut' ter—position of single
vowel letter)
purest* (root with *e* dropped + ending; pure—final *e*)

This famous fable should be part of every child's literary heritage, since "killing the goose that laid the golden eggs" is an allusion used by English-speaking people the world over. The behavior of the foolish, greedy farmer in the fable explains the significance of the saying. Nine-year-olds are not too young to appreciate the implication of the story events—hasty, thoughtless desire for gain may often destroy the opportunity for future profit.

PREPARING FOR READING

Establishing background: Ask children if they have ever heard anyone talk about "killing the goose that laid the golden eggs," and encourage them to tell what they think the expression means. Then comment that today's story, "The Golden Eggs," is an Aesop fable that explains the saying, and suggest that children read the fable to find out what the saying means.

INTERPRETING THE STORY

Pages 279-282: After silent reading, have children tell the moral of this fable. Comment that the moral is sometimes stated "Much wants more, and loses all" and let pupils explain how this saying fits the fable. Then ask pupils what they think the expression "killing the goose that laid the golden eggs" means. If necessary, help youngsters conclude that often something that may be valuable is wasted or destroyed through greediness, thoughtlessness, or haste. You might suggest an example of this generalization (such as chasing the birds from one's yard, forgetting that they eat many insects) and encourage children to think of other examples.

Then have youngsters tell what kind of people the farmer and his wife were in the first part of the story and how possessing the rare goose changed them. Discuss with children the meaning of such expressions as "overcome with rapture," "conceal this rare treasure," "couple's rapture knew no bounds," "bewitched by dazzling dreams of rare wealth." Did pupils use the glossary or sentence context to derive the meaning of the new word *rare?* Which entry word, *rare*[1] or *rare*[2], fits the context of this story?

In conclusion, suggest that pupils reread the second paragraph on page 282 and discuss the farmer's boasting and his grand plans for spending his great wealth before he has it. Ask children what girl in another of Aesop's fables the farmer reminds them of. Youngsters will probably mention the foolish milkmaid in "The Milkmaid and Her Pail." Recall the moral of that fable (Don't count your chickens before they are hatched) and ask how it applies to the farmer in today's story. The use of page 74 of the *Think-and-Do Book* gives pupils further experience in generalizing. After they have read a fable, children are asked to decide which of several morals or old sayings the fable illustrates.

Oral interpretation: Children will enjoy reading this story in the form of a play, with a narrator and two youngsters taking the parts of the farmer and his wife. Before the oral reading, skim the story with pupils, helping them plan how to bring out the bewilderment and excitement of the couple as revealed in their conversations on pages 280 and 281 (point out that the short lines in "G-G-G-Goose," "S-S-S-Solid," and "I-I-In" indicate stuttering) and the boastfulness, greediness, and despair in the farmer's speeches on the last page.

EXTENDING SKILLS AND ABILITIES

Memory based on association: To introduce this exercise, explain that you will read some speeches from the stories in this unit. Encourage pupils to listen carefully and to form vivid mental pictures of what was happening in the story at the time the words were spoken. As you read each of the quotations on this and the following page, ask which story it brings to mind. (Suggest that children refer to the table of contents, if necessary, to recall the story title.) Then have pupils tell who was speaking, when in the story he made the speech, and why he made it (what had happened to prompt the character's comment).

1. "I never dreamed of so much happiness when I was an ugly duckling!"
2. "Beware! Beware! Strange things happen in this enchanted place."
3. "We cannot live in that house any more. In the kitchen a horrible witch scratched me with her sharp nails."

4, "Cock-a-doodle-doo! Cock-a-doodle-doo! I know how to flatter, too!"
5 "I vow the witches have told you my name!"
6 "If I had not been so greedy, I could have improved my good fortune."
7 "Nature always knows best what is good for the world."
8 "A princess is a princess, and a promise is a promise."
9 "But he is so ugly. It's a pity he can't be made over."
10 "I confess that I have fooled you. But it was the only way I could please you."

EVALUATING SKILLS AND ABILITIES

You may want to start now to record and summarize your informal evaluation of each child's progress. To begin, it would be helpful to ask yourself the questions on pages 248-249 of the *Guidebook* for the new *Times and Places* and to record the answers. In view of the skills and understandings that have been developed and emphasized at Book Four² level, you will also want to record the answers to the following questions. (The page references in parentheses after each question indicate pages in this *Guidebook* on which there is an italic insert pointing out the importance of the skill or understanding involved.)

> Does he try to use independently any pronunciation key he may encounter in a glossary, dictionary, or encyclopedia? (page 106)
>
> Is he able to generalize the meaning of an unknown word from reading all its definitions and to paraphrase the wording of the definitions and the context, when necessary, to fuse the meaning of the word with the sentence in which it appears? (page 172)
>
> Does he locate and use source materials independently when the need arises? (pages 153-154)
>
> Is he able to perceive pertinent relationships that enable him not only to compare past times with the present but to note significant points of comparison within a given period of past time? (page 148)

When such personal observations are checked against pupils' responses on the pages in the *Think-and-Do Book*, you will be better able to judge the type of guidance needed as well as the rate at which the child can proceed with success at the next level of The New Basic Reading Program.

Think-and-Do Book: Use page 74.

EXTENDING INTERESTS

Enjoying literature: By now, children are accustomed to the idea that a fable is told to teach a lesson—that the moral is usually the last sentence of the fable and is often written just below the fable for emphasis. You might read a fable from *Time for Fairy Tales* (pages 224-230 in the revised edition) and see whether pupils can supply the moral. If you use "The Wolf in Sheep's Clothing," for example, children who are adept at generalizing may express the moral in this way: "You can't always tell what people are like from the way they look." Pupils who are satisfied with "The sheep were foolish to think the wolf was a sheep just because he was wearing a sheep's skin" might be led to state the moral in more general terms—for example, "You can't tell about people just by looking at what they wear." You may find that some pupils cannot arrive at a generalization at all, for fables are the most difficult of all forms of literature for children. If the activity does not succeed, read the moral at the end of the fable and have pupils tell how they might apply it in their lives.

Independent supplementary reading: In addition to reading aloud some of their favorite selections from other readers, children might also like to illustrate a few with the idea of displaying the pictures as advertisements for stories they think their classmates would enjoy. Each illustration should bear the title of the selection, the book in which it is found, and the number of the page on which it begins.

Cinder Lad   PAGES 283-293

Attack Words: *creaked* earthquake* sneered* armor* elder* realm* gallant** (glossary)

cin′der* slip′per y* (position of single vowel letter)

knight* (*i* followed by *gh*)

claimed* (root + ending; claim—two vowel letters together)

fur′ther* (vowel followed by *r*)

The theme of this old Norse tale is one that has long been a favorite of storytellers—that of the lowly, misunderstood person who finally comes into his own. Cinder Lad, with amusing nonchalance typical of story characters in Norse folk tales, three times braves magic, earthshaking rumblings and collects three gallant steeds that later help him win a rich reward. The plot and characterizations of this story will undoubtedly remind young readers of "Cinderella." And they will rejoice at Cinder Lad's triumph over his contemptuous brothers and his fabulous reward just as they did at Cinderella's good fortune.

PREPARING FOR READING

Establishing background: Explain that the last story in the book is an old Norse folk tale that had long been a favorite with Norwegian people before it ever came to be written down. Have pupils note the story title in the table of contents and ask which well-known fairy story the title "Cinder Lad" reminds them of. When children mention "Cinderella," comment, "Although most of the story events in 'Cinder Lad' are quite different from those in 'Cinderella' I think you'll find that several of the characters in today's story and something that happens at the end of the story will remind you of 'Cinderella.'"

INTERPRETING THE STORY

Pages 283-287: Have the first subtitle read, and ask pupils to read as far as the next subtitle to find out what the mystery of the hayfield was and how Cinder Lad solved it. You might recall with pupils the repetitive style or structure used in many folk tales, and suggest that they notice how repetition of story incidents is used in this tale.

After silent reading, ask children to tell what had been happening to the farmer's prize hayfield and what he decided to do to protect his crop. Then lead children to discuss what happened when the two elder sons were sent to watch the meadow. Ask, "How did Cinder Lad solve the mystery of the hayfield? What did Cinder Lad's brothers think of him? What do you think of Cinder Lad? [You might talk over the amusing nonchalance of Cinder Lad's remark on page 284. What does it reveal about the difference between Cinder Lad and his brothers?] Do you think his brothers would have believed him if he had told them what happened at the meadow?" Then discuss the repetition of story events that have occurred so far. Did pupils note the recurring pattern of threes? (three brothers, Cinder Lad's three trips to the hayfield, the three horses) Before youngsters resume silent reading of the story, clarify the meaning of such phrases as "Midsummer's Eve" (explain that Midsummer's Eve was thought to be a night when many magic events were likely to occur), "took to his heels," "a spanking big horse" (if necessary, suggest that pupils consult the dictionary for the meaning of *spanking* in this context), "proceeded to conceal," "questioned him closely."

Pages 287-293: Have the second subtitle read and ask, "What do you suppose the trials will be? How many would you guess there might be? Do you suppose Cinder Lad and the three fine horses he concealed will take part in them?" Allow a few moments for conjectures and then suggest that pupils finish the story to see whether they were right.

When children have finished, ask, "What was the purpose of the trials? How many trials were there? Did you expect there might be three? Why? At what point in the story did you first guess that it was Cinder Lad who was the mysterious knight? What gave you the clue?" Then discuss the two elder brothers' treatment of Cinder Lad. Ask pupils to find and read aloud passages that tell what he did and said that prevented his brothers from ever suspecting that he was the winning knight at each trial. Why did no one recognize Cinder Lad at the trials? Then encourage youngsters to tell how Cinder Lad was proclaimed the winner of the princess' hand and of the Southern half of the king's realm. Ask, "Did you like the way this story ended? Why?"

In conclusion, ask, "How did the events at the end of this story remind you of the way 'Cinderella' ended?" The marriage of a humble peasant lad or lass to a princess or a prince is a familiar characteristic of folk tales, and youngsters undoubtedly can recall other tales that tell of such marriages. Children will enjoy thinking of other points of comparison between "Cinder Lad" and "Cinderella," for example, the sneering older brothers in "Cinder Lad" and the haughty stepsisters in "Cinderella," Cinder Lad's three trials on the glass hill and Cinderella's three excursions to the king's ball, the royal search in each story to uncover the identity of the person who deserves the reward. Perhaps most obvious is the theme of both stories—the eventual triumph of a lowly, misunderstood young brother or sister.

Oral interpretation: As they read this story aloud, children will have many opportunities to use varying tones of voice to bring out the mood and sensory imagery of the narrative passages and the emotional reactions of the characters in their speeches. Encourage pupils to skim the story to decide how they would bring out the sneering tones of the brothers' speeches, the mysterious sounds and happenings at the hayfield on Midsummer's Eve, the excitement of the three trials at the glass hill, and the satisfying outcome of the king's search for the knight in the golden armor.

EVALUATING SKILLS AND ABILITIES

The results of the Basic Reading Test to accompany *More Times and Places* will provide an objective check of children's mastery of reading skills. Careful personal observations and evaluations combined with the results obtained on this test will clearly indicate those youngsters who will experience no difficulty at Book Five[1] level as well as those children who may continue to need special help. For example, youngsters who have evidenced weaknesses in specific skills will profit from further teaching and review of the "Extending Skills and Abilities" exercises in this *Guidebook*, which give background for similar ones at the next level (see also the italic insert on pages 212-213).

Think-and-Do Book: Use pages 75, 76, and 77. Children's responses on page 76 will give you an objective check of their ability to use partial word form clues and context as aids to rapid word recognition. On page 77 pupils use sensory imagery and association as a basis for recalling stories they have read in Unit 4.

EXTENDING INTERESTS

Enjoying literature: Ask pupils whether "Cinder Lad" reminds them of any other folk tales besides "Cinderella." Some children may be reminded of the story "Tattercoats," one of the most delightful of the many variations on the "Cinderella" theme. If youngsters are not familiar with it, you will want to read it aloud and have pupils tell in what ways it is similar to "Cinderella." "Tattercoats" can be found in *Time for Fairy Tales*.

Those children who have not had an opportunity to relate or read aloud one of their favorite stories from the library books that they have been reading might be given time to do so now.

CONCLUDING ACTIVITIES

Summarizing the book: Look over the story titles in the table of contents with the children, and with the aid of the unit titles help them generalize about the kind of stories in each unit. Then continue with such questions as:

1. Which unit of stories did you enjoy most? Why?
2. Of all the places we read about in the first unit, which would you like most to visit? Why?
3. Do you think that when they were children, the famous Americans we read about were much different from you or the story characters in the first unit? What makes you think they were not?

4. Which of the animal stories did you like best? Why?
5. How do you feel about the fact that some of the animals we read about are becoming scarce in this country? What can boys and girls do to protect wild animal and plant life?
6. Do you think the famous Americans in the third unit might have read or heard the stories we just finished reading in the last unit? What makes you think so?
7. From what you know of these famous Americans, which of the old tales do you think they might have liked best? Why? (This question will challenge superior pupils. They may reason, for example, that Clara Barton might have preferred "The Ugly Duckling" or "Cinder Lad" because of her sympathy for people in trouble, or that P. T. Barnum would have laughed heartily at "Tyll's Masterpiece" because he enjoyed a good joke whether it was played on him or on someone else. Noah Webster, on the other hand, might have shown a preference for the three fables in the unit, since he was a teacher at heart and liked to teach in an entertaining way. If no one is able to offer any suggestions in answer to this question, do not press the point. The thinking skills involved may be too advanced for all your pupils.)

Encourage youngsters to reread their favorite stories. Perhaps, too, they would like to repeat their dramatization of "The Four Musicians" or the puppet performance of "Rumpelstiltskin" for another class.

Bibliography

SELECTIONS FROM OTHER READERS[1]

Unit one: Young Citizens Here and There

"Sandy Smith," pages 90-96, "The Little Cactus," pages 234-241, "The Winner," pages 266-273, *Beyond Treasure Valley* (book 3^1), American Book, 1958.

"Judy's Vacation," pages 103-114, *Do and Dare* (book 3^2), Heath, 1955.

"The Dinner Bell," pages 246-263, *Looking Ahead* (book 3^1), Houghton, 1957.

"Fun along the Creek," pages 100-113, *Once upon a Storytime* (book 3^2), Lyons, 1954.

"Jeremy Rides the Tractor," pages 57-63, *Good Times Today* (book 3^1), Macmillan, 1957.

"The Bottle That Went to Sea," pages 10-20, *Story Carnival* (book 3), Singer, 1960.

"Louise and Red," pages 7-22, "Jack and the Navajo Boy," pages 93-100, "Watching the Sheep," pages 101-110, The New *Under the Sun* (book 3), University, 1954.

*"Let's Make Gus Smile," pages 46-52, "Slow Poke," pages 106-113, *Along Friendly Roads* (book 3^2), American Book, 1958.

*"Scary Night on the River," pages 10-15, "A Race with the Ice," pages 117-124, *American Adventures* (book 4), American Book, 1959.

*"Old Tom," pages 199-209, "Little Vic," pages 336-345, *Roads to Everywhere* (book 4), Ginn, 1961.

*"It Rained for a Week," pages 24-33, "Chinatown Cat," pages 62-72, "The Jar of Tassai," pages 165-174, *Luck and Pluck* (book 4), Heath, 1955.

*"Meals for Mickey," pages 156-166, *The Brave and Free* (book 6), Heath, 1955.

*"Law of the Timber," pages 112-126, *High Roads* (book 4), Houghton, 1957.

*"Herbert's Can Collection," pages 135-150, *Helping Others* (book 4), Lippincott, 1954.

*"Patsy and Her Pet Lambs," pages 73-80, *Good Times Tomorrow* (book 3^2), Macmillan, 1957.

---

[1] See the "Extending Interests" sections of the lesson plans. Starring of selections is explained on page 44 of this *Guidebook*.

*"Pinto's Luck," pages 60-69, "In the North Woods," pages 70-80, "For Love of the Widgeon," pages 237-248, *Sharing Adventures* (book 4), Macmillan, 1957.

*"Danny's Wish Comes True," pages 32-42, *Story Carnival* (book 3), Singer, 1960.

*"The Painted Horse," pages 56-62, "The Bookshop Mystery," pages 63-70, "Two Hearts," pages 79-85, *Across the Valley* (book 3²), Winston, 1960.

**"Coronado's Ghost," pages 256-264, *Adventures Here and There* (book 5), American Book, 1959.

**"Homemade Fiddle," pages 199-208, "Gloucester Boy," pages 224-236, *Trails to Treasure* (book 5), Ginn, 1961.

**"Lost in the Marshlands!" pages 10-22, "Two Against the Sea," pages 23-25, *Wings to Adventure* (book 6), Ginn, 1961.

**"Corn-Belt Billy," pages 144-155, *The Brave and Free* (book 6), Heath, 1955.

**"Mr. Songcatcher Comes By," pages 35-47, "Whitey and Jinglebob," pages 87-98, *Sailing Ahead* (book 5), Lippincott, 1954.

**"Wild Dog," pages 172-190, "Race on Ice," pages 319-334, *Moving Forward* (book 6), Lippincott, 1954.

**"Joseph Decides for Himself," pages 204-216, *Days of Adventure* (book 5), Lyons, 1956.

**"Skiing," pages 193-200, *The World I Know* (book 5), Macmillan, 1957.

**"The Wood Lot," pages 5-20, "The Letter," pages 21-39, *Runaway Home* (book 6), Row, 1957.

**"The Ranch at Heber's Crossing," pages 82-91, *Across the Blue Bridge* (book 5), Singer, 1960.

Unit two: The Great Outdoors

"Trouble on Smoke Mountain," pages 122-128, "Clever Mother Squirrel," pages 170-176, *Beyond Treasure Valley* (book 3¹), American Book, 1958.

"Fish for Breakfast," pages 156-163, *Friends Far and Near* (book 3²), Ginn, 1961.

"The Tornado," pages 162-170, *Fun and Frolic* (book 3¹), Heath, 1955.

"Lions That Bark," pages 38-43, "Indian Whale Hunters," pages 104-114, "The Beaver at Work," pages 176-182, *Stories from Everywhere* (book 3¹), Lyons, 1954.

"In a National Park," pages 115-142, "Peder's Gull," pages 146-160, "The Twin Fawns," pages 161-172, *Once upon a Storytime* (book 3²), Lyons, 1954.

"The Adventure in the Cornfield," pages 104-113, *Good Times Today* (book 3¹), Macmillan, 1957.

"Baby Bears," pages 63-70, *Story Carnival* (book 3), Singer, 1960.

"Finding Flag," pages 171-180, The New *Under the Sun* (book 3), University, 1954.

"Prairietown, U. S. A.," pages 208-214, *Across the Valley* (book 3²), Winston, 1960.

*"Honk, the Moose," pages 29-38, *Believe and Make-Believe* (book 4), Allyn, 1957.

*"The Reindeer Roundup," pages 144-151, *American Adventures* (book 4), American Book, 1959.

*"A Baby Whale's Adventure," pages 174-185, "Blackie and Mr. Darting Hawk," pages 186-193, *Friends Far and Near* (book 3²), Ginn, 1961.

*"A Sea Family," pages 231-237, "The Snowshoe Rabbit Escapes," pages 238-247, *Roads to Everywhere* (book 4), Ginn, 1961.

*"No Fun for Henry," pages 228-235, *High Roads* (book 4), Houghton, 1957.

*"Corbie," pages 365-382, *From Every Land* (book 6), Laidlaw, 1955.

*"Wild Moose," pages 203-204, *Once upon a Storytime* (book 3²), Lyons, 1954.

*"Exploring Bird Creek," pages 187-202, "The Back Country," pages 331-339, *Meeting New Friends* (book 4), Lyons, 1956.

*"At the Animal Inn," pages 275-282, "Old Charley," pages 293-303, *Sharing Adventures* (book 4), Macmillan, 1957.

*"Baby Hippo Sees His World," pages 3-14, *The World I Know* (book 5), Macmillan, 1957.

*"A Surprise for Old Mary," pages 3-11, *Stories from Near and Far* (book 4), Scribners, 1951.

*"The Beautiful Duck," pages 36-42, *Across the Valley* (book 3²), Winston, 1960.

**"Carca," pages 22-28, "Little Chuck Becomes a Friend," pages 40-50, *Believe and Make-Believe* (book 4), Allyn, 1957.

**"On Arctic Ice," pages 152-158, *American Adventures* (book 4), American Book, 1959.

**"Rack's Victory," pages 80-89, *Adventures Now and Then* (book 6), American Book, 1959.

**"The Trail of the Sandhill Stag," pages 342-352, *Wings to Adventure* (book 6), Ginn, 1961.

**"Kelly Mentioned Bears," pages 8-20, *Bright Peaks* (book 6), Houghton, 1957.

**"Bob Visits the Plains," pages 340-356, "A Hard-Working Toad-Frog," pages 361-368, *Meeting New Friends* (book 4), Lyons, 1956.

**"Raggylug," pages 196-199, *Days of Adventure* (book 5), Lyons, 1956.

**"Jago," pages 283-291, *Sharing Adventures* (book 4), Macmillan, 1957.

**"Oliver's Other World," pages 99-114, *The World I Know* (book 5), Macmillan, 1957.

**"The Black Stallion and the Red Mare," pages 49-62, *Stories Old and New* (book 6), Scribners, 1951.

Unit three: Famous Americans of Other Times

"The Little Cook," pages 25-31, *Story Caravan* (book 3²), Allyn, 1957.

"Daniel Boone Leads the Way," pages 129-135, *Believe and Make-Believe* (book 4), Allyn, 1957.

"Daniel Boone's Cat," pages 272-282, *Do and Dare* (book 3²), Heath, 1955.

"It's Ideas That Count," pages 142-152, *Climbing Higher* (book 3²), Houghton, 1957.

"Will Ropes a Turkey," pages 104-108, *High Roads* (book 4), Houghton, 1957.

*"New Homes in Kentucky," pages 74-80, *Along Friendly Roads* (book 3²), American Book, 1958.

*"A Christmas Gift for the General," pages 23-30, "The Music Maker," pages 191-199, *American Adventures* (book 4), American Book, 1959.

*"Daniel Boone," pages 57-67, "Twelve Seconds," pages 122-131, *Roads to Everywhere* (book 4), Ginn, 1961.

*"The Best Captain on Lake Erie," pages 144-154, *Do and Dare* (book 3²), Heath, 1955.

*"A Heroine of the Great Snow," pages 57-69, "Pocahontas," pages 205-213, *On the Trail of Adventure* (book 4), Laidlaw, 1955.

*"They Came to Trade," pages 91-96, "The Iron Stove," pages 112-119, "The Landlord's Mistake," pages 270-273, "Abe and Austin," pages 276-283, "Lee, of Virginia," pages 308-316, *Meeting New Friends* (book 4), Lyons, 1956.

*"Stevie's Flute," pages 239-252, *Story Carnival* (book 3), Singer, 1960.

*"The Girl Who Could," pages 172-176, *Across the Valley* (book 3²), Winston, 1960.

**"Abe Lincoln and His Sister," pages 148-160, *Finding the Way* (book 5), Allyn, 1957.

**"Sacajawea," pages 62-68, *American Adventures* (book 4), American Book, 1959.

**"America's Lafayette," pages 122-127, *Adventures Here and There* (book 5), American Book, 1959.

**"A Girl Who Loved the Stars," pages 140-149, "Henry Can Fix It," pages 151-160, *Trails to Treasure* (book 5), Ginn, 1961.

**"The Boy Who Put the World on Wheels," page 287, *Bright Peaks* (book 6), Houghton, 1957.

**"The Boy Who Saved a Regiment," pages 164-177, *On the Trail of Adventure* (book 4), Laidlaw, 1955.

**"A Hero of Our Navy," pages 202-222, "Master of Music," pages 293-298, *The World Around Us* (book 5), Laidlaw, 1955.

**"Pioneer and President," pages 176-184, "The Soldier Who Loved Peace," pages 186-197, "Real-Men Artists," pages 331-342, *From Every Land* (book 6), Laidlaw, 1955.

**"A Gift for Young Abe," pages 26-33, *Moving Forward* (book 6), Lippincott, 1954.

**"Journey up a Wild River," pages 276-302, "Cody's Boy," pages 317-329, *Days of Adventure* (book 5), Lyons, 1956.

**"The Young Dreamer," pages 25-36, "Sequoyah's Great Invention," pages 152-161, "Snowshoe Thompson," pages 164-173, *Stories to Remember* (book 6), Lyons, 1956.

**"The First Made-in-America Toys," pages 365-373, *On to Adventure* (book 6), Sanborn, 1953.

**"Mr. President," pages 349-354, *Stories Old and New* (book 6), Scribners, 1951.

**"Justin Morgan and the President," pages 74-83, "Tad Lincoln and the Goat," pages 273-283, *Aboard the Story Rocket* (book 6), Singer, 1960.

Unit four: Old Tales from Everywhere

"The Real Princess," pages 45-48, "The Purple Horse," pages 49-59, *Story Caravan* (book 3²), Allyn, 1957.

"Long Nose," pages 83-89, "The Gold Bird," pages 114-121, "Why Night Follows Day," pages 162-169, *Beyond Treasure Valley* (book 3¹), American Book, 1958.

"The Three Feathers," pages 118-128, *Friends Far and Near* (book 3²), Ginn, 1961.

"The Good Flea and the Wicked King," pages 274-280, "Pekka and the Rogues," pages 295-303, *Fun and Frolic* (book 3¹), Heath, 1955.

"The Brave Tin Soldier," pages 175-184, *Do and Dare* (book 3²), Heath, 1955.

"The Stonecutter," pages 265-271, *Looking Ahead* (book 3¹), Houghton, 1957.

"The Fast Sooner Hound," pages 161-183, "The Seven Sticks," pages 200-202, *Climbing Higher* (book 3²), Houghton, 1957.

"The Lion," pages 258-261, *Once upon a Storytime* (book 3²), Lyons, 1954.

"The Half-Chick," pages 111-117, *Story Carnival* (book 3), Singer, 1960.

"Almost Like Magic," pages 24-29, *Into the Wind* (book 3¹), Winston, 1960.

*"The Little Copper Princess," pages 114-126, *Believe and Make-Believe* (book 4), Allyn, 1957.

*"The Giant with the Gray Feathers," pages 90-96, *American Adventures* (book 4), American Book, 1959.

*"The Princess and the Fisherman," pages 143-154, *Friends Far and Near* (book 3²), Ginn, 1961.

*"The Brave Little Tailor, pages 74-85, "Bruce and the Spider," pages 90-91, *Roads to Everywhere* (book 4), Ginn, 1961.

*"The Nose," pages 342-354, *Luck and Pluck* (book 4), Heath, 1955.

*"The Catnip Man's Adventure," pages 372-376, "The Hungry Wolf," pages 393-395, *Meeting New Friends* (book 4), Lyons, 1956.

*"The Boy Who Found a Pebble," pages 142-152, "The Little Birch Twig," pages 306-315, *From Sea to Sea* (book 3¹), Silver, 1946.

*"The Tinder Box," pages 128-137, *Story Carnival* (book 3), Singer, 1960.

*"A Man Named Charles," pages 29-35, "The Little Red House," pages 86-92, "The Chain of Gold," pages 216-224, *Across the Valley* (book 3²), Winston, 1960.

**"Mr. Crow Takes a Wife," pages 133-139, "The Man and the Alligator," pages 256-263, *American Adventures* (book 4), American Book, 1959.

**"Beauty and the Beast," pages 192-201, "The Power of Kindness," pages 250-255, "The Bravest of All," pages 274-282, *Adventures Here and There* (book 5), American Book, 1959.

**"The Bell of Atri," pages 56-60, *Sky Lines* (book 5), Houghton, 1957.

**"The Search for the Beautiful," pages 85-97, *On the Trail of Adventure* (book 4), Laidlaw, 1955.

**"Jan the Prince," pages 297-312, *From Every Land* (book 6), Laidlaw, 1955.

**"Why the Evergreen Trees Never Lose Their Leaves," pages 206-210, *Helping Others* (book 4), Lippincott, 1954.

**"The Proud Salmon," pages 189-191, *Sailing Ahead* (book 5), Lippincott, 1954.

**"Nail Soup," pages 377-380, *Meeting New Friends* (book 4), Lyons, 1956.

**"The Man Whose Trade Was Tricks," pages 131-139, *The World I Know* (book 5), Macmillan, 1957.

**"Why Rabbits Have No Tails," pages 122-125, *Aboard the Story Rocket* (book 6), Singer, 1960.

LIBRARY BOOKS FOR CHILDREN[1]

Unit one: Young Citizens Here and There

Here's a Penny. Carolyn Haywood. Harcourt.
Penny and Peter. Carolyn Haywood. Harcourt.
Penny Goes to Camp. Carolyn Haywood. Morrow.
When the Moon Is New. Laura Bannon. Whitman.
*Cowboy Boots. Shannon Garst. Abingdon.
*Peachtree Island. Mildred Lawrence. Harcourt.
*The School Train. Helen Acker. Abelard.
*Told under Spacious Skies. Association for Childhood Education. Macmillan.
**A Place for Peter. Elizabeth Yates. Coward.
**Across Canada. Clare Bice. Macmillan.
**Blue Willow. Doris Gates. Viking.
**Maggie Rose, Her Birthday Christmas. Ruth Sawyer. Harper.
**Mountain Born. Elizabeth Yates. Coward.
**Prairie School. Lois Lenski. Lippincott.

Unit two: The Great Outdoors

Dash and Dart. Mary and Conrad Buff. Viking.
Spike, the Story of a Whitetail Deer. Robert McClung. Morrow.
The Wild Little Honker. Dorothy Childs Hogner. Walck.
*Honk, the Moose. Phil Stong. Dodd.
*Star of Wild Horse Canyon. Clyde R. Bulla. Crowell.
*The Blind Colt. Glen Rounds. Holiday; Cadmus.
*The Stolen Pony. Glen Rounds. Holiday; Cadmus.
**An Otter's Story. Emil Liers. Viking.
**Brighty of the Grand Canyon. Marguerite Henry. Rand.
**Let Them Live. Dorothy P. Lathrop. Macmillan.
**Snow Dog. Jim Kjelgaard. Grosset.
**The Biggest Bear on Earth. Harold McCracken. Lippincott.

Unit three: Famous Americans of Other Times

Buffalo Bill. Ingri and Edgar Parin d'Aulaire. Doubleday.
Martin and Abraham Lincoln. Catherine C. Coblentz. Childrens Press; Cadmus.
Tom Edison: Boy Inventor. Sue Guthridge. Bobbs.
*Abe Lincoln: Frontier Boy. Augusta Stevenson. Bobbs.
*Benjamin Franklin. Ingri and Edgar Parin d'Aulaire. Doubleday.

---

[1] This section of the bibliography contains the library books listed in the bibliography of *More Times and Places*, with publishers' names added. For your convenience, the books have been listed in the order of difficulty and starred as are the "Selections from Other Readers" (see page 44). Additional library books, which are suggested in specific lesson plans, are listed on page 229 of this *Guidebook*.

Boat Builder, the Story of Robert Fulton. Clara Ingram Judson. Scribners.

**Clara Barton: Girl Nurse*. Augusta Stevenson. Bobbs.

George Washington: An Initial Biography. Genevieve Foster. Scribners.

George Washington: Boy Leader. Augusta Stevenson. Bobbs.

Kit Carson, Mountain Man. Margaret E. Bell. Morrow.

The Story of Daniel Boone. William O. Steele. Grosset.

The Story of Thomas Alva Edison. Enid La Monte Meadowcroft. Grosset.

**Abraham Lincoln: An Initial Biography*. Genevieve Foster. Scribners.

**Abraham Lincoln, Friend of the People*. Clara Ingram Judson. Follett.

**Betsy Ross and the Flag*. Jane Mayer. Random; Cadmus.

**George Washington, Leader of the People*. Clara Ingram Judson. Follett.

**The Story of John Paul Jones*. Iris Vinton. Grosset.

**The Story of Mad Anthony Wayne*. Hazel Wilson. Grosset.

Unit four: Old Tales from Everywhere

Chanticleer and the Fox. Geoffrey Chaucer. Adapted and illustrated by Barbara Cooney. Crowell.

Dick Whittington and His Cat. Marcia Brown. Scribners.

Gone Is Gone. Retold and illustrated by Wanda Gág. Coward.

Peter and the Wolf. Serge Prokofieff. Illustrated by Warren Chappell. Knopf.

Puss in Boots. Charles Perrault. Illustrated by Marcia Brown. Scribners.

The Emperor's New Clothes. Hans Christian Andersen. Illustrated by Virginia Lee Burton. Houghton; Cadmus.

The Steadfast Tin Soldier. Hans Christian Andersen. Translated by M. R. James. Illustrated by Marcia Brown. Scribners.

The Ugly Duckling. Hans Christian Andersen. Translated by R. P. Keigwin. Illustrated by Johannes Larsen. Macmillan.

More Tales from Grimm. Translated and illustrated by Wanda Gág. Coward.

Picture Tales from Spain. Retold by Ruth Sawyer. Lippincott.

Tales from Grimm. Translated and illustrated by Wanda Gág. Coward; Cadmus.

Tales of Faraway Folk. Babette Deutsch and Avrahm Yarmolinsky. Harper.

Three Gay Tales from Grimm. Translated and illustrated by Wanda Gág. Coward; Cadmus.

**Aesop's Fables*. George Tyler Townsend and Thomas James. Lippincott.

**Andersen's Fairy Tales*. Hans Christian Andersen. Translated by Mrs. E. V. Lucas and Mrs. H. B. Paull. Grosset.

**Chimney Corner Fairy Tales*. Edited by Veronica S. Hutchinson. Putnam.

**East o' the Sun and West o' the Moon*. Peter Asbjörnsen and Jörgen Moe. Retold by Gudrun Thorne-Thomsen. Row.

**English Fairy Tales*. Collected by Joseph Jacobs. Putnam.

**Giants and Witches and a Dragon or Two*. Compiled by Phyllis R. Fenner. Knopf.

**Grimms' Fairy Tales*. Jacob and Wilhelm Grimm. Retold by Mrs. E. V. Lucas, Lucy Crane, and Marian Edwardes. Grosset.

**More English Fairy Tales*. Collected and edited by Joseph Jacobs. Putnam.

**Padre Porko, the Gentlemanly Pig*. Robert Davis. Holiday.
**Princesses and Peasant Boys*. Selected by Phyllis R. Fenner. Knopf.
**The Three Sneezes and Other Swiss Tales*. Roger Duvoisin. Knopf.
**Time to Laugh*. Selected by Phyllis R. Fenner. Knopf.

ADDITIONAL LIBRARY BOOKS REFERRED TO IN THIS GUIDEBOOK

Abraham Lincoln. Ingri and Edgar Parin d'Aulaire. Doubleday.
Deer Mountain Hideaway. E. H. Lansing. Crowell; Cadmus.
**The Wahoo Bobcat*. Joseph Wharton Lippincott. Lippincott.

REFERENCE BOOKS

Britannica Junior. Encyclopaedia Britannica.
Compton's Pictured Encyclopedia. Compton.
Jordan, Emil L. *Hammond's Nature Atlas of America*. Hammond.
Parker, Bertha Morris. *Saving Our Wild Life*. Row.
————. *The Golden Treasury of Natural History*. Simon.
———— and Park, Thomas. *Animal Travels*. Row.
The World Book Encyclopedia. Field.

COLLECTIONS OF STORIES AND POEMS

Arbuthnot, May Hill, comp. *Time for Fairy Tales, Old and New*, Revised Edition. Scott, Foresman.
————. *Time for Poetry*, Revised Edition. Scott, Foresman.
————. *Time for Poetry*. General Edition, Revised. Scott, Foresman.
————. *Time for True Tales, and Almost True*, Revised Edition. Scott, Foresman.
Association for Childhood Education, Literature Committee. *Told under the Stars and Stripes*. Macmillan.
Behn, Harry. *The Little Hill*. Harcourt.
————. *Windy Morning*. Harcourt.
Field, Rachel. *Taxis and Toadstools*. Doubleday.
Jagendorf, M. *Tyll Ulenspiegel's Merry Pranks*. Vanguard.
McCord, David. *Far and Few*. Little.

RECORDS

Emperor's New Clothes. Young People's Records YPR 1007-8 (78 and 45 rpm).
Hans Christian Andersen. Decca DL 8479 (33⅓ rpm).
Midsummer Night's Dream. Children's Record Guild CRG 205 (78 and 45 rpm).
Music of American Indians. RCA E-89 (78 rpm), and WE-89 (45 rpm).
"Peter and the Wolf." RCA LM-1803 (33⅓ rpm), Columbia ML-5183 (33⅓ rpm).
"Till Eulenspiegel's Merry Pranks." RCA LM-2077 (33⅓ rpm), Decca DL 9529 (33⅓ rpm).

MOTION PICTURE FILMS

"Chumming with Chipmunks." Bray Studios.

"Common Animals of the Woods." EBFilms.

"Giants of the North." Bray Studios.

"Maple Sugar Time." NFB Canada.

"The Bear and Its Relatives." Coronet Films.

"The Story of Maple Syrup." University of Michigan.

BOOKS FOR THE TEACHER

Anderson, Irving H., and Dearborn, Walter F. *The Psychology of the Teaching of Reading*. Ronald. 1952.

Arbuthnot, May Hill. *Children and Books*, Revised Edition. Scott, Foresman. 1957.

———. *Keeping Up with Children and Books*. Scott, Foresman. 1959.

Artley, A. Sterl. *Your Child Learns to Read*. Scott, Foresman. 1953.

Betts, Emmett A. *Foundations of Reading Instruction*. American Book. 1954.

Bond, Guy L., and Tinker, Miles A. *Reading Difficulties, Their Diagnosis and Correction*. Appleton. 1957.

Bond, Guy L., and Wagner, Eva Bond. *Teaching the Child to Read*, Third Edition. Macmillan. 1960.

Breckenridge, Marian E., and Vincent, E. Lee. *Child Development*, Fourth Edition. Saunders. 1960.

Burton, William. *Reading in Child Development*. Bobbs. 1956.

Commission on the English Curriculum, National Council of Teachers of English. *Language Arts for Today's Children*. Appleton. 1954.

———. *The English Language Arts*. Appleton. 1952.

De Boer, John J., and Dallmann, Martha. *The Teaching of Reading*. Holt. 1960.

D'Evelyn, Katherine E. *Individual Parent-Teacher Conferences, a Manual for Teachers of Young Children*. Teachers College. 1945.

Eaton, Anne Thaxter. *Treasure for the Taking*, Revised Edition. Viking. 1957.

Elementary Teachers Guide to Free Curriculum Materials. Educators Progress Service. Revised annually.

Gesell, Arnold, and Ilg, Frances L. *The Child from Five to Ten*. Harper. 1946.

Gray, Lillian, and Reese, Dora. *Teaching Children to Read*. Ronald. 1957.

Gray, William S., ed. *Promoting Growth Toward Maturity in Interpreting What Is Read*. Supplementary Educational Monographs, no. 74. University of Chicago Press. 1951.

———. *On Their Own in Reading*, Revised Edition. Scott, Foresman. 1960.

Harris, Albert J. *How to Increase Reading Ability*, Third Edition. Longmans. 1956.

Jenkins, Gladys Gardner, and others. *These Are Your Children*, Expanded Edition. Scott, Foresman. 1953.

Jersild, Arthur T. *Child Psychology*, Fifth Edition. Prentice-Hall. 1960.

The Junior Reviewers Catalog of the Best Books for Children. Latest edition. Junior Reviewers.

Larrick, Nancy. *A Teacher's Guide to Children's Books.* Merrill. 1960.

Leonard, Edith M.; VanDeman, Dorothy D.; and Miles, Lillian E. *Counseling with Parents, in Early Childhood Education.* Macmillan. 1954.

Robinson, Helen M., ed. *Sequential Development of Reading Abilities.* Supplementary Educational Monographs, no. 90. University of Chicago Press. 1960.

Rue, Eloise, comp. *Subject Index to Books for Intermediate Grades,* Second Edition. A. L. A. 1950.

Russell, David H. *Children Learn to Read.* Ginn. 1949.

Witty, Paul, ed. *Development in and Through Reading.* Sixtieth Yearbook of the National Society for the Study of Education, Part 1. University of Chicago Press. 1961.

DIRECTORY OF PUBLISHERS

ABELARD. Abelard-Schuman Limited, New York, N. Y.

ABINGDON. Abingdon Press, New York, N. Y.

A. L. A. American Library Association, Chicago, Ill.

ALLYN. Allyn and Bacon, Inc., Englewood Cliffs, N. J.

AMERICAN BOOK. American Book Company, New York, N. Y.

APPLETON. Appleton-Century-Crofts, Inc., New York, N. Y.

BOBBS. The Bobbs-Merrill Company, Inc., Indianapolis, Ind.

BRAY STUDIOS. Bray Studios, Inc., New York, N. Y.

CADMUS. E. M. Hale and Company, Eau Claire, Wis.

CHILDRENS PRESS. Childrens Press, Chicago, Ill.

CHILDREN'S RECORD GUILD. Children's Record Guild, New York, N. Y.

COLUMBIA. Columbia Records, Inc., New York, N. Y.

COMPTON. F. E. Compton & Company, Chicago, Ill.

CORONET FILMS. Coronet Films, Chicago, Ill.

COWARD. Coward-McCann, Inc., New York, N. Y.

CROWELL. Thomas Y. Crowell Company, New York, N. Y.

DECCA. Decca Records, Inc., New York, N. Y.

DOUBLEDAY. Doubleday & Company, Inc., Garden City, N. Y.

EBFILMS. Encyclopaedia Britannica Films, Inc., Wilmette, Ill.

EDUCATORS PROGRESS SERVICE. Educators Progress Service, Randolph, Wis.

ENCYCLOPAEDIA BRITANNICA. Encyclopaedia Britannica, Inc., Chicago, Ill.

FIELD. Field Enterprises Educational Corporation, Chicago, Ill.

FOLLETT. Follett Publishing Company, Chicago, Ill.

GINN. Ginn and Company, Boston, Mass.

GROSSET. Grosset & Dunlap, Inc., New York, N. Y.

HARCOURT. Harcourt, Brace & World, Inc., New York, N. Y.

HARPER. Harper & Brothers, New York, N. Y.

HEATH. D. C. Heath and Company, Boston, Mass.

HOLIDAY. Holiday House, New York, N. Y.

HOLT. Holt, Rinehart and Winston, Inc., New York, N. Y.

HOUGHTON. Houghton Mifflin Company, Boston, Mass.

JUNIOR REVIEWERS. Junior Reviewers, Aspen, Colo.

KNOPF. Alfred A. Knopf, Inc., New York, N. Y.

LAIDLAW. Laidlaw Brothers, River Forest, Ill.

LIPPINCOTT. J. B. Lippincott Company, Philadelphia, Pa.

LITTLE. Little, Brown and Company, Boston, Mass.

LONGMANS. Longmans, Green & Co., Inc., New York, N. Y.

LYONS. Lyons and Carnahan, Chicago, Ill.

MACMILLAN. The Macmillan Company, New York, N. Y.

MERRILL. Charles E. Merrill Books, Inc., Columbus, Ohio.

MORROW. William Morrow and Company, Inc., New York, N. Y.

NFB CANADA. National Film Board of Canada, New York, N. Y.

PRENTICE-HALL. Prentice-Hall, Inc., Englewood Cliffs, N. J.

PUTNAM. G. P. Putnam's Sons, New York, N. Y.

RAND. Rand McNally & Company, Skokie, Ill.

RANDOM. Random House, New York, N. Y.

RCA. RCA Victor Division, Radio Corporation of America, Camden, N. J.

RONALD. The Ronald Press Company, New York, N. Y.

ROW. Row, Peterson and Company, Evanston, Ill.

SANBORN. Benj. H. Sanborn & Co., division of L. W. Singer Company, Inc. See SINGER.

SAUNDERS. W. B. Saunders Company, Philadelphia, Pa.

SCOTT, FORESMAN. Scott, Foresman and Company, Chicago, Ill.

SCRIBNERS. Charles Scribner's Sons. New York, N. Y.

SILVER. Silver Burdett Company, Morristown, N. J.

SIMON. Simon and Schuster, Inc., New York, N. Y.

SINGER. The L. W. Singer Company, Inc., Syracuse, N. Y.

TEACHERS COLLEGE. Teachers College, Bureau of Publications, Columbia University, New York, N. Y.

UNIVERSITY. The University Publishing Co., Lincoln, Neb.

UNIVERSITY OF CHICAGO PRESS. University of Chicago Press, Chicago, Ill.

UNIVERSITY OF MICHIGAN. University of Michigan, Audio-Visual Education Center, Ann Arbor, Mich.

VANGUARD. The Vanguard Press, Inc., New York, N. Y.

VIKING. The Viking Press, Inc., New York, N. Y.

WALCK. Henry Z. Walck, Inc., New York, N. Y.

WHITMAN. Albert Whitman & Co., Chicago, Ill.

WINSTON. Holt, Rinehart and Winston, Inc., New York, N. Y.

YOUNG PEOPLE'S RECORDS. Young People's Records, Inc., New York, N. Y.

Index of Skills

Page numbers in lightface type refer to exercises in the "Extending Skills and Abilities" section of the lesson plan. Numbers in boldface type refer to pages on which the specific skill is emphasized or applied in other sections of the lesson plan.

On all pages marked with an asterisk, the skill is specifically applied in locating or using source material. The separate abilities to identify a key word or topic, to use an index, to select relevant source materials, to outline, and so on (often referred to as research or study skills), are dependent on the application of such fundamental interpretative skills as interpreting main ideas, evaluating ideas in light of the author's purpose, comprehending phrase and sentence meaning, and perceiving relationships.

PROMOTING GROWTH IN INTERPRETATIVE SKILLS

Interpreting the main idea, pages **59-61,** 67*, **82,** 88-89, 95-96, **104,** 107-108*, **112, 114,** 115-116*, **124*,** 124-125, **126*, 133-134*, 135-136, 137*,** 148-150*, 153*, 158*, 171-172, **174*,** 191, **202,** 205, 214-215. See also the "Interpreting the Story" section of all other lesson plans. (Think-and-Do, pages 2, 7, 17*, 23*, 36, 37*, 41, 42-43*, 57, 64, 69, 74, 75)

Recognizing emotional reactions, motives, and inner drives of story characters, pages **40, 47-48, 55, 63, 65-67, 76,** 89-90, 110-111, **114-115, 128, 155, 157-158, 162,** 163, 171-172, 181, 195-196, **206** (Think-and-Do, pages 5, 9, 11, 36, 53, 59)

Interpreting ideas implied but not directly stated, pages 55, **72,** 72-73, **83, 100, 115,** 116, **128, 129,** 132, **136, 143-144,** 158, **160-161,** 167, 171-172, 195-196, **202,** 202-203, **208, 214.** See also the "Interpreting the Story" section of all other lesson plans. (Think-and-Do, pages 3, 5, 11, 19, 33*, 41, 44*, 56, 71*)

Recognizing story problem or plot structure, pages **46-47, 59-61,** 61, 88-89, 95-96, **104, 123,** 124-125, **186, 189,** 206-207, **218-219** (Think-and-Do, pages 3, 69)

Comprehending phrase and sentence meaning, pages 55, 68, 78, 101, 115-116*, 125-126, 132, 132-133, **137***, 158*, 163, **171**, 172-173, 177-178, 191, 196, 199, **202**, 211-212, 212, **214-215, 218.** See also the "Interpreting the Story" section of all other lesson plans. **(Think-and-Do,** pages 6, 9, 10, 12, 22, 26, 29*, 34, 35, 38, 55, 56, 60, 63, 64, 65, 73, 74, 75)

Recognizing connotations or denotations of words, pages 55, 62, **109,** 110-111, 132-133, **143,** 177-178, **195,** 196, 199, **202, 218 (Think-and-Do,** pages 5, 8, 9, 26, 30, 34, 38, 68)

Interpreting figurative, idiomatic, and picturesque language, pages 55, **100, 104,** 110-111, **122,** 132-133, **171,** 199, **202, 210-211, 218 (Think-and-Do,** pages 38, 66, 68)

Identifying author's purpose, pages 110-111, **147,** 163, **189, 190, 198,** 199, **201, 202, 214, 215, 216-217 (Think-and-Do,** pages 1, 24*, 31*, 34, 41, 69, 74, 75)

Evaluating and reacting to ideas in light of author's purpose, pages 67*, **69***, **107-108***, **109,** 110-111, 115-116*, **126***, **129-130***, **133-134***, **137***, **141,** 148-150*, 153*, 163, **190, 195, 198,** 199, **202, 214, 215, 216-217 (Think-and-Do,** pages 31*, 34, 41, 71*)

Identifying elements of style

Figurative, idiomatic, or picturesque language, pages 55, **104,** 110-111, 132-133, 199, 206-207, **210-211 (Think-and-Do,** pages 34, 66, 68)

Refrain or repetition, pages **186,** 206-207, **218-219**

Forming and reacting to sensory images, pages **39-40,** 62, **76, 87, 100, 102, 104, 109,** 110-111, **114, 118,** 124-125, **128, 136, 162, 187, 190, 202, 210-211 (Think-and-Do,** pages 8, 12, 13*, 19, 34, 42-43*, 45, 77)

Anticipating outcomes, pages **38-39, 53, 59-61, 114, 135, 161-162, 176, 186, 194, 198, 209, 218-219.** See also the "Interpreting the Story" section of all other lesson plans. **(Think-and-Do,** pages 3, 69)

Identifying and evaluating character traits,[1] pages 49, **63, 77, 82-83, 89-90, 105, 115, 144, 145, 153, 155, 157,** 163, **166, 169,** 171-172, **174,** 181, **199, 215, 220-221 (Think-and-Do,** pages 57, 60)

Making judgments and drawing conclusions,[1] pages **40-41,** 48, 54, 62, 83, **89-90, 95, 110,** 114-115, **128-129, 129-130, 132, 136, 138, 144, 153, 157-158, 160-161,** 163, **166-167, 176,** 181, **190, 195, 202, 208, 220-221 (Think-and-Do,** pages 9, 11, 12, 13*, 19, 20*, 31*, 33*, 41, 60, 61)

Generalizing,[1] pages **40-41,** 48, 61, **66, 77,** 83, **88, 89-90, 95, 96, 105, 110, 124, 128-129, 138, 147-148,** 191, **195,** 199, **214, 215, 216-217, 220-221 (Think-and-Do,** pages 28*, 31*, 33*, 46, 60, 64, 74, 75)

---

[1] Children grow through reading as they evaluate character traits, evaluate ideas gained from reading, draw valid conclusions, and formulate generalizations that will serve as guiding principles in their own future conduct.

Perceiving relationships[1]

Analogous, pages **51, 63, 89-90**, 105, **112, 123-124, 129-130, 131-132, 134, 138, 145, 147-148, 153**, 178, 191, **198, 199, 211, 219** (Think-and-Do, pages 2, 24*, 28*, 33*, 39*, 40, 57, 64, 74, 75)

Cause-effect, pages **48, 54, 55, 72, 89-90, 104-105, 110**, 116, **129-130, 143-144, 147, 147-148, 157, 160-161**, 162, 171-172, **210-211, 220-221.** See also the "Interpreting the Story" section of all other lesson plans. (Think-and-Do, pages 13*, 19, 20*, 56, 59)

Class, pages **124, 138, 189, 198, 201, 206**, 206-207 (Think-and-Do, pages 28*, 33*, 40)

General-specific, pages 95-96 (**Think-and-Do, pages 1, 58***)

Part-whole, pages **64, 88-89, 95-96, 109, 131, 148-150** (Think-and-Do, pages 12, 42-43*)

Place or space, pages **46, 52-53, 64, 75-76, 81, 89-90**, 113, **123, 129-130, 131, 137, 142, 147, 147-148** (Think-and-Do, pages 18, 19)

Sequence, pages 83-84, 88-89, 95-96, 148-150 (**Think-and-Do, pages 15, 48*, 50***)

Time, pages 83-84, **142, 143-144, 147, 147-148**, 148-150, 158, **160-161, 163, 167, 171, 176, 180** (Think-and-Do, pages 42-43*, 48*, 50*, 61, 62*)

Comparing and contrasting,[2] pages **51, 55, 62, 63, 69, 70, 77, 79, 89-90**, 102, 105, **107, 112**, 114-115, 118-119, **121-122, 123-124, 128-129, 130, 131-132, 133-134*, 134, 138, 143-144, 145, 147-148, 153*, 160-161, 166-167, 178, 181, 190, 198, 199**, 206-207, **211, 215, 219, 220** (Think-and-Do, pages 2, 19, 24*, 33*, 39*, 45, 51, 64, 74)

Identifying and reacting to the mood or tone of a passage, story, or poem, pages **41, 49, 51, 66-67, 74, 77, 94, 97-98, 100, 109**, 110-111, **115, 121-122, 137**, 169, 196-197, **204, 206, 210-211, 215** (Think-and-Do, page 34)

Understanding the function of phrasing, cadence, and stress in oral interpretation, pages **49, 121-122, 130, 206** (Think-and-Do, pages 36, 53)

Projecting idea, mood, or tone in oral interpretation, pages **41, 49, 66-67, 77, 100, 115, 121-122, 130, 147, 157, 187, 190-191, 195, 198, 206, 211, 215, 219**

Strengthening memory based on

Association, pages 88-89, **89-90**, 95-96, 105, **129-130, 138**, 178, 188, 207, **210-211, 215-216** (Think-and-Do, pages 9, 19, 24*, 40, 45, 61, 63, 70, 77)

---

[1] The ability to perceive relationships and to summarize and organize ideas is basic to using a written outline form. Formal outlining is merely a method of recording a systematic organization of ideas in terms of specific relationships.

[2] Possibly nothing contributes more to the child's growth through reading than his ability to compare ideas or experiences gained from reading one selection with ideas gained from reading other sources or with his direct experience. Basic to this ability is the perceiving of relationships. For example, in Unit 3 of this book, the child is led not only to compare past times with the present but also to note comparisons and contrasts within a given period of past time as they are revealed in stories about the lives of famous Americans.

Logical relationships: cause-effect—pages **89-90, 129-130, 160-161,** 195-196, **220-221;** class—pages **124, 138;** part-whole—pages 83-84, 88-89, 95-96, 188, **210-211,** 215-216; sequence—pages 83-84, 95-96; time—pages 83-84, 148-150, **180 (Think-and-Do,** pages 2, 15, 24*, 28*, 40, 48*, 50*, 56, 61, 62*)

Sensory imagery, pages **76,** 83-84, **210-211,** 215-216 **(Think-and-Do,** pages 19, 24*, 45, 77)

Summarizing and organizing ideas for the purpose of remembering,[1] pages **66, 69, 76,** 83-84, 88-89, **89-90,** 95-96, **104,** 124-125, **129-130, 135-136, 138,** 158, 167, **176, 180, 210-211 (Think-and-Do,** pages 1, 17*, 28*, 33*, 37*, 40, 48*, 50*, 58*, 62*)

PROMOTING GROWTH IN WORD-PERCEPTION SKILLS

Strengthening memory of word forms based on

Association of meaning, pages 62, 67-68, 96-97, 125-126, **131,** 172-173, 177-178, 211-212, 212 **(Think-and-Do,** pages 5, 8, 10, 26, 30, 35, 55, 60, 65, 68, 70, 73)

Careful scrutiny or imagery of form, pages 191-192, 211-212 **(Think-and-Do,** pages 46, 70, 73, 76)

Using context clues to

Determine specific word meanings, pages 67-68, 172-173, 177-178, 196, 211-212 **(Think-and-Do,** pages 26, 35, 55, 73)

Check word analysis, pages 84-85 **(Think-and-Do,** pages 14, 16, 65, 67)

Select appropriate defined meanings and pronunciations in dictionary, pages **66,** 77-78, **87,** 101-102, 132-133 **(Think-and-Do,** pages 22, 38, 55)

Developing and applying phonetic skills and understandings

Auditory perception of language sounds

Consonants and vowels, pages 42-43, 49-51, 55-57, 73-74, 84-85, 167-168 **(Think-and-Do,** pages 4, 6, 16, 47, 49, 54)

Syllables, pages 42-43, 84-85 **(Think-and-Do,** page 67)

Accent, pages 42-43, 84-85, 154, 154-155, 199-200, 203 **(Think-and-Do,** pages 16, 67)

Blending

Consonant and vowel sounds, pages 49-51, 55-57, 73-74, 79, 84-85, 101-102, 105-107, 111-112, 119-120, 207-208 **(Think-and-Do,** pages 4, 6, 9, 14, 16, 22, 25, 27, 32, 47, 49, 54, 67, 72)

---

[1] There are many ways of organizing ideas (in sequence, in order of importance, for example). The biographical chart (page 149 of this *Guidebook*) is a simple, concrete representation of time relationships emphasized throughout Unit 3. The chart form serves as an effective device for helping children summarize and organize ideas for the purpose of remembering.

Understandings that aid in determining accent (see list of understandings below), pages 42-43, 84-85, 101-102, 154, 154-155, 158-160, 163-164, 167-168, 199-200, 203 (**Think-and-Do**, pages 16, 22, 47, 49, 52, 67)

Accent affects vowel sounds in syllables

In words of two or more syllables, one syllable is accented more than the other or others

In words of three or more syllables, one of the first two syllables is accented[1]

In inflected or derived forms, the primary accent usually falls on or within the root word

Using visual clues to vowel sound or syllabication as clues to accent

Two like consonant letters following the first vowel letter are a clue to an accented first syllable and to a short vowel sound in that syllable (hol' low, glit' ter, cot' ton), pages 154, 154-155, 158-159, 163 (**Think-and-Do**, pages 47, 54)

The letters **ck** following a single vowel letter are a clue to an accented first syllable and to a short vowel sound in that syllable (jack' et, crick' et, chuck' le), pages 167-168 (**Think-and-Do**, page 54)

If the final syllable in a word ends in **le** preceded by a consonant, the final syllable is unaccented (ea' gle, ma' ple, ri' fle), pages 163-164, 167-168 (**Think-and-Do**, pages 52, 54)

Two vowel letters together or two vowel letters, one of which is final **e**, in the last syllable may be a clue to an accented final syllable and a long vowel sound in that syllable (ob tain', re late', re quire'), pages 158-160, 163, 167-168 (**Think-and-Do**, pages 49, 54)

In words ending in final **e** preceded by **c** or **g**, final **e** is a clue to the soft sound of **c** or **g** but not necessarily a clue to accent or to a long vowel sound (ad vice', no' tice, ar range', mes' sage), pages 158-160 (**Think-and-Do**, page 49)

Developing and applying structural skills and understandings

Root words are meaning units in inflected and derived forms, pages 67-69, 77-79, 96-97, 125-126, 177-178, 196 (**Think-and-Do**, pages 10, 14, 21, 35, 55, 65)

Prefixes and suffixes are meaning units,[2] pages 67-69 (dis-, im-, un-, re-; -less, -y, -ful, -ness, -er, -ish, -ly, -en), 96-97 (fore-; -ward), 125-126, 177-178 (-or), 196 (**Think-and-Do**, pages 10, 21, 65)

---

[1] In longer words where there is a secondary as well as a primary accent, often the secondary accent falls on the first or second syllable.

[2] At this level the child begins to develop understanding of the grammatical function of suffixes as well as their function as meaning units.

Combining structural and phonetic analysis

Using visual clues to the vowel sound in a one-syllable root word in an inflected or derived form

A single vowel letter followed by one consonant letter before an ending or a suffix[1] is a clue to a long vowel sound and a dropped final **e** in the root word (hoping, diner), pages 158-160 (**Think-and-Do,** page 49)

A single vowel letter followed by two like consonant letters (other than **r**) before an ending or a suffix is a clue to a short vowel sound in the root word (hopping, fussy), pages 77-78, 154-155, 158-159 (**Think-and-Do,** page 47)

Two vowel letters followed by a single consonant letter are a clue to a long vowel sound, unless the vowel letters form a special two-letter vowel symbol (oo, ou, ow, oi, au, aw, etc.), pages 158-160 (**Think-and-Do,** page 49)

Using visual clues to vowel sound or syllabication as clues to accent in a two-syllable root word in an inflected or derived form

Two like consonants before an ending or suffix are a clue to an accented final syllable in the root word and to a short vowel sound in that syllable unless the vowel sound is controlled by the **r** sound (per mit′ ting, oc cur′ ring), pages 77-78, 154, 154-155, 158-159, 163 (**Think-and-Do,** page 47)

A single consonant following a single vowel before an ending or suffix is usually a clue to the schwa sound in an unaccented final syllable (la′ bel ing, slum′ ber ing) or it may be a clue to a long vowel sound and a dropped **e** in an accented final syllable of the root word (se cur′ ing, de scrib′ ing), pages 158-160, 163-164 (**Think-and-Do,** pages 49, 52)

Developing and applying dictionary skills and understandings

Locating entries[2]

Recognizing alphabetical sequence or general alphabetical position, pages 67*, 115-116* (**Think-and-Do,** pages 23*, 29*)

Identifying root words in inflected and derived forms, pages 77-79. See also all entries under "Root words are meaning units in inflected and derived forms."

Deriving meanings

Using context clues to select appropriate definitions. See head under "Using context clues."

Generalizing word meanings, pages 172-173, 212 (**Think-and-Do,** pages 9, 55, 60)

---

[1] This principle applies only when the ending or suffix begins with a vowel letter.

[2] The same basic skills needed to locate an entry in a dictionary are used in locating entries in an encyclopedia or in other indexed source material.

Comprehending definitions in light of context, pages **37, 66,** *77-79,* 101-102, 132-133, 172-173, 212 **(Think-and-Do,** pages 9, 22, 38, 55, 60)

Adapting definitions in light of context, pages *77-78,* 132-133, 172-173, 212 **(Think-and-Do,** page *55)*

Deriving pronunciations

Identifying the basic sound units in our language, pages *42-43, 49-51, 55-57,* 73-74, 105-107, 111-112, 119-120, 207-208 **(Think-and-Do,** pages 4, 6, 16, 25, 27, 32, 47, 49, 54, 72)

Identifying accent in spoken language. See "Auditory perception of language sounds—Accent."

Blending consonant and vowel sounds and blending syllables into word wholes. See all entries under "Blending."

Formulating generalizations that aid in interpreting dictionary pronunciations

There are consonant and vowel sounds in our language, pages *42-43, 55-57,* 73-74, 105-107, 207-208

Meaning may affect pronunciation, pages **87,** 101-102 **(Think-and-Do,** page 22)

In dictionary pronunciations a consonant letter symbol stands for its most common sound, pages *42-43, 55-57,* 105-107, 111-112

In dictionary pronunciations each symbol stands for a sound, pages *42-43, 49-51, 55-57,* 73-74, 105-107, 111-112, 207-208

Understanding the function of special pronunciation symbols (accent mark, diacritical marks, the schwa, etc.), pages *42-43, 49-51, 55-57,* 73-74, 105-107, 111-112, 119-120, 203

Understanding the function of pronunciation keys, pages *42-43, 49-51, 55-57,* 73-74, 105-107, 111-112, 119-120 **(Think-and-Do,** pages 4, 6, 25)

Interpreting pronunciation symbols (using pronunciation keys, accent marks, etc., to determine the pronunciation of words), pages **37-38,** *49-51, 55-57,* 79, 101-102, 105-107, 111-112, 119-120, 144, 203, 207-208 **(Think-and-Do,** pages 4, 6, 9, 22, 25, 27, 32, 54, 55, 72)

1 2 3 4 5 6 7 8 9 10 11 12 13 14 15 16 17 18 19 20 21 22 23 24 25   SI   70 69 68 67 66 65 64 63 62 61

More Times and Places

The 1962 Edition

William S. Gray, Marion Monroe,
A. Sterl Artley, May Hill Arbuthnot

SCOTT, FORESMAN AND COMPANY

Chicago   Atlanta   Dallas   Palo Alto   Fair Lawn, N. J.

Stories

Young Citizens Here and There

The Great Outdoors

Famous Americans of Other Times

Old Tales from Everywhere

3

Young Citizens
Here and There

Unwelcome Passengers

Penny and Peter were sitting on the dock near their seaside cottage. It was easy to see how Penny got his name. In the brilliant sunshine his hair shone like a new penny.

"It seems funny not to be out sailing on the last day of our vacation," he remarked.

"I know," said his brother Peter. "But Father put the sailboat away before he left. I wish he hadn't had to leave early."

After lunch the boys would be returning to the city with their mother. But now they did not know what to do with themselves.

6

Finally Peter had an idea. "Let's take the rowboat," he said. "Let's get some crabs and surprise Mother. Maybe we can have them for lunch."

"Oh, yes!" cried Penny. "I love crabs. But we must catch some fish for bait first."

After getting their fishing lines, the boys caught several fish at the end of the dock. Then they rowed out a short distance in the shallow water and sat motionless in the boat, waiting for crabs. They waited a long time. Finally Penny sighed impatiently.

"There don't seem to be any crabs today," he grumbled.

"Sometimes they all come at once," Peter said. "Let's wait a little longer."

Suddenly the shallow water by the rowboat was full of crabs. Peter grabbed a small net and scooped up a crab that was nibbling at the bait tied on his line.

"Got one!" he shouted. "A big one!"

"Me, too!" cried Penny. "Quick, get it!"

Peter scooped up crabs as fast as he could and dropped them into a basket in the boat.

"Aren't they beauties!" exclaimed Penny. "And won't Mother be surprised to see us bringing home crabs for lunch!"

Peter glanced at the cottage. "Look," he said, frowning. "It's too late to cook the crabs for lunch. Mother's already put out the time-to-eat signal. The old red sweater is hanging on the porch."

Penny's face clouded with disappointment. Then it brightened. "We might take the crabs back to town with us," Penny suggested. "I do hate to waste these crabs."

Peter guided the rowboat up to the dock. After tying the boat securely, the boys lifted out the bushel basket of crabs and carried it across the beach to the house.

"Hi, Mother!" cried Penny. "Look at the beautiful crabs we caught. Almost fifty."

"My goodness!" said his mother. "What shall we do with all those crabs? We are leaving on the two o'clock train."

"Why not take them home with us?" asked Peter. "We could keep them in this basket with some seaweed over them."

"Oh, no," said his mother. "You can't take animals in passenger cars."

"But that rule is for pets," argued Peter. "These crabs aren't pets. They're food."

"Well, can I depend on you boys to take charge of them?" asked their mother. "I've a shopping bag full of odds and ends that I want to take. With the bag and the suitcase, I can't handle anything more."

"We'll take care of the crabs all right," promised the boys.

After a hasty sandwich lunch, the family waited near the door for a taxicab to take them to the train. The boys' mother looked doubtfully at her shopping bag. It was full of half-used packages of flour, salt, tea, and other things. Sticking out of the bag were a pancake turner and a big cooking spoon.

"I hate to take all these things on the train," she said. "But I don't like to leave anything behind that I can use at home."

When the taxi came, everyone piled in.

"You're sure you have plenty of seaweed on the crabs, Peter?" asked his mother.

"Oh, sure, sure," Peter said as he looked at the basket on his lap.

When the taxicab arrived at the station, the train was already there. It was hard to get the heavy basket up the train steps, but the boys finally managed it.

Their mother led the way to a couple of vacant seats facing each other near one end of the car. She put the shopping bag and the suitcase on the shelf for baggage.

"Now, boys," she said, "you'll have to put the basket of crabs on the floor. Just do the best you can with your feet and legs. After all, the crabs were your idea."

As Penny and Peter lowered the crabs to the floor, the train started with a jerk. Penny dropped his end of the basket, and the basket promptly tipped over.

Then what excitement there was! Nearly all the crabs and seaweed spilled out into the aisle. The crabs began scrambling off in every direction. Bits of damp seaweed were still clinging to them.

"E-e-e-e-k!" squealed a frightened woman. "That seaweed's alive! It's walking!"

"No, it isn't!" shrieked another woman. "I mean it's crabs! Watch out!"

Children screamed. Some people began to jump up on the seats. Others blocked the aisle as they ran from the scurrying crabs.

Peter righted the basket. Penny cried, "Oh, Mother! Oh, Mother! Oh, Mother!"

"Stop moaning and do something," said his mother. "Get me that shopping bag."

She pulled the pancake turner out of the shopping bag and went after a nearby crab. She scooped it up, but it slid off.

Meanwhile, the other crabs were getting farther and farther away. Everyone in the car was either standing or kneeling on the seats. They were all watching the crabs.

"I need the big cooking spoon, too," said the boys' mother. "Hand it to me, Peter."

Peter handed her the spoon. She put the pancake turner under one crab and the big spoon on top of it. Then she was able to lift the crab back into the basket.

She started to go after another crab, but Peter, looking rather ashamed, stopped her. "Penny and I will get them, Mother. We said we'd take care of the crabs."

The two boys went crawling up and down the aisle. Peter had the pancake turner in one hand and the big spoon in the other. As Penny chased the crabs out from under the seats, Peter went after them. Frequently the crabs slid off the pancake turner before Peter could capture them with the big spoon. But by the time the train was halfway home, all the crabs were back in the basket.

"Well!" cried Peter as he sank down into his seat. "Now I know why there's a rule against taking animals in passenger cars."

"Me, too," said Penny wearily. "But I'm glad we didn't lose those crabs. I do love crabs—cooked ones, I mean."

A Christmas to Remember

It was a few days before Christmas. But as Jane Wallace swept the ranch-house porch, her thoughts were not very cheerful.

Six months ago, when her father had told the family that they were moving to a ranch out West, Jane had been glad. And at first she had loved their new home. Every day was bright and sunny, with plenty of time to play and to learn about ranch life.

But lately the family had had nothing but misfortunes. Some of the cattle had taken sick and died, and the hot desert winds had ruined the garden.

Now Mr. Wallace was away, trying to get more cattle. Jane felt sure he would not be back for Christmas. And her mother was too discouraged and too busy taking care of the ranch to make any Christmas plans.

"It doesn't seem right for Tim and Ann not to have a Christmas this year," Jane said to herself. "I've had plenty of good Christmases. But the twins are too little to remember our holiday fun back East. If they're to celebrate Christmas this year, I guess I'll have to be Santa Claus."

Jane leaned on her broom, thinking hard.

"The main thing," she decided, "is to get a Christmas tree. But where can I find a real one? Nothing but cactus and mesquite grows around here."

As Jane went about her duties, she kept wondering how to provide a Christmas tree. Then suddenly she stopped wondering.

"Why, it can be just any kind of a tree," she thought. "It can even be a mesquite bush. Only it has to look pretty. It has to *look* like a Christmas tree, with lots of pretty trimmings."

Jane hurried into the kitchen. "Mother!" she cried. "Where is our box of Christmas-tree ornaments?"

"I'm sorry, dear," replied Mrs. Wallace. "Those ornaments were all broken when our things got here. I must have packed them carelessly."

Jane sighed bitterly.

"Were you thinking of having a Christmas tree?" asked Mrs. Wallace, noting Jane's disappointment.

"Yes, Mother," Jane replied. "The twins are old enough now to remember Christmas. They should have a tree and gifts."

"You're right, Jane," said Mrs. Wallace. "But where can we get a tree? How can we provide gifts?"

Just then the twins rushed in. "Lunch!" they cried hungrily.

"We'll have it ready in a few moments," said their mother. "We'll have scrambled eggs and ham if you'll bring in some eggs."

As the twins dashed out to the henhouse, the wrinkles in Mrs. Wallace's forehead deepened in thought.

"My granny used to *make* pretties for her family's tree," she told Jane. "But I——"

Then Mrs. Wallace laughed. "Eggs!" she exclaimed. "Granny made ornaments from eggshells!"

Quickly Mrs. Wallace explained to Jane how this was done.

After lunch, while the two youngsters were taking their naps, Jane set to work with a dozen eggs. She poked a darning needle into the ends of each egg. After making holes a quarter of an inch wide, she held the egg over a bowl. Then she blew very gently into one end of the egg. The insides ran out the other end into the bowl, leaving an empty eggshell.

Jane dyed the shells with some Easter-egg dye that Mrs. Wallace found. "They'll make lovely ornaments," Jane said to her mother with satisfaction. "Your granny was very clever."

The girl's plans for Christmas grew and grew. She made lots of fancy cookies, some to eat and some to hang on the tree. One she cut like a big star. That was to go at the very top of the tree.

All the next day Jane kept trying to think of presents for the twins. Then Tim ran in with a round blue stone he had found.

"It's like a ball," he said. "I wish it would bounce like the one I lost."

"A ball," Jane repeated to herself. "Why, I'll *make* Timmy a ball."

She found yarn in her mother's scrap bag and wound it tightly into a ball. Then she covered the yarn with bright-colored scraps of cloth.

"It won't bounce like the rubber ball Tim lost," she thought. "But it's mighty pretty."

The yarn gave Jane another idea. "I'll make a stocking doll for Ann," she decided.

Finally it was the night before Christmas. The twins were in bed, and Mrs. Wallace was making a special Christmas pudding. Now it was time for Jane to find a tree and trim it. She stepped outside the house. Then she gave a little cry of delight.

The shining moon made the night almost as light as day. The desert sand looked snowy white, with dark pools where the cactus and mesquite cast their shadows.

"Why, the desert is beautiful!" the girl murmured. "It's as beautiful as our white Christmases back home."

But she must not linger. Running to the barn, Jane got a short-handled ax. Nearby she found just the mesquite tree she wanted. It was small enough for her to chop down with a few blows of the ax.

Jane carried the tree into the house and fixed it securely in a box filled with sand. Then she covered the box with pillowcases and scattered soap flakes over them to look like snow. With a darning needle, she ran strings through the cookies and the dyed egg-shells and then tied them to the branches.

Just as Jane finished, her mother came in. Mrs. Wallace gazed at the tree in amazement.

"Was your grandmother's tree any prettier than this?" Jane asked.

"No, dear," said her mother gently. "I'm sure no tree could be prettier than yours."

The next morning the twins' delight repaid Jane for all her work. The youngsters were enchanted with the tree and with their gifts.

Later, as they were all starting to eat their Christmas dinner, there was a sound at the door. Tim ran to open it.

"It's Daddy!" he shouted happily.

"Well!" said Mr. Wallace when he saw the tree. "I hurried back home to bring your Christmas, but apparently it's already here."

"It's Jane's idea," said her mother. "She thought the twins should have a tree. It's the first one they can remember."

"Look in my bag, Jane," said her father, smiling tenderly. "You will find some other things to help them remember Christmas."

Mr. Wallace had brought gifts for all his family, and they were so excited they could hardly eat their dinner.

That night when Jane helped her mother tuck the twins into bed, she smiled happily.

"They won't forget this first Christmas in the desert," she said. "None of us will."

Adventure in the Swamps

Johnny was a farm boy who lived near the Santee River swamps. One morning after breakfast he was sitting on the front steps, idly roping a gatepost. He pretended that the post was an alligator he was attempting to capture.

Ever since Johnny's big brother Henry had caught and tamed an alligator, Johnny had wanted one, too. Today he intended to get it.

He coiled the rope and tossed it over one shoulder. Then he went slowly out the gate, singing loudly.

Johnny sang so loudly, in fact, that his mother did not notice he had left the porch. The boy headed for the Santee River. He was thinking only about his alligator.

"I hope my 'gator won't be hiding in his cave under the riverbank," Johnny said to himself. "If he is, I'll just have to wait till he comes out."

As Johnny walked along, he remembered all the exciting things Henry had told him about alligators. At the same time, however, he began to feel a little guilty. His mother had told him it was dangerous for him to go alone into the swamps. But he had been so eager to catch an alligator that until now he had forgotten her warning.

"There's nothing to be afraid of in the swamps," Johnny argued aloud with himself. "And if Henry can catch a 'gator, I guess I can, too. Besides, I'm almost there. It would be a shame to turn back now."

The sound of his own voice encouraged the boy. He began to whistle. Before long he reached the swamp, still carrying the coiled rope over his shoulder.

Johnny walked along under cypress trees dripping with moss. He smelled the blossoms of the tupelo trees, where bees were busily gathering honey. His glance darted around eagerly. He wanted to catch all the sights of the Santee swamp.

He saw a turtle sunning itself on a big cypress log and tossed a stick at it. Then he came to a clump of leafy bushes heavy with ripe, juicy berries. On any other day he would have stopped to eat his fill. But today he was after his 'gator.

Johnny stopped just long enough to grab a handful of the tasty berries. Then the boy saw bees buzzing about a hollow tupelo tree. He wondered if that was where they had stored their honey. He would come back later and find out, for no honey is sweeter than tupelo honey from the swamps.

"Ah, coon tracks!" he said as he spied tiny footprints. "I'll come again next winter and try to catch him. If he's a big coon, I'll trade him to Henry for his fiddle. Henry wants a coon hide." Then Johnny forgot about the coon. He had seen his 'gator!

It was a river alligator, about four feet in length. Johnny felt sure that he would be able to handle it. The alligator was sliding through the broom grass toward the river. Johnny was lucky. He had not expected to find his 'gator out of water.

Then the alligator saw Johnny. It lay dead still. Johnny noticed that it looked like an old cypress log.

The boy crept toward it cautiously, getting his rope ready to throw. But the alligator saw Johnny coming. It slid off toward the riverbank again.

Johnny coiled his rope and threw it at the animal. The rope caught on a tupelo tree. While the boy was getting it untangled, the alligator slid forward several yards nearer the river.

Again Johnny tried, and again he missed. He started to try a third time.

Suddenly he heard a warning rattle from behind a cypress log. Turning around, he saw eight feet of coiled rattlesnake and a broad, wicked-looking head. Johnny did not linger. He got away fast.

He did not stop to kill the snake, for he knew his 'gator was heading for the water. It had only a few yards to go. Once again Johnny threw his rope. It landed squarely about the alligator's thick neck, like a collar. Johnny felt very proud. Now he could pull his prize home. He would show Henry!

The alligator struggled fiercely against the rope. It flopped about, trying to get loose. Johnny grasped the rope more tightly. He pulled hard as the alligator squirmed to free itself from the rope.

Suddenly the alligator hooked its big tail around a young tree. Johnny could not budge the animal. It just lay and stared at Johnny with unblinking, snakelike eyes.

Henry had said that if a 'gator makes up his mind he won't budge, he just won't. So Johnny calmly sat down to wait until the alligator would unhook.

Johnny still grasped the rope tightly. He was keeping well out of reach of that tail. He knew that an alligator defends itself by slapping with its tail. And its slap is no gentle pat.

Finally the alligator unhooked its big tail. As Johnny started pulling again, he did not see something move in the nearby bushes.

Then the bushes parted, and a fierce wild pig appeared. Her wicked eyes flashed, and she was grunting furiously.

Panic seized Johnny as the pig opened her ugly mouth. He looked about frantically for a tree.

But no tree was near enough for Johnny to climb before the beast could reach him. Tightening his grasp on the rope, he moved farther away from the pig. How he wished that he had paid attention to his mother's warning!

Suddenly the angry pig lunged at Johnny. The alligator was now between him and the pig, but apparently the pig had not noticed it. The alligator gave a quick flip of its tail, and the pig tumbled over.

As the pig got up and tore madly into the swamp, Johnny laughed out loud. He felt much better. He was thankful to be alive.

Johnny looked at his alligator. Again it stared back with unblinking, snakelike eyes.

"I've changed my mind," Johnny said. "You're my 'gator all right. But you saved my life, so I'll repay you by leaving you here. You'd miss this old Santee swamp."

Johnny went up as close to the alligator as he dared. He took out his knife and cut off part of the rope. Then he started for home, singing. The alligator slid off through the grass.

Judy's Chickens

Judy Woods stood by the door of her very own chicken house. Carefully she counted her chickens as they ate their breakfast.

"Eighty-two, eighty-three—but where is the eighty-fourth?" Judy peered anxiously into the dimness of the chicken house.

She was convinced that her chickens were the finest in the whole world. She had fed and watered them ever since they were pale-yellow fluffy balls only two days old. Now they were three months old and ready to be sold. Judy's father was taking them to the market in Clayborn tomorrow.

"Oh, dear," sighed Judy. "I hope nothing has happened to one of my chickens."

Just then the eighty-fourth chicken ran out from behind the chicken house.

"Judy! It's time for school," cried Mrs. Woods from the back porch.

Judy shut the chicken-house door and ran to get her bicycle. It would not do to be late for school this Thursday. Her teacher was to give the class directions for their Easter trip to the St. Louis zoo on Saturday.

Hopping on her bike, Judy waved good-by to her mother and rode swiftly off.

Soon Judy came to the tiny farm where her good friend Mrs. Pepper lived all alone. Mrs. Pepper was feeding her chickens.

"Good morning!" Judy called gaily.

"Hello!" Mrs. Pepper called back. "I'm going to Clayborn this afternoon. Maybe I can get a summer job in the factory there."

"Well, good luck!" Judy shouted as she sped on down the road.

Before long she came to the Banks farm, which was a chicken farm like most of the others in that region. Mary Banks and her brother Bob were coming down the walk on their bicycles.

"Say, Judy," said Bob, "did you hear the radio broadcast this morning? There was a tornado just two miles away last night."

"I hope we never have one here," Mary said with a shiver.

"Me, too," said Judy. "It might kill my chickens. I'm counting on the money that Dad gets for them to pay for my St. Louis trip."

"You and your old chickens," laughed Bob. "You'd think they were made of gold. And wouldn't one of your chickens look funny with all the feathers blown off it!"

"Oh, don't mind him, Judy," said Mary. "He's always teasing me, too."

The children hurried on to the little white schoolhouse. When all the pupils were in their seats, the teacher told them the final plans for the St. Louis trip. Judy felt as though she could hardly wait. She had been looking forward to this wonderful trip ever since it had first been mentioned.

Four o'clock came at last. Judy dashed out to her bicycle. She was so eager to see if her chickens were all right that she did not even wait for Mary.

Without warning, something cold hit her on the nose as she rode along. Then something bounced off her forehead. Tiny hailstones were falling from dark, puffy clouds. More hailstones hit her face—bigger ones.

"My poor chickens!" she gasped. "They're outside! I closed the chicken-house door, and they can't get in."

She passed the Banks farm. Mr. and Mrs. Banks were running about, closing up their chicken houses.

Judy looked at the sky. A huge cloud in the west looked ugly and purple. It curved and moved around like boiling syrup.

Now Judy was passing Mrs. Pepper's tiny farm. The chickens were pressing against their house. Their door was closed, too.

"Why doesn't Mrs. Pepper let them in?" the girl wondered. Then she remembered. Mrs. Pepper had gone to Clayborn.

As Judy rode on, the hail ceased. There was a queer yellow light everywhere, and a peculiar quiet. Judy looked at the western sky again. The huge cloud was closer now, and it had something long like an elephant's trunk hanging from it.

Judy stared at the cloud in panic. "That really must be a tornado cloud," she thought. "My chickens will all be killed!"

Her father and mother would not know that she had closed her chicken-house door. And they would not notice it because the chicken house was almost hidden behind the barn.

Judy sped on, her heart pounding. How could she go to St. Louis if all her chickens were killed? Then she thought of her good friend Mrs. Pepper. *Her* chicken money paid for most of her living. What would she do if her chickens were blown away?

It was a difficult choice for Judy to make, but she did not hesitate long. She turned around and rode back to the tiny farm. If she never went to St. Louis, she could not let Mrs. Pepper lose her precious chickens.

Judy opened the chicken-house door, and the clucking chickens scurried inside.

Then a blinding rain began to fall, and the wind blew fiercely. It was too late for Judy to go home now. She hurried inside with the chickens and shut the door tight.

Judy watched the storm anxiously. The wind was slashing at the trees, breaking off branches and whipping them through the air.

"Oh, my poor chickens!" Judy cried again.

Suddenly all was quiet, and the sun came out. Judy opened the door cautiously. To the west the sky was blue. To the east the dark clouds were hurrying away.

Once more the girl mounted her bicycle. The muddy road made the going hard. Here and there tree limbs lay on the road. Then she had to get off and push her bicycle around them. But finally she reached home.

"Judy!" her mother cried, hurrying out of the house. "Where have you been?"

Judy headed for her chicken house.

"I'll tell you later, Mother," she called back. "I have to see if my chickens are all right. I left the door of their house shut. They couldn't get in out of the tornado!"

"Wait, Judy!" cried her mother. "Your chickens are safe. The tornado didn't hurt anything around here. It passed through the woods."

The girl was so happy that she whirled her mother around in a little dance.

"Stop, Judy," laughed Mrs. Woods. "Tell me—where were you during the storm?"

Judy giggled. "I was in Mrs. Pepper's chicken house with the chickens," she said. "I stopped there to let her chickens into their house. The wind must have blown the door shut while she was gone. I was afraid the tornado would carry them away."

Mrs. Woods looked at her daughter with pride. "Mrs. Pepper will be thankful she has such a good friend," she said. "Now come inside and try on your Easter dress."

"It will be my St. Louis zoo dress, too," said Judy, skipping gaily up the steps.

Maple-Sugar Time

"Why did Mother and Dad have to choose Vermont to move to?" Robert Huff grumbled to himself. "There's nothing to do here but skate, skate, skate! At home we might be playing baseball by this time."

It was the first Saturday in March. The Huff family had left New York City for their new home in Vermont only two weeks ago. Now Robert was going with Jason Peters and Ben Dickson to the skating pond.

"See the crows!" cried Jason as some big black birds flapped over the bare trees.

"That means spring," said Ben. "The sap will be running soon if it warms up a bit."

"What's so wonderful about sap?" Robert asked. "All I hear in this old town is maple trees and sap, maple syrup, maple sugar."

Ben and Jason stared at Robert. After a moment Jason said, "If that's the way you feel about our town, we won't bother you."

The two boys ran toward the pond and left Robert standing alone in the path. Angrily he walked back to town.

During the weekend the sun shone warmly in the daytime, but the nights were cold. It was good sap-running weather.

When Robert arrived at school on Monday morning, not even the teacher was there.

"It must be a special Vermont holiday," Robert decided.

Just then a sled load of laughing boys and girls came along the road. "Come and help us scatter buckets at Peters' Woods," a girl called. "No school till the sap-run is over."

"I'm too busy," Robert replied, although he really had nothing to do.

But as the sled went by with its load of shining buckets and cheerful boys and girls, Robert suddenly felt lonesome.

On his way home Robert passed Peters'
Woods. When he saw all the people working there, he stopped to watch. Mr. Peters
was boring a hole in the south side of a tree,
where most of the branches grew. After the
hole was bored and blown free of sawdust,
his grandson Jason fitted a steel spout into
it, hammering the spout in firmly.

Then Ben Dickson hooked a bucket on the
spout. Over the bucket he put a cover that
was shaped like a tiny roof. "To keep the
snow and dirt out," Robert guessed.

Mr. Peters and the two boys went on to
the next tree. Nearby other teams of three
were boring holes, fitting spouts, and hanging buckets.

Robert thought the work looked like fun. But he was too stubborn to offer Jason and Ben his help. He walked on down the road.

Soon he came to a little shack. It was a sap house, or sugar house, where the sap was boiled into syrup.

A sled stood before the shack. On the sled was a tank with a pipe leading down to another tank where the sap was stored until it could be boiled into syrup. The driver was letting the sap pour down the pipe.

"Hello, Robert," called the man. "Have you come to see how we make syrup?"

Robert recognized Mr. Swift, who worked in the bank. "Why, hello, Mr. Swift," the boy said. "Is the bank closed?"

"Everything's closed for the sap-running," replied Mr. Swift. "We have to gather and boil the sap into syrup in a few days. This sap weather usually doesn't last long."

He closed the tap on the pipe and started to drive the tank back for more sap.

"Maybe I can help you," offered Robert.

"Sure, hop on," said Mr. Swift. "You can empty buckets into this tank. It takes forty gallons of sap to make one gallon of syrup. That's a lot of emptying."

Mr. Swift chuckled. "I was the first one in town to have my buckets scattered. I'll start my boiling tonight."

After helping Mr. Swift all day, Robert ached with weariness. He felt as though he had emptied thousands of gallons of sap. But after eating dinner, he felt fine.

"Dad!" he cried. "Why don't we go down to watch Mr. Swift boil his sap?"

"I'd like to, Son. But I must write some important letters. You go ahead, though."

Robert put on his warmest sweater and jacket and went down to the sugar house. Its windows were glowing brightly.

Mr. Swift was not in the sugar house. But Robert saw a long pan on top of a narrow wood stove. Under a cloud of steam, gallons of maple sap boiled in the pan.

While Robert watched, he began to notice that the sap was boiling more slowly than it had at first. "The fire must be getting low," he thought. "I wonder if I shouldn't add some wood."

Robert watched a little longer. Only a few bubbles broke the surface of the sap. Quickly the boy threw some wood into the stove. The sap started to bubble violently.

"What if it boils over?" Robert worried as the bubbles rose higher and higher.

The boiling sap was almost even with the top of the pan. Robert knew that he would have to do something. He jerked open the stove door and tried to pull out some of the wood. Immediately the flames leaped out at him. He banged the door shut with his foot.

Now the syrup was beginning to boil over.

"Maybe I should take out some sap," he thought. As he looked frantically around the shack, he noticed a pitcher containing a little cream. Robert grabbed the pitcher. Dipping it quickly into the pan, cream and all, he lifted out a pitcherful of sap.

The bubbling sap quieted down at once and fell an inch or two in the pan.

"How mysterious!" Robert thought. "I didn't take out *that* much sap. Maybe Mr. Swift can explain the mystery."

Robert ran to the door and looked down the snowy path. It was empty.

Suddenly he heard a cry, "Help! Help!" Guided by the voice, Robert raced into the woods. There he found Mr. Swift limping painfully along.

"I've hurt my leg," he moaned. "I must get back to the shack. I'm afraid the syrup is ruined by this time."

"Here," said Robert, "lean on me. Don't worry about the syrup. It's all right now. I built up the fire to keep the syrup boiling. Then it began to boil over, so I used your pitcher. It worked like magic."

"Now tell me something," said Mr. Swift as he limped to the shack. "How did a city boy like you know that mixing a little cream in the sap would keep it from boiling over?"

"Cream!" cried Robert. "Why, I *didn't* know. So that's what did the trick!"

The next day everyone in the Vermont town knew how Robert had saved the syrup. On his arrival at the shack to help Mr. Swift, he found Jason and Ben already there.

"We came to help, too," said Jason. He added gruffly, "You didn't do so badly last night—for a city boy."

"Would you like to come to our sugaring-off party Thursday?" Ben asked. "That's when we make maple-sugar candy for everyone who helped during the sap-run."

"I certainly would like to come," Robert replied. "I want to taste this fine maple sugar that my home town makes."

"Have some right now," offered Mr. Swift. "I boiled down a small panful of syrup into sugar last night after you'd gone. I thought you might like to try some!"

The Quiet Mountains

"Oo-oooo-ooh!" screamed a train whistle.

"That will be Number Nine coming in," Sarah thought as she stood looking out her window at Mount Stephen. "Father will be home to breakfast soon."

All day long and all night, too, the sound of engines could be heard in Field, a small railroad town in Canada. The town lay in a deep valley, with the Rocky Mountains rising steeply on both sides.

Along the bottom of this narrow valley ran the Kicking Horse River, the highway, and the railway.

From "Train Whistles in the Mountains" in *Across Canada* by Clare Bice. Copyright, 1949, by The Macmillan Company. Adapted by permission of the publishers.

Sarah gave a last look at the snow-capped mountain and went downstairs to breakfast. Her father was just coming in from the railroad yards. "Numbers Fifteen and Sixteen will be taken off next week," he announced. "The vacation season is just about over."

"I wish people would really stop off here at Field," Sarah said. "They just stay a few minutes while the pushers are hooked on."

The extra engines were called "pushers," though they really helped *pull* the trains up the mountains. It took two and frequently three of the pushers to haul a train up the mountain pass and through the tunnels.

"Oh, by the way, Sarah," said her father. "Your friend Molly wants to see you. I saw her when I came from the roundhouse."

Later that forenoon, as Sarah was going to the grocery store, she met Molly.

"Guess what!" Molly cried. "A man has rented our front bedroom. His name is Mr. Brooks, and he paints pictures. He's going up the valley this afternoon to paint. So I asked if you and I could go along."

"What did he say?" asked Sarah eagerly.

"He said that he'd be pleased to have
our company," Molly answered.

"Oh, good!" said Sarah. "Perhaps he'll
paint Mount Stephen. There's a fine view
way up the highway."

After lunch the three of them crossed the
bridge over the river at Field and walked
for a while along the road that wound up the
left side of the valley. Looking back across
the valley, they saw Mount Stephen rising
ten thousand feet into the sky. At the base
of the mountain snuggled the town of Field.

"See how the train curves around the sides
of Stephen," Molly pointed out to Mr. Brooks.

Just then a truck drove up behind them.

"It's our neighbor, Mr. White!" exclaimed Sarah. "If he'll give us a lift, we can go much higher. Then we'll get a better view of the top of Mount Stephen."

Mr. White drove the girls and Mr. Brooks on up the curving slope. After a while they crossed a bridge back to the right side of the valley. When they came to a level spot, Sarah cried, "This is the view I meant!"

Mr. White let his three passengers out. After promising to pick them up on his way back, he drove on up the sloping road.

"Look! Isn't that nice?" said Sarah.

"It certainly is!" cried Mr. Brooks. "It will be a lovely, peaceful view to paint."

He started unpacking his paints at once. Sarah thought that perhaps she and Molly should leave Mr. Brooks in quiet to paint his picture. So she said, "Molly, there's a fine fossil bed a little farther up the road. We might look for some interesting fossils while Mr. Brooks paints."

"I'm going to stay and watch," Molly said.

Sarah would have preferred to stay, too. But now that she had mentioned the fossil bed, she decided to go there by herself.

She walked up the curving mountain road, feeling a bit lonely and uneasy. Near Field she did not mind walking alone, but she was not so familiar with this part of the valley. What if she should meet a grizzly! She was not afraid of black bears, but she had a deep fear of grizzlies.

She felt better when she came to a spot where the railway track crossed the road— she was used to railroads. And nearby were two houses where the track workers lived.

The fossil bed could not be far off now. Sarah kept on walking, though now and then little noises in the woods made her jump.

Then Sarah saw a bear in the bushes by the road! The girl's heart skipped a beat, and she stopped still. But it was a black bear, not a grizzly. Followed by two cubs, the bear came out onto the highway. After staring at Sarah for a moment, she hustled her cubs into the woods.

Shivering, Sarah hurried on to the fossil bed. There she saw some pebbles that were like curious little animals. People said that long, long ago they had really been animals. But they had been buried in the mud for so long that they had turned to stone.

Sarah picked up half a dozen fossils and put them in her sweater pocket. Suddenly she heard a rumble farther up the road.

The rumble grew louder and louder. Now she could see something about a quarter of a mile ahead. A landslide was starting down the steep slope above the railroad track.

As Sarah watched, a piece of the mountain seemed to fall away. It went crashing and rumbling down, carrying with it huge rocks and trees. Finally it landed right across the railroad track!

The earth and rocks continued to slide for several minutes. Sarah stood glued to the ground. Then she remembered that Molly's father would be bringing his pusher engine down this track soon!

Sarah turned and ran back down the road as fast as her legs could carry her. One of the track workers' houses at the crossing would surely have a telephone. If she could call the station at Field, she thought, then Molly's father would be warned that the track was buried under a slide.

She pounded frantically on the door of the first house. No answer. She pushed open the door and rushed in. No one was there. But on the wall was a telephone!

"Hello! Hello!" Sarah shouted loudly into the mouthpiece. "Is this Field? I'm at the highway crossing. . . . Yes, that's right. . . . There's a landslide across the track about a quarter of a mile up beyond the fossil bed. . . . You know already? . . . Oh, I forgot that the signal wire would warn you. . . . That's fine. . . . Good-by."

Slowly Sarah hung up the receiver. She leaned against the wall, trying to steady her shaking knees and trembling lips. The man at Field had said that the trains would be stopped before they got to the buried track. There would be no wreck.

When Sarah joined Mr. Brooks and Molly, they were looking at his completed painting. Molly was pointing at it and saying something to Mr. Brooks. Apparently they had not heard the noise of the landslide.

"Hello," Mr. Brooks greeted Sarah. "Did you get some good fossils? I hope Mr. White comes back soon to pick us up. I thought I heard thunder a while ago."

But Sarah could think of nothing except the picture. She gazed at it eagerly.

"I'm afraid my painting isn't very good," said Mr. Brooks, frowning.

"Oh, it *is* good!" Sarah exclaimed. "It's— it's perfect, I think."

"No," insisted Mr. Brooks, "it isn't what I wanted to paint. It doesn't show the silence and peace of these mountains."

Silence? Peace? Sarah smiled to herself. The mountains might look quiet and peaceful to Mr. Brooks. But he had not met a bear or seen a dangerous landslide. How amazed he would be when he learned of the exciting things that had just happened to her on these mountains!

Alarm in the Night

After a warm, sunny day the Southern California night was sharp with sudden cold. Now the moon was turning the leaves in the Pages' orange grove to bright silver.

In her room thirteen-year-old Susan Page switched on the bedside radio. If she kept the radio turned low, she could listen to her favorite program, "California Pinto."

As the story went on, Susan listened with growing delight. "How wonderful it would be to own a pony!" she thought. Suddenly the radio program was interrupted.

"ATTENTION, FRUIT GROWERS!" came the radio announcer's voice. "The temperature in Southern California may drop to freezing before morning. Light your orchard heaters to save your crops!"

Susan drew a frightened breath. Suppose their oranges should freeze! For a moment she thought of waking her mother and her younger brother Joey. But her mother had been up very early that morning helping Dad pick oranges. She needed her night's rest. And Joey would know less about saving the rest of the crop than Susan herself did.

"Oh, dear," the girl sighed. "If only Dad were here!"

That afternoon Mr. Page had gone to take part of his orange crop to market in town. He would not come back until tomorrow. Susan had often helped in the orange groves, but she had never lighted the heaters.

"Maybe the temperature won't drop after all," she thought. "This California weather changes quickly in the orange belt. And if the temperature does fall dangerously low, our own frost-alarm bell will ring."

With this comforting thought, Susan was soon fast asleep. In her dreams she was riding a swift pinto.

All at once she awakened with a start. A bell was ringing loudly. "The frost alarm!" she cried. "The temperature did drop."

Susan heard running footsteps in the hall followed by a knock on her door.

"Mother says to get up!" shouted Joey. "Our oranges will freeze!"

After Susan had pulled on her sweater and blue jeans, Mrs. Page came by. "We'll have to light the orchard heaters," she told the children. "I know they are kept filled with oil, but I've never lit them."

"I know how," Susan said encouragingly. "I've watched Dad do it. He lit them with a can with a long spout. Dad called the can a torch. He filled the can with oil. Then he lit the end of the spout and touched the flame to the heater."

"Joey is a little young for that kind of work," Mrs. Page said doubtfully. "But I need all the help I can get. He'll just have to be extra careful."

They all started immediately to the shed near the grove. Here the torches were kept. Susan helped her mother fill them with oil.

"When we light the heaters," Susan told Joey, "warm smoke comes out the pipe in each heater and floats up under the trees. This blanket of smoke keeps the oranges from freezing."

With torches in hand, the three of them hastened toward the trees. Mrs. Page lit the wick of each torch. Quickly they began to light the iron heaters.

As they went farther in among the trees, the warm, gassy smoke drifting up from the oil heaters made it a little hard to breathe. Mrs. Page heard a choking sound.

"Joey!" she called. "Are you all right?"

"My throat and eyes burn," Joey replied.

"Go back to the house, then," ordered his mother.

"No," said the boy bravely. "I want to help."

Finally the last heater was lit. The whole grove was now protected by a light cloud of warm, smoky air.

With relief Mrs. Page put out the flames of the torches. Then she and the children left the orange grove and threw themselves down on the ground to rest. The cold air chilled them now, but they were too weary to get up.

"Your throat and eyes will be all right," Mrs. Page comforted Joey. "But that was a hard night's work. I don't know what I would have done without your help, children. I never could have lit all those heaters in time to save the oranges."

At last Mrs. Page said, "We'd better go back to the house." And through the dim light of early morning they stumbled home.

Shortly afterwards the rumble of a truck was heard outside. Then the door opened.

"Anyone home?" boomed Mr. Page's voice. "I saw smoke in the grove as I approached the house. There must be a fine ranch hand around here."

Mr. Page turned to his wife. "Did you manage all those heaters by yourself?"

"The children did just as much as I did," said Mrs. Page. "They were a great help."

"Well, I'm proud of all of you," said Mr. Page. "I heard the frost warning over the radio. I started to hurry home, but my truck broke down on a mountain detour. I was sure we'd lose our fruit."

Then he smiled. "Would you two like to go over to the corral of the Double-X ranch this morning?" he asked the children.

"The Double-X?" said Susan. "What for?"

"Every good ranch hand needs a horse," replied her father. "I know two fine ponies there that are just begging for a new home."

"You mean they're for us?" cried Joey.

"Of course," said Mr. Page. "Well, what are we waiting for?"

"Just to catch our breath!" replied Susan.

The School Train

In a one-room cabin deep in the northern forests a trapper named Antoine lived with his two motherless sons, Tony and John.

One snowy November night Antoine said, "Boys, it's time for me to set out my trap-lines or we won't have any furs to sell at the trading post. I may be gone for a month or two. I don't like to leave you, but we must have money for food and clothes."

"Don't worry, Papa," said red-haired Tony. "John and I can manage."

Antoine banked the fire in the stove, and the boys got into their wooden bunks. Soon they were fast asleep.

The next morning Antoine said, "I've told Ace Stone that I'm leaving today. So if you need help, go to him."

The boys nodded. They had always liked the fisherman who lived five miles away.

Shortly after the trapper had gone, Ace pounded on the door of the cabin.

"I've thought of something you might like to do while your father is away," he said.

"What is it?" asked both boys at once.

"Well," Ace began, "there's a supply train that goes to the lumber camps. One of the cars is a schoolroom for boys and girls who live in the forest. There are books, desks, and a teacher!"

"John and I have never been to a school," Tony burst out. "How I wish we could learn to read and write!"

Ace smiled. "The train leaves the school car in a camp while it is delivering supplies farther on," he continued. "Then it returns later to take the school car to another camp. The car is at Pine Camp now, twenty miles away. I can't take you to it this time, but when it returns to Pine Camp, I will."

"When do you suppose the school car will come back to Pine Camp?" asked John.

"I'm not sure," replied Ace. "But it will be soon. Maybe two or three weeks. Then we'll go."

After Ace had left, Tony and John talked over the news. "Let's not wait for Ace to take us to the school car," suggested Tony. "Let's go by ourselves tomorrow."

Early the next morning they collected the things necessary for their trip. Besides a tent, they packed sleeping bags, cans of milk and vegetables, a saucepan for cooking, and some extra clothes.

Just as the boys were ready to go, Tony thought of something. "Suppose Papa comes home before we get back from the school," he said. "Or suppose Ace comes by and we are not here. They would worry."

"We must leave a message," John said.

"How?" inquired Tony. "We can't write. And neither Papa nor Ace can read."

"Watch!" said John. Taking a small piece of blackened wood from the stove, he began to draw on the clean table top.

Quickly John finished the picture-message. He had drawn a train and the figures of two boys heading toward it.

"That will tell Papa and Ace where we've gone," he said.

Both boys knew the forest and the trail to Pine Camp. But traveling was difficult, especially in the deep forest. For three long days the boys walked steadily. They camped out each night and built fires to heat their food. At dusk on the third day they arrived at the camp. There they met a man.

"Hello," he said. "Where are you from?"

"From our cabin twenty miles away," Tony said. "We've come to see the school car."

"Fine!" said the man. "I'm Mr. Chalmers, the teacher. Come, I'll show you the car. Mrs. Chalmers and I live in the car with our daughter Mary."

The school car was on a nearby railroad siding. As they all walked toward it, the boys told the teacher their names and how they happened to be there.

To the boys' surprise the car contained three rooms. The first was a tiny kitchen. Next was a larger room with some chairs, day beds, and a table. There Mr. Chalmers introduced the boys to his wife and daughter. They welcomed Tony and John warmly.

Then the boys saw the schoolroom. There were blackboards, two rows of desks, maps of the world, and cases of books.

"May we camp by the car and go to school while Papa is trapping?" asked Tony.

"Yes, indeed," replied the teacher. "We shall be glad to have you in the class."

That night Tony and John ate supper with the teacher's family. "Tonight," said Mr. Chalmers, "you'd better sleep in the schoolroom. It's too late to put up your tent."

Early the next morning the boys set up their tent and cooked breakfast over a fire. When the school bell rang, they hurried into the car with the children from the lumber camp. In all, there were thirteen pupils, six of whom were Indians.

"Good morning," said the teacher. Then he told the pupils about Tony and John and their twenty-mile walk to join the school.

"Now," said Mr. Chalmers, "we will stand and sing the song of Canada."

Tony and John stumbled over the words, but they enjoyed singing with the others.

After the song came reading and writing lessons. Then Mr. Chalmers read a story. Tony liked the story very much. He decided that even though learning printed words was hard, he wanted to be able to read stories for himself as soon as possible.

During the lunch hour the other children gathered around Tony and John. "Tell us again about your trip through the forest," they demanded eagerly. Soon the children were all talking together like old friends.

The next two weeks sped quickly by. Then it was time for the supply train to pick up the school car and take it farther into the wilderness.

"The car will not be back for two weeks," Mr. Chalmers explained to the pupils. "So you must work at home those two weeks."

That night Tony asked his brother, "Shall we go back home while the car is gone?"

"Let's talk to Mrs. Chalmers," John said.

A little later they did. "I have a plan," said Tony shyly. "I thought we could travel with the school car to the next camp. Then we could keep on going to school."

"That's a fine plan, boys," Mrs. Chalmers told them. "I'm sure your father would like you to get all the schooling you can."

When the school car left the camp Friday, Tony and John were on it. The boys were thrilled to be riding on a train. And they were looking forward to going to school with the children of the new lumber camp.

Two weeks later the car was returned to Pine Camp. Monday morning the pupils all met in the school car. Tony and John were delighted to see their old friends again.

As the singing started, the boys noticed the arrival of two men at the door. It was Ace Stone and their father!

"Papa!" cried the boys, rushing to greet Antoine.

"The boys' father returned home two days ago," Ace explained to Mr. Chalmers. "He found a picture-message in his cabin. So that's how we knew where the boys were."

"We are very proud of these boys," said Mr. Chalmers. Quickly he picked up a small book and handed it to Tony. "Here, show your father how you can read," he said.

Taking the thin book, Tony read it easily from cover to cover. Then Mr. Chalmers gave it to John, who also read it through.

Antoine beamed at his sons. "I—I cannot say how I feel," he stammered. His voice was choked with happiness.

Mr. Chalmers praised the boys' fine work at school. "I hope they will keep coming," he said.

"I will see that they do," promised their father seriously.

"Oh, good!" cried John. "Then Tony and I can learn to read much thicker books!"

A Camp in the Canyon

The moment the Howard family laid eyes on the clearing in the canyon, they decided that it was a perfect place to camp. Thick pine forests grew on either side, and beyond them rose the high canyon walls.

While Mr. Howard chopped wood for a fire, Mrs. Howard started supper. Jill went to a nearby spring for a pail of water, and Tom built a rock stove not far from the tent.

As Tom was starting the fire, he heard a sharp voice call, "Say, there!"

A boy about Tom's own age had entered the clearing. Over his shoulder he carried a trout rod.

"Hello," said Tom in a friendly voice.

The boy pointed his trout rod at the fire. "Put that out," he said sternly. "You can't build fires here."

His tone made Tom a little angry. "Who are you?" he asked.

"I'm Louis Cook," replied the boy. "This is my dad's land. He won't permit campers."

Hearing the boys, Mr. Howard came over. "Hello," he said. "What's the trouble?"

"Dad won't permit campers on his land," Louis repeated. "Campers start forest fires."

"Well, we are always very careful about fires," said Mr. Howard, smiling. "We have built this rock stove in the open, and we never go off and leave a fire burning. If you tell your father that, maybe he'll permit us to camp here for a few days."

"Dad isn't home," answered the boy in the same unfriendly tone as before.

"All right," replied Mr. Howard. "We'll find another place for our camp."

As the boy walked away, Mr. Howard put out the fire. Then the family packed their things and left in search of another spot.

"There are plenty of good places to camp," said Mr. Howard. "We'll find one soon."

Fortunately they found one before dark on a ranch farther up the canyon. "We'll ask permission this time," said Mr. Howard as he drove to the ranch house.

To the family's relief, the rancher agreed to let them stay. "I think I can recognize good campers," he added. "You don't look like careless folks who would leave fires to destroy the forests."

The Howards promised that they would be careful. Soon they were settled in the new place. Tom and Jill did not like it so well as the first place, but at least they knew that they were welcome.

The moon was up before they had finished eating supper. The calmness of the summer night was broken only by the faint chirping of the crickets.

The next day all the family explored the canyon. It proved to be very exciting.

Tom discovered a deserted shack in which pack rats had hidden their stolen treasures. There were brass pins, a gold buckle, and other shiny objects. Nearby was a stream where Mr. Howard could cast for trout.

Small animals and brilliantly colored birds kept Jill busy with her camera. Once the family startled a dainty fawn. As the fawn leaped out of sight, bluejays scolded them noisily.

One morning Tom and Jill climbed up to the fire tower of the ranger station. Dick Sharp, the ranger on lookout duty, let them look through his field glasses at the timber region below. How close it looked! Then he explained how field glasses and airplanes helped the rangers patrol the forests.

"A fire patrol is always on duty," he said. "We must watch for the first sign of a fire, for it could ruin acres and acres of timber. Electric storms and careless campers cause us the most worry."

Jill looked out over the pine forests that seemed to meet the western sky.

"Don't you ever get lonesome?" she asked the ranger.

"We haven't time to get lonesome," Dick Sharp answered with a smile. "We're far too busy. Patrolling these forests is quite a job, even with the help of planes."

Jill and Tom thanked the ranger for his kindness and started home. As they left, he added, "I know you'll help us prevent fires. Remember, a single careless act may start a fire that could destroy all this fine timber."

Halfway down the canyon, Tom suddenly stopped. "I smell something burning!" he exclaimed.

They hurried along, looking on every side for a curl of smoke or a blaze. Finally they discovered a patch of burning moss.

"Get some water! Quick!" Tom said.

A few steps away was a brook. But they had nothing to hold water, not even a cap.

"Oh, look!" Jill cried in alarm as a patch of dry pine needles burst into flames.

"Let's try to stamp the fire out!" cried Tom. "Our boots are heavy."

The two were so busy at their task that they did not see Louis Cook running toward them with his trout rod. Not until a dry branch snapped beneath his feet did the two children look up.

"Hi!" Tom shouted. "Come and help us put this fire out."

Louis threw down his trout rod. "So you *did* start a fire!" he cried angrily.

"We didn't start it," Jill denied.

"Well," said Louis, "whether you did or not, we'll have to put it out." Pulling off his sweater, he soaked it in the brook and handed it to Jill. "Beat the flames with it," he said. "We boys can use our shirts."

Quickly both boys peeled off their woolen shirts. For a time all three fought the fire desperately.

"It's no use," Louis said, throwing down his shirt. "We can't stop it. I wish I had a shovel. I could dig a ditch around the fire. A lot of timber will be burned unless the patrol sees this fire soon."

"I'll go and get Dad," said Jill. "He'll know what to do."

"Good!" cried Louis. "Your brother and I will keep working. But hurry!"

"Tell Dad to bring a shovel," Tom called as Jill sped toward the camp.

Twenty minutes later Jill returned with her father. With them were Mr. Cook and other ranchers. By this time the rangers who patrolled the region had arrived on a truck with their fire-fighting tools. They were already fighting the fire.

Mr. Howard put Jill in the rangers' truck, which was parked at a safe distance.

Then he joined the men who were digging a ditch to prevent the fire from spreading. Two of the rangers were slashing away the brushwood that was catching fire from the flying sparks. Other rangers were beating the blazing grass with sacks that had been soaked in the brook. Tom and Louis were beating the grass, too, working together like old friends.

A stiff breeze fanned the fire toward the south. For three hours the men fought on. Their faces were scorched and blackened by the heat and smoke. Then it began to rain. The light sprinkle grew into a steady downpour. Soon the entire canyon was soaked.

"The timber's safe!" shouted a ranger, and the men ceased work in weary relief.

Mr. Cook took off his scorched gloves and shook hands with Mr. Howard. "Thanks for your help," he said. "If all campers were like your family, I'd put up signs saying *Welcome* instead of *Keep Out*. After this you may camp on my land any time."

The
Great Outdoors

A Zoo Without Bars

The full October moon splashed light and shadow over a wide, grassy meadow. In this shadowy light three children were advancing quietly across the meadow.

"Every wild thing that walks at night will be out under this moon," Jim, the older boy, said. "I'm going to give a talk in school Tuesday on the wild animals around here. We ought to see a lot of them tonight."

"Do you suppose we'll see a fox?" asked his sister June eagerly.

"Not if he sees us first," Jim said softly. "Remember, we must be very quiet."

Jim continued, "I found a rabbit run this morning. Let's go there and watch."

Soon the children were lying comfortably on a fallen tree that was screened by two bushes. David yawned loudly.

"Shhhh," June told her younger brother. "Don't make so much noise."

"Look carefully," Jim whispered. "You can see how the tall grass has been eaten away and pushed down to form open tunnels. This place is full of these rabbit trails."

Five minutes later June noticed something that made her stiffen. She grabbed Jim's hand and pointed.

"Skunk," Jim told her, and chuckled softly. "He isn't at all afraid of us. And he isn't as bad as most people think. He eats insects and small animals that are harmful to crops. I think he deserves the few eggs he gobbles up when he visits farms."

The neat black-and-white creature walked carelessly through the grass. Occasionally he paused to sniff and scratch in the earth. Then he settled down to do some serious digging.

"What's he found?" asked David.

The question was answered when a mouse jumped between the skunk's feet. But the tiny mouse was too slow to escape the sharp teeth that snapped on him.

"That skunk will eat a dozen more mice before morning," Jim remarked. "Maybe a few crickets, too."

Slowly the skunk walked on. He vanished from sight in the tall grass.

A moment later June caught her breath as a steady thump, thump, thump sounded from the meadow.

She drew closer to Jim. "What's that?" she whispered uneasily. "It sounds like a giant walking."

"It's a rabbit kicking the ground," replied Jim. "Something has alarmed him—maybe the skunk. He's sending a message to the other rabbits around here to watch out for possible danger. He isn't quite sure what's going on. So he drums on the ground with his hind legs to warn his friends."

"Oh," sighed June in relief. "I thought it must be something huge and dangerous."

There was a slight movement in a grass tunnel, and a rabbit hopped out. He began nibbling on a clump of clover. Soon he was joined by another rabbit, and another, and another.

June wiggled with delight. "Look!" she said softly. "It's a bunny party!"

Jim pressed her arm for silence.

"Just wait," he said with a low chuckle. "You really *will* see a party."

All at once the rabbits began leaping high into the air. Then they bounded in circles. Their powerful hind legs acted as springs beneath them.

Gradually the rabbits formed one big circle like a merry-go-round. Each animal seemed to be trying to leap higher than the others.

Just how long this play might have lasted none of the watchers knew. For suddenly a shadow crossed the moon, and the meadow was filled with thumps of alarm and fleeing rabbits. The shadow took clearer shape. It swooped close to the ground and then rose again on strong wings.

"Don't be frightened," Jim whispered. "It was just an owl after a mouse."

For a long time there was no sound but the hoarse croaking of frogs from a nearby pond. The children waited quietly. Then suddenly Jim pointed across the grass.

"Fox!" he breathed. "Don't make a sound. He's just looking over the ground before he starts his hunt. If he hears us, he'll be gone in a flash."

Against the moonlit sky June could see a slim, motionless body. It was a red fox. His ears stood up, and his nose sniffed the air for scents of food or danger. But the wind blew too strongly to carry the scent of people to his keen nose.

After a last look around, the fox began to advance slyly through the tall grass.

"I'm going to try something," Jim muttered softly. "Don't move a muscle."

Quickly he lowered his head and drew his lips together. June almost shrieked aloud at the mouselike squeak that came from her brother's mouth.

Then she forgot her alarm as she watched the fox. He sat down and stared right in the direction of the children.

Jim squeaked again.

The fox came trotting toward them. His ears stood up stiffly, and his nose twitched.

Suddenly he hesitated and looked around him. He was now so close that June could see his whiskers jerking rapidly. The fox was trying hard to pick up the scent of the mouse. He was certain that the mouse was very near.

Just then there came a thump and a loud yell from the ground beside the log. The fox barked with fright and bolted.

"Oh-ooooo!" howled David. "I fell out of bed. Who moved my bed outdoors?"

Jim pulled David to his feet and dusted him off. David blinked in surprise.

"You're a fine one to go animal-watching!" June scolded. "You have been sleeping on that log for an hour. And you had to pick this minute to roll off and scare the fox!"

"What fox?" David mumbled sleepily. "All I saw was a skunk catching a mouse."

Jim laughed. "We may as well go home. No animal that heard David yell will come out of hiding tonight. But now that we know about this zoo without bars, we must come again. Next time, though, David must take a long nap before we come."

The Wild Colt's Lesson

War Paint was a wild colt whose spotted hide looked as if brushfuls of paint had been spilled all over it. With a herd of wild horses, he wandered over the broad western plains as free as the wind.

The favorite sport of the frisky colts was a kind of boxing. Standing up on their hind legs, the youngsters would paw at each other with their forefeet. This play helped them become sure-footed. It also taught them how to defend themselves in time of danger.

Occasionally during their play the lively animals would pause to snatch a mouthful of grass. Then back they would go again to their boxing.

When the colts tired of their sport, they would settle down to steady grazing close to the herd.

One day War Paint and his partner, Nosey, started off to explore a deep gully. They had not gone very far when War Paint heard his mother whinny to him. Nosey went on, but War Paint hesitated. Then Nosey looked back. He seemed to be saying, "Oh, come on. Let's see what's in this gully."

So War Paint paid no more attention to his mother's warning whinny. He pranced boldly after his partner.

The colts went a short distance into the gully. Then suddenly a stone came rattling down a bank. The startled animals whirled. There stood a prairie wolf, ready to pounce!

Instantly the terrified colts started back
toward the herd, trying to seek escape up
the rocky cliff. Nosey deserted his partner
and bolted up the gully to safety.

War Paint started to follow Nosey. The
wolf headed him off and lunged at his hind
legs in fury.

The spotted colt dodged this way and that
in terror. But the crafty wolf dodged, too.
Once more the beast lunged furiously at the
colt's hind legs. War Paint slashed out with
his heels to defend himself.

War Paint saved his legs, but the wolf's powerful jaws scraped his side. Squealing with pain, the colt tried again to flee from the gully. His playful adventure had become a desperate fight for life.

Fiercely the killer sprang after the injured colt. War Paint was wild with terror. He was cornered again. The big wolf lunged a third time. Fortunately, War Paint leaped high in the air just as the wolf threw himself forward.

The wolf was so intent on his prey that he did not hear the pounding hoofs at the top of the gully. Suddenly a black thunderbolt shot down the side of the rocky cliff. With ears laid back and teeth bared, War Paint's mother plunged to his rescue.

Caught completely off guard, the wolf had no chance to escape. The enraged mare gave a lightninglike lunge and sank her teeth into the wolf's hide. Then with a quick toss of her head she cast the wolf into a big clump of sharp-thorned cactus. He lay quite still. Apparently he was badly injured.

The black mare's eyes gleamed with fury. Instantly she plunged into the cactus after the wolf. Her powerful forefeet were ready to slash the enemy and teach him the lesson he deserved. But just in time the wolf got to his feet and limped swiftly away.

War Paint's mother did not try to follow him. Instead, she turned to her trembling colt and whinnied. When the colt whinnied in reply, she nosed him over gently.

As soon as the mare found that War Paint was not badly injured, she snorted loudly as if to scold him. Then she gave him a little bite on his shoulder and pushed him gently on the forehead.

"There, my son," the mare seemed to be saying. "I hope that you have learned your lesson."

A Falls and a Fawn

"Isn't a waterfall the most beautiful thing in the world?" Joyce shouted to her brother.

"Well, a mountain is splendid, too," Phil replied. "But I guess nothing beats a waterfall for noise. If this fence weren't here, I could get really close to the falls."

"This fence keeps people from falling over the cliff," said Joyce. "So you stay here."

Phil suddenly pointed downward. "Look!" he cried. "See the fawn on those rocks!"

Joyce stared down at the mossy rocks on the bank near the base of the falls.

"Why, sure enough!" she exclaimed. "It's a baby fawn! See how still it's standing."

Just then a doe appeared in the bushes behind the rocks. With short, quick steps she advanced toward the rocks. Then she turned and hurried back into the shadows of the bushes.

After the doe had done this several times, Joyce cried, "Something must be wrong!"

"It sort of looks like it," Phil agreed. "That doe must be trying to get the fawn to follow her. I wonder why it just stands there."

"Maybe it can't get away!" Joyce cried. "Maybe it's caught in the rocks!"

"Here's where we could use an elevator," Phil remarked. "But say! There must be a trail down to the bottom of the falls. I'll ask Dad if we have time to go down to the fawn before lunch."

Phil ran quickly to a distant picnic table. Joyce waited by the railing, watching with pity the timid fawn and its worried mother.

Phil came panting back. "Dad is looking for a place to get drinking water," he said. "But Mother says it's all right if we hurry. I brought the rope that we tied around our picnic basket. We may need it."

Phil and Joyce soon spied the trail and started downward. At the trail's end they found themselves on the edge of a rushing stream. But they were on one side of the falls, while the fawn was on the other side. And between the fawn and the children was the whirlpool made by the water that came flooding down the cliff.

Just then the fawn noticed the children. It stood watching them with startled eyes.

"What shall we do now?" wailed Joyce.

"Well," said Phil, "we'll have to get over to the other side of the falls somehow. But we mustn't risk falling into the whirlpool. It's too dangerous."

"I know," said Joyce. "But how *can* we get across?"

Phil stepped closer to the wall of water that was roaring down into the stream and examined the rock behind it.

"Look!" he exclaimed. "This rock is all hollowed out behind the falls. See how it makes a little passageway!"

Joyce looked eagerly. Behind the waterfall was an opening like a low tunnel. The cliff made a wall on one side. The rushing falls made the other wall.

The children ducked their heads and went into the passageway. If they bent over just a little, they could walk easily along its rock floor. Directly behind the falls the path was perfectly dry and level.

Halfway through the narrow passageway Joyce stopped and stared out at the wall of water in front of her.

"Just think!" she cried. "We're behind a waterfall! It sparkles like diamonds!"

"Just like a girl," Phil muttered. "Come on, we have work to do."

"Just like a boy!" Joyce laughed as she followed Phil through the passage.

When the children came out from behind the falls, the tiny fawn remained motionless. But as Phil and Joyce drew nearer, its eyes rolled with terror.

"Its hoof is caught between two rocks," Joyce cried.

"I believe I can move this rock a little," Phil said as he knelt down by the fawn.

When he moved the rock, the fawn pulled its leg free and leaped into the stream.

"No, no!" Joyce shrieked. "You're going toward the whirlpool!"

Phil leaned out to grab the fawn, but it plunged still closer to the whirlpool.

"We'll have to do something quick!" cried Phil desperately. "He'll drown!"

"Use the rope!" Joyce yelled.

"I can tie a slipknot," Phil said, "but I'm not sure I can throw it around him."

Quickly he made a loop in the rope and tossed it at the struggling fawn. But the rope fell short and dropped into the water.

Three times Phil tried. Each time the rope fell short.

In a flash Phil pulled off his shoes and socks. He waded out in the shallow water near the rocks and tossed the rope again. This time the loop encircled the fawn's thin neck.

Gently Phil pulled the animal to the shore. Joyce knelt and held its trembling body while Phil took the rope from its neck.

"Now run to your mother," Joyce said.

As the animal bounded away, the children caught a glimpse of the doe. She had been waiting in the bushes all this time.

Just then the children heard a shout. It was their father, who was leaning over the railing high above them. When Joyce and Phil looked up, he pointed a finger at his open mouth.

"Food!" cried Phil, hurriedly putting on his socks and shoes. "I certainly can use some. How about you, Joyce?"

But his sister was already scrambling up the steep trail to hot dogs, potato chips, and chocolate pie.

Bushy Tail's Escape

One by one the pale stars appeared in the sky over the forest. The midsummer night was filled with soft, mysterious sounds as small woodland creatures crept cautiously out from their hiding places.

They were risking their lives in search of food. Silent-winged owls waited in the dark branches of the trees, ready to pounce on any mouse or wood rat that ventured forth. Weasels and foxes prowled the forest trails. They were preying on weaker animals that were unable to defend themselves.

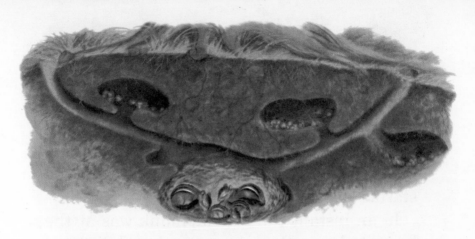

Hidden underground in their den beneath an old stump, a father and mother chipmunk and their babies were sound asleep. Even Bushy Tail, the frisky one, lay quietly.

Occasionally sounds from the forest above came faintly into the burrow. Then the old chipmunks stirred uneasily in their sleep.

The doorway of the burrow was small, and the tunnel that led to the chipmunks' den was long and narrow. So the chipmunks had little to dread from most night prowlers.

But the weasel is one prowler from which chipmunks are never safe. His body is so slim that he can squeeze his way into the deepest part of a chipmunk's burrow. His sharp eyes can see the slightest movement in the grass. And his nose is as keen as the nose of a fox.

Tonight, while the chipmunks were asleep, danger was very near. A weasel was slyly making his way toward their burrow.

Presently the father chipmunk woke up. Something warned him of danger, and he started up the tunnel at once.

In an instant the old chipmunk was at the burrow door. Here he paused and listened intently. He heard no sound, and at first he saw nothing alarming.

Then suddenly on the dim hillside below him Father Chipmunk's eyes caught a slight movement. A slim, dark form was sneaking through the shadows and moving toward the burrow. One glance told the chipmunk of his danger. That long, slim body belonged to his most dreaded enemy—the weasel.

Father Chipmunk fled back down the tunnel to the den. There he turned and looked up the narrow passageway. At the entrance a faint light shone. The sly weasel could enter the den only through this passage. As long as the chipmunk could see that round patch of light, he and his family would be secure from their enemy.

But in a moment the small patch of light was blacked out. The dreaded weasel had found the opening into the burrow!

The old chipmunk did not hesitate. After barking a warning to his family, he fled up a back tunnel to a secret door. Through this door escape was possible.

Mother Chipmunk and the little ones woke in terror and scurried after him. In their haste to flee through the secret door, they scratched and clawed each other frantically.

Meanwhile, the weasel was trying to enter the front door of the burrow. The entrance was tight, even for his slim body.

Squirming and twisting, the crafty weasel finally managed to force his way down into the tunnel. His greedy eyes shone cruelly as his keen nose caught the scent of the chipmunks' tracks. That scent promised to lead him to a tasty meal.

But when he reached the den, it was empty! The chipmunks had fled. Only their tracks to the secret tunnel now remained. Eagerly sniffing these tracks, the weasel forced his way toward the secret door.

Bushy Tail had been the last chipmunk to escape from the tunnel. When he found himself outside, he was filled with fresh terror. His family had vanished!

Then the little chipmunk saw the weasel coming out the secret door. Bushy Tail ran swiftly toward an old hollow tree. Among its roots were many familiar hiding places. If only he could reach those roots in time!

Suddenly Bushy Tail looked back. What he saw increased his panic. Close behind him two small, greedy eyes gleamed through the darkness. The crafty weasel was near and would soon pounce upon him!

All at once the silence of the night was broken by the fierce hunting cry of a great horned owl. The bird swooped from a giant oak nearby. Straight as an arrow it dived at those two gleaming eyes. There was a rustling in the shadows. Then all was still. The dreaded weasel would prowl no more, for the owl had seized its prey.

Bushy Tail was safe now as he bolted for the roots of the hollow tree. At a burrow entrance his nose caught a familiar scent. Pausing, he twitched his tail happily. Bushy Tail had found his family!

Billy and the Loons

As another fish flopped into the bottom of the canoe, Billy Grayson's eyes shone.

"That's a good catch, isn't it, Chief?" he asked his companion.

The Indian guide's face wrinkled into a smile as he looked at the boy's eager face.

"You're doing all right, Billy," he said in his soft voice. "And when we get ashore, I'll show you how to clean your fish."

"Will I be a woodsman then?" asked ten-year-old Billy hopefully.

"You'll be on the way, son, on the way," Chief told him encouragingly.

Billy fished in silence for a while. Then
he asked, "What else do I have to do before
I'm a real woodsman?"

"Well," his companion replied, "you really
should sleep outdoors at least once. Sleeping on the ground toughens you up.

"It's nice to sleep by a lake. You hear
the waves talking and the wind whispering
through the pines. You might even hear the
loons calling before you drop off to sleep.

"Then," the guide's soft voice went on, "if
you wake up very early, you might see the
loons dance. Lots of woodsmen have tried
but failed to see the loons dance. But you
might be one who does."

"I'll ask Dad when we go ashore if I may sleep out," Billy said. "Do you think he'll let me?"

The Indian smiled. "Your dad is a wise man," he replied. "He will say 'Yes.'"

With a quiet stroke of the paddle, Chief turned the canoe toward the spot where the Graysons were camping. In a space partly surrounded by tall trees, Billy could see the ring of stones for a fire. Soon Chief would be cooking the fish that Billy had caught.

As soon as he ran ashore, the boy asked his father's permission to sleep outdoors. Mr. Grayson agreed at once. Mrs. Grayson said, "Oh, Billy!" But she quickly added, "Be sure to take enough blankets, Son."

The boy was almost too excited to eat his supper. But the fish he had caught tasted delicious. He managed to eat an amazing number.

At dusk Billy shouldered his blanket roll. He was eager to start on his adventure.

"I'll go and help Billy find a good place to sleep," the Indian guide told Mr. and Mrs. Grayson.

Leading the way, the Indian walked until he found a little hollow under a great pine. The lake shore was close by, and the water lapped gently against the rocks. Soon the blankets were spread, and Billy rolled himself up in them.

"Would you like to keep the lantern?" the guide asked.

Billy wanted very much to keep it. But he shook his head.

The Indian looked at Billy silently for a minute. "Good boy!" he said. And taking the lantern, he moved quietly away.

"How quiet it is!" thought Billy, looking upward at a star that twinkled through the branches of the pine tree. Then a breeze whispered, and the waves broke sleepily on the rocky shore. Far away a loon called. The boy smiled and was soon fast asleep.

Billy woke suddenly to the dim, gray light of dawn. A mist lay over the lake. Above him the pine needles dripped water. He had never been awake so early before, and the swirling mist made everything seem strange. He was not exactly afraid, but he was glad he had not awakened in the dark.

Suddenly from the water nearby came a loon's loud cry. Then another and another could be heard. The cries sounded like wild laughter.

Billy rolled over quietly. He did not want to risk frightening the loons away. Now he could see the lake without even raising his head. How near the loons had sounded! He peered out into the swirling mist, wishing he could see better.

Gradually the mist rose higher. There, right before Billy's eyes, were the loons.

"One, two, six, eight, ten!" Billy counted aloud. "I wish Dad and Mother and Chief could see those birds!"

Again wild laughter rose from the water. Against the mist, Billy could see the loons' thin necks and pointed bills.

As the boy watched eagerly, he saw the big birds form into two lines opposite each other, about ten or eleven feet apart.

"Will they dance?" wondered Billy. "Am I really going to see the loons dance?"

For a moment the opposite lines of birds
remained quietly facing each other across
the lane of water. Then the two loons at
one end moved toward each other and turned
to face the lane.

Suddenly these two birds rose half out of
the lake and swept down the lane. Their
black wings beat the water, and their feet
churned it to foam. At the foot of the line
the two birds took their places. Afterwards
they filled the air with their laughter.

Now the next pair churned down the lane
and laughed wildly. The dance was
repeated again and again, while
Billy hardly ventured
to breathe.

Then there was a sudden crackling rustle above him, like the rustle of stiff silk. An eagle swooped down over the misty lake. At once the loons dived. The eagle flew off, and only the foaming water was left.

Billy lay very still for a long time. But the loons did not reappear on the surface of the lake. After a while Billy rolled up his blankets and started back toward the camp. He walked very quietly, for he did not want to wake his parents.

As the boy approached the tents, he could smell smoke. Sitting by a crackling fire was the Indian guide.

"Oh, Chief!" Billy whispered. "Did you hear the loons? I saw them! I saw their dance!"

Chief turned slowly, his eyes intent and serious. "I saw the dance, too, son. Don't ever forget it. It may be a long time until you see that dance again."

"And I slept outdoors by myself!" Billy cried. "Am I a real woodsman yet?"

"I believe so," the Indian told him. "I believe you're a grown-up woodsman now!"

Wilderness Partners

A huge grizzly bear sat perfectly still in a shallow stream. His eyes were fixed on the clear water swirling about his forepaws.

The bear ate many kinds of food. But he chose only what he considered the tastiest. And of all the foods that he ate, he liked fish the best. Because he had roamed the wilderness for so long, he knew when the trout chose to swim upriver to another pool. He knew also that they passed through the stream right where he was sitting. It was their highway between two pools.

Now a large trout was swimming toward him. The bear raised his head. His keen eyes followed the trout's gleaming back as the fish fought its way upstream.

Nearer and nearer came the trout. Then suddenly its way was blocked by the bear's solid form. The trout paused. An instant later it lunged forward through the water swirling around the grizzly's forepaws.

With amazing speed for anything so large, the grizzly slapped the water with his huge forepaw. The force of the slap caused a spout of water to squirt upward. The trout rose with the water.

It landed on a rock by the stream. As
the grizzly started toward it, the nearby
bushes parted. Out walked a woolly puppy.
His eyes were alert, and his ears stood up
sharply. His face, with its gray and white
markings, showed that he was a Husky.

Without heeding the big grizzly, the puppy
pounced on the flopping fish. He pinned it
down with his forepaws and sank his sharp
teeth into its smooth sides. Then, walking
backward, he began to drag the trout toward
the bushes.

Over the big grizzly's face came a look of complete astonishment. Then his surprise turned to anger. With a snort the enraged animal scrambled up the bank. He halted just before he reached the puppy.

The puppy had stopped, too. Seemingly he had sensed the bear's anger and had dropped the stolen fish.

Now the Husky moved back a few steps. His tail twitching, he watched the bear sniff at the gasping trout.

The grizzly bit the big trout in half and swallowed the part with the head. Then he turned to the other half. He bit it off just above the tail. The tail he left lying on the bank.

It looked as if the bear were offering the pup a reward for not eating his catch. But actually the grizzly did not like fish tails.

Finished with his meal, the bear shuffled over to sniff at the Husky.

The puppy sat perfectly still. Somehow he sensed that now he had nothing to fear from the grizzly. He was right. Although the bear was a terrible enemy when angered, most of the time he was friendly. His good nature sprang from the fact that he was so much stronger than all the other wilderness animals. After a few moments the grizzly ambled back to the stream.

The hungry pup gobbled up the fish tail and lay down to wait. If the bear caught more trout, the Husky would have more tails to eat. He would have a good meal before he continued his search for the wild mother Husky from whom he had wandered.

The Magic Coat

Tawny, a baby mountain lion, first opened his eyes in a dusky den on Mount Grizzly. His brownish-yellow fur was sprinkled with dark spots, and he was as soft and round-eyed as any kitten.

Like all kittens, Tawny did not want his mother to wash him. "Mew!" he cried in his small, high-pitched voice. And he kicked as hard as he knew how.

But Tawny's mother held him fast in her forepaws as she licked the warm milk from his whiskers. "Mmmmm," she purred.

Tawny squirmed and twisted, but it was useless. His mother went on cleaning and smoothing every part of his plump body.

Then came his sister Leone's turn. His twin had the same black spots on her back. She had the same black tip to her nose, and the same black rings encircled her tail. But Leone was smaller than Tawny.

The two kittens lived in a cave on a steep ledge. At first they were too weak even to walk. They had to shove themselves along on their stomachs with their hind legs. But soon they were strong enough to play games.

"Ffft!" Tawny would call in cat language.

"Ffft!" Leone would reply.

Then the mischievous kittens pretended to fight. With backs humped and tails bushed out in make-believe anger, they would leap at each other. Away they would go, rolling in a furry ball.

One day Tawny's mother was out hunting, and Leone was asleep in the cave. Tawny sat at the mouth of the cave, lazily enjoying the sunshine. His eyelids were almost closed. Suddenly they snapped open alertly.

Just out of Tawny's reach was
a butterfly. Tawny leaped for it.
But he did not catch the butterfly.
Instead, the kitten turned completely over.
Missing the ledge, he pitched downward to
the ground below.

The earth was soft and springy with pine
needles. Tawny was not hurt by the fall,
but he could not get back up into the den.
The ledge was too high for him to jump up
on it. Nor could he dig his claws into the
hard surface to climb up.

Frightened, Tawny crouched in the shade
of some low bushes. Then he saw a coyote
sneaking toward him. The animal's hungry
look increased Tawny's terror.

"Ffftt!" hissed Tawny, ready to fight for his life. But the coyote only crept nearer. His greedy eyes never left the little hump of fur crouched at the foot of the ledge.

All at once the furry hump lunged forward. The kitten startled the larger animal with a stinging slap of his paw.

Uttering a loud "Yiii!" the coyote backed out of reach. Instantly Tawny scrambled up a nearby tree trunk. Trembling, he clung to the rough bark while the coyote crouched below, watching the kitten intently.

But soon poor Tawny felt his claws giving way under the weight of his fat body. As the coyote gazed at him hungrily, he began to slide down the tree trunk.

Then, not far away, Tawny could hear his mother coming. He gave a wail of despair. His cry was small and high-pitched, but it reached his mother's ears.

There was a flash of red-brown fur. The big mountain lion was rushing to her baby's rescue. She reached the tree just as the coyote was jumping up toward Tawny.

"Grrr!" she threatened, growling deep in her throat.

The coyote fled, his tail between his legs.

Quickly Tawny's mother looked her baby over. Then she picked him up by the loose skin on the back of his neck. She carried him in her mouth to the foot of the ledge.

The door of her den was a few feet above. But with little effort she leaped the entire distance. Grabbing the edge of the rock with her great forepaws, she drew herself up over it. She did not drop Tawny until she was far back in the snug cave.

One bright morning the mother cat taught her babies a game. Tawny and Leone were napping just outside the back opening to the cave. When they woke, their mother was nowhere in sight. At least the two kittens could not find her.

This was very strange. Sniffing around, they could smell their mother's warm fur. They stood listening, their wee tails twitching. Surely they could hear her breathing.

Tawny was confused. His eyes searched the ground. Then he looked up. What had become of his mother?

"Grrr!" called the mother cat, rolling the sound in her throat. The call came from a branch above Tawny. The leaves stirred. Now the kittens could see their mother!

There she lay, crouching along the limb of a large tree. Her white underside was pressed close against the bark. And it was almost impossible to see her brownish fur among the brown branches. It was just as though she had a magic coat that hid her.

"Mmm!" purred the mother cat, watching her youngsters' surprise.

She would play this game with her babies many times. By and by they would learn that they, too, had magic coats to protect them from threatening enemies.

But now it was time to eat. The great mountain lion leaped to the ground to see what she could catch for supper.

Tawny scampered back into the cave with his twin. He was still too young to hunt. But he would learn. Soon he would be able to seek his own food. And he would learn how to keep from being preyed upon by the other wild animals.

Willie the Moose

Willie shoved his head around the corner of a low log building that stood in a snow-covered clearing. The moose peered at the spot he had just left so hurriedly.

A moment before he had tried to drive off the Clayton family's two frisky young dogs by kicking at them. Unhappily his flying hoof had hit Mr. Clayton's leg.

Now from behind the logging-camp stable Willie could see the lumberman rubbing his leg and glaring about. Herbert and Kitty Clayton were running from the family cabin toward their father.

"This is the last straw!" Mr. Clayton told the children angrily. "We'll simply have to get rid of Willie."

"But, Dad," argued Kitty, "it was just an accident. Willie didn't mean to kick you."

"Of course not," Herbert added. "We saw the dogs bothering him. You just happened to be in the way of Willie's hoof."

But Mr. Clayton was determined to get rid of the moose. "We've no place to cage him up, and he's too big and strong to run loose like a pet any longer. No telling when he might injure somebody seriously."

Kitty's forehead wrinkled with concern.

"What do you intend to do with Willie?" she asked anxiously.

"I'll just have to run that moose off into the woods," her father answered.

"Oh, no!" Kitty wailed in despair. "Poor Willie!"

Followed by the children, Mr. Clayton limped toward the cabin. "Herbert," he said, "remember now. I want you and Kitty to stay away from Willie. I'll get rid of him as soon as I can."

The Claytons had found Willie in the woods when he was a helpless, week-old calf. Ever since they had treated him kindly. Herbert and Kitty had fed and cared for him. They had spent most of their time with him when they were not attending the country school two miles away.

But as the moose grew older, he seemed to take charge of the children. He never let them out of his sight as they swam in the lake or picked berries or roamed through the woods.

Now the moose's young charges seemed to be deserting him. Puzzled, Willie watched them go to their cabin. Then he ambled off toward the camp kitchen. The door was shut against the bitter cold, but even outside the smell of food was sweet and tempting.

The moose nosed the latch until he finally lifted it. Then he butted the door with his antlers, and it swung open.

Charlie, the logging-camp cook, was making flapjacks. "Hi, Willie!" shouted the cook. "Have some of your favorite food!" With that Charlie tossed a flapjack at the moose.

Willie gobbled up the flapjack and waited in the doorway for more.

Charlie tossed him several more flapjacks. Finally the cook said, "That's all, Willie. Now get out!"

"Moo-oo-oooo!" Willie bellowed.

"I'll *moo* you!" Charlie said. Picking up a dishpan full of water, he flung the water right in Willie's face.

"Get out!" yelled the cook. "Go before you eat up all the family's lunch!"

Willie backed out the door so fast that he sat down. Before he could get on his feet, the water dripping down his nose and chin had frozen into long, icy whiskers.

The next day Mr. Clayton tied one end of a rope around Willie's neck. He fastened the other end to his car and drove off along a logging trail. The children watched sadly as Willie was swallowed up by the forest.

Mile after mile the moose followed along at the end of the rope, his long legs churning like a windmill. At last he grew tired and began to fight the rope that encircled his neck. As the automobile bounced over a small pit in the trail, the moose gave an extra hard pull. The rope broke, and Willie regained his freedom.

He bounded off among the trees and ran until Mr. Clayton was far behind. Then the moose lay down and took a nap. When he woke, he felt hungry and lonesome. So he began walking toward the Clayton camp.

Suddenly he stopped and sniffed. There was a smell of flapjacks in the air!

Following his nose, he walked on until he almost stumbled upon a tent skillfully hidden by brushwood. Around a fire three men were sitting. They were all gobbling up stacks of delicious-smelling flapjacks.

Overcome with hunger, Willie mooed loudly
and ran straight toward the men. At his
unexpected appearance, they dropped everything and scattered into the woods.

Willie immediately ate up every flapjack
in sight. Then he ambled on toward home.

He had a long way to go. But even though
this part of the forest was strange to him,
he managed to keep on the right trail.

When he was half a mile from the Clayton
camp, he noticed a peculiar scarlet glow in
the darkening sky above the trees. The red
glow broadened as Willie stared.

Now the moose could smell burning logs.
He ran bellowing to the bunkhouse. Then
he sped to the Clayton cabin and set up an
unearthly noise.

There were cries of "Fire! The stable's
on fire!" as the loggers streamed from the
bunkhouse. Mr. Clayton quickly joined them.
Finally Herbert and Kitty came rushing out,
buttoning on their heavy coats.

"Why, Willie is back!" cried Kitty. She
and Herbert patted him fondly.

With the moose standing beside them, the
two children watched as their father and
his loggers fought the fire.

After the fire was out, Mr. Clayton said, "It's lucky that the blaze was discovered so soon."

"It was Willie who discovered the fire," Charlie said.

"Willie!" exclaimed Mr. Clayton.

"Yes," answered Charlie. "It was Willie's bellowing that gave the alarm."

"Well," said Herbert, "this proves that we need Willie here. He would make a splendid fire chief."

Mr. Clayton grinned. "I'll have to change my mind about Willie," he admitted. "He's certainly won the right to stay with us."

The next day the moose strutted about the camp with a large sign encircling his neck. The sign said, "Willie Clayton, Fire Chief."

A Dangerous Surprise

The mother sea otter was on the alert. She held herself straight up in the water. One third of her glossy brown body rose above the waving blue-green surface of the rock-walled cove. Although the water was deep, she stood so straight that it looked as if she were standing on the bottom.

Occasionally she twitched her black nose and white whiskers. Her eyes followed her plump, woolly baby intently as he practiced swimming for the first time alone.

Adapted by permission of the publisher, J. B. Lippincott Company, from *The Last of the Sea Otters* by Harold McCracken. Copyright, 1942, by Harold McCracken.

Learning to swim was like a game to the baby sea otter. He paddled his short front legs furiously. He wiggled his whole body as he splashed the water into foam with his hind feet and tail.

Every time his face went under water he snorted and shook his head hard. Once he tried to dive but came up choking. With a little look of fright in his eyes he rolled over on his back for a brief rest while he recovered his breath.

The days passed swiftly for the little sea otter. He was always learning something. Every day he learned something new that he could do or should not do. Nearly every day he saw some new creature that lived in the sea or flew in the air.

But his world was still a very small one. It did not go beyond the rocky cliffs that walled the cove where he and his mother lived.

Swimming under water was the young sea otter's favorite sport. Everything appeared different in the strange world beneath the surface.

One day the little otter was gliding gracefully under water past the rocky sides of the cove. He poked his black nose exploringly along the ledges.

On one ledge crawled an odd-looking crab. Its arms were almost as long as the baby otter's whole body. It moved them slowly, as if it were tired.

The sea otter stopped for a moment to watch this queer creature. Then he shot up to the surface briefly to get a fresh breath of air. He tried to jump clear out of the water as he had seen his mother do.
Then down he went again
to find something else.

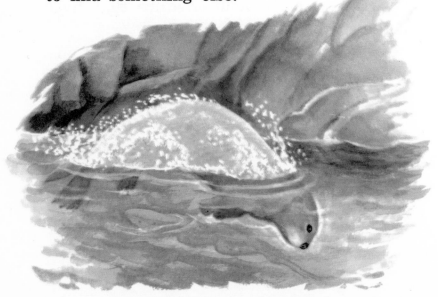

There was only one place in the entire cove where he was forbidden to go. This was around a large ledge that overhung the water near a small beach. The top of the ledge was smooth and level. To the young sea otter it looked like the nicest place in all the cove to lie and sleep.

When he was younger, he had crawled out on this ledge several times. Each time his mother had barked a stern warning. Then she had come to him as fast as she could. Grabbing him in her teeth, she had carried him away quickly. As she put him down, she had bumped him very roughly with her snout.

"You stay away from there!" she seemed to be saying.

The little otter had never seen anything dangerous near this forbidden ledge. But his mother's warnings had made him curious and doubly eager to go back. There must be something very unusual there. It was probably under the water.

The otter determined to go to the ledge at his first chance.

One day the mother sea otter was floating on her back out in the center of the cove. She was playing with a bunch of seaweed. Purring contentedly, she tossed the seaweed into the air, first with one paw, then with the other.

When the young otter saw that his mother was not watching, he took a deep breath. Then he dived and swam quickly toward the forbidden place.

As he glided along through the water, he met a school of small, flat fish that had wandered into the cove. They were about the size of his hind feet. Occasionally he had seen these fish before. He had always tried to catch one then. Now he scarcely noticed them.

Eagerly he approached the big ledge. His little nose pointed straight ahead. His eyes tried to pierce the dark underwater shadows before him. Then his heart began to beat fast, and he slowed his speed.

Once the youngster faltered and started to double back. But he saw nothing frightening, and he went closer.

It was like a cave beneath the overhanging ledge. To the youngster it looked like a good place to explore. But it was very dark. He swam up almost to the entrance. Peering inside, he thought he saw something move.

Suddenly the whole cave seemed to come alive. The most startling thing the young otter had ever seen rushed out upon him. The foaming water appeared to be filled with long wiggling arms lined with suckers. In the center of these arms was a shapeless body with two great eyes at the top. The arms shot out at the young sea otter as if to throw themselves around him.

It was an octopus. For a long time this octopus had been waiting in its underwater cave for something like a baby sea otter to swim near. Now it was ready to grab its prey for a wonderful feast.

The frightened otter whirled in the water to make a desperate dash for safety. But one of the octopus' long arms slipped around the back part of his body. Frantically the otter struggled to get free as the octopus tried to fasten the suckers of its arm upon him. Fortunately, the thick, woolly hair on the otter's body prevented the suckers from taking a firm hold.

Suddenly, with a quick movement, the otter broke the hold of the octopus. He was free of the deadly suckers! He was saved!

He swam to the surface faster than he had ever traveled before. When his head came up into the air, he sped to his mother.

From his frightened look she sensed what had happened. She nosed him over to make certain he was uninjured. Then she rolled over on her back again. She was sure he would never go to the forbidden ledge again.

Gray Wing and Nika

From their wilderness home in the North flew a wedge of splendid big Canada geese. They were winging their way southward for the winter.

Led by a wise old gander, they flew over mountains and the silvery ribbon of a wide river. Straight to a forest-edged lake the gander piloted his flock of sixty geese. This lake had always been as secure for them as their far-off northern home. Each year the birds rested here for a day or so. Then they flew on to their southern feeding grounds.

Near the middle of the wedge of soaring
Canadas flew Gray Wing, a splendid young
gander. His back and wings were darker
than those of his companions. In the rays of
the western sun his glossy feathers shone
like satin.

Flying near Gray Wing was graceful Nika,
his mate.

When the geese were directly over the lake,
the wedge spread out. The birds began to
settle for the night upon the calm water.

The geese woke at dawn. Paddling close to shore, they began to feed on the wild rice, which was plentiful that autumn season. Gray Wing and Nika swam about with the other geese, concealed by the morning mist. The gray birds were fearless, for they had never been bothered on this peaceful lake.

Slowly the sky lightened. The mist began to rise, and the shoreline appeared. There, concealed in the reeds, were two men with guns. As the fog lifted, they saw the flock of splendid geese.

The hunters lost no time. Instantly two shots burst out. A great outcry rose from the startled geese. With a heavy rustling of wings they started upward in desperate flight.

There was a second burst of shot. Now the geese mounted rapidly. Above their outcry rose the call of their leader, the wise old gander.

High overhead the birds circled. Then they headed southward through the protecting mist. Of the sixty geese, all but three were in the wedge. One of these was Nika.

At the first shots one goose had flopped head downward into the water, a huddle of limp feathers. Another bird had faltered and dropped when the guns had blazed away the second time.

At that moment Nika, rising swiftly from the lake, had felt a blow on her left wing. This was followed by a sharp pain. Nika had faltered, then steadied herself. Now she was attempting to beat her way upward.

But she could not reach the swiftly flying wedge. She called out to the flock. Only Gray Wing, her mate, heeded her wild cry. Looking back, he discovered that Nika was missing from the wedge.

Gray Wing uttered an answering cry. He turned, left the flying wedge, and swooped down toward Nika. By this time she was barely above the treetops, for the pain in her injured wing was increasing.

The rest of the geese soared on. From the misty sky the honking of the flock came back, high and clear. Then the cries grew fainter and fainter. Gradually the sounds died away.

Soon Nika's strength was spent. So she and her mate dropped down to a little pond, where the reeds and rice concealed them.

Fortunately, only Nika's wing was injured, but she was weak from the pain. When she had recovered some of her strength, both geese began to feed on the wild rice.

It was noon when a few tame ducks from a nearby farm came to the pond. They were marching in a single line behind a handsome green-headed drake. Gray Wing and Nika watched the ducks and the drake wade out into the water. Presently the northern birds ventured forth from the rice stalks and reeds near the shore.

As the geese swam out to join the tame
fowls, they were suddenly frightened by a
herd of cows approaching the pond to drink.
Gray Wing rose up. But Nika's attempt to
follow was in vain. Her injured wing could
not bear her weight.

Gray Wing wheeled and flew back to Nika.
Again they hid in the reeds near the shore.

Young Frank Gordon, who drove the cows, was much excited. He hurried back to the farm where he lived with his Aunt Lizzie and Uncle Peter. Breathlessly he told them about the two wild geese. When Aunt Lizzie Gordon heard her nephew's report, she said that the visitors were not to be harmed.

The next day Frank took some corn from the crib. He scattered it beside the pond where the two strangers could find it. As he watched the geese eating the grain, he wished he could make pets of them.

Gray Wing and Nika remained among the rice and reeds while Nika's wing mended. Gradually it grew stronger. But Nika could not yet fly. After frequent attempts to lead her away, Nika's faithful mate always came back to her.

One morning the two big Canadas heard a distant honking. A large flock of geese was flying southward. Nika tried to rise and join them. But she could not. Faithful Gray Wing did not desert her. He stayed with her, ready to help her and to protect her from harm.

The last days of autumn passed swiftly. Then one night a storm swept in from the northwest. It was followed by a day of icy rain and bitter cold. Aunt Lizzie Gordon thought immediately of the big gray geese. They must be sheltered from the fury of the winter storms. So Frank went out and left a trail of corn on the ground. In this way the birds were coaxed into a pen.

The geese no longer had their freedom, but they were safe with the other fowls. As the season advanced, they seemed to grow used to their pen. Frequently they were allowed to run loose in the barnyard. They came fearlessly at Frank's call.

Uncle Peter grumbled because the geese ate so much grain. Once he suggested roast goose for Christmas. But Aunt Lizzie gave him such a scolding that he quickly insisted it was only a joke. And that was his last remark about roast goose.

One morning there was a wild honking in the barnyard. Nika was trying her wings! For fifty yards she circled upward. Then, faltering, she swooped to the ground.

By the end of winter Nika had recovered from her wound and was able to fly again. On the first warm spring day she and Gray Wing grew restless. They were longing for the freedom of their northern home.

One day a familiar call came from the sky. A large wedge of Canada geese was flying directly overhead. They were returning from their winter home in the South.

Their cries urged Gray Wing and Nika to join their flight to freedom. The two geese hissed in their pen and beat their splendid wings against the wire. But it was in vain. They could not escape.

Three days later a big wind storm struck
suddenly during the night. Much damage
was caused on the farm by the harsh blasts.
Big branches were torn from the trees, and
shingles were blown off the farmhouse roof.
The weather vane was twisted off the barn.

When Frank Gordon woke the next morning, he heard the fowls making a great deal
of noise. He dressed quickly and ran to the
shed where the Canadas were kept at night.
There Frank saw that the wind had blown a
big tree limb against the door, smashing it
completely. The geese had escaped.

Then far overhead the boy heard a faint
honking. Immediately there were answering
cries from Gray Wing and Nika. He looked
up just in time. Upward swept the two big
birds to join the wedge of Canadas. Up, up
they went—flying free at last.

Famous Americans
of Other Times

George Grows Up

"George," called Mrs. Washington one day from the farmhouse door. "I want you to help me clean out the storehouse. It hasn't been done since your father died."

The storehouse was a small building, near the kitchen, where many things that were not used every day were kept. Cleaning it seemed a tedious job to the lively thirteen-year-old boy, but George Washington did as his mother asked.

In a dark corner of the storehouse, George found something strange made of iron rods. He examined it closely.

"What is this?" he asked his mother.

When she saw what he was holding, she said, "That's your father's surveying chain. Did you never see it before? Your father used it to measure the land he bought. He wanted to make sure that all the boundary lines were actually right."

"May I keep this?" George asked.

"If you like," answered Mrs. Washington. Then she hurried away on an errand.

"I will talk with Lawrence about learning surveying," George thought.

Lawrence Washington, who was George's older half-brother, lived at Mount Vernon. Shortly after George's fourteenth birthday the lad had a chance to go to Mount Vernon. As soon as he could arrange it, he talked to his brother alone.

"I would like to give up school and learn surveying, Lawrence," George said. "School is tedious and boring. I want to learn what I need for a *man's* work."

"I have been thinking about your future," Lawrence replied. "Your mother will not permit you to go to school in England as I did. But perhaps you could go to sea."

"To sea!" George cried. "Oh, Lawrence, that would be wonderful! But will Mother let me go?" he added in sudden dismay.

"I will ride back with you tomorrow and ask her," Lawrence said.

The next day he asked Mrs. Washington's permission for George to go to sea.

She settled the matter at once. "George is not to go!" she said firmly.

For a time George was disappointed. But at last he forgot about going to sea. He did not forget, however, about wanting to learn surveying.

One day George learned that an excellent surveyor, Mr. Byrne, lived in a nearby town.

"He might teach me," the boy thought.

The next day George went to Mr. Byrne's house. His knock was answered at once by a friendly-looking man.

"I'm looking for Surveyor Byrne," George announced.

"You have found him," the man answered with a smile. Then he motioned for George to enter.

"I am George Washington. Perhaps you knew my father," said George.

"So I did," Mr. Byrne replied. "I helped your father with several surveys. But that was some time ago."

"Yes, sir," George replied politely. "And now I want to be a surveyor, too. Would you teach me? I can figure very well, and I can draw a good map."

"Surveying is not all a gentleman's work," Mr. Byrne told him. "You'd have hours of tramping in the mud, climbing mountains, and wading shallow creeks. You'd hardly care for that."

"I like the outdoors, sir," George said. "What you say makes me want to learn all the more."

Mr. Byrne made up his mind quickly. "All right, George," he said. "Come tomorrow. Wear your top boots. You'll need them."

"Shall I bring my chain?" George asked.

"No," said Mr. Byrne, "you'll use mine."

From that time on George went on many surveying trips with Mr. Byrne. George learned to measure the boundaries of a piece of land and to set out corner poles or use trees as boundary markers.

He learned to draw maps of the boundaries he had measured, showing all the rivers and creeks. His drawing was always neat and his lettering clear. Sometimes he would just describe a boundary line in writing. The line might be between a maple tree and an oak, or between two spruces and an apple tree.

When George was almost sixteen, William Fairfax, who lived near Mount Vernon, had a visitor from England. It was his cousin, Lord Fairfax. He owned thousands of acres of wilderness land in the West.

One morning when George was at Mount Vernon, he and Lawrence rode over to call on Lord Fairfax. They found him striding excitedly up and down the room. The pages of a letter in his hand shook as he walked.

"People are moving onto my land without paying for it!" he cried angrily. "They say that the land is vacant and belongs to anyone who wants it."

"You cannot do anything about it until you have your land surveyed," William advised. "You must know your boundary lines."

"Then let's make a survey," snapped the land owner. It was decided to do so at once.

"I hear that George is doing well with his surveying," William Fairfax told Lawrence. "Why not have him accompany the surveying party?"

Turning to the boy, William asked, "How about it, George?"

George's eyes gleamed. "I should like it
very much, sir," he answered.

The surveying party left on their trip in
the month of March. In charge was one of
the best surveyors in Virginia. George's
work was to describe the boundary lines in
writing. His earlier training proved to be
a great help to the party.

George was sorry when the five-week trip
was ended. There was a thrill about the
wilderness that he had never known before.
He wondered how and when he would take
such a journey again.

After the survey, George was recognized as a grown-up among the men around Mount Vernon. They asked his advice about the new wilderness land and discovered that he had noticed more about the soil than had the head surveyor. Now when the men talked about land, George joined in.

"I should like to own land in the West," Lawrence remarked at dinner one day.

"What does land sell for, George?" Lord Fairfax, who was a dinner guest, inquired.

"Oh, the price is cheap," George replied. "You can get a hundred acres for about six or seven pounds in English money."

The talk soon changed to soil and crops. About these, too, George knew a great deal.

After Lord Fairfax had gone, Lawrence put his hand on George's shoulder.

"You know, George," he said, "I've been sorry that you were not sent to school in England. But I begin to see that what you have learned here in Virginia may be worth more than what many other young men learn abroad. Virginia has a great future. And I expect you to have a big part in it."

The Boy Hunter

Daniel Boone was only ten when he asked his father for a gun.

"I reckon you're a little young for that," drawled his father. "You'll have to wait a couple of years longer."

While George Washington was learning to be a surveyor in Virginia, Daniel was growing up in a neighboring region. Like George, Daniel lived on a farm. But the Boone farm was on the edge of a thick forest.

Daniel had loved the forest as long as he could remember. When he was little more than a baby, he tramped through the woods while his father and older brothers hunted game for the family's table. At the age of ten Daniel knew the forest almost as well as he knew his own barnyard.

To Daniel two years seemed a long time to wait for a rifle. So he made himself a hunting weapon. He uprooted a slender tree and sharpened one end of it to a point. At the very first chance he got, he started off into the woods with his homemade weapon.

The boy did not come home empty-handed. He brought a couple of wild birds.

"Oh!" cried Mrs. Boone. "They'll make a fine supper for us. How did you manage to get them, Dan?"

"With this," answered Daniel. Proudly he held up the weapon he had made.

Daniel had little time to spend hunting with his new weapon. He had many chores and duties at home. But whenever he found an opportunity, the lad would slip off into the woods.

There Daniel learned many things that he could not learn in school. For one thing, he learned to read signs. By looking closely at the ground or brush, he could tell whether some wild animal had passed that way lately. He could even tell what kind of animal it was and track it to its hiding place.

He could also tell from the appearance of footprints whether a white man or an Indian had been roaming the forest.

Two years passed. At last the day came when Daniel's father provided him with a rifle. The lad was delighted. Now, more than ever, he tried to find time to go off into the woods. He soon became so skillful with his gun that he was praised far and wide as a hunter.

One November morning Daniel finished his chores quickly and shouldered his precious rifle. He had decided to go hunting.

Calling to his favorite dog, Daniel started into the woods. The boy's family was not worried to see him go off alone. They were used to his hunting trips, and the game he brought home was welcome. They supposed that he would be back by sunset. But darkness fell, and Daniel was still absent.

At supper Mr. Boone said, "Well, I reckon Dan can take care of himself."

"Yes," agreed the boy's mother. "He'll be back by tomorrow."

But he was not. When Daniel was still absent on the second day, his family began to be concerned. Late in the afternoon a searching party started off into the woods.

The searchers soon found the trail of the missing lad. A short time later they lost it. The boys in the party shouted, and the men fired their rifles, hoping that Daniel would answer. But they heard nothing.

At dusk one of the party caught sight of a distant plume of smoke. The searchers hurried toward it.

Guided by the smoke, the party came upon a rough shack built of tree limbs, dry grass, and brushwood. Daniel was inside, cooking his supper. Skins of animals that he had shot were scattered on the floor of the hut.

Daniel looked up at the men opposite him. "What's all the excitement?" he asked.

"Why, we thought you were lost, Dan!" exclaimed Mr. Boone. "Didn't you hear the guns go off?"

The lad had been so intent on his cooking that he had scarcely heeded the shots of the searchers. "Oh," he said, "I heard all the shooting. But I thought some hunters were after deer. You needn't have worried. I can take care of myself."

And so he could. For the rest of his life he continued to roam the forests. As the settlers came in and cut down the trees, he kept moving west. Finally he had moved far beyond the Ohio valley.

Even Daniel's last home was built in the midst of a wilderness. There he watched his sons and daughters grow up. There he spent his happiest days, hunting and trapping in the woods he had always loved.

The Spelling Bee

"Spell *porridge*," said the schoolmaster.

"*Porridge.* P-o-r-r-i-d-g-e," slowly spelled the entire class.

It was a bare, dreary country schoolroom in New England, in the year 1770. There were no wall maps, pictures, or bookshelves to make the room pleasant. There were no pictures in the schoolbooks to make learning easier. There was a fireplace in the room. But it scorched the faces of those near it and left those a few feet away shivering.

As the teacher pronounced the words, he did not see the pupils passing a note around.

From one long bench to the other went the note, and from one child to the next. Each boy and girl read the note eagerly. It was an invitation.

Come to my house to a Spelling Bee and Taffy Pull Friday night at candle-lighting.

Noah Webster

Blue eyes and brown turned toward the tall, slender boy with a high forehead and dark-red hair who had given the invitation. There was high excitement at the thought of another spelling contest and taffy pull at Noah Webster's house.

Upon their arrival Friday at the Webster home, the young guests found a half-circle of vacant chairs arranged before the fireplace. When the boys and girls took their places, the flames from the great logs shone upon happy faces. Spelling at the Websters' was a jolly party, not a tedious task.

Noah's younger sister and brother were seated with the guests. Noah stood opposite them, his back to the fire. He looked very serious.

Noah began to give out the words from a
list he had made. His gray eyes gleamed.
His square jaw was firm. Spelling to Noah
Webster was a very important matter.

The delightful odor of boiling taffy came
from a huge kettle over the fire. But the
real business of the evening had everyone's
attention.

"Color," Noah pronounced and motioned to
Rebecca Hooker. She sat in the first chair
next to Noah's sister, Jerusha.

"C-o-l-o-u-r," Rebecca answered.

"Wrong! Leave the circle," said Noah.

The other children giggled. They all knew why Noah had put Rebecca out of the circle. The schoolmaster taught them to spell in the English manner—c-o-l-o-u-r, o-d-o-u-r.

But Noah Webster was a loyal American. He believed that the better way of spelling words like *color* and *odor* was the simpler New England way—without the *u*.

Next it was Jerusha's turn to take the word *color*. "C-o-l-o-r," spelled Jerusha as she moved into Rebecca's vacant chair.

The spelling bee went on. Noah gave out words familiar to the New England people. Some of these were *stall, cupboard, rescue, pitch, soul, opossum, mischief, cousin.*

Finally only Jerusha was left. The other children did not mind. "What else could be expected," they thought, "from a girl who has Noah Webster for a brother!"

Now came the more interesting part of the evening. With a piece of black, scorched wood, Noah drew a picture of a bear on the pine walls of the kitchen. As he drew, he told a story about the picture and wrote the difficult words on the wall.

Noah's audience crowded admiringly about
him. Because of the story and the picture,
his pupils could easily remember the spelling of these words.

Before long Noah had almost covered the
kitchen walls with pictures and words. Then
the pine walls were scrubbed, but the words
remained clearly in the minds of those boys
and girls. It was a pleasure to learn by
Noah's way of teaching.

Now the party grew noisier. Games were
played. The taffy was pulled and eaten with
delight.

As the Websters' tall grandfather clock was striking nine, the guests began to put on their wraps. Soon they departed, their lanterns in their hands. Walking along the dark roads, they complained about the high prices they had to pay for schoolbooks.

"I shall have no new shoes all winter," Rebecca said sadly. "That's because Father had to buy me an arithmetic and a Bible for school. Books should be cheaper."

"I reckon Noah Webster is smart enough to make a book," said Betsy Hand. "Noah knows so many words. He draws very good pictures, too."

"Noah make a book? You must be out of your wits!" William Duke exclaimed.

The others agreed. Noah Webster could draw pictures that certainly made spelling fun. But no one with any wits at all would think that Noah could write a book. What a comical idea!

But they would not have laughed if they could have seen into the future. When they grew up, their own children used a spelling book that Noah Webster had made.

The book contained lists of words used every day by American boys and girls. It also contained pictures and stories that helped pupils remember the words. When the children used this book, learning how to spell was no longer a dreary task for them.

Thousands of Webster spellers were taken by settlers to all parts of the country. The books went west, south, and north. They went in stagecoaches, covered wagons, ox-carts, puffing little steam trains, and aboard river boats.

Meanwhile, Noah Webster himself went from farms to villages, and from villages to towns, explaining his speller to the teachers. Soon he carried with him a dictionary that he had made. It, too, had pictures to help explain the meanings of words.

With his speller and his dictionary, Noah taught countless numbers of boys and girls who lived far beyond the kitchen walls of his New England home.

Fulton's Folly

It was a hot afternoon in the late spring of 1779. Young Robert Fulton was going out fishing with his friend Christopher and Christopher's father.

Robert frowned as he pushed the long pole into the creek bottom and shoved with all his strength. The boys had worked all day. Both were tired. But there was still more work to be done before they could enjoy any fishing.

Their heavy, flat-bottomed boat had to be poled a long way up the shallow stream. Besides being heavy, the boat was awkward and hard to steer.

Adapted and reprinted from *Boat Builder, the Story of Robert Fulton* by Clara Ingram Judson; copyright, 1940, by Charles Scribner's Sons; used by permission of the publishers.

"There should be an easier way to move a boat than this!" Robert said impatiently.

Christopher looked at Robert in surprise. "But we have to use either oars or a pole. We can't go upstream any other way."

"I should think an engine could be used to move a boat," Robert argued. "People use steam engines to do all kinds of work now. Why not move a boat with one?"

"Have you lost your wits?" Christopher's father cried. "The engine's weight would sink a boat. No one will ever move a boat very far with steam."

After the boys had finally poled the boat to the fishing spot, they took a swim to cool off. Afterwards they caught a good string of fish. But the idea that there should be a better way to move a boat upstream still lingered in Robert's mind.

Several weeks later Christopher's father wanted to go fishing again. But when he came to the creek bank, his boat was gone. A sound up the creek caught his attention. Coming toward him around a bend was his boat.

Something odd was fastened to each side
of the boat. Robert was standing up in the
center, turning a strange-shaped rod.

"They work!" Christopher called. "The
paddles work!" His father was speechless.
Had those boys ruined his boat?

Christopher took a pole from the bottom of
the boat and steered toward the bank.

Then Robert spoke up. "I was sure that
there must be a better way to move a boat.
I invented a way, and Christopher helped
me fix up your boat. You turn this crank
to move the two paddles on the sides. Then
the paddles move the boat. It's really very
simple. Won't you try it, sir?"

Christopher's father looked doubtful. "No, you do it," he said, stepping into the boat.

So after Christopher had turned the boat around, Robert worked the crank. Slowly but steadily they moved upstream.

The invention was a great success. All the village boys wanted rides. They were even willing to turn the crank for a chance to go on the boat. Every evening villagers came to watch the boat sweep upstream with delighted boys cranking the paddles.

Though Robert was excited by the success of his invention, he did not forget his idea of boats run by steam. If a hand-turned crank moved a boat, he reasoned, why wouldn't a steam engine do the task even better? But for years he did nothing about his idea. He was more interested in other things.

The lad had always been skillful at drawing and painting. When he was seventeen, he began to earn his living by painting and selling pictures. Later he went abroad in a sailing ship to study art in England. For many years he remained there and became an excellent painter.

All over England and in France there was talk of steam engines and of the work they could do. People said that there was great need to move things faster by water.

Fulton's interest in a steam-run boat was renewed by this talk. Many other men had attacked the problem of building such a boat but had failed to solve it completely. Fulton felt sure he could do it. In France he met a man who helped him develop his ideas, and he actually built a steam-powered boat.

The boat was small, and there was little space for passengers. People jeered at it. But it amazed the watching crowds by running under its own power for several miles upriver and back to the dock.

Fulton was encouraged by this success. So he decided to leave France and build a steamboat in the United States. He wanted to build one that would carry passengers and cargo. In the autumn of 1806, after twenty years abroad, he sailed for New York.

Immediately upon his arrival he started to work. He arranged to have the new boat built in a New York shipyard. He ordered the engine from England.

Work on the new steamboat went swiftly. By the following spring it was well along. The engine came from England. After being carefully checked, it was put in place.

In July the boat was nearing completion. Great crowds gathered to look at it. They jeered just as the people had done earlier in France. They called the new steamboat "Fulton's Folly."

"It will never work," they said gleefully.

By the late summer of 1807 the boat was ready to be tested. Fulton invited some of his friends to make the first trip with him. The boat was to run upriver for a distance of one hundred fifty miles.

The day of the test was clear and warm. Curious throngs lined the riverbank to watch Fulton prove his folly.

"How people will laugh at us if the boat doesn't go!" said the passengers on deck.

Suddenly a bell rang, and ropes were cast off. Fulton gave the signal to start. The engine began to rumble, while all the people held their breath. Then the engine stopped. There was no sound but the lapping of the water against the boat.

On the bank the watchers began to laugh.

"Told you she wouldn't go!" they jeered. "Now look at Fulton's Folly!"

Meanwhile, all the passengers wondered if they should go ashore. Then Fulton stepped up on a deck seat and spoke loudly enough to be heard on the dock.

"Do not be annoyed by the delay, friends. Give me half an hour. I'll get us going, or we'll give up the trip for the day."

Fulton stepped down and went to examine the engine. Soon he found what the trouble was and corrected it. A few minutes later the paddle wheel began to turn, and the boat started upriver.

At first all the watchers were speechless. Then the silence ended in a shout of triumph echoing from shore to ship and back again. Men tossed hats into the air. Women waved their handkerchiefs and hugged each other with excitement. All the passengers on the boat rushed to shake Fulton's hand.

Robert Fulton was excited, too. He had proved that his steamboat would really go! Now people and cargoes could travel safely and cheaply over the lakes and rivers of the United States. And someday a steamboat would cross the ocean.

How a Song Named a Flag

In the year 1814 a large new flag waved over the fort guarding the city of Baltimore.

"It's a grand flag," said Mary Pickersgill, who had made it. "It's a strong flag, too," Mary boasted. "Those broad stripes will never tear apart. I fastened them thread by thread, to hold together forever, like our United States."

Caroline Pickersgill regarded the flag with shining eyes and echoed her mother's words. "Yes, it's a grand flag," she said. Her own skillful sewing had helped make the brilliant banner in the Pickersgill flag shop.

The huge flag was about thirty-three feet long and twenty-seven feet wide. This was the largest flag that Mary Pickersgill had ever made. It could be seen from both land and sea.

In the streets of Baltimore the citizens looked up thankfully at the huge flag waving over the fort. "As long as it waves, we'll be safe," they thought.

One day a small ship was sailing past the fort. On it was a young man who forgot all else as he admired the bright banner. How magnificent it looked against the sky!

At the sight Francis Scott Key bared his head. "A star-spangled banner!" he said to himself. Then he added a wish, "Long may it wave."

The United States was again at war with England. The nearby city of Washington had been attacked, and some Americans had been captured.

Among these prisoners was an old doctor whom everyone loved. He was being held on an enemy ship. Naturally many Americans were anxious for Dr. Beans' safety.

Francis Scott Key was sailing to rescue the prisoner. Key's ship carried a flag of truce to protect it from being fired upon by the enemy ships. But first he must find the ship on which Dr. Beans was held.

At last the English warships were found. The officer in charge of them permitted Dr. Beans to go aboard the truce ship at once. But the truce ship was forced to stay with the English fleet, which was preparing for a surprise attack on the fort that guarded Baltimore. Dr. Beans, Francis Scott Key, and another American aboard the truce ship spent a dreary week of anxious waiting.

Finally the English fleet sailed to attack, and the United States truce ship was taken along.

The truce ship was held back of the warships. The three Americans on deck took
turns watching the battle through a powerful
spyglass.

When the warships first started to bomb
the fort, no guns answered from the shore.
The three loyal watchers groaned. Then the
enemy fleet moved up closer. Immediately
the guns of the fort roared violently.

The warships moved back, badly damaged.
Francis Key felt encouraged. All day long
he stood on the ship's deck. His eyes were
glued to the Stars and Stripes, still waving
over the fort.

Before midnight the enemy renewed their attack. Again the Americans on the deck of the distant truce ship watched the firing. By the light of the bursting bombs they saw their star-spangled flag clearly.

Just before dawn the bombing ceased, and Francis Scott Key waited anxiously to see the fort. At daybreak he´cried in triumph, "It's there! The flag is still there!"

In the meantime, under cover of darkness, the enemy fleet had sailed away. Now the truce ship was free to return to Baltimore. On the way Key was busy writing something on a piece of paper.

"Listen!" he cried, showing the paper to his companions. He sang the words on it to an old, familiar tune. His friends joined in and sang, too.

> 'Tis the star-spangled banner.
> Oh, long may it wave
> O'er the land of the free
> And the home of the brave.

People all over the country began singing Francis Scott Key's song. People still sing it. It is called "The Star-Spangled Banner."

A Boy and His Book

Pigeon Creek was a lonely place when the pioneers began to settle in Indiana. But as young Abraham Lincoln tramped across a field, he was thinking how much he loved his new home in the Indiana wilderness.

The Lincoln cabin was roughly built. At night from his bed in the loft, the lad could see the sky through the cracks between the logs. Great white stars shone down on him. Sometimes the yellow moon lighted his room like a bright candle. Sometimes on warm summer nights cooling raindrops fell gently over his face. In winter feathery flakes of snow fell on his pillow.

Today the sturdy youth was hurrying home with good news. A school was starting nine miles from Pigeon Creek. Abe meant to go and get some book learning.

Early the next morning Abe and his older sister Sally got ready for the long walk to school. Nancy, their mother, saw that they were neat and clean. Then she sent them off with a loving pat.

"Now go and learn all you can," she told them. And away they went. They were both dressed in clothing made entirely by their mother. She had even made Abe's coonskin cap. His boots were made from bearskin.

After a few days of school Sally tired of
the daily eighteen-mile walk. She did not go
any more. But young Abraham considered
no distance too great if only he could learn
to spell and write and to read books.

About a month later the school closed so
that pupils could help with the spring plant-
ing. Abe was much disappointed. He knew,
however, that the pioneer farmers of Indiana
needed all the help they could get to plow
their fields and to raise and harvest their
crops.

Abe was big and sturdy for a boy of his
age. He tried his best to do a man's work.
But as he worked, he never stopped thinking
about books. He never stopped wishing that
he knew what they contained.

The next year a strange illness brought
sorrow to the community at Pigeon Creek.
The illness was so terrible that many people
died. Abe's mother was one of them.

For a long time after her death the boy
did not go to school. He spent all his time
helping Sally with the housework or hunting
and fishing.

Then one day Mr. Lincoln brought home a new wife with three children of her own.

The new wife was a good mother to Abe and Sally. She knew how much Abe wanted book learning and sent him back to school. But in the Indiana wilderness, school was open for just a few weeks during the winter season. And Abe was often absent while he helped his father chop wood or pull fodder.

In those few weeks of school the boy learned reading, writing, spelling, and some arithmetic. He liked reading best of all, but books were scarce in Pigeon Creek.

The Lincoln family owned only two books—
a Bible and an arithmetic. The Bible was
hard to read, and Abe often stumbled over
the words. The arithmetic was easier. He
studied it from cover to cover.

Abe borrowed every book anyone would
lend him. He read each one until he knew
it almost by heart.

One cold day he tramped five miles over
rough fields to help a farmer pull cornstalks
for fodder. When he came in to dinner at
noon, he saw a book on a table.

"Could I borrow it?" he asked.

Abe's eyes sparkled with pleasure when
he left with the book tucked under his arm.
At home he swallowed his supper quickly.
Then he stretched out flat on the floor with
his borrowed book. He read until midnight
by the light of the crackling fire.

When Abe went up to his bed in the loft, he tucked the book between two logs of the wall. At dawn, when he reached for it, his fingers touched something wet and cold.

The book was soaked with snow that had blown in through the cracks. Now it was ruined! The only honest thing he could do was to go and tell the owner. The boy did not hesitate. He set out without waiting for breakfast or combing his hair.

Abe told the farmer his sad story. "Oh, please, sir," he said anxiously, "I'll pull fodder or do anything you say to make up for spoiling your book."

"Well," drawled the farmer, "I reckon two days' work will pay for it. Pull fodder for two days and keep the book."

So Abe toiled for two days. He did not mind that his back ached and his hands were stiff with cold. The precious book was his! It was a story about George Washington.

Years afterwards Abraham Lincoln often told about the Washington book. "It helped me become President of the United States," he always said.

A Great Showman

One winter day in 1824 a lad of fourteen stood on a narrow street in a New England village. He was listening to a group of excited men. In the center of the group was a neighbor who had just returned from a visit to the world beyond the village. The man had been forty miles from home, and everyone was inquiring about his trip.

"How did you find the roads?"

"What places are there along the way to get food and rest for man and horse?"

"What do people outside our village talk about? How do they entertain themselves?"

The boy was even more curious than the others. Soon he had an opportunity to ask the question that was on his mind.

"John," he said, "didn't you see anything new or strange outside?"

"Yes, Taylor," the man replied. "I saw ə dog that had two tails."

"Honestly?" asked Taylor in amazement. "That is very curious."

A thought occurred to Taylor Barnum. If only he had that dog, he could make a lot of dimes and nickels exhibiting it.

"Do you think I could buy the dog?" the youth asked eagerly.

"Why, yes," John said slowly. "I guess five or ten dollars would buy him."

"Then I'll start out in the morning to find him," Taylor declared.

"Well, see me before you go," John said. "I might think of something to help you."

The next morning Taylor mounted one of his father's sturdy horses and started off to seek the strange animal. But before he left the village, he remembered to stop to see his neighbor.

"Well, John, I'm off to find that dog," the boy said. "Have you any advice?"

"Y-yes," drawled his neighbor. "I forgot to mention that the dog with two tails was coming from behind the counter in a meat market. He carried one tail in his mouth."

The joke about the two-tailed dog became famous in the small community. But Taylor was not angry. Playing jokes was one way that the people could entertain themselves. It was their chief amusement.

The Barnum family had very little money. So Taylor, the oldest of the children, got a job working in a store. He was good at it, too. He had a witty way of talking about his goods. And because the customers were entertained, they bought things they did not really need.

As Taylor Barnum grew older, he roamed all over the country, working at many kinds of jobs. But he was always interested in collecting strange things for people to see.

Once when Barnum was working in New York City, he walked by a place where many odd animals and curious objects were being exhibited. People were paying ten cents to look at this collection. But Barnum thought that he could make the business pay much better if he owned it.

The owner was willing to sell Barnum the entire collection for twelve thousand dollars. Barnum arranged to pay for it out of his earnings.

When he took charge, only the two words *American Museum* were on the outside of the building. There was nothing else outside to attract attention to the museum or to advertise it. But that was soon changed.

One morning passers-by blinked their eyes in surprise. Immense bright-colored signs, covering the front of the museum, captured their attention. Each sign described one of the exhibits inside the building.

A band played all day. At night big gaslights shone on the signs. Tickets cost a
quarter, and people swarmed inside. There
they saw wild beasts and strange birds, such
as pelicans and parrots. There were freaks,
too, one of which was a two-headed calf.

There were also lifelike wooden figures of
famous people from all parts of the world.
Almost every kind of machine that had been
invented was exhibited.

The American Museum attracted sightseers
from everywhere. It was the talk of New
York. "What will Barnum do next?" was
on everybody's tongue.

Business was so good that Barnum sent men to faraway countries to find new and freakish things for his collection. Besides odd-looking animals, there were magicians, stiltwalkers, tightrope walkers, and sword swallowers.

There were giant men and women and tiny people called midgets. One famous midget was especially small. He was less than two feet tall. Barnum named him Tom Thumb.

Tom Thumb was very quick-witted. He said many clever things and could perform clever tricks, too. He attracted so much attention in America that Barnum decided to take him abroad. The midget was exhibited to curious throngs all over the world. He was even presented to the Queen of England.

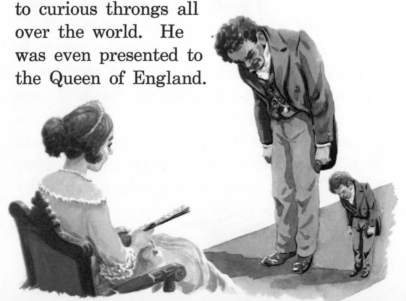

Soon Barnum became very rich. He now used his full name, Phineas Taylor Barnum.

When Phineas was about sixty years old, he started a traveling circus. This circus required a tent so large that everyone was amazed at its size. Instead of one ring for performers, the "big top" had two.

Phineas Taylor Barnum's big show became more famous than before when an enormous elephant named Jumbo joined it. By that time the big top had three rings.

Three acts all going at once! No wonder audiences swarmed to Barnum's big top!

Never had there been so large a collection of freaks. Never had one show contained so many people, so many horses, so many monkeys, giraffes, lions, tigers, and other wild animals, or so many clowns. And the people never tired of seeing Tom Thumb, the midget, and Jumbo, the huge elephant.

Phineas Taylor Barnum grew so famous that people went to his circus to see *him* as well as Tom Thumb, Jumbo, and all the freaks. Barnum was always ready to talk to people. They fondly called him "Old P. T."

Often Barnum would sit in the audience with groups of children. One of his great delights was watching their amusement.

Of course there were other circuses, too. Soon the owner of the biggest of these was persuaded to join with Barnum. Together they made the Greatest Show on Earth. It traveled over the country for many years. Even today some people still talk about Jumbo, Tom Thumb, and P. T. Barnum—the greatest showman who ever lived.

Nothing for Herself

One Saturday there was big excitement at the Barton farm. The barnyard was filled with men. The whole community had come with tools and ladders to help the Bartons raise a new barn. By noon the timbers of the frame were in place, and the siding had been nailed to the lower story.

Mrs. Barton, with her three daughters, served dinner in the yard. Clara Barton, the youngest daughter, poured the milk and passed the bread.

Just as dinner was over, everyone looked up at the barn. There was David Barton climbing up the frame.

"How wonderful David is!" thought Clara. "He is so strong! He can do anything."

The lad reached the top of the frame and stepped out onto a board. As he stood on the board, it broke and David fell.

For a while no one thought that he was badly hurt. He just had a headache.

"No broken bones," announced the doctor after examining the sturdy youth. "He'll be all right."

But after a month had passed, David still had a headache. It gradually grew worse, and at last he could not get out of bed. He lay there with a high temperature.

The whole family waited on David. But Clara was the only one he wanted near him. Every night she rested on a pile of quilts beside David's bed. She hardly slept at all. Weeks went by, and David's illness became steadily worse. There were times when he did not recognize people.

Then at last he began to improve. "Why aren't you in school?" he asked Clara.

"I didn't want to go, David. I wanted to stay with you until you were well."

"That may be a long time," David replied. "The doctor doesn't come any more. Everybody thinks I'll never get well. Everyone has given me up!"

"No, David," cried Clara earnestly. "I'll never give you up!"

David moaned feebly. "I'm so tired," he sighed. "Read to me, Clara."

Slowly and softly the girl started to read from the Bible. She read until her brother fell asleep.

For over a year David had to stay in bed. The young nurse never left her patient for more than an hour or two at a time.

When David had finally recovered, Mrs. Barton began to worry about Clara.

"Now you are not so well as David," she said. "You didn't grow an inch or put on any weight all during David's illness. And you try to hide from people. You seem to be afraid of them."

"It's because I can't get used to seeing people," Clara replied. "I didn't see anyone except the family for all those months that I was David's nurse."

"You'll have to catch up with the times," Mr. Barton told Clara. "You are so far behind that I'll bet you don't even know who the President of the United States is!"

"I'll bet I do. Andy Jackson!"

"Right!" her father chuckled. "You always were a smart girl."

Soon Clara returned to school. She had excellent teachers and rapidly caught up in her studies. But she could not overcome her shyness with people whom she did not know.

"How can we help Clara have a happy future?" her mother asked a friend who was visiting the family. "Clara deserves all the good she can get out of life."

"She may always be shy," the guest said. "Probably she will never be interested in getting things for herself. Her happiness lies in helping the people who need her. For others she will fight fearlessly. Whatever she undertakes, she'll never fail."

After Clara grew up, she began to teach. She did not fail. She was very patient and kind to her young pupils, and she never gave up trying to teach them all the things they should know.

After teaching fifteen years, Clara began another task. The country was torn apart by a violent war. Clara determined to do something to help save the lives of wounded men. They required care before they were taken from the battlefields to hospitals.

It seemed an impossible task for a woman to undertake, but again Clara did not fail. She kept trying till she obtained permission to take supplies to the dreary battlefields.

Clara gave first aid to the wounded before they were moved to hospitals. To keep them from starving, she cooked food over an open fire on the battlefield.

Soon she had people to assist her. Some of them collected first-aid supplies, clothing, food, and money. They sent these things to Clara. Then other people helped give out the supplies on battlefields and in hospitals and prison camps.

When the war ended in 1865, Clara's work for her country was not over. She began a task that required the aid of the government. Clara did not hesitate. Determined to see President Abraham Lincoln, she went to the White House in Washington.

"Mr. President," Clara said earnestly, "I receive hundreds of letters from families and friends of missing soldiers. They all want to know if their men are dead or if they are in hospitals. It is just impossible for me to answer all the questions.

"The newspaper lists of dead and wounded are often wrong. The government ought to have a department to supply correct lists. People deserve to know what has become of their missing loved ones."

Clara did not speak to President Lincoln in vain. "The government will assist you in your work," he promised.

Before long, Clara obtained an office, with government workers to search for news of missing soldiers. Now at last she was able to answer all the letters she received about them, and her replies often brought comfort to saddened families. Once more Clara did not fail those who needed her help.

Even when this job was completed, Clara Barton did not stop toiling for others. She crossed the ocean and worked as a nurse in another war. This time she was with a new group known as the Red Cross. The group aided the wounded soldiers of any country that agreed to the Red Cross rules.

"If I live to return to America," Clara said, "I shall try to make the people understand the purpose of the Red Cross. I'll try to get America to join the Red Cross."

This was not an easy task. Clara had to ask the aid of three Presidents before she succeeded. At last the American Red Cross was started, with Clara Barton at its head. The shy young nurse had become the most famous and best-loved woman in America.

Night Is Turned into Day

"Mother, may I have some money?" Tom Edison asked as he came into the kitchen.

"Money!" his mother echoed in surprise. "What on earth did you do with that whole silver dollar you had last week?"

"I spent it on stuff to make a bomb," the boy replied. "Now I need more money to buy things for my inventions."

"Then you'll have to earn it," said Mrs. Edison. "But not now. Now, I want you to get me some stovewood. And you haven't filled the lamps yet. They're on the back porch. Trim the wicks, too."

"Smelly old things!" the boy muttered as he went out to the porch. He lifted the can containing coal oil and poured the smelly oil carefully into each lamp. Then he trimmed the greasy wicks and cleaned the dirty glass chimneys.

When the job was finished, he carried the lamps into the house and placed them in the rooms where they belonged.

"There!" he said, setting the last lamp on the kitchen table. "That poky job is done! I should think there'd be a better way to light houses than with oil lamps."

"In the cities they have gaslights," said his mother. "But even if we had them here in Port Huron, I know what you would say. You'd say they ought to be improved."

"Guess I would " Thomas Edison drawled calmly. "Gas can kill you if you breathe it. It's even more dangerous than these awful coal-oil lamps "

"Well, you can worry about better ways to light the Port Huron houses while you get me some stovewood!" his mother said.

"All right," the boy replied with a grin.

But while he filled the woodbox, he was not thinking about new ways to light houses. He was wondering how to earn some money. This was not easy in the little community of Port Huron. He wished he could earn enough money to obtain everything he needed for his workshop and inventions.

The boy's wish came true, but not until twenty years later. By that time Thomas Alva Edison owned one of the biggest workshops in the world. The Port Huron youth had grown rich and famous by inventing new machines. Yet he still worked day and night on other new ideas.

It was twelve o'clock one October night in the year 1879. In Edison's workshop men were still talking. Edison sat humped over a table. At last he rose from his chair.

"That's all for now, boys," he announced. "You fellows build the power plant that I've described so we can obtain more electricity. I'll continue my experimenting with the bulb. I'm going to invent a good electric light if it takes me all the rest of my life. People need bright, safe lights for their houses."

As the others departed, he seated himself again. He sat motionless, staring absently at the wall.

"I'll bet he'll sit there all night, thinking about his light bulb," said one of the men as he left. "When you consider how long he's experimented on that light, you'd think he'd be extremely discouraged."

"Not Thomas Alva Edison!" another man declared. "He never gets discouraged."

But Edison was discouraged. Nearly a year had passed since he had undertaken to make an electric light that could be used in homes. Nearly a year of hard, steady toil, and still the job seemed to be nowhere near completion!

One kind of electric light had already been invented by someone else. But that kind of light burned out quickly. It was so bright that it hurt the eyes. And it was unsafe to use indoors.

Edison's aim was to invent a more useful, cheaper light that would be safe anywhere. He had decided to use a glass bulb for his light. For months he had been searching for the right material to burn in the glass bulb. He needed something that would glow steadily when electricity went through it.

"Every material I have experimented with has blown out, burned up, or broken when we've tested it," he thought. "I might try cotton thread again. The last time we tried it, we hadn't discovered that we had to get all the air out of the bulb before we turned on the electricity."

Locking his hands behind his head, Edison began to think of a new way to use cotton thread. The dim, gray light of dawn lit up the windows before he stood up.

"I believe I've got it," he said under his breath. "It will be worth a try anyway."

Yawning and stretching, he shoved to one side the many things on his table. Then he lay down with his head on a book. He slept soundly until his men returned to work a few hours later.

With renewed hope Thomas Edison began to experiment again with cotton thread. He prepared the little pieces of thread in a new way this time.

After many tedious trials, one prepared thread was put into an airtight glass bulb. When Edison turned on the electricity to test the bulb, it glowed brightly.

"I'll bet that cotton thread won't work," said one man. "It will go to pieces like the other materials we've experimented with."

But as the minutes and hours ticked on, it glowed steadily. Edison watched closely. All night and all the next day he sat beside the bulb.

His helpers went about doing their work as usual. But they stopped often to exclaim over the wonderful light. When they found the little lamp still burning on the second day, they became so excited that they could not work at all.

Shortly after noon the new lamp burned out. Everyone glanced at the clock.

"Forty hours!" one workman shouted in triumph. "It's burned forty hours!"

"Yes, forty hours!" Edison echoed joyfully. "If I can make a lamp that will burn forty hours, I can make a lamp that will burn a week."

Two months later, on New Year's Eve, there was a great display of Thomas Alva Edison's lamps. Over three thousand people had been attracted to the brilliant sight.

Electric lights shone brightly on both sides of the street that led to Edison's workshop. Electric lights blazed from the windows of buildings and houses. The brightness of the display seemed to turn night into day!

"Electric light is safer than gas or oil or candles," people said. "Someday it will be cheaper, too. And there are no chimneys to clean or wicks to trim!"

Inside the workshop there were displays of lights being moved about on long cords. One bulb was even burning under water.

As the throngs departed, they exclaimed, "It's astonishing! Thomas Alva Edison is indeed a wizard!"

Old Tales
from Everywhere

The Four Musicians

There was once a donkey who had worked for his master faithfully many years. But now he was feeble and unfit for work. So his master had decided to put an end to the faithful animal. The donkey realized what was going to happen and ran away.

"I shall go to the city," he said. "There I can probably get work as a musician. My body may have grown feeble, but my voice is as strong as ever."

He had not gone far when he spied a dog lying by the road. The dog was panting as if he had run a long way.

"My friend, what makes you pant so?" the donkey asked.

"Ah, me!" said the dog. "My master was
going to put an end to me because I am old
and weak and can no longer make myself
useful in hunting. So I ran away. But how
am I to gain a living now?"

"Listen!" said the donkey. "I am going
to the city to be a musician. Why don't you
accompany me and see what you can do in
the same line of work?"

The dog wagged his tail and accepted the
donkey's invitation. They went on together
and soon came to a cat sitting by the road.
She looked as dismal as three wet days.

"What is the matter with you, my good
lady?" asked the donkey. "You look quite
out of spirits."

"Ah!" said the cat. "How can I be cheerful when my life is in danger? I am getting old and feeble, and my teeth are no longer sharp enough to catch mice. So today my mistress threatened to drown me. It was my good fortune to get away from her. But I do not know what is to become of me!"

"Leave your cruel mistress," replied the donkey. "Come with us to the city and be a musician. You have always understood music. Therefore, you ought to be able to make a good living by entertaining people."

The cat liked the idea and went on with the donkey and the dog. As they passed a farmyard, a rooster flew up on the gate.

"Cock-a-doodle-doo!" he screamed.

"Splendid!" cried the donkey. "Upon my word, you make a fine noise! What is all the crowing about?"

"I was only announcing fair weather for our washing day," said the rooster. "I do that every week. But my mistress doesn't thank me for my trouble. She has told the cook that I must be made into stew for the guests who are coming tomorrow."

"You, too, have a cruel mistress," said the donkey. "Come with us, Master Chanticleer. We are going to the city to be musicians. You possess a good voice. If all of us sing tunes together, we should have no trouble finding an audience. So come along."

It was more than a day's journey to the city. The four animals decided, therefore, to spend the night in the woods. The dog and the donkey lay down under an oak tree. The cat climbed up in the branches. And the rooster flew up to the very top.

Before the rooster went to sleep, he looked around to see that everything was all right. In so doing, he saw a little light shining in the distance.

"There must be a house not far off," he called to his companions. "I see a light."

"Then let us go there," said the donkey. "I am not used to sleeping in a forest. The sooner we find a better place, the happier I shall be."

"Yes," said the dog. "And we are hungry and thirsty, without even a crust of bread. Perhaps we shall find some food there."

The cat and the rooster came down from the tree, and they all paraded toward the house, with Chanticleer in the lead.

When they reached the house, the donkey, being the tallest, looked in the window.

"Well, what do you see?" asked the dog.

"I see that the house belongs to thieves," said the donkey. "Swords and guns are on the walls, and chests of money on the floor. The thieves are all sitting at a table that is loaded with good things to eat and drink."

"Those things to eat and drink would just suit us," declared the rooster.

"Indeed they would," replied the donkey. "But we cannot get at them unless we first manage to drive the thieves away."

The animals soon hit upon a plan. The donkey stood with his forefeet on the window ledge. The dog climbed on the donkey's back. The cat jumped up on the dog's back. And the rooster perched on the shoulders of the cat. Then they began their music.

"Heee-eee-aw!" squawked the donkey.

"Bow-wow!" barked the dog.

"Meow! Meow!" cried the cat.

"Cock-a-doodle-doo!" crowed the rooster.

At the completion of their song, they burst through the window. The thieves, thinking an ugly troll was about to attack them, fled in panic.

At once the animals proceeded to eat the good food. Then they put out the light, and each found a sleeping place to his liking.

The donkey lay down in the yard. The dog stretched out inside the house by the door. The cat curled up on the hearth. And the cock flew up and slept on the chimney.

About midnight the thieves came sneaking back toward the house. All was quiet.

"I think we ran away without reason," the thieves' captain said. "But let us take no risks. You stay outside while I see if we are likely to have any more trouble."

He entered the kitchen quietly. The cat was now awake, watching with shining eyes.

The thief thought the cat's eyes were two live coals. He reached down to get a light by touching a match to them. Now the cat did not enjoy that sort of thing. She sprang into the thief's face, scratching wildly.

He cried out in terror and ran toward the door. There the dog bit him in the leg.

But the man managed to get out into the yard. At once the donkey knocked him down with a kick. Then the rooster, awakened by the noise, cried out, "Cock-a-doodle-doo! Cock-a-doodle-doo!"

Crawling away to the other thieves, the captain said, "We cannot live in that house any more. In the kitchen a horrible witch scratched me with her sharp nails. By the door a man pierced my leg with a knife. In the yard a tar-black giant beat me with a stick. And on the roof a fellow kept shouting, "Toss him up to me!"

So the thieves went away and never came back. The four musicians were so pleased with their new quarters that they did not go to the city. They stayed where they were. And they may be there to this very day.

A Barber's Discovery

Once there lived in a village a very fine
barber named Garo. As he served his customers, Garo was always glad to give them
advice. And as long as there was hair to
cut or a beard to trim, he never ran out of
things to say.

In those days a barber traveled from house
to house, like a peddler, to do his work. So
old Garo had a chance to observe just what
was occurring. For this reason his advice
was considered excellent.

Because Garo gave so much advice, people thought that he was very wise indeed. And you may be sure that Garo himself agreed with them. He felt that he had no equal.

One November afternoon Garo was resting beneath a great oak tree. His head leaned comfortably against the bark as he gazed at a nearby field. There pumpkins lay yellow and fat in the sunshine. Garo observed how the fat pumpkins clung to slender vines that wandered here and there like pieces of lost string.

Yawning sleepily, the barber happened to glance upward. From the branches of the oak tree hung hundreds of tiny brown acorns. They were ready to fall at the first harsh blast of winter wind.

Suddenly Garo wrinkled up his forehead. Then he squinted his eyes and stroked his beard. He always did these things when he had made a discovery.

"Lo and behold!" he exclaimed. "Nature has made a big mistake! Observe these tiny acorns. They hang on branches that are sturdy enough to bear the weight of an ox.

But big pumpkins grow on stringlike vines. How foolish! Even a simpleton knows that heavy pumpkins should grow on sturdy oaks and dainty acorns on slender vines."

Old Garo lay there, stroking his beard and squinting. How his customers would marvel when he told them of his discovery! "It's a pity I wasn't around when the world began," he said to himself. "I could have provided Nature with good advice." And so saying, the barber folded his hands over his fat stomach and fell into a deep slumber.

His stomach under his yellow shirt looked a great deal like one of those huge pumpkins. And his puffy brown nose did not look very different from one of the acorns on the oak branches above his head.

Garo began to snore loudly, just as he always did when he slumbered. As he snored, he smiled. He was dreaming of his wonderful discovery.

All of a sudden an acorn was loosened by the wind. Down it fell from a high branch. It landed on Garo's nose with a loud plop, right in the middle of a snore.

The startled barber's snore turned to an angry snort. Then he caught a glimpse of the acorn that had plopped down on his nose, making it red and sore. Gently rubbing his nose with his fingers, he stared at the acorn thoughtfully.

Finally, still rubbing his sore nose, Garo said meekly, "How foolish I was even to consider giving advice to Nature! And how sore my nose would be if that acorn had been a pumpkin! Nature always knows best what is good for the world."

With that wise and solemn remark, he set out for home.

Tyll's Masterpiece

This is a tale about merry Tyll, who lived by his wits. His chief interest was helping people recognize their follies so that they would act more wisely in the future. To do this, he often played tricks upon people.

One day he was riding his donkey along a lonely road. Suddenly the beast stopped.

Tyll got down and pulled at the reins with might and main, but the donkey refused to move. So Tyll stripped some branches from a berry bush and mounted the donkey again. Then he stretched out his arm and held the branches before the animal's mouth.

The donkey, seeing food so close, began to amble after it. In this way Tyll coaxed the beast on until they came to the marble castle of a nobleman.

The nobleman happened to see Tyll riding along in this strange manner.

"Fellow with the merry face and strange ways," the great man called to Tyll, "what work do you do?"

"Noble lord," Tyll replied humbly, "I am a portrait painter."

"Oho!" cried the nobleman. "I am looking for just such a person. Would you like to be my court painter?"

"Gladly, my lord," said Tyll. "But if I am to live at your court, I must be as well fed and as well dressed as the other members."

"That is fair enough," said the nobleman. "Come with me."

Soon Tyll found himself dressed in robes of fine material. Then he was served at a table loaded with plates of rich food.

After dinner the nobleman said, "I want you to paint portraits of me, my wife, and all the members of my court."

"My lord," Tyll answered humbly, "your desire is my command. I will undertake to paint such portraits for two hundred gold coins."

The next morning Tyll asked that all the people whom he was to paint should pass separately before him.

First came a fat duke. "You must paint me without my fat, as I looked when I was young. Or else," the duke hissed, "I shall have you punished!"

Next came an old lady in waiting, thin and ugly. "Master painter," she threatened, "if your painting of me is not beautiful, you will find yourself in prison."

Then a young lady in waiting came along. She had yellow hair and fresh pink cheeks. But two of her front teeth were gone.

"Master," she said, "you must paint me smiling, with no teeth missing. If you don't, I shall have you put to death."

And so it went. Each and every member of the court who passed Tyll threatened him harshly. At the end of the line came the noble lord himself.

"Tyll," he said, "I am paying you well for these portraits. See to it, therefore, that each is a perfect likeness of its owner. If not, you will receive a dreadful punishment. I will accept no excuses."

Then he departed. Left alone, Tyll began to feel extremely worried.

"Surely no man was ever given such a difficult task," Tyll thought in distress. "I must paint each person as he wishes to look. Yet each portrait must be a perfect likeness. If I fail, I'll be imprisoned or put to death. And I thought the life of a painter was a merry one!"

Tyll thought and thought until at last he found a way out of his troubles.

"Ho, my fine ladies and gentlemen!" he cried. "I shall treat you to such portraits as were never painted before!"

Immediately he asked the nobleman for a big room with large blank walls. He also demanded that long curtains be hung over the walls from ceiling to floor. And finally he asked for three painters to assist him.

He was given the room, the curtains, and the three helpers. Then Tyll and his fellows locked themselves in, refusing to see anyone while they worked.

For thirty days the four painters lived in the room in great comfort. They were served the finest foods that the castle cooks could prepare.

On the thirty-first day the nobleman stuck his nose in the door.

"Ho, there, Tyll!" he said. "How is the painting coming along?"

"Fine, noble lord," Tyll replied.

"May I see it?"

"Not yet, my lord," Tyll answered.

After forty days the nobleman peeped in again.

"Ho, there, Tyll!" he shouted. "Is today the day?"

"My lord, the painting is almost finished," said Tyll. "But no one may enter yet."

After fifty days the noble lord became enraged. He walked right in and found the curtains drawn over the walls.

"This is nonsense!" he boomed. "Show me the painting this very instant!"

"Certainly, my lord," Tyll replied meekly. "But first you must call together here all the noble ladies and gentlemen whom I have painted."

The nobleman did so. Presently all the members of his court had gathered before the drawn curtains.

"Most noble lord," Tyll announced, "you are all about to see a brilliant masterpiece. Here are perfect likenesses painted in magic colors. I learned the great secret of these colors from a famous magician. They can be seen only by those of noble birth. But if there are common people here, they will see only a blank wall."

Then Tyll drew the curtains apart. The people stood speechless, their eyes opened wide. All they saw was a white, blank wall.

Tyll pretended to point out people on the blank wall, describing their faces and their clothes. No one dared to disagree with him. Each was afraid to say that he saw nothing.

Suddenly the Court Fool cried out, "You may call me a common fellow. I don't mind a bit. But I see only a white, blank wall."

After a brief silence Tyll burst out laughing. "When a fool is honest and tells the truth, it's time for wise men to listen. I confess that I have fooled you. But it was the only way I could please you."

With a shamefaced smile, the master of the castle spoke. "You are a clever fellow, Tyll. All of us told you how to paint our portraits. You showed us our folly.

"Here is your money. Now leave before some of my people forget the lesson they have learned and decide to punish you."

Tyll went quickly. When he was a good distance from the castle, he spoke to his donkey. "My friend, listen and learn. The secret of life is laughter. Fifty men were ready to kill me, but I laughed them out of it. Laughter makes life easy and gay."

Chanticleer and the Fox

Once upon a time a poor woman lived in a small cottage near a wood. She had little enough to eat. But she considered herself extremely fortunate to have a cow, a pig, and a few chickens.

Among her chickens was a very handsome rooster named Chanticleer. As he strutted about the barnyard, his comb looked as red as fire. His glossy feathers were as yellow as gold. For loud crowing he had no equal in all the neighborhood. And if there ever could be a King of Roosters, Chanticleer was certainly that king.

One night Chanticleer was perched by his wife in the chicken house. Suddenly he began to moan and mumble in his sleep. Then he groaned as though in great distress. He made such a fuss that his wife woke from her slumber. Looking at him with concern, she cried, "Chanticleer! What is wrong?"

Her cries woke Chanticleer. The rooster gave a start and flapped his wings loudly.

"Oh, my dear!" he exclaimed, his comb stiff with terror. "I've had a most horrible dream. You simply cannot imagine how it frightened me!"

In a shaking voice he continued, "I was in the yard, looking for worms or crickets. All at once I beheld a strange beast lurking there. He looked like a dog, but his manner was extremely fierce. He was yellowish-red in color, and he had a long, plumy tail and a pointed snout. His eyes glowed like coals of fire, and his dismal howls were terrible to hear."

"Simpleton!" said Chanticleer's wife ·in a scornful voice. "Why make a fuss about a ridiculous dream? Everybody knows that dreams are caused by eating too much rich food. Really you are sillier than a goose."

Such talk hurt Chanticleer's pride. So he began to relate all the dreams he had ever heard of that had come true. He was trying to prove to his wife that dreams often warned of future happenings. But she would not listen to him.

"Not *your* dreams," she said scornfully. "Quit fussing and go back to sleep."

"Yes, my dear," said Chanticleer meekly, for he was too weary to keep on arguing. So they slumbered peacefully until morning.

At the first streak of light, Chanticleer was fully awake. He flew down from his perch and strutted out to the barnyard in a royal manner. Flapping his wings, he hopped up to his usual perch on the fence. Then he started to crow.

"Cock-a-doodle-doo! Cock-a-doodle-doo!
Time for work and breakfast, too."

All the hens came down from their perches. Cackling loudly, they began to look for juicy insects. Chanticleer puffed up with pride as he saw how they scurried to obey him. He strutted up and down in the barnyard, his comb standing up like a king's crown. Whenever he ate an insect, he crowed loudly. He wanted to remind the hens that his alert eye was upon them.

The rays of the sun grew hotter and hotter. Chanticleer decided he would stop looking for insects and take a dust bath. Hastily swallowing one last cricket, he went down to the end of the fence. Here the dirt was as loose as ashes. It was cool and dry and especially good to wallow in.

While Chanticleer was wallowing in the dust, a strange beast came sneaking through the gate. It had yellowish-red fur, a long, pointed snout, and a plumy tail.

Now Chanticleer did not know it, but this was a sly old fox. He had been lurking in the bushes all morning, waiting for just this opportunity to catch Chanticleer alone.

"Good morning, Mr. Chanticleer," said the crafty fox as he regarded the rooster with watchful eyes.

When Chanticleer beheld the horrible beast
of his dreams, he started up in terror. But
the fox spoke again before Chanticleer had
recovered from his fright.

"Don't be afraid of me," coaxed the fox
in a persuading tone. "I just want a chance
to win your friendship. Why, I came here
this morning for that very reason. I knew
both your father and mother well. I've even
entertained them for dinner in my home."

The fox laughed to himself as he made this
remark. He remembered with satisfaction
what had occurred at that dinner. Chanticleer's parents had made him a tasty meal.
He was sure their plump son would satisfy
his appetite equally well.

"Your father had the finest voice I ever heard," the fox went on. "He used to stand on tiptoe, stretch out his neck, and crow with his eyes shut. I'm sure your voice equals your father's. Please, dear Mr. Chanticleer, display your friendship by letting me hear you crow."

The vain bird was much flattered. Acting on the suggestion of the crafty fox, he rose from the dust-wallow. Then he hopped up on the fence, stretched out his neck, shut his eyes, and began to crow.

Of course this was just the opportunity that the fox wanted. Before Chanticleer had finished crowing, the fox jumped up into the air and grabbed the cock by the neck. Then he flung Chanticleer over his shoulder and made off toward the woods at a great rate of speed.

The hens saw the fleeing fox and began to cackle their loudest. The old woman came running from her house to see what all the cackling was about.

"Alas! Alack!" she cried in distress. "A fox has caught Chanticleer. Help! Help!"

Down the road ran the old woman, shrieking in alarm. The farmers dropped their rakes and hoes and came to join the chase. A cow and her calf, three hogs, two sheep, and a black dog accompanied them, mooing and grunting and bleating and barking.

Wasps and other insects swarmed overhead, buzzing angrily. Even the crows stopped eating the corn and began cawing harshly. But it was in vain. The fox kept well ahead of them all.

Then to confuse his pursuers, he ran into a flock of geese. The terrified fowls ran hither and thither, hissing and squawking.

Poor Chanticleer looked around for an opportunity to escape. Suddenly a brilliant idea came to him. Peering around the fox's snout, he said meekly, "Those silly, confused people will never catch up with you at this rate. No creature runs as fast as a fox. They should know better than to pursue you. Why don't you tell them to stop?"

The old fox was flattered by Chanticleer's praise. He acted on the suggestion at once. "Stop!" he shouted at his pursuers.

The minute the fox opened his mouth, the rooster flapped his wings wildly, flew up on the limb of a tree, and crowed:

"Cock-a-doodle-doo! Cock-a-doodle-doo!
I know how to flatter, too!"

Then the fox realized he had been fooled by his own trick. From his pointed snout to the tip of his tail he was a picture of shame. Chanticleer went home in triumph, but he promised himself never again to crow with his eyes shut or to be fooled by sly flattery.

The Seven Dancing Stars

A long, long time ago, when the world was young, a tribe of Indians dwelt in the midst of a forest. One day all the wild creatures disappeared from the forest as if by magic. Not even the most skillful hunter could bring home meat for the cooking-pots.

The tribe roamed far and wide, seeking new hunting grounds. But wherever they went, the animals vanished.

At last Chief Big Hawk called his tribe together. Briefly he related what the Great Spirit had made known to him.

"The Great Spirit will lead us toward the setting sun," Big Hawk said. "Far beyond towering cliffs is a lake, the home of many beavers. There we shall find fish that leap into nets as eagerly as bees seek blossoms. Bear and deer grow fat in the forest. Our cooking-pots will never be empty."

So once more the squaws gathered together their few belongings. At daybreak the tribe set out for the new hunting grounds.

At last they reached the lake where the Great Spirit had led them. On the shore Big Hawk stopped and raised his right hand.

"Let us all give thanks," he said earnestly. "Thank the Great Spirit for aiding us on our journey. May He be with us as we build our wigwams. May He give us good hunting and years of peace."

The Great Spirit was kind to the Indians, and they dwelt peacefully in their wigwams beside the lake. Meat was plentiful. Even an old squaw would not have returned from the woods empty-handed.

As the weather grew colder, the squaws of the tribe were busy preparing food for the coming winter. So the children were often left to find their own amusement.

One day Little Eagle, Big Hawk's eldest son, went with his seven brothers deep into the forest. There they came upon an open circle where the ground was as level as if it had been tramped upon by a thousand feet. The children gave no thought to how such an open place happened to be in the midst of a thick forest. They began a joyous dance.

Day after day they returned to dance in the mysterious circle, telling no one about it. One day as they danced, they heard a voice.

"Beware! Beware!" it called. "Strange things happen in this enchanted place."

Turning quickly, the children saw a tall, stern-looking figure. The stranger wore a robe of white feathers, and his long white hair shone like silver. "Leave this place," he warned the children solemnly. "Remember my words and never return."

The happy children paid no heed to the stranger's solemn warning. Instead, they went merrily on with their dance.

"Let us bring food tomorrow," suggested Little Eagle, who was always ready to eat. "Then we can feast as well as dance."

His seven brothers agreed. But when they asked their mother for the food, she seemed vexed and refused to prepare it. "Eat in the wigwam as you should," she said.

The brothers had to do without their feast, but they returned to the circle to dance as before. At the completion of their dance a strange thing happened. The startled children found themselves rising into the air—up, up.

As they soared over the wigwams, their mother saw them. The squaw pleaded with them to come back. She promised them any food they desired.

Hearing his mother's words, Little Eagle glanced toward the earth. Instantly there was a blinding flash. Little Eagle had been turned into a falling star! Down to earth he plunged in a streak of light.

But his seven brothers did not look back. They all reached the sky and became stars. There they shine and twinkle to this day, a band of seven dancing stars.

Rumpelstiltskin

A Spinner of Gold

There was once a poor miller who had a beautiful daughter. He loved her dearly and was so proud of her that he could not help boasting about her.

One day a stranger came to the mill with a sack of corn to be ground into meal. He saw the dainty lass in the doorway. As he beheld her lovely face, he remarked, "I wish I had a daughter as beautiful as she."

The miller rubbed his mealy hands together and glanced at his daughter standing in the sunshine. He observed how the sun's rays, shining on her yellow hair, framed her head with golden light. He began to boast again.

"Yes, I consider her a lass in a thousand. She can spin straw into gold."

The stranger marveled at this news. He spread the tale far and wide, and soon it reached the ears of the king. Immediately the astonished king sent for the miller, telling him to fetch his daughter to the palace with him. So the miller obeyed.

"I have heard," said the king, "that this maiden can spin straw into gold. She must show if this be true. If she fails, beware, for you shall be punished."

The miller's tongue stuck in his throat, and he almost choked with fear. He dared not tell the truth about his careless boast.

The king led the dainty lass into a stable. There a spinning wheel and many bundles of straw had been placed. He looked at her and smiled. "You have straw enough here," he said. "Spin it into gold before morning."

Then he barred the door and departed.

The lass looked at the spinning wheel, and she looked at the straw. Then she thought of the punishment her father would receive the next day. Sinking down on a bench, she started to weep. In the midst of her sobs she heard a slight rustle. From underneath the straw popped a tiny man with a pointed hat on his head. He had a brown, withered face, a long red nose, and a rusty-red beard that swept down below his belt.

He regarded the maiden with piercing eyes. "Why all this fuss?" he asked harshly.

The miller's daughter was so surprised at the sight of this mere wisp of a man that she stopped crying and told him the truth.

"Pooh!" jeered the dwarf. "Spin straw into gold? That's no trouble. How will you repay me if I spin it?"

The maid had never before seen so odd and ugly a man. But his little needle-sharp eyes had such cunning that she half suspected he could do what he said. So she promised to give him her necklace.

With that, the tiny dwarf whirled dizzily on his toes. Then sitting down on a stool by the spinning wheel, he began to spin.

Whrr, whrrr, whrrr! The straw seemed to swish through the air as if caught up in a high wind. In a moment, behold! All the straw was spun into shining gold thread.

Then the long-nosed dwarf rose from his stool. Accepting the necklace, he poked it into a leather pouch, and off he went.

The next morning when the king saw all the golden thread, he was extremely pleased. But his greed increased with every glance at the shining heap.

"Well and fair," said he. "Well and fair. You shall have another trial."

Then once more he led the poor lass to a stable. This one was half-filled with straw.

"When that is spun into gold," said the king, "you shall have praise indeed. If you fail, beware of terrible punishment."

Though the king really pitied the girl, his greedy heart did not melt. He said nothing more. Turning on his heel, he went out of the stable and barred the door.

The poor maid was now greatly distressed. Yesterday's straw had been only a handful compared with today's. "Oh, if only that long-nosed dwarf were here to assist me!" she moaned.

Sadly she sat down at the wheel and tried to spin. But the straw remained only straw. "Alas and alack! There is no hope for me," she thought. But lo! To her great relief the withered dwarf appeared once more.

"Ah!" said he. "What's wrong now?"

When she told him, he combed his rusty-red beard with his bony fingers. Then he asked, "What shall I have as a reward this time if I spin for you?" She promised him the pearl ring on her finger.

He flung his beard over his shoulder and snapped his fingers. Then he plopped himself down on the stool and began to spin.

Whrrr, whrrr, whrrr went the wheel as the straw turned into golden thread. And smaller and smaller grew the heap of straw. Before dawn it was all spun, and the dwarf had vanished before the king's arrival.

The king marveled at the sight. But even yet his greedy mind was not satisfied.

"Well and fair," he said. "Only one more trial, my dear, and you shall toil no more."

This time the stable was heaped to its roof with straw.

"Spin that into gold," said the king, "and tomorrow you shall be queen."

With a glance over his shoulder he went out, barred the door, and left her to herself.

The maid sat down and looked hopelessly at the immense heap of straw. "Ah, me!" she sighed. "To spin all that into gold would require the efforts of a hundred little men."

"What, what, what!" cried a voice. In an instant little Master Long-Nose appeared for the third time.

But this time the poor trembling lass had nothing left to offer the dwarf for his work. He stared at her in silence for a moment. Then he said, "Promise me your first child if you ever have one, and tomorrow you shall be queen."

The maiden could not help being amused at such an idea. She did not suspect that she would ever be queen. So she solemnly gave the promise required of her.

The sly dwarf raised himself on his toes and whirled around nine times. After that he sat down at the wheel, whistling a tune.

Whrr, whrr, whrrr went the wheel like a swarm of bees buzzing about a hive. All night long the dwarf sat busily spinning the straw. By sunrise the heaps of straw had disappeared. They had all been spun into gold. Then the ugly little man skipped away on his wispy legs.

The king kept his promise and made the miller's daughter his queen. So she lived happily and in great comfort at the king's fine palace. When her first child was born, the young queen's joy was beyond compare.

A New Bargain

Some time after the birth of her child, the
joyous life of the queen was changed. One
day she knelt in the apple orchard, playing
happily with her baby daughter. All at once
her happiness turned to fear. Behold, there
beside her was the dwarf! It seemed as if
he had sprung from the trunk of a crooked
apple tree nearby.

The dwarf slyly regarded the baby. "Ah! A pretty thing," he said. "And mine!"

Until now the poor queen had forgotten the promise she had made in her desperate trouble. She began to plead earnestly with the dwarf. "I will grant you anything else you ask. Only free me from my promise and let me keep my darling child."

"Nay, nay!" he refused. "A princess is a princess, and a promise is a promise. But I'll make another bargain with you. You shall have three days and nine chances to guess my name. If you have not guessed it by noon of the third day, the child shall be mine." And he disappeared as mysteriously as he had come.

All night long the queen lay wide-awake, wondering what name the ugly dwarf could possess. The next morning she went sadly to the orchard. Exactly at noon the dwarf appeared.

"Ah, Madam!" said he. "Now what's my name?" And the queen guessed the silliest names she could think of—Bumpetyboomery, Catalawampus.

But at each one the dwarf shook his head. The queen thought for a moment. Then she said a third name that popped into her mind, "Nickerruckerrubblegrubb."

The dwarf broke into a hoot of laughter. "Madam, that is not my name," he squeaked. And off he went.

Promptly at noon the next day the dwarf appeared. This time the queen guessed the three queerest names she could think of— Long-Nose, Little-Body, and Lean-Legs.

At each name the little man jiggled about, clapping his hands with glee.

"Nay, nay, Madam," he cried. "One more day, three more guesses, and the child will be mine."

On returning to the palace, the queen sent for a messenger who was sharp of hearing and as keen of eye as a hawk. She told him what the little dwarf looked like, with his withered face, wispy legs, long nose, rusty beard, and pointed hat. Then she ordered the messenger to ride like the wind, hither and thither, in search of the dwarf, and to find out his name.

"Learn his name," she said, "and immense wealth shall be yours. If you fail, you may expect to be punished harshly."

The messenger lingered not even a moment. He flung himself into the saddle and raced away on his fleet-footed steed. All night he rode hither and thither. At last, just before daybreak, he found himself at a crossroads. There he stopped and looked about.

Just beyond the crossroads the messenger could see a tiny hut. A fire burned before it. Dancing around the fire was an ugly elf. He had a withered face, wispy legs, a long nose, and a rusty-red beard flowing down below his belt.

One glimpse of the ugly, troll-like man convinced the messenger that this was the very dwarf whom the queen had sent him to find. He dismounted and crept near the fire.

The dwarf was singing a joyous tune as he danced by the firelight.

"Today I build a fire and bake.
Tomorrow the queen's child I'll take
No other one is called the same,
For Rumpelstiltskin is my name."

The messenger, lurking behind a big tree,
listened carefully. He wanted to be certain
of the dwarf's long name.

Then, delighted beyond measure, he crept
silently back to his horse. He had barely
sprung to his saddle when his steed lunged
forward. Speedily the messenger galloped
off to tell his news to the queen.

The queen was seated on her throne when the messenger arrived. He knelt at her feet and related to her what he had seen. After that he whispered the name he had heard.

The queen was almost overcome with joy. Immediately she dressed in her finest satin robe and velvet cloak. She even wore her most beautiful jewels. Then she went to the orchard to wait for the ugly dwarf. The royal nurse carried the baby princess, as if the child were to be given to the dwarf.

At the stroke of noon the horrible little man appeared. As usual, he had popped out from behind the mossy old apple tree. This time he wore a plume in his hat. Over his arm was a dainty shawl he had fetched to wrap about the baby.

"Ah, Madam!" cried the dwarf. "Three more guesses and the baby is mine!"

Again the queen pleaded with him. She promised him any treasure except her child. But the enraged dwarf would not listen to her. He shouted violently:

"A bargain's a bargain. A vow's a vow
To the last word of it. Answer me now."

266

Smiling to herself, the queen first guessed, "Wheat-Straw."

The dwarf laughed in scornful amusement. Next she guessed, "Heaps of Gold."

The dwarf laughed louder. And then the queen smiled gleefully. She motioned for the withered dwarf to come closer. "How about Rumpelstiltskin?" she murmured.

The dwarf stared at her a moment, as if all in a wink he had been turned to stone. Then he trembled with rage and disappointment. "I vow the witches have told you my name!" he screamed.

He stamped on the ground so hard that one thin leg pierced the earth and sank into it up to the knee. Try as he might, he could not draw it out. In his fury Rumpelstiltskin grasped his other leg, trying to pull himself free. He jerked with such force that he nearly tore himself in two. But he never was able to pull himself out.

The Ugly Duckling

Mother Duck's Queer Baby

It was midsummer. The soft air was filled with the odor of clover blossoms and other flowers that grew in a meadow. In the midst of the meadow was a deep, blue lake.

Among some slender reeds near the water's edge a duck was sitting on her nest. Her eggs were just beginning to crack open.

"Cheep! Cheep! Cheep! Cheep!" One after another the ducklings came to life and began to poke out their heads.

"Quack! Quack!" replied their admiring mother. Soon the ducklings tried to quack, too, as they ran hither and thither.

All around them lay the beautiful green world. Their mother let them look as much as they liked because green is good for the eyes. "How big the world is!" they said.

"Don't think this is the whole world," the mother duck told them. "It stretches a long, long way beyond this farm. Though I must say I've never been to the end of it myself.

"I hope you are all here," she continued. Then she lifted herself off the nest to see if all the eggs had hatched. But the biggest one had not hatched yet.

"Well, well," sighed Mother Duck. "I've never known an egg to take so long." And she settled herself on the nest again.

"How are you getting along?" called an old duck who had come for a friendly chat.

"This last egg is taking such a long time!" replied Mother Duck. "The shell will not crack open."

"Let me see the egg that will not hatch," said the old duck. "It may be a turkey's egg. The farmer's wife put one in my nest once. What trouble I had when it hatched! The creature was afraid to go near the water.

"Yes, that's a turkey's egg," she added as Mother Duck rose up from the nest. "Leave it alone. You should be teaching the ducklings to swim."

"Oh, I'll be patient and sit on it a little longer," replied Mother Duck.

"Well, I won't argue with you," said the old duck, waddling away. "I gave my advice only because of our long friendship."

At last the big egg cracked. "Cheep!" said the young one as he tumbled out of the shell. How big and ugly he was!

"What a huge duckling!" said his mother. "None of the others looked like that. Can he possibly be a turkey? Well, we shall soon find out. Into the water he shall go, even if I have to push him into it myself."

The next day was gloriously fine, and the mother duck took her family to swim.

Splash! Into the water she plopped.

"Quack, quack," she called loudly, and one after another the ducklings jumped in. The water went over their heads, but they came up to the surface again and floated properly. Their legs seemed to go of themselves quite naturally, and there they were, swimming about. Even the ugly gray one had sprung in eagerly and was swimming as well as the rest.

"Well, that is no turkey, at any rate," said Mother Duck in relief. "How well he uses his legs! How smoothly he glides along! He is my own child after all."

Then she called to the ducklings, "Come with me. I will take you into the world and introduce you to the duck yard. Keep close to me and beware of the cat."

Off she started, giving advice to the ducklings trailing along behind her.

"Remember to quack properly," said she. "Don't turn your toes in! Well-behaved ducklings turn their toes out, just as I do. Now bend your necks and say 'Quack!'"

At the duck yard the ducklings all did as they were told. But when the other fowls saw the ugly one, they hissed at him.

"Ugh, ugh!" they said. "What a frightful object he is!" Then a drake rushed at the poor creature and bit him in the neck.

"Let him alone," said the mother. "He's not bothering you."

"I know," said the drake. "But he is so ugly. It's a pity he can't be made over."

"His looks will improve as he grows older," said his mother. "He was in the egg too long. That's why he isn't properly shaped."

But his looks did not improve, and he had a miserable time. The ducks pecked him till he was sore all over. Even his brothers and sisters found fault with him.

Finally the poor creature could endure it no longer. At the first opportunity he went through a hedge and escaped from them all.

The Search for a Home and Friends

The ugly duckling wandered about till he came to a hut near the edge of a swamp. It was November now, and the wind whistled fiercely around the poor, ugly bird. He saw that the door was half open, and he ventured inside without permission.

An old woman dwelt there with her cat and her hen. "Meow," said the cat in a scornful manner. "What do you want?"

"Just a place for shelter from the wind's cold blasts," said the duckling humbly.

"Can you lay eggs?" demanded the hen.

"No, I can't lay eggs."

"Can you purr?" asked the cat.

"No, I can't purr," replied the duckling.

"Well, if you can't lay eggs or purr, what can you do?" inquired the hen. She was convinced that the duckling was hopelessly stupid.

"I can swim and dive," said the duckling.

"Swim and dive!" exclaimed the cat and the hen in amusement. "Who cares to swim and dive? This is not the proper place for anyone who cannot lay eggs or purr. Go away, you useless creature!"

So the duckling departed and stayed in the reeds near a lake where the wild ducks lived. But he was so ugly that he frightened them away. After that he was always alone.

Winter set in. Dead leaves filled the air, and icy blasts howled. Dark clouds, heavy with snow, coasted across the sky.

One dismal day some enormous birds rose out of the reeds. They were swans.

The ugly duckling had never seen anything like these big birds before. They were all dazzling white with long, gracefully curved necks. Uttering strange cries, they spread their wings and circled in the air above the lake. They were preparing to fly southward, away from the region of ice and snow.

As the swans circled overhead, the duckling glided around and around in the water to watch them. Suddenly a curious sadness came over him. Then he uttered a cry so loud and strange that it frightened him.

The dismal winter days soon grew bitterly cold, and the duckling had to keep swimming to prevent the water from freezing around him. He paddled faster and faster, but at last he was so tired that he stopped moving. Soon he was a prisoner in solid ice.

Early the next morning a farmer found the helpless duckling. The man broke the ice and carried the bird home. There in the big warm kitchen the duckling began to stir about. The children made a fuss over him and tried to pet him. But the duckling was afraid and sought to escape from them.

Plop! He landed right in the milk pail, spilling milk over the floor. Next he upset the butter. Then he dived into the flour.

The two children pursued him, laughing and shouting. Their mother shrieked and slashed at him with the broom. Finally the confused bird managed to get out the door and creep off. For the rest of the winter he lurked in the midst of a swamp, without the friendship of any living creature.

In the spring when the sun had begun to shine warmly, the ugly duckling again found himself by a lake. Robins and wrens were singing joyously. Bright butterflies danced in the air.

The dazzling sunshine filled the duckling with joy. He spread his wings wide. They had grown stronger now, and to his surprise they carried him up into the air.

Up, up the bird soared. Before long he was flying over a shining pool surrounded by flowering bushes and peach and pear trees in full blossom. The odor of flowers filled the air with a glorious sweetness.

Suddenly from under the flowering bushes three dazzling white swans came swimming. They floated along as lightly as butterflies. When the duckling recognized them, the same sadness came over him. He felt he had no choice but to go to them, even though they might peck him to death.

Down he flew and swam toward the three swans. They glided out to meet him, their white feathers gleaming. The poor duckling bowed his head. He was ready to endure any punishment, however harsh it might be.

Then he saw himself mirrored in the pool. Lo! He was no longer a gray bird, awkward and ugly. He himself was a swan!

Good fortune was his at last, and instantly all his troubles were forgotten. The other swans stroked his glossy feathers lovingly with their bills. Then some children came running. "See the new swan!" they cried. "He is much handsomer than the others."

The young swan held his graceful head high. His heart beat with rapture as he exclaimed, "I never dreamed of so much happiness when I was an ugly duckling!"

The Golden Eggs

Many, many years ago a farmer and his good wife dwelt in a humble cottage beside a winding stream. The couple lacked many things that their richer neighbors enjoyed. But they were always willing to share what they had.

No matter how little they had themselves, they always spared a bit of food for the wild creatures that drank from the stream. The good wife never neglected to toss a handful of crumbs to the robins and wrens. She also scattered grain on the riverbank for the wild fowls.

One day a splendid wild goose flew down to the farmyard. She did not fly off again but made herself quite at home. Soon she had settled down in a dust-wallow with the hens.

The next morning when the wife heard the hens cackling, she went out to get the eggs. She saw the big wild goose fly off a nest, looking extremely wise.

"Oho!" exclaimed the woman. "A goose egg! It will fetch a good price."

She hurried to the nest. There in the hay lay an egg of solid gold! The woman was so excited that she screamed for her husband, who was weeding a cabbage patch.

"G-G-G-Goose! S-S-S-Solid gold egg!" she stuttered, almost speechless.

"Have the fairies bewitched your tongue?" he asked. "What are you stuttering about?"

Speaking more calmly, she said, "The wild goose has just laid an egg of solid gold."

"Solid gold!" cried the man. "Where?"

"I-I-In the barn," she stuttered.

"Simpleton!" shrieked her husband. "Do you lack good sense? Why did you leave a solid gold egg in the barn, where a common thief might steal it?"

He rushed into the barn and picked up the golden egg. How it glittered! The farmer was nearly overcome with rapture.

"We must conceal this rare treasure," he cried. "Some dishonest person will try to steal it."

They chose a hiding place under the clay bricks of the hearth. Marveling at their good fortune, they thought about the egg all day. They neglected their work and forgot to feed their chickens and the wild creatures. When night came, they could not sleep for wondering if they would find another gold egg the following day.

The next morning they rose before dawn. Carrying a lantern, they ran to the barn. There lay a second glittering egg of solid gold. The couple's rapture knew no bounds as they regarded the treasure.

Day after day the wild goose laid an egg of purest gold. Day after day the greedy partners buried the egg and lingered in the house to guard the treasure. They neglected their work. They forgot that the chickens and wild fowls lacked food. They were bewitched by dazzling dreams of rare wealth.

"I shall soon be the wealthiest man in all the land," boasted the farmer. Hooking his thumbs over his belt, he tried to reckon the worth of his treasure. He could buy choice food, fine horses, a carriage, and anything else he chose. But suddenly he felt that he could not endure waiting another instant for this great wealth.

"I'll cut the goose open and get all her eggs at once," he cried. So he rushed out and killed the goose. Cutting her open, he discovered she was like any common goose!

"Alas and alack!" he cried in despair. "Why did I kill the goose that laid the golden eggs? If I had not been so greedy, I could have improved my good fortune. At least I've learned a lesson. Things worth having are worth waiting for."

Cinder Lad

The Mystery of the Hayfield

Once there was a man who had a meadow that he prized highly for its fine hay. But one Midsummer's Eve, when the grass was at its best, the meadow was eaten down to the ground. It looked like a pasture where a whole flock of sheep had been grazing.

The same thing occurred a second year. The poor man felt that he could not endure having his crop ruined a third time. So the next year on Midsummer's Eve, he told his sons that one of them must hide in the barn to watch the hayfield.

The eldest son went off to the barn. As he watched the hay, suddenly there came the sound of booming thunder. Then the very planks of the floor rattled and creaked as if from the shock of an earthquake. The lad took to his heels in fright. Nor did he dare to look around until he got home. So the hay disappeared again.

The fourth year on Midsummer's Eve, the next eldest son went to guard the meadow.

Again came the booming thunder. The lad took to his heels as if bewitched, and the hay was destroyed as before.

On Midsummer's Eve of the fifth year, the turn came to Cinder Lad, the youngest son. But when he prepared to go, his brothers sneered at him. "What a fine guard you'll make!" they cried. "All you've ever done is sit on a stool among the cinders."

In spite of their teasing, Cinder Lad did not despair but went to the barn. Soon the booming and creaking and quaking began.

"Well," said Cinder Lad, "if nothing worse than this happens, I can stand it."

But the uproar grew worse. Suddenly the booming and the quaking ceased. The air was deathly still. Instead of fleeing, Cinder Lad tiptoed to the half-open barn door and peeked out.

There stood a spanking big horse. It was eating away as if it would never stop. One glance convinced Cinder Lad that this was no ordinary horse. It wore bright-colored harness, and beside it lay a sword and a suit of glittering brass armor for a knight.

"Ah!" said the lad. "So it's you who eats our grass. Well, I'll attend to you." And he proceeded to conceal both horse and armor in a secret place.

When Cinder Lad got home, his father and brothers questioned him closely. But he did not relate his true adventures. He merely claimed that he had heard nothing frightening. The brothers suspected that he was not telling the truth. However, there was the meadow grass, still thick and green.

The next year on Midsummer's Eve, the two elder brothers again lacked courage to watch the meadow. So Cinder Lad went to the barn. A storm came up as before. But compared to these violent creaks and blasts, last year's uproar had been a mere whisper.

All at once the air was still. Cinder Lad looked out. There stood another giant steed. He, too, was eating away at a great rate. He was far handsomer than the horse that had appeared the year before, and of a size rarely seen. Beside him lay a suit of silver armor for a knight.

"Ah!" said the lad. "So now it's you who eats our grass. I'll attend to you." He led this horse to the place where he had hidden the other. Then he returned home.

Again his elder brothers sneered at him. "Well," said one of them, "I suppose you'll claim there's no damage to our hayfield."

"That I do!" declared Cinder Lad. And he showed no further concern in the matter.

But the others, suspecting his word, went to the meadow. Lo and behold! There stood the grass, thicker and greener than ever.

The next year the two elder brothers were still afraid. So Cinder Lad was required to watch the field. Again came the peals of thunder, the creaking and quaking, and the silence. When the brave lad looked out, he saw a horse far finer and glossier than the others. Near him lay armor of purest gold.

Cinder Lad proceeded to hide the horse and went to report that the hay was safe.

The Trials at the Glass Hill

The king of the country where Cinder Lad dwelt had a daughter who was beautiful beyond compare. The king proclaimed that the princess should marry the first man in the realm who could ride up a glass hill as slippery as ice.

The king further proclaimed that the princess would sit at the top of the hill holding three golden apples in her lap. Whoever could ride up the slippery hill and carry off the golden apples was to claim the princess for his bride and half the kingdom besides.

Everyone—young or old, rich or poor—was invited to attend the trials.

Knights and princes from the whole realm
accepted the king's invitation, and everyone
came to watch the rare sight. The two elder
brothers, neglecting their work, were among
the watchers. But they had refused sneer-
ingly to let Cinder Lad accompany them.

All day long the gallant noblemen sought to
climb the glass hill. No one, however, could
proceed even twice the length of his horse.
So the king announced that no further trials
would be held until the next day.

Suddenly a knight in glittering brass armor
appeared. Up the slippery hill he charged
at full speed. Sparks flew from the hoofs
of his splendid horse as he proceeded about
a third of the way.

When the princess beheld the knight in the brass armor, she wished that he might claim her for his wife. But the horse came a third of the way and no farther. Then back he slipped. Quickly the princess flung one of her golden apples after the strange knight. It fell right into his lap.

When the knight reached the foot of the hill, he galloped off before anyone could prevent his disappearance.

The next day the two brothers, neglecting their work as before, set off to attend the trials. Cinder Lad pleaded to go with them. They would have none of him.

Once again the knights and princes tried to urge their steeds up the hill. They rode and slipped and slipped and rode. But not one could force his panting horse up the steep slope.

All at once a knight in silver armor came riding into the midst of the watching throng. His horse was black and of uncommon size. Straight toward the slippery hill the knight charged, riding directly up two-thirds of the way.

Suddenly the black horse wheeled with his
forefeet in the air.

The princess gazed with rapture at the
gallant rider. Before he had turned around,
she had sprung to her feet and thrown the
second apple to him. But as soon as the
knight reached the foot of the hill, he rode
swiftly away.

On the third day everything occurred as
on the two days before. Cinder Lad again
begged to go with his brothers. Again they
would not permit him to accompany them.

The gallant knights renewed their efforts to climb the hill. No one could improve on his attempt of the day before. No one got farther than a quarter of the way up.

At last a knight came riding on a horse so huge that no one had ever seen its equal. This mysterious knight wore armor of pure gold. It was so bright that the sun's rays gleamed from it a mile off.

Up the slippery hill he went at full speed. He took the third apple from the princess in triumph. Then he rode down and was gone before anyone could halt him.

Now when the elder brothers got home that evening, they told and retold the tale of the knight in golden armor. Cinder Lad listened as if bewitched.

"I vow no one has ever possessed such glorious armor before!" one brother cried. "Not even in the whole world!"

"I-I wish I could have seen him," Cinder Lad stuttered.

"You!" sneered the eldest brother. "Why, the knight wouldn't even have glanced at a stuttering simpleton like you."

The next day the king's messenger sought out all the knights, ordering them to come to the palace. Among them the king hoped to find the one who had climbed the hill.

So to the palace they all came. But not a single one possessed a golden apple. Nor could any of them explain the disappearance of the mysterious knight.

"Alas! Alack!" cried the king in despair. "Where is the gallant knight in the golden armor?"

Then the king commanded that everybody in all the realm should be sought out and brought to the palace. There were knights and ladies, cooks, carpenters, innkeepers, bootblacks, maid-servants, and many others. But none had seen the golden apples. No one knew who the golden knight might be, for his armor had covered him from head to toe. Therefore no one had caught even a glimpse of his face.

The two brothers of Cinder Lad were the last ones to be questioned. But of course they knew nothing of the golden apples nor of the knight.

"Is there no one else in all my kingdom?" asked the despairing king. "I am requiring every one of my people to come before me."

"Oh," said the eldest brother, "there's our young brother. But he could not have seen the golden apples. I'm sure he has not left his chimney corner for the last three days."

"Never mind that," said the king. "Fetch him to me without further delay."

The two brothers ran home to fetch Cinder Lad. They dragged him to the king, dressed just as he was in a ragged old cloak.

"Speak out, lad," ordered the king when Cinder Lad came to the foot of the throne. "Have you seen the golden apples?"

"Yes, Your Majesty," replied Cinder Lad. "I have the apples. Here is the first one. Here is the second. And here is the third."

The youth took off his ragged cloak. Now he stood before the king dressed in glorious armor of pure gold.

"Ah!" exclaimed the king in great delight. "You shall marry my daughter and rule the southern half of my realm. So gallant a knight well deserves a rich reward."

BOOKS TO READ

Here are some good books that provide more of the same fun and adventure we find in *More Times and Places*.

Young Citizens Here and There

Across Canada.　Clare Bice.
This book contains eight interesting stories, all by the same author, about boys and girls who live in different parts of Canada.　The story called "The Quiet Mountains" in *More Times and Places* is taken from this book.

Blue Willow.　Doris Gates.
Janey belongs to a family of crop harvesters who have always moved about from place to place, following the crops. Janey longs for a real home worthy of her precious blue willow plate. She finally wins such a home for her family, and finds true friends among her California neighbors.

Cowboy Boots.　Shannon Garst.
Here is a story about a city boy's visit to a ranch and his struggles to earn the right to be called a cowboy.

Here's a Penny.　Carolyn Haywood.
This is the first of three very funny books about Penny and Peter, whom you have already met in *More Times and Places*. The two boys become brothers by being adopted into the same family.　*Penny and Peter*, from which the story "Unwelcome Passengers" was taken, and *Penny Goes to Camp* contain more of the brothers' amusing adventures.

Maggie Rose, Her Birthday Christmas.　Ruth Sawyer.
Maggie Rose is a little New England girl who is determined to have a very special Christmas birthday party.　Her lazy, loving family think she is clever but do nothing to help her with her exciting plans until her hard-earned money is stolen.　How she has her wonderful party at last makes a funny, sad, and beautiful Christmas story.

Mountain Born.   Elizabeth Yates.

This is the first of two books about Peter, whose father has a mountain farm in New England.   In this book Peter learns to care for the sheep and has some very exciting adventures. In the second book, *A Place for Peter*, the boy proves that he can be trusted with important farm tasks and is finally recognized as his father's partner.

Peachtree Island.   Mildred Lawrence.

Cissie, who has no parents, spends a year on her uncle's peach orchard in the Great Lakes region.   She thinks her uncle prefers boys to girls, and does all she can to make him change his mind.   Her success brings Cissie a very happy surprise.

Prairie School.   Lois Lenski.

Here is the true and exciting story of a group of school children and their teacher.   It tells of their troubles and courage during a hard, snowy winter on the prairies of South Dakota.

The School Train.   Helen Acker.

Two brothers, the sons of a fur-trapper, walk twenty miles through the deep forests of Canada to catch up with the school train.   The story by the same name in *More Times and Places* is a shortened form of this unusual book.

Told under Spacious Skies.   Association for Childhood Education.   This collection of twenty-seven stories, by well-known authors, is about children living in different regions of the United States.   Each story tells about something that has to do with a special region.

When the Moon Is New.   Laura Bannon.

An Indian girl in Florida is promised a big surprise "when the moon is new."   She hopes that the surprise will be a sewing machine, but it turns out to be something much better.   You will enjoy the pictures of the Florida Everglades and of the colorful Indian costumes.

The Great Outdoors

An Otter's Story.   Emil Liers.
   The author of this book has pet otters.   In writing about the life of two young river otters, he shows us how harmless and playful these animals are.   The things that happen in the story are based on actual facts.

Brighty of the Grand Canyon.   Marguerite Henry.
   A little wild burro called Brighty is the hero of this story. All by himself, he makes a now-famous trail from the top to the bottom of the Grand Canyon.   Brighty has many adventures, among them a fight with a mountain lion.   You will enjoy the funny pictures showing how Uncle Jim takes care of Brighty's wounds.   Part of the story is a mystery, and Uncle Jim is the one who solves it.

Dash and Dart.   Mary and Conrad Buff.
   This beautiful picture-story of the first year in the life of twin fawns tells how the young fawns learn the things they should know.   Occasionally the authors feel that the fawns think as people do.   For example, Dash admires his father's big, handsome antlers but does not realize what is happening when his own antlers begin to grow.

Honk, the Moose.   Phil Stong.
   Honk will be one of your favorite animals after you have read this very funny story.   It is about a wild moose that moves into a village stable for the winter and makes himself at home.   Not even the village policemen can manage to get him out.

Let Them Live.   Dorothy P. Lathrop.
   You will understand why the author is famous for her beautiful pictures when you see this book.   *Let Them Live* explains why such wild animals as red foxes, beavers, wood ducks, sea otters, black bears, fur seals, and mountain lions should not be hunted and killed as they are today.

Snow Dog.　Jim Kjelgaard.
The Husky puppy of "Wilderness Partners" in *More Times and Places* is the "snow dog" of this story.　The book will tell you how he later meets a northern trapper who tries hard to make friends with the dog.　You will like the exciting ending.

Spike, the Story of a Whitetail Deer.　Robert McClung.
All the facts in Mr. McClung's stories are correct, and this deer story is one of his best.　It tells how a deer changes in appearance as he grows older, and how he learns to take care of himself.　It also describes the dangers he faces from forest fires and from hunters who do not obey the game laws.

Star of Wild Horse Canyon.　Clyde R. Bulla.
Here a boy has a chance to see a herd of wild horses captured, and later to train one of them himself.　One stormy night the horse, Star, disappears.　What do you suppose happens when Danny discovers that someone is hiding Star from him?

The Biggest Bear on Earth.　Harold McCracken.
An Alaskan brown bear cub whose mother is killed grows up to be the biggest bear in the world and certainly one of the smartest and strongest.　After a fight with another huge bear, he rules as king of the forest.

The Blind Colt.　Glen Rounds.
You cannot help liking this fine story of how a colt learns to get along without sight and of a young boy's understanding love for him.　You will also want to read *The Stolen Pony*, by the same author.

The Wild Little Honker.　Dorothy Childs Hogner.
A family of wild geese settles down contentedly on a river in New York State.　Only Little Honker scorns their easy life.　Finally he flies off with some geese that are returning to their home in the far North.

Famous Americans of Other Times

Abraham Lincoln: An Initial Biography. Genevieve Foster.
  This book and *George Washington: An Initial Biography*, by
  the same author, will tell you about the lives of two of our
  country's best-loved men. Both of these fine books have
  pictures by the author.

Benjamin Franklin. Ingri and Edgar Parin d'Aulaire.
  It is hard to tell the whole story of Franklin's life in a short
  book with large pictures, but this one tells a surprising
  amount. Be sure to notice Franklin's sayings tucked away
  around the borders of the pages.

Betsy Ross and the Flag. Jane Mayer.
  How we first got our flag is not known exactly, but here is a
  well-known story told in an interesting way.

Boat Builder, the Story of Robert Fulton. Clara Ingram Judson.
  Robert Fulton's life was indeed a busy one. Here Mrs.
  Judson describes his youth and his work both as an artist
  and as an inventor. "Fulton's Folly" in *More Times and
  Places* is taken from *Boat Builder.*

Buffalo Bill. Ingri and Edgar Parin d'Aulaire.
  Buffalo Bill was a mighty man of the plains and a showman
  as well. In this book you will follow his exciting life from
  childhood to his days with circuses and rodeos. The pictures
  are large and colorful.

Clara Barton: Girl Nurse. Augusta Stevenson.
  This is a story about Clara Barton's childhood. The author
  has also written about the childhoods of other famous Americans. You will like *Abe Lincoln: Frontier Boy* and *George
  Washington: Boy Leader.*

George Washington, Leader of the People. Clara Ingram Judson.
  In this book, from which the story "George Grows Up" in
  More Times and Places is taken, the author makes George
  Washington seem as real as if he were still alive. You will

enjoy equally well Mrs. Judson's *Abraham Lincoln, Friend of the People.*

Kit Carson, Mountain Man.   Margaret E. Bell.
The old days of the West are brought to life in this book about one of our country's greatest scouts and hunters. Again and again young Kit Carson was refused a chance to prove his scouting skill to the fur-trapping mountain men, but success came at last.

Martin and Abraham Lincoln.   Catherine C. Coblentz.
This is the true story of a boy who was given comfort in time of trouble by a kindly man who turned out to be the President of the United States.

The Story of Daniel Boone.   William O. Steele.
Here you will read about Daniel's boyhood, his adventures with the Indians, and the settling of Kentucky.

The Story of John Paul Jones.   Iris Vinton.
This book will tell you how a lively boy named John Paul Jones grew up to be one of America's most famous heroes of the sea.

The Story of Mad Anthony Wayne.   Hazel Wilson.
Anthony Wayne was one of George Washington's greatest and most daring generals.   In this story of his life you will learn of his great concern for the well-being of his men, and of their willingness to follow him on his maddest adventures.

The Story of Thomas Alva Edison.   Enid La Monte Meadowcroft.   The author tells in an entertaining way about Edison's experiments, from a boyhood attempt to turn a friend into a balloon to his invention of moving pictures.   The Edison story in *More Times and Places* is from this book.

Tom Edison: Boy Inventor.   Sue Guthridge.
Here is another good book about Thomas Edison.   This one is entirely about his childhood.

Old Tales from Everywhere

Aesop's Fables. George Tyler Townsend and Thomas James. There are many other beautiful books containing Aesop's fables, but you will especially like the pictures in this book and the way the fables are told.

Andersen's Fairy Tales. Hans Christian Andersen. Retold by Mrs. E. V. Lucas and Mrs. H. B. Paull. Andersen was a famous writer of fairy tales, and there are many thick books full of his stories. There are also small books, with just one story beautifully pictured, that you may prefer. Try these: *The Emperor's New Clothes* (pictures by Virginia Lee Burton); *The Steadfast Tin Soldier* (pictures by Marcia Brown); *The Ugly Duckling* (pictures by Johannes Larsen).

Chanticleer and the Fox. Geoffrey Chaucer. Retold by Barbara Cooney. This story was written by Chaucer, an Englishman, more than six hundred years ago. Barbara Cooney has retold it in more modern language. She has also drawn the beautiful pictures, which show the people and the countryside of England as they looked in Chaucer's day.

Chimney Corner Fairy Tales. Veronica S. Hutchinson. Here is a good collection of a few favorite stories with pleasant pictures.

East o' the Sun and West o' the Moon. Peter Asbjörnsen and Jörgen Moe. Retold by Gudrun Thorne-Thomsen. This book contains twenty-five old tales from Norway. They are retold simply, and you will enjoy reading them.

English Fairy Tales. Joseph Jacobs. Forty-three old English fairy tales appear in this book, and another forty-four in *More English Fairy Tales*. A small book called *Dick Whittington and His Cat* contains only this one famous old English tale, retold by Marcia Brown. Be sure to read it.

Grimm's Fairy Tales. Jacob and Wilhelm Grimm. Retold by Mrs. E. V. Lucas, Lucy Crane, and Marian Edwardes. Among the most exciting fairy tales are those collected by the Grimm brothers. Here are many of their stories, with amusing pictures. Other good collections with fewer stories are *Tales from Grimm*, *More Tales from Grimm*, and *Three Gay Tales from Grimm*, by Wanda Gág. *Gone Is Gone*, also by Wanda Gág, is just one tale.

Padre Porko, the Gentlemanly Pig. Robert Davis.
The "gentlemanly pig" of these amusing old tales from Spain has to get the other animals out of trouble.

Peter and the Wolf. Serge Prokofieff.
Some of you will be familiar with this fairy tale from hearing it on the radio or on a record. Here it is in a small book, with delightful pictures by Warren Chappell. The book also contains some important parts of the music.

Picture Tales from Spain. Retold by Ruth Sawyer.
These eleven easy-to-read tales are fun to tell and still more fun to act out.

Puss in Boots. Charles Perrault.
The pictures by Marcia Brown make this one of the gayest and handsomest books you have ever seen. It is easy to read, too.

Tales of Faraway Folk. Babette Deutsch and Avrahm Yarmolinsky. You are sure to be entertained by these tales from many lands.

The Three Sneezes and Other Swiss Tales. Roger Duvoisin.
Here are some exciting old Swiss tales, simply told.

Time to Laugh. Phyllis R. Fenner.
These stories, collected from many parts of the world, show that laughter is the same everywhere. Two of Phyllis Fenner's other collections are *Giants and Witches and a Dragon or Two* and *Princesses and Peasant Boys*.

GLOSSARY

Full Pronunciation Key

The pronunciation of each word is shown just after the word, in this way: **ab bre vi ate** (ə brē′vi āt). The letters and signs used are pronounced as in the words below. The mark ′ is placed after a syllable with primary or heavy accent, as in the example above. The mark ′ after a syllable shows a secondary or lighter accent, as in **ab bre vi a tion** (ə brē′vi ā′shən).

a	hat, cap	j	jam, enjoy	u	cup, butter
ā	age, face	k	kind, seek	u̇	full, put
ã	care, air	l	land, coal	ü	rule, move
ä	father, far	m	me, am	ū	use, music
		n	no, in		
b	bad, rob	ng	long, bring		
ch	child, much			v	very, save
d	did, red	o	hot, rock	w	will, woman
		ō	open, go	y	young, yet
e	let, best	ô	order, all	z	zero, breeze
ē	equal, be	oi	oil, voice	zh	measure, seizure
er	term, learn	ou	house, out		
				ə	represents:
f	fat, if	p	paper, cup		a in about
g	go, bag	r	run, try		e in taken
h	he, how	s	say, yes		i in pencil
		sh	she, rush		o in lemon
i	it, pin	t	tell, it		u in circus
ī	ice, five	th	thin, both		
		ᴛʜ	then, smooth		

This pronunciation key is from the *Thorndike-Barnhart Beginning Dictionary*. Special acknowledgment is made to Clarence L. Barnhart, editor of the Thorndike-Barnhart Dictionaries, for his assistance in the preparation of this glossary.

a broad (ə brôd′), outside one's country: *He is going abroad this summer to travel in England.*

ac com pa ny (ə kum′pə ni), **1.** go along with. **2.** be or happen along with: *The rain was accompanied by a high wind.*

a corn (ā′kôrn), the nut of an oak tree.

Acorn

ad vance (ad vans′), **1.** move forward. **2.** forward movement: *The army's advance was very slow.* **3. In advance** means (**1**) in front. (**2**) ahead of time.

a lert (ə lèrt′), **1.** watchful; wide-awake. **2.** lively. **3. On the alert** means watchful.

al li ga tor (al′ə gā′tər), large crawling animal with a long body, four short legs, a thick skin, and a long tail. See the picture. Alligators live in rivers and swamps of warm parts of America.

Alligator (12 ft. long)

am ble (am′bəl), go in a slow, easy way.

ap par ent ly (ə par′ənt li), **1.** as far as one can tell; seemingly. **2.** clearly; plainly.

ar mor (är′mər), covering worn to protect the body in fighting.

ar riv al (ə rīv′əl), coming: *She is waiting for the arrival of the train.*

as sist (ə sist′), help.

at tack (ə tak′), **1.** set upon to hurt; go against as an enemy: *The dog attacked the cat.* **2.** begin to work on: *attack a hard lesson.* **3.** attacking: *The attack of the enemy took us by surprise.*

au di ence (ô′di əns), all the people gathered in a place or building to hear or see (someone or something).

ban ner (ban′ər), flag: *Robert carried our school banner in the parade.*

be held (bi held′), saw: *They beheld the approaching storm.*

be hold (bi hōld′), see; look; take notice: *Behold! the king!*

belt (belt), **1.** strip of leather, cloth, etc., worn around the body to hold in or support clothes. **2.** region in which certain crops or plants grow well: *The wheat belt is the region where wheat is grown.*

be ware (bi wãr′), be careful; be on your guard against: *Beware! danger is here. Beware the dog!*

be witch (bi wich′), **1.** put under a spell; use magic on: *The wicked fairy bewitched the princess, and made her fall into a long sleep.* **2.** delight very much: *We were all bewitched by our pretty little cousin.*

blast (blast), **1.** strong sudden rush of wind or air: *the icy blasts of winter.* **2.** sound made by blowing a horn or trumpet: *We heard the blast of the trumpet.*

bolt (bōlt), dash off; run away.

bore[1] (bôr), make a hole by means of a tool that keeps turning, or as a worm does in fruit.

bore

bore² (bôr), make weary by tiresome talk or by being dull: *This book bores me, so I shall not finish it.* .

bound a ry (boun′də ri), anything that shows the border of a piece of land or a region: *A river sometimes forms the boundary between two states.*

brief (brēf), short.

bril liant (bril′yənt), **1.** very bright; sparkling. **2.** splendid.

cac tus (kak′təs), thorny plant without leaves. Cactuses grow in dry, hot regions.

Common cactus

can yon (kan′yən), narrow valley with high, steep sides, usually with a stream at the bottom.

cease (sēs), stop.

coil (koil), **1.** wind round and round into a circle, a pile, or a curl: *A snake can coil itself up or coil around a branch. A wire spring is evenly coiled.* **2.** anything that is coiled: *a coil of rope.*

com mu ni ty (kə mū′nə ti), the people of any small region or town: *This lake provides water for six communities.*

com pan ion (kəm pan′yən), one who goes along with or accompanies another; one who shares in what another is doing: *The twins were companions in work and play.*

com ple tion (kəm plē′shən), **1.** finishing; act of completing: *After the completion of the job, the workman went home.* **2.** being

creak

finished or completed: *The work is near completion.*

con ceal (kən sēl′), hide.

con cern (kən sėrn′), **1.** interest. **2.** worry.

con fuse (kən fūz′), **1.** mix up; throw into disorder: *So many people talking to me at once confused me.* **2.** mistake (one thing for another): *People often confuse Mary with her sister.*

con sid er (kən sid′ər), **1.** think about in order to decide: *Take time to consider the problem.* **2.** think to be: *I consider him an able man.* **3.** allow for; take into account: *This watch runs well, if you consider how old it is.*

con vince (kən vins′), make someone feel sure; persuade firmly.

coon (kün), raccoon, a small grayish animal with a bushy ringed tail.

cove (kōv), small bay; mouth of a creek; inlet on the shore.

coy o te (kī ō′ti or kī′ōt), prairie wolf of western North America.

crab (krab), water animal with eight legs, two claws, and a broad, flat, shell covering. Many kinds of crabs are good to eat.

Crab

craft y (kraf′ti), clever at fooling others; sly: *the crafty fox.*

creak (krēk), **1.** squeak loudly. **2.** creaking noise.

304

cricket — earnest

crick et (krik'it), black insect of the grasshopper family.

crouch (krouch), **1.** stoop low with bent legs like an animal ready to spring, or like a person hiding. **2.** shrink down in fear.

cy press (sī'prəs), evergreen tree with hard wood and dark leaves.

deck (dek), floor of a ship.

de part (di pärt'), go away; leave: *We arrived in the village in the morning, and departed at night.*

de spair (di spãr'), **1.** loss of hope; a being without hope; a dreadful feeling that nothing good can happen: *Despair seized us as we felt the boat sinking under us.* **2.** lose hope: *The doctors despaired of saving the child's life.*

des per ate (des'pər it), **1.** hopeless. **2.** ready to run any risk: *a desperate thief.*

de ter mine (di tėr'mən), make up one's mind very firmly: *He determined to become the best Scout in his troop.*

dis mal (diz'məl), **1.** dark; gloomy: *A damp cave or a rainy day is dismal.* **2.** dreary; miserable: *Sickness or bad luck often makes a person feel dismal.*

dis play (dis plā'), **1.** show: *He displayed his good nature by answering all our questions.* **2.** planned showing of a thing, for some special purpose: *Grade 4 had two displays of children's drawings.*

dis tress (dis tres'), **1.** great pain or sorrow; worry; trouble. **2.** make unhappy; worry.

dou ble (dub'əl), **1.** twice as much, as large, as strong, etc. **2.** made of two like parts; in a pair: *double doors.* **3.** bend or turn sharply backward: *The fox doubled on his track and escaped the dogs.*

Dr., Doctor.

drake (drāk), male duck.

drawl (drôl), **1.** talk in a slow, lazy way. **2.** slow, lazy way of talking.

dread (dred), **1.** look forward to with fear or dislike; fear greatly: *Cats dread water.* **2.** fear, especially fear of something that will happen, or may happen.

dread ful (dred'fəl), causing dread; terrible; fearful.

drear y (drēr'i), gloomy and dull; without cheer.

dusk (dusk), **1.** the time just before dark. **2.** shade; gloom.

dwarf (dwôrf), **1.** person, animal, or plant much smaller than the usual size for its kind. **2.** in fairy tales, an ugly little man with magic power.

dwelt (dwelt), lived; made one's home: *We have dwelt in the country for years.*

ear nest (ėr'nist), **1.** strong and firm in purpose; serious: *An earnest pupil has his mind on his work.* **2.** **In earnest** means determined; serious.

hat, āge, cãre, fär; let, bē, tėrm; it, īce; hot, ōpen, ôrder; oil, out; cup, pùt, rüle, ūse; takən

305

earth quake (ėrth′kwāk′), shaking or sliding of the ground, caused by changes far beneath the earth's surface: *Earthquakes sometimes destroy whole cities.*

ech o (ek′ō), repeat; be heard again.

eld er (el′dər), older.

eld est (el′dist), oldest. .

en dure (en dür′ or en dūr′), 1. last; keep on: *A gold ring will endure for a thousand years.* 2. bear; stand: *Those brave men endured much pain.*

en rage (en rāj′), make very angry; make furious.

ex hib it (eg zib′it), 1. show to the public: *You should exhibit your roses in the Flower Show.* 2. something shown to the public: *Their exhibit of corn at the fair won the prize.*

ex per i ment (eks per′ə ment for 1, eks per′ə mənt for 2), 1. try in order to find out; make tests: *That man is experimenting with dyes to get the color that he wants.* 2. trial or test to find out something: *a cooking experiment.*

ex treme ly (eks trēm′li), much more than usual; very.

faith ful (fāth′fəl), loyal: *a faithful friend, a faithful servant.*

fal ter (fôl′tər), 1. hesitate; lose courage: *The soldiers faltered for a moment as their captain fell.* 2. become unsteady in movement.

fa mil iar (fə mil′yər), 1. well known: *The words of the old song were familiar to everyone.* 2. well acquainted: *He was familiar with several languages.*

fee ble (fē′bəl), weak: *a feeble old man, a feeble cry.*

fetch (fech), go and get; bring: *Please fetch me my glasses.*

flap jack (flap′jak′), pancake.

fled (fled), 1. ran away: *The thieves fled, but they were soon caught.* 2. went quickly.

flee (flē), 1. run away. 2. go quickly.

fleet[1] (flēt), ships under one command; ships sailing together: *the United States fleet.*

fleet[2] (flēt), fast moving; rapid.

fod der (fod′ər), coarse food for horses, cattle, etc. Hay and cornstalks with their leaves are fodder.

fol ly (fol′i), 1. being foolish; lack of sense: *It is folly to eat too much on the picnic.* 2. foolish practice, act, or idea; something silly: *"You are too old for such follies," said Mother.*

for tune (fôr′chən), 1. great deal of money; riches. 2. luck; chance.

fos sil (fos′əl), the hardened remains of an animal or plant. Fossils of ferns are found in coal.

frame (frām), 1. support over which something is stretched or built: *the frame of a house.* 2. put a border around: *to frame a picture.*

freak (frēk), something very queer or unusual: *A green leaf growing in the middle of a rose would be called a freak of nature.*

fre quent (frē′kwənt for 1, fri kwent′ for 2), 1. happening often, near together, or every little while: *Storms are frequent in March.* **2.** be often in; go to often: *Frogs frequent ponds.*

fre quent ly (frē′kwənt li), often.

fu ture (fū′chər), **1.** the time to come. **2.** coming: *We hope your future years will all be happy.*

gal lant (gal′ənt), brave.

gan der (gan′dər), male goose.

glimpse (glimps), **1.** very brief view; short look: *I got a glimpse of the falls as our train went by.* **2.** catch a brief view of.

glit ter (glit′ər), **1.** shine with a bright, sparkling light. **2.** bright, sparkling light.

glo ri ous (glô′ri əs), magnificent; splendid.

gloss y (glôs′i), smooth and shiny.

gov ern ment (guv′ərn mənt), person or persons ruling or managing a country at any time.

grad u al ly (graj′ü əl i), little by little.

griz zly (griz′li), **1.** grayish. **2.** a large, fierce, gray or brownish-gray bear of western North America.

gul ly (gul′i), little steep valley; ditch.

Grizzly bear
(about 8 ft. long)

harsh (härsh), **1.** rough to the touch, taste, eye, or ear: *a harsh voice.* **2.** cruel.

heed (hēd), **1.** take notice of: *Now heed what I say.* **2.** careful attention; notice: *She pays heed to her clothes.*

hes i tate (hez′ə tāt), **1.** hold back; feel doubtful; be undecided. **2.** stop an instant; pause.

hith er (hiℸн′ər), **1.** here. **2. Hither and thither** means here and there.

hum ble (hum′bəl), **1.** simple; not important; not grand: *We live in a humble cottage of one room.* **2.** not proud.

hum bly (hum′bli), in a humble manner.

Husk y or **husk y** (hus′ki), Eskimo dog.

im prove (im prüv′), **1.** make better: *You could improve your handwriting if you tried.* **2.** become better: *His health is improving.*

in tent (in tent′), **1.** paying close attention; earnest. **2.** much interested: *She is intent on doing her best.*

jeer (jēr), make fun in a rude or unkind way: *Do not jeer at the mistakes or misfortunes of others.*

keen (kēn), **1.** so shaped as to cut well: *a keen knife.* **2.** sharp; cutting: *keen wind, keen pain.* **3.** able to do its work quickly and exactly: *a keen mind, keen eyes.*

---

hat, āge, cãre, fär; let, bē, tėrm; it, īce; hot, ōpen, ôrder; oil, out; cup, pút, rüle, ūse; takən

lack (lak),   1. have no; be without.   2. have not enough.

lamp (lamp),   a gas, oil, or electric light. See the picture.

lass (las),   girl; young girl.

Oil lamp

ledge (lej),   1. narrow shelf: *a window ledge.*   2. shelf of rock.

lin ger (ling′gər), stay on; go slowly, as if unwilling to leave.

lo (lō),   look! see!

loon (lün),   large diving bird that has a loud, wild cry. See the picture.

Loon (about 32 in. long)

lord (lôrd),   1. owner, ruler, or master; person who has the power.   2. title of some noblemen.

lunge (lunj),   1. sudden forward movement.   2. move forward suddenly.

lurk (lėrk),   stay about without attracting attention; be hidden: *A tiger was lurking in the forest outside the village.*

mad am (mad′əm),   polite title used in speaking to a lady or of a lady.

mare (mãr),   female horse.

mar vel (mär′vəl),   1. something wonderful: *The airplane, radio, and television are among the marvels of science.*   2. wonder greatly.

ma te ri al (mə tēr′i əl),   what a thing is made from or done with: *dress material, building materials, writing materials.*

meek (mēk),   1. gentle; patient; not easily angered.   2. giving in tamely when ordered about.

mes quite (mes kēt′),   tree or shrub common in the southwestern United States: *Cattle eat mesquite pods.*

midg et (mij′it),   very small person; dwarf.

midst (midst),   middle. **In our midst** means among us.

mid sum mer (mid′sum′ər),   1. the middle of summer.   2. the time near June 21.   3. in the middle of summer.

mu se um (mū zē′əm),   building or rooms in which collections or objects of interest are kept and exhibited.

neg lect (ni glekt′),   1. give too little care or attention to.   2. leave undone.   3. fail: *Don't neglect to water the plants.*

no ble man (nō′bəl mən),   man of noble title or birth.

ob serve (əb zėrv′),   1. notice: *Did you observe anything strange about that man?*   2. examine closely; study.

oc ca sion al ly (ə kā′zhən əl i), now and then; once in a while.

oc cur (ə kėr′),   1. happen; take place: *Storms often occur in winter.*   2. come to mind; suggest itself: *A new idea suddenly occurred to me.*

oc to pus (ok′tə pəs),   sea animal having a soft body and eight arms with suckers on them.

o dor (ō′dər),   smell: *the odor of roses.*

op por tu ni ty (op/ər tü/nə ti or op/ər tū/nə ti),   good chance: *I had an opportunity to earn some money picking berries.*

op po site (op/ə zit), across from; facing: *The teacher's desk was opposite the door.*

or chard (ôr/chərd),   **1.** piece of ground on which fruit trees are grown. **2.** The trees in an orchard.

o ver come (ō/vər kum/), **1.** get the better of: *We can overcome difficulties. Overcome by the sight of so much candy, the child grabbed for it.* **2.** made weak or helpless: *The child was overcome by weariness and slept.*

pan ic (pan/ik),   sudden, terrible fear.

pa trol (pə trōl/),   **1.** go the rounds as a watchman or a policeman does: *The camp was carefully patrolled.* **2.** men who patrol: *The patrol was changed at midnight.*

pause (pôz),   stop for a time; wait: *He made a short pause and then went on reading. The dog paused when he heard me.*

peer (pēr),   **1.** look closely to see clearly, as a near-sighted person does: *She peered at the tag to read the price.* **2.** peep out: *The sun was peering from behind a cloud.*

per mis sion (pər mish/ən), consent; leave; permitting: *He asked the teacher's permission to go early.*

per mit (pər mit/ for 1, pėr/mit for 2),   **1.** let; allow: *Mr. Bell permitted us to swim in his pond.* **2.** written order giving permission to do something: *Have you a permit to fish in the lake?*

pierce (pērs),   **1.** make a hole in; bore into or through: *A nail pierced the tire of our car.* **2.** make a way through with the eye or mind: *to pierce a disguise, to pierce a mystery.*

pi ty (pit/i),   **1.** sorrow for another's distress or suffering; a feeling for the sorrows of others. **2.** feel sorry for: *Ann pitied any child who was hurt or hungry.* **3.** cause for pity or distress: *It is a pity to be kept in the house in fine weather.*

plead (plēd),   ask earnestly; beg: *The busy man pleaded for more time to finish the job.*

plume (plüm),   **1.** a large, long feather; feather. **2.** something like a large soft feather: *a plume of smoke.*

por trait (pôr/trit or pôr/trāt), picture of a person.

pos sess (pə zes/),   own; have: *The farmer possessed many acres of land.*

pounce (pouns),   jump suddenly and seize: *The cat pounced upon the mouse.*

prey (prā),   **1.** animal hunted or seized for food: *Mice and birds are the prey of cats.* **2. Prey on** or **prey upon** means hunt or kill for food: *Cats prey upon mice.*

---

hat, āge, cãre, fär; let, bē, tėrm; it, īce; hot, ōpen, ôrder; oil, out; cup, put, rüle, ūse; takən

pro ceed (prə sēd′),　　1. move forward: *The train proceeded at the same speed as before.* 2. carry on any act: *The man proceeded to light his pipe.*

prop er (prop′ər), correct; right; fitting: *Night is the proper time to sleep, and bed is the proper place.*

prop er ly (prop′ər li),　　in a proper, correct, or fitting manner: *Eat properly.*

prove (prüv), 1. show that something is true or right: *Prove these answers.* 2. turn out; be found to be: *The book proved interesting.*

prowl (proul),　　go about slowly and secretly, hunting for something to eat or steal: *Many wild animals prowl at night.*

pur sue (pər sü′),　　chase: *The policeman pursued the robbers.*

pur su er (pər sü′ər),　　one who pursues.

quake (kwāk), 1. shake; tremble: *The young girl quaked with fear.* 2. a shaking; a trembling.

rang er (rān′jər),　　person employed to guard a forest region.

rap ture (rap′chər),　　very great joy: *The mother gazed with rapture at her long-lost son.*

rare[1] (rãr), 1. not usually found; few: *Storks and peacocks are rare in the United States.* 2. not happening often: *Snowstorms are rare in Florida.* 3. unusually good: *Edison had rare powers as an inventor.*

rare[2] (rãr),　　not cooked much: *a rare piece of meat.*

rare ly (rãr′li),　　not often.

realm (relm),　　1. kingdom. 2. region.

reck on (rek′ən),　　1. find the number or value of; count: *You must reckon the cost before you decide.* 2. consider; judge: *He is reckoned a fine speller.* 3. think; suppose: *The man said, "I reckon it's going to rain."*

re cov er (ri kuv′ər), 1. get back (something lost, taken away, or stolen): *to recover a purse.* 2. get well; get over: *Ann is recovering from a long illness. The boy quickly recovered from his fright.*

reed (rēd),　　a kind of tall grass with a hollow stalk that grows in wet places.

re gard (ri gärd′),　　1. consider; think of: *He is regarded as the best doctor in town.* 2. look at; watch: *The cat regarded me anxiously when I picked up her kittens.* 3. a look; a steady look: *The man's regard seemed fixed upon some distant object.*

re gion (rē′jən),　　1. any large part of the earth. 2. place; space.

re late (ri lāt′),　　1. tell; report: *The traveler related his adventures.* 2. connect in thought or meaning. *"Better"* and *"best"* are related to *"good."* 3. **Be related** sometimes means belong to the same family: *Cousins are related.*

re lief (ri lēf′),　　1. the freeing from pain, worry, or difficulty. 2. aid; help.

re new (ri nü′ or ri nū′), 1. make new or strong again; make like new. 2. begin again: *He renewed his efforts to open the window.*

310

re quire (ri kwīr´),   **1.** need: *We require more spoons for our party.* **2.** demand; order; command: *The rules required us all to be present.*

risk (risk),   **1.** chance of harm or loss; danger: *He rescued the dog at the risk of his own life. If you drive carefully, there is no risk of being fined.* **2.** take the risk of: *The children risked drowning when they swam in the deep river.*

roam (rōm),   go about with no special plan or aim; wander: *to roam through the fields.*

rus tle (rus´əl),   **1.** sound that leaves make when moved by the wind; sound like this. **2.** make a light, soft sound: *Her silk dress rustled when she walked.* **3.** move or stir (something) so that it makes such a sound.

sap[1] (sap),   the liquid that circulates through a plant, carrying water, food, etc. as blood does in animals.

sap[2] (sap),   weaken; use up: *The extreme heat sapped her strength.*

scorch (skôrch), **1.** burn slightly; burn on the outside: *The fire scorched the boys' faces.* **2.** slight burn.

scorn ful (skôrn´fəl),   making fun of; mocking: *He spoke of our old car in a scornful voice.*

se cure (si kūr´),   **1.** safe: *This is a secure hiding place.* **2.** firm: *Are the boards of this bridge*

secure? **3.** get; obtain: *We have secured our tickets for the play.*

sense (sens), **1.** feel; understand: *Mother sensed that Father was tired.* **2.** understanding, intelligence: *He hasn't sense enough to come in when it rains.*

shal low (shal´ō),   not deep: *shallow water, a shallow dish.*

shove (shuv),   **1.** push roughly: *The people shoved to get on the crowded car.* **2.** push: *Tom gave the boat a shove which sent it far out into the water.*

slash (slash),   **1.** cut with a sweeping stroke of a sword, knife, whip, or ax. **2.** make a slashing stroke. **3.** reduce a great deal.

slight (slīt), **1.** not much; small: *I have a slight headache.* **2.** not big; slender.

slope (slōp),   **1.** go up or down as shown in the picture: *The land slopes toward the sea. The house has a sloping roof.* **2.** any surface, line, or land that goes up or down from a level: *If you roll a ball up a slope, it will roll down again.*

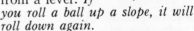
Slope of a hill

sneer (snēr),   make fun of or mock by looks or words: *The mean girls sneered at poor Jane's clothes.*

snout (snout),   long nose of an animal; the nose and mouth of an animal: *the snout of a pig.*

---

hat, āge, cãre, fär; let, bē, tėrm; it, īce; hot, ōpen, ôrder; oil, out; cup, put, rüle, ūse; takən

sol emn (sol/əm),　　serious; earnest: *He gave his solemn promise never to return.*

sol id (sol/id),　　**1.** strongly put together; hard; firm: *They were glad to leave the boat and put their feet on solid ground.* **2.** alike throughout: *The ring was solid gold.*

sought (sôt),　　**1.** looked for; hunted: *For days she sought a safe hiding place.* **2.** tried: *The bird sought to escape from the cage.*

span gle (spang/gəl),　　sprinkle with small bright bits: *The sky is spangled with stars.*

spir it (spir/it),　　**1.** supernatural being. God is a spirit. **2. Spirits** means state of mind: *He is in good spirits.* **Out of spirits** means sad; gloomy.

spout (spout),　　**1.** flow out with force: *Water spouted from the break in the pipe.* **2.** stream: *A spout of water shot up from a hole in the pipe.* **3.** tube or lip by which liquid is poured. A teapot has a spout.

SPOUT

squaw (skwô),　　American Indian woman or wife.

steed (stēd),　　**1.** horse, especially a riding horse. **2.** a high-spirited horse.

strut (strut),　　walk, in a vain, important way: *The rooster struts about the barnyard.*

stur dy (stėr/di),　　strong.

suck er (suk/ər),　　part of an animal that is used for sucking or holding fast to things.

sur vey (sər vā/ for 1, sėr/vā for 2),　　**1.** measure for size, shape, place, boundaries, etc.: *Men are surveying the land before it is divided into house lots.* **2.** careful measurement: *Surveys showed that the northern boundary was not correct.*

sur vey ing (sər vā/ing),　　the act or business of making surveys of land.

sur vey or (sər vā/ər),　　person who surveys.

sus pect (səs pekt/ for 1 and 2, sus/pekt for 3),　　**1.** imagine to be so; think likely: *The mouse suspected danger and did not touch the trap. I suspect that some accident has delayed him.* **2.** doubt. **3.** person suspected.

swamp (swomp),　　wet, soft land.

swan (swon),　　large, graceful water bird with a long, slender, curving neck.

swarm (swôrm),　　**1.** large group of insects flying about together. Swan (nearly 5 ft. long with the head and neck) **2.** fly or move in great numbers: *The flies swarmed about us.*

swirl (swėrl),　　move with a twisting motion; whirl: *dust swirling in the air.*

swoop (swüp),　　come down with a rush, as a hawk does; sweep rapidly down (upon) in sudden attack.

syr up (sir/əp or sėr/əp),　　a thick, sweet liquid. Maple syrup is made from the sap of maple trees.

te di ous (tē′di əs or tē′jəs), long and tiring: *A long boring talk is tedious.*

tem per a ture (tem′pər ə chər), 1. degree of heat or cold. The temperature of freezing water is 32 degrees Fahrenheit. 2. a body temperature higher than normal (98.6 degrees).

ter ror (ter′ər), great fear: *The child has a terror of thunder.*

thith er (thiŦH′ər), there.

threat en (thret′ən), 1. say what will be done to punish or harm: *The farmer threatened to shoot any dog that killed one of his sheep.* 2. give warning of coming trouble: *The clouds threaten rain.* 3. be a cause of possible harm to: *A flood threatened the city.*

throng (thrông), crowd: *Great throngs of people came to see the President.*

thun der bolt (thun′dər bōlt′), 1. flash of lightning and the thunder that follows it. 2. something sudden, startling, and terrifying.

toil (toil), 1. hard work. 2. work hard.

tor na do (tôr nā′dō), violent whirlwind that often destroys things.

tri al (trī′əl), trying or testing: *He gave the machine another trial to see if it would work.*

tribe (trīb), group of people living together under the same leaders: *America was once the home of many tribes of Indians.*

tri umph (trī′umf), joy because of victory or success: *He took home his prize in triumph.*

trout (trout), fresh-water food and game fish.

truce (trüs), a stop in fighting; peace for a short time: *A truce was declared between the armies.*

tu pe lo (tü′pə lō), large North American tree with strong wood.

un der take (un′dər tāk′), 1. try; attempt. 2. agree to do; promise.

vain (vān), 1. having too much pride: *She is vain of her beauty.* 2. of no use; unsuccessful: *She made vain attempts to reach her mother on the telephone.* 3. **In vain** means without success: *The drowning man shouted in vain, for no one was near.*

val ley (val′i), 1. low land between hills or mountains: *Most large valleys have rivers running through them.* 2. wide region drained by a great river: *the Ohio valley.*

ven ture (ven′chər), 1. dare: *No one ventured to interrupt the speaker.* 2. dare to say, go, make, or try something: *In spite of the storm, the boys ventured outside.*

vi o lent (vī′ə lənt), 1. rough; forceful: *a violent blow.* 2. showing or caused by very strong feeling or action: *violent language, a violent war.*

vi o lent ly (vī′ə lənt li), in a violent way.

---

hat, āge, cãre, fär; let, bē, tèrm; it, īce; hot, ōpen, ôrder; oil, out; cup, put, rüle, ūse; taken

vow (vou), **1.** solemn promise. **2.** declare earnestly or forcefully: *She vowed she would never leave home again.*

wal low (wol⁄ō), **1.** roll about: *The pigs wallowed in the mud.* **2.** place where an animal wallows.

weap on (wep⁄ən), thing used in fighting or attacking. Swords, arrows, clubs, guns, claws, horns, teeth, and stings are weapons.

wea sel (wē⁄zəl), a small, quick, sly animal with a slim body and short legs. Weasels eat rats, mice, birds, and eggs.

Weasel (6 to 8 in. long without the tail)

wedge (wej), **1.** something shaped like the letter V: *Wild geese fly in a wedge.* **2.** thrust or pack in tightly: *He wedged himself through the narrow window. The man's foot was wedged between the rocks, so that he could not get away.*

whin ny (hwin⁄i), **1.** sound that a horse makes. **2.** make such a sound.

wick (wik), the part of an oil lamp, candle, or torch that is lighted.

wig wam (wig⁄wom), hut of poles covered with bark, mats, or skins, made by American Indians.

Candle cut to show the wick

wil der ness (wil⁄dər nis), wild place; region with few or no people living in it.

wisp (wisp), **1.** small bunch: *a wisp of hay.* **2.** small portion of anything: *a wisp of hair; a wisp of smoke.* **3.** little thing: *a wisp of a girl.*

wit (wit), understanding; mind; sense: *People with quick wits learn easily. The child was out of his wits with fright.*

with er (wiŦH⁄ər), dry up; wrinkle: *Flowers wither after they are cut. Age had withered the old woman's face.*

wit ty (wit⁄i), amusing and clever: *He makes witty remarks.*

---

hat, āge, cãre, fär; let, bē, term; it, īce; hot, ōpen, ôrder; oil, out; cup, pu̇t, rüle, ūse; takən

TO THE TEACHER

More Times and Places, Book 4², with its accompanying *Guidebook* and *Think-and-Do Book*, continues The New Basic Reading Program for the middle grades. It is designed for approximately one semester's use whenever the child has successfully completed the new *Times and Places*.

More Times and Places contains 513 words not introduced by the end of Book 4¹ of The New Basic Reading Program. Each of these new words is used four or more times in this book, and there is a maximum of four new words to a page. The majority of words introduced in the new *Times and Places* are further repeated in *More Times and Places*.

The 513 new words in this book are listed below. The following forms of known words are not counted as new (including those forms made by changing *y* to *i* or *f* to *v*, dropping the final *e*, or doubling the final consonant in the root word): forms made by adding or dropping the inflectional endings *s*, *es*, *ed*, *ing*, *n*, and *en*, and *er*, *est* of comparison; possessives; forms made by adding or dropping the prefixes *dis-*, *im-*, *re-*, or *un-* and the suffixes *-en*, *-er*, *-ful*, *-ish*, *-less*, *-ly*, *-ness*, or *-y*, and *-teen*, *-th*, or *-ty* of numerals; compounds made up of known words; contractions. Also, homographs are not counted as separate words; for example, if *fleet* meaning "ships under one command" has been introduced, *fleet* meaning "fast moving or rapid" is not counted as a separate word. Nonsense words as well as syllables that represent sounds are not counted as new.

The red asterisks indicate 472 words that boys and girls can attack independently by applying the word-attack skills developed in The New Basic Reading Program and by using the pronunciations in the glossary of *More Times and Places*. Those starred words printed in italics in the vocabulary list are defined in the glossary. The type of analysis that pupils can use in unlocking each attack word is indicated in the *Guidebook* for *More Times and Places*.

VOCABULARY LIST

UNIT I

6 *brilliant* *
7 *crabs* *
   shallow *
   motionless *
8 sweater
9 *guided* *
   securely *
   argued *
10 *lap* *
11 *vacant* *
12 *moaning* *
   meanwhile *

13 *frequently* *
   capture *
14 ruined
15 *cactus* *
— *mesquite* *
   duties *
   provide *
16 ornaments *
   bitterly *
   forehead
17 youngsters
   quarter
18 . . . . .
19 . . . . .

20 *linger* *
21 *apparently* *
22 *swamps* *
   Santee *
   alligator *
   coiled *
23 'gator *
   encouraged *
24 *cypress* *
   moss *
   blossoms *
   tupelo *
25 hollow *
   coon *

26 rattlesnake *
27 grasped *
   defends *
28 *panic* *
29 *lunged* *
30 *peered* *
   dimness *
   convinced *
31 St.
   Louis
32 sped *
   region *
   tornado *

315

33 curved *
    syrup *
34 ceased *
    western *
35 hesitate *
36 slashing *
37 . . . . .
38 Vermont *
    Jason *
    sap *
39 buckets *
    lonesome *
40 boring *
    spout *
41 tank *
    pipe *
    recognized
42 gallons *
43 bubbles *
    violently *
44 pitcher *
    containing *
45 . . . . .
46 arrival *
47 Stephen
    railroad *
    valley *
48 season *
49 . . . . .
50 slope *
    level *
    peaceful *
51 fossil *
    familiar *
    grizzly *
52 buried *
    rumble *
53 . . . . .
54 receiver *
55 . . . . .
56 southern
    California

57 temperature *
    freezing *
    orchard *
    belt *
58 comforting
    oil *
    lit *
    torch *
59 wick *
60 choking *
    throat *
    relief *
61 boomed *
62 double *
63 northern *
    Antoine
    November *
    papa *
64 Ace *
    supply *
    lumber *
    pine *
65 message *
66 dusk *
67 Chalmers *
68 whom *
69 wilderness *
70 . . . . .
71 praised *
72 canyon *
    Howard
73 trout *
    rod *
    permit *
74 permission *
    crickets *
75 proved *
    dainty *
76 ranger *
    timber *
    patrol *
77 . . . . .
78 fought *
    desperately *

79 . . . . .
80 scorched *

Unit II

81 . . . . .
82 advancing *
83 skunk *
    insects *
    deserves *
84 occasionally *
    paused *
85 slight *
    movement *
86 gradually *
    fleeing *
    swooped *
87 slim *
    keen *
88 twitched *
    bolted *
89 . . . . .
90 war
    forefeet *
91 partner *
    gully *
    whinny *
    pounce *
92 cliff *
    fury *
    terror *
    crafty *
93 injured *
    intent *
    prey *
    rescue *
94 enraged *
    mare *
    gleamed *
95 splendid *
    downward *
96 distant *
    pity *

97 . . . . .
98 risk *
    passageway *
    directly *
99 knelt *
100 . . . . .
101 encircled *
    glimpse *
102 midsummer *
    ventured *
    weasels *
    prowled *
103 dread *
104 sneaking *
    fled *
105 . . . . .
106 force *
    greedy *
    roots *
    increased *
107 rustling *
108 loons *
    companion *
109 . . . . .
110 . . . . .
111 lantern *
112 upward *
    dawn *
    mist *
    swirling *
113 opposite *
114 lane *
    foam *
115 eagle *
116 forepaws *
    chose *
    considered *
    roamed *
117 solid *
118 alert *
    Husky *
    heeding *
119 anger *
    sensed *

316

120 swallowed *
nature *
ambled *
121 tawny *
pitched *
purred *
122 Leone's
ledge *
shove *
humped *
123 butterfly *
crouched *
coyote *
124 hissed *
uttering *
125 *despair* *
threatened *
126 *confused* *
127 . . . . .
128 Willie *
Herbert *
129 *determined* *
concern *
130 attending *
Charlie *
flapjacks *
131 flung *
132 freedom *
skillfully *
133 *overcome* *
appearance *
134 . . . . .
135 *strutted* *
136 *glossy* *
cove *
137 *brief* *
recovered *
138 gliding *
139 forbidden *
snout *
140 *pierce* *
faltered *
141 *suckers* *

142 *octopus* *
143 Nika
wedge *
southward *
gander *
144 rays *
145 rice *
concealed *
reeds *
146 . . . . .
147 *drake* *
148 fowls *
vain *
149 Frank *
Gordon *
Lizzie *
faithful *
150 . . . . .
151 . . . . .
152 *harsh* *
blasts *

Unit III

153 famous *
Americans
154 *tedious* *
155 *surveying* *
boundary *
156 Lawrence
Vernon *
future *
England
157 *surveyor* *
Byrne
158 tramping *
159 describe *
160 William *
Fairfax *
lord *
accompany *
161 Virginia

162 *abroad* *
163 Daniel
Boone *
reckon *
drawled *
164 rifle *
weapon *
slender *
165 *opportunity* *
166 absent *
167 *plume* *
168 *midst* *
169 *dreary* *
170 invitation *
taffy *
Noah
Webster *
171 *odor* *
Rebecca *
Jerusha *
172 manner *
173 *audience* *
174 *departed* *
arithmetic *
Bible *
wits *
175 . . . . .
176 Fulton's *
folly *
Christopher
177 . . . . .
178 speechless *
invented *
crank *
179 invention *
ship *
180 France *
renewed *
attacked *
jeered *
181 *completion* *
tested *

182 *throngs* *
deck *
183 *triumph* *
echoing *
184 Baltimore *
Pickersgill *
regarded *
banner *
185 Francis *
Scott *
spangled *
186 prisoners
Dr. *
truce *
fleet *
187 battle *
bomb *
188 tune *
189 pigeon
Indiana
Abraham *
Lincoln *
190 *sturdy* *
youth
Abe *
191 illness *
community *
death *
192 *fodder* *
193 . . . . .
194 honest
combing *
toiled *
195 entertain *
196 Taylor *
occurred *
Barnum *
exhibiting *
197 amusement *
198 collection *
museum *
attract *

317

ACKNOWLEDGMENTS

For permission to adapt and use copyrighted material, grateful acknowledgment is made to the following:

To the author and publishers for "Unwelcome Passengers," adapted from *Penny and Peter* by Carolyn Haywood, copyright, 1946, by Harcourt, Brace and Company, Inc.; to the author for "A Christmas to Remember" by Catherine Blanton in *American Junior Red Cross News;* to the publishers for "Adventure in the Swamps" from "The Alligator's Tail" by Idella Purnell, copyright, 1938, by Story Parade, Inc., reprinted by permission; to the author for "Judy's Chickens" from "Rosina's Chickens" and for "Maple-Sugar Time" from "Maple Sugar Surprise" by Gladys Relyea Saxon in *American Junior Red Cross News;* to the author and publishers for "Alarm in the Night" by Fleur Conkling in *Children's Activities;* to the author and publishers for "The School Train" from *The School Train* by Helen Acker, published by Abelard Press, Inc.; to Mrs. Graham Doar for "A Camp in the Canyon" from "Fires Start in the Fall" by Eleanor Hammond in *Junior World.*

To the author for "Zoo Without Bars" by Garald Lagard in *American Childhood;* to the author and publishers for "A Falls and a Fawn" by Dorothy Dill Mason in *Trails for Juniors;* to the publishers for "Bushy Tail's Escape" from *Bushy Tail* by Alice Crew Gall and Fleming Crew, copyright, 1941, by Oxford University Press, Inc.; to the publishers for "Billy and the Loons" by Laura E. Wiggins, copyright, 1950, by Story Parade, Inc., reprinted by permission; to the publishers for "Wilderness Partners" from *Snow Dog* by Jim Kjelgaard, published by Holiday House; to the author for "The Magic Coat" from *Tawny Goes Hunting* by Allen Chaffee, published by Random House, Inc.; to Lantern Press, Inc., for "Willie the Moose" from *Young Readers Animal Stories*, copyright, 1950, by Adolph Regli; to the author and publishers for "Gray Wing and Nika" from "In the Wake of the Storm" by William H. Bunce in *Trails.*

To the author and publishers for "George Grows Up" from *George Washington, Leader of the People* by Clara Ingram Judson, published by Wilcox & Follett Company; to the publishers for "The Boy Hunter" by Clarence M. Lindsay, copyright, 1949, by Story Parade, Inc., reprinted by permission; to the author and publishers for "The Spelling Bee," adapted from *Homespun Playdays* by Carolyn Sherwin Bailey, copyright, 1941, by Carolyn Sherwin Bailey, reprinted by permission of The Viking Press, Inc., New York; to the author for "How a Song Named a Flag" by Fannie R. Buchanan in *Story Parade;* to the author for "A Boy and His Book" from "A Little Lad of Long Ago" by Alice E. Allen in *Good Housekeeping;* to the author and publishers for "A Great Showman" from *The Boy's Life of Barnum* by Harvey W. Root, publishod by Harper & Brothers; to the author for "Nothing for Herself" from *The Story of Clara Barton of the Red Cross* by Jeannette Covert Nolan, published by Julian Messner, Inc.; to the author and publishers for "Night Is Turned into Day" from *The Story of Thomas Alva Edison* by Enid La Monte Meadowcroft, Grosset & Dunlap Signature Books, 1952.

To Mrs. Clifton Johnson for "The Four Musicians" from *The Oak Tree Fairy Book*, edited by Clifton Johnson, copyright, 1933; to the publisher for "Tyll's Masterpiece" from *Tyll Ulenspiegel's Merry Pranks* by M. Jagendorf, copyright, 1938, by Vanguard Press, Inc., used by permission of the publisher; to James B. Pinker and Son, Inc., Agents, for "Rumpelstiltskin" from *Told Again* by Walter de la Mare.

ILLUSTRATIONS

The pictures in this book were made by Seymour Fleishman (cover, pp. 1, 175, 249-253); Henry M. Picken (pp. 2-3, 38-55, 63-71, 82-89, 108-126); Brinton Turkle (pp. 5, 14-21, 56-62, 81, 153, 219); Fred Scott-Wood (pp. 6-12, 30-36, 95-100); John Merryweather (pp. 22-28, 90-93, 169-173, 189-209); I. Heilbron (pp. 72-79, 267, 274, 278, 290); Earl Sherwan (pp. 102-107, 136-141); Willard Arnold (pp. 128-135, 220-226, 270, 277); L. M. Henderson (pp. 143-152); Raymon Naylor (pp. 154-168, 176-187, 211-218); Mary Gehr (pp. 232-238); Nell Smock (pp. 240-248); Keith Ward (pp. 228-231, 256-265); E. Segner (pp. 268-269, 272-273, 276); Milo Winter (pp. 280-281, 285-288).